CONTENTS

In loving memory of my father, Paul Levin (1931 – 2004), who gave me everything and took nothing. He would have loved to flip through this and I always imagined giving him a copy.

CHAPTER 1 – ALGEBRA

1.1. – TYPES OF NUMBERS

Natural Numbers (N): **N** = {_, __, __, __, __…}

Integers (Z): **Z** = {…,__, __, __, __, __, 0, __, __, __, __, __…}

Rational Numbers (Q): **Q** = $\{\frac{a}{b}, a, b \in Z\}$

Numbers that **can** be written as _______being both the numerator and the denominator_______.

Examples: $\frac{1}{1}, \frac{2}{3}, \frac{-7}{3}, \frac{4}{-1}, \frac{\_\_}{\_\_}$, ______, ______ …

Irrational Numbers (Q'): **Q'** $\neq \{\frac{a}{b}, a, b \in Z\}$ Numbers that _______ be written as fractions, being both the _______ and _______ Integers.

Examples: __, __, __ …

Real Numbers (R): **R** = **Q** + **Q'** (Rationals and Irrationals)

Represented in a Venn diagram:

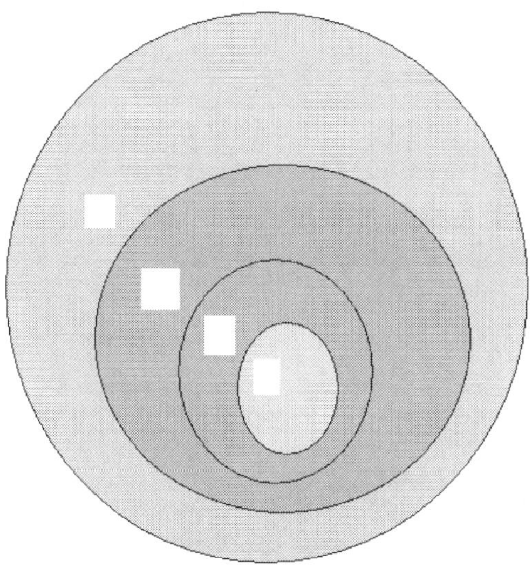

Exercises:

1. Natural numbers are contained in the ___________ numbers.
2. Integer numbers are contained in the ___________ numbers
3. Rational numbers are contained in the ___________ numbers.
4. Irrational numbers are located _____________________________.

5. Shade the area in which the irrational numbers are located:

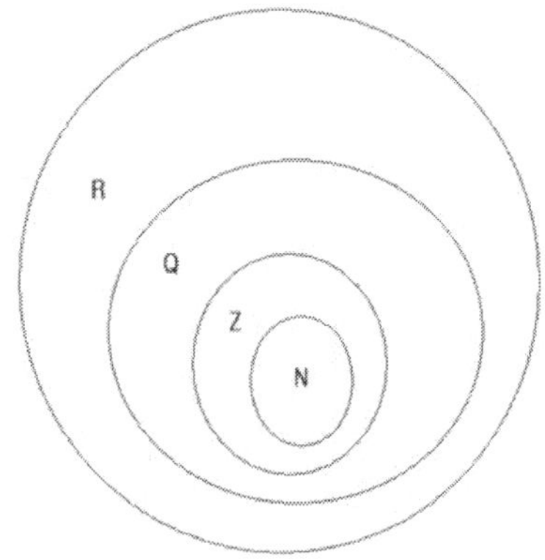

6. True or False:

   a. All Natural numbers are Integers: ____

   b. All Real numbers are Natural: ____

   c. All Rational numbers are Real: ____

   d. All Real numbers are Rational: ____

   e. All Integer numbers are Rational: ____

   f. All Real numbers are Irrational: ____

   g. Some Irrational numbers are Real and some are not: ____

   h. Some Irrational numbers are Integers: ____

   i. Some integers are negative: ____

   j. Some Irrationals are negative: ____

   k. Some Natural numbers are negative: ____

7. Fill the chart with yes or no (follow the example):

Number	**Natural**	**Integer**	**Rational**	**Real**
-2	no	yes	yes	yes
Π				
$-3.121212....$				
-15.16				
$\sqrt{3}$				
$-2\frac{2}{5}$				
$\sqrt[3]{8}$				

8. Fill the numbers column with appropriate numbers and yes or no.

Number	Natural	Integer	Rational	Real
	no	yes		
		no	yes	yes
	yes	yes	yes	
			no	yes
		no	yes	yes
			yes	
	no			
		yes	no	

4. Convert the following numbers into the form: $\frac{n}{m}$

1. 0.333… =

2. 1.111… =

3. 5.3 =

4. 5.2828… =

5. –2.3535… =

6. 42.67 =

7. 12.355355… =

8. –31.44 =

9. $0.125125\ldots =$

13. $1.123123\ldots =$

10. $3.22332233\ldots =$

14. $1.22565656\ldots =$

11. $1115.36 =$

15. $1.5696969\ldots =$

12. $122.53 =$

16. $5.540404040\ldots =$

5. Given the following diagram:

Write the following numbers in the appropriate location in the diagram:

a. 2.2
b. -5
c. 3
d. $\frac{1}{3}$
e. 5
f. -3.3
g. $1.111\ldots$
h. $\frac{1}{\sqrt{3}}$
i. 2π
j. $1+2\pi$
k. $\sqrt{2}+3$
l. $\frac{4}{2}$

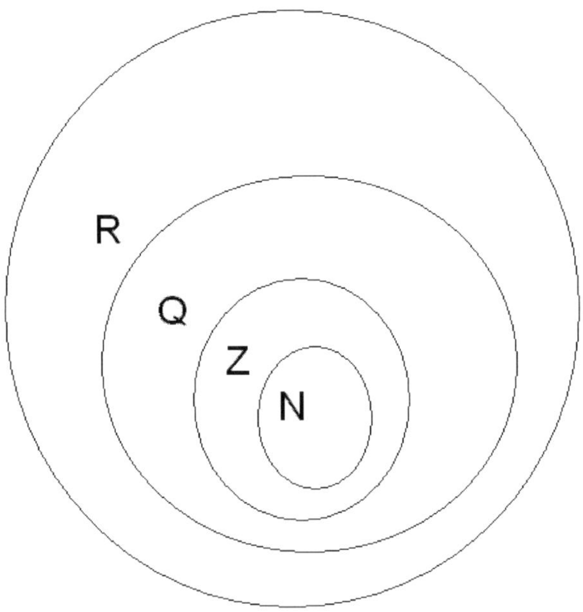

6. Circle the right option. The number –2 is:

   a. Integer and Natural.
   b. Positive
   c. Integer and Rational
   d. Natural and Real
   e. Natural and Rational
   f. None of the above

7. Circle the right option. The number 3.41414141..... is:

   a. Integer and Natural.
   b. Natural
   c. Integer and Real
   d. Rational and Integer
   e. Rational
   f. None of the above

8. Circle the right option. The number 3.41 is:

   a. Integer and Natural.
   b. Integer
   c. Rational and Real
   d. Integer and Real
   e. Rational and negative
   f. None of the above

9. Circle the right option. The number $\sqrt{31}$ is:

   a. Integer and Natural.
   b. Integer
   c. Decimal
   d. Integer and Real
   e. Rational
   f. Irrational

10. Circle the right option. The number 5 is:

    a. Natural.
    b. Integer
    c. Real
    d. Integer and Natural
    e. Rational and Natural
    f. All of the above

1.2. – INTERVAL NOTATION

$x \ni (a, b]$ or $\{x| a < x \leq b\}$ means x is between a and b, not including a and including b.

Exercises:

1. Represent the following Intervals on the real line:

a. $x \ni (2, 5]$

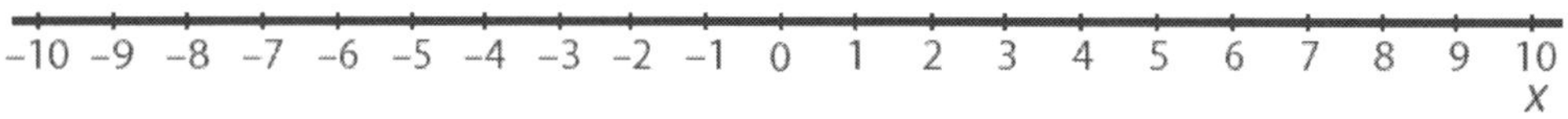

b. $x \ni (3,6)$

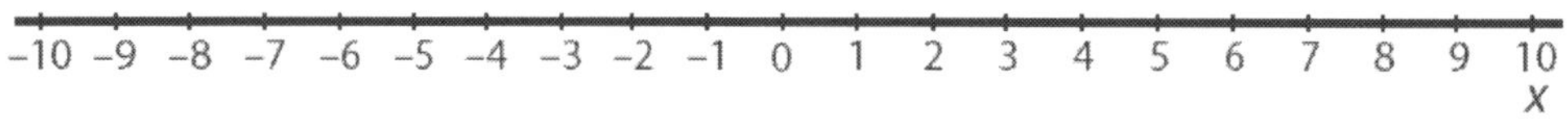

c. $x \ni [-5,9]$

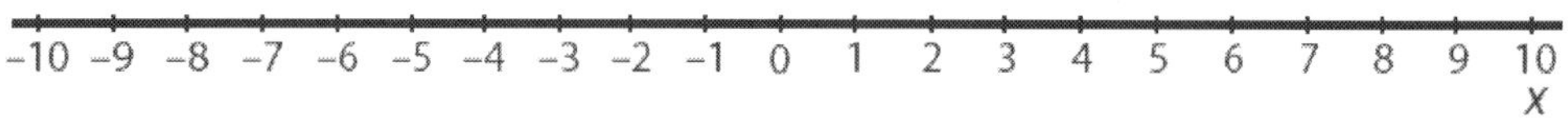

d. $x \ni [-8,-1)$

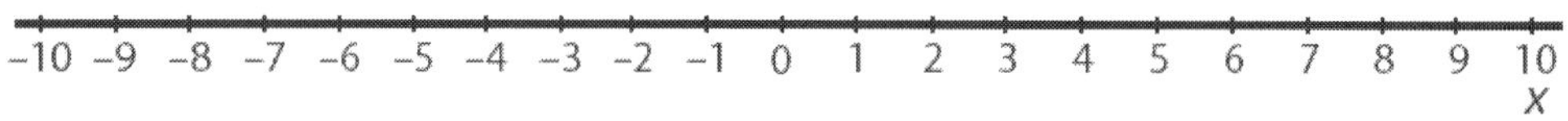

e. $x \ni [-\infty,-1)$

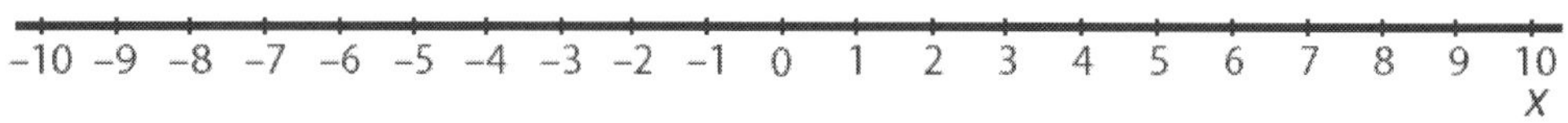

f. $x \ni [-\infty,6]$

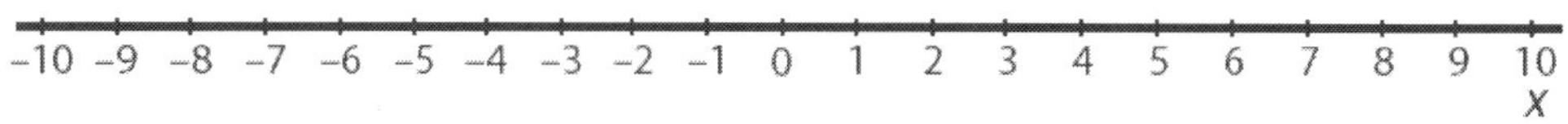

g. $x \ni (6, \infty]$

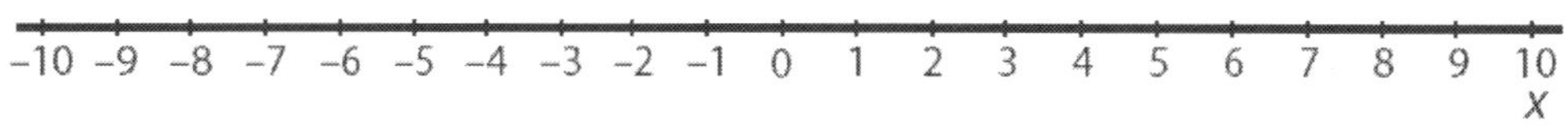

h. $\{x| 7 < x < 9\}$

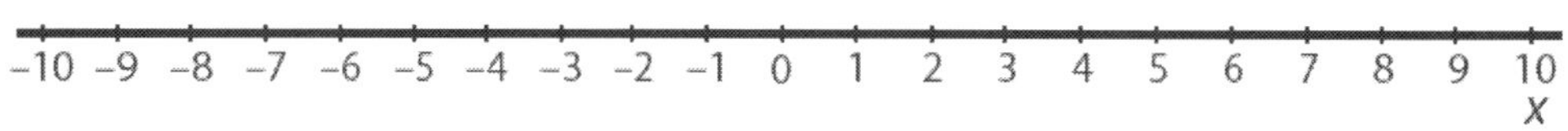

i. $\{x| -7 < x < -2\}$

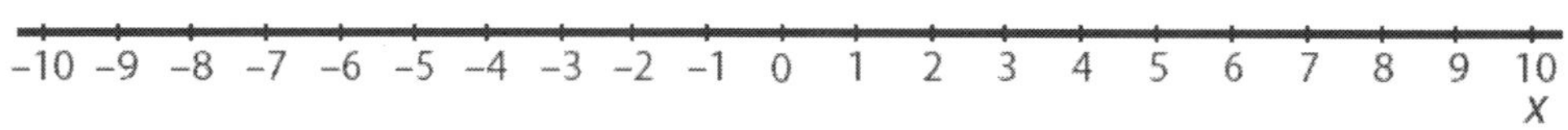

j. $\{x|\ 1 < x < 2\}$

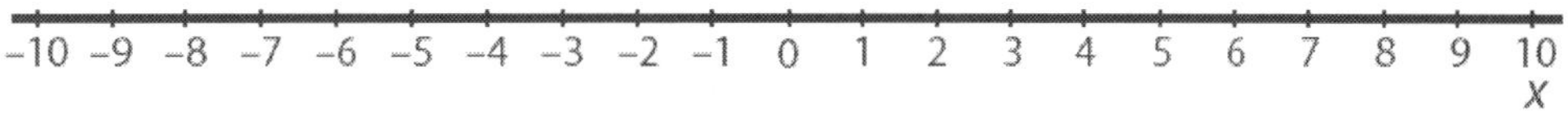

k. $\{x|\ \infty < x < 2\}$

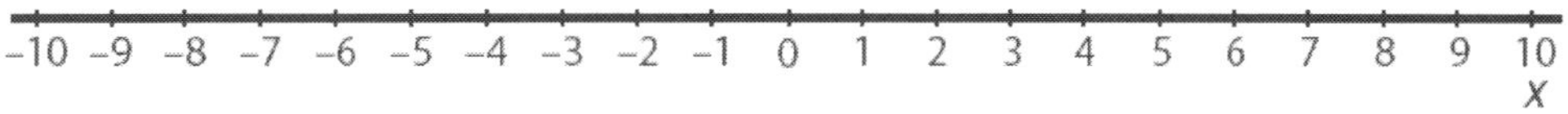

l. $\{x|\ 1 < x < \infty\}$

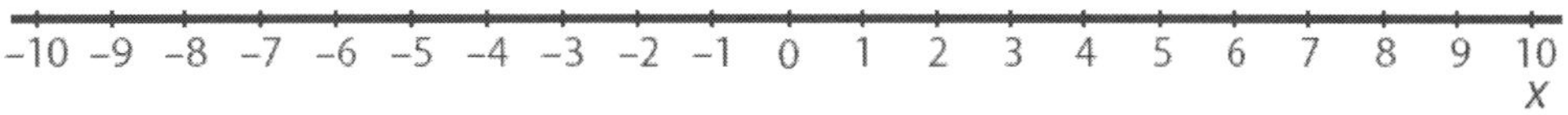

2. Write each one of the Intervals using all types of notations:

a. x ∍ (4, 5)

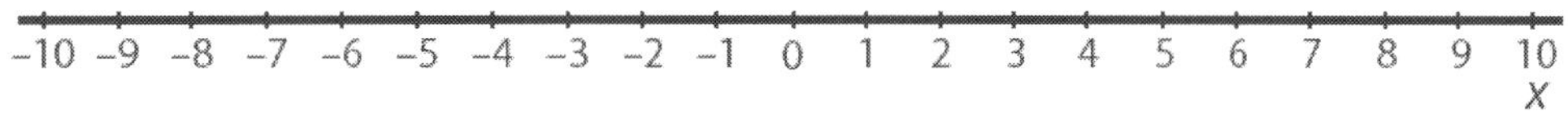

b. x ∍ (–∞, 5)

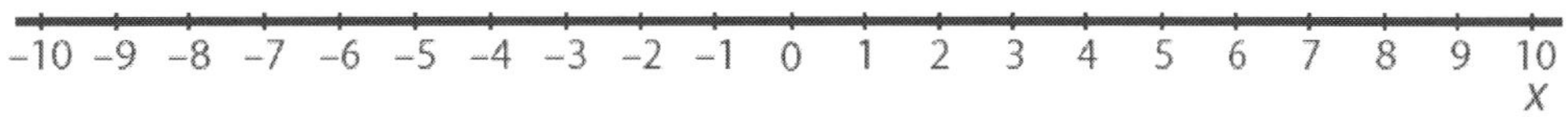

c. x ∍ (4, 5)

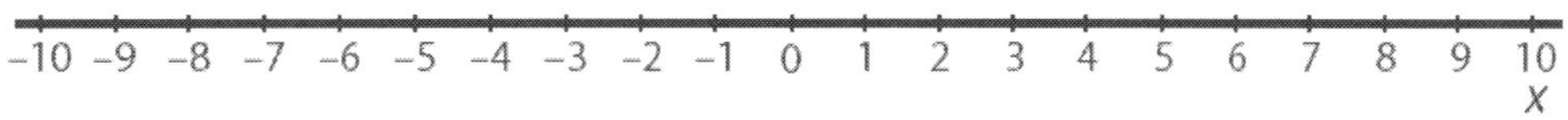

d. x ∍ (3, ∞]

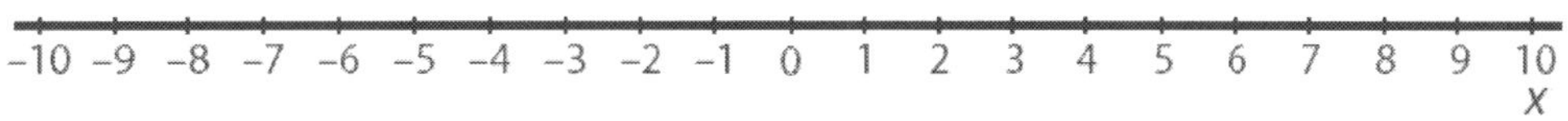

e. x ∍]–5,9]

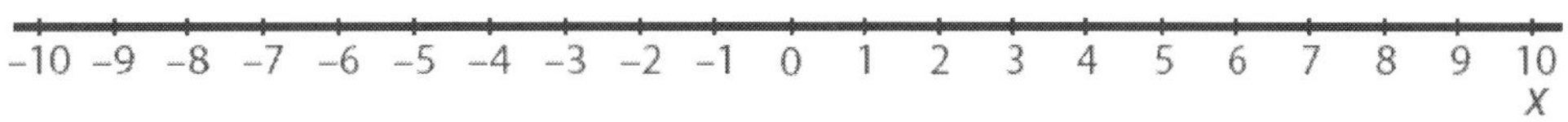

f. x ∍ [–8,–1[

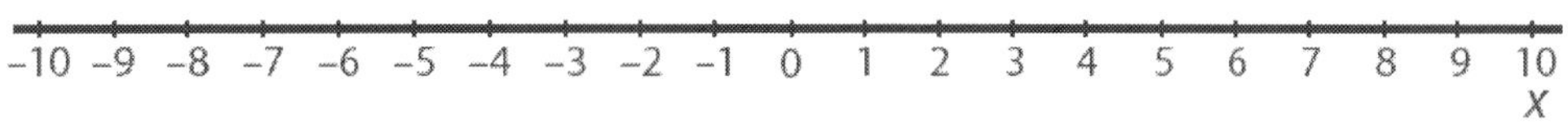

g. $\{x|\ 7 < x < 9\}$

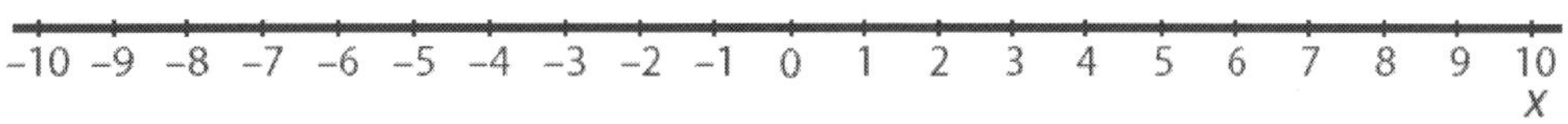

h. $\{x|\ -7 < x < -2\}$

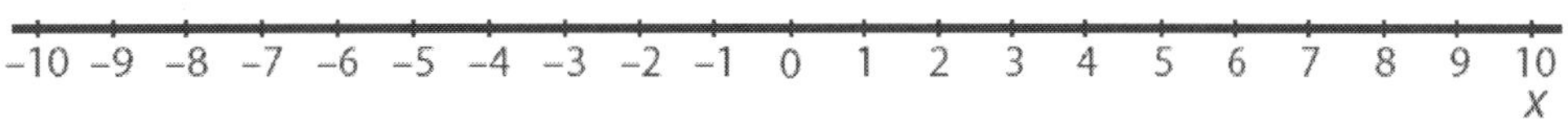

3.

a. Solve the inequality $3x - 7 \leq 2$

b. Solve the inequality $-x < -2$.

c. Represent both solutions on the real line:

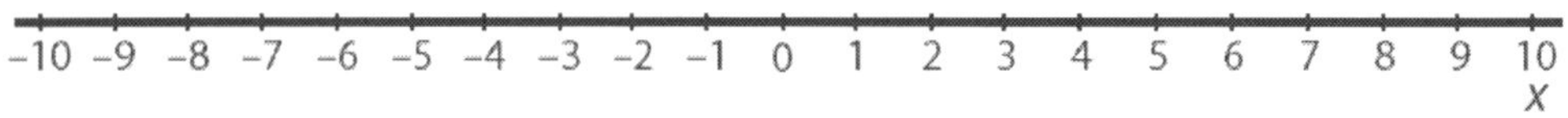

d. State their intersection: ______________________________.

4.

a. Solve the inequality $5x - 2 \leq 2$

b. Solve the inequality $-2x + 1 > -2$.

c. Represent both solutions on the real line:

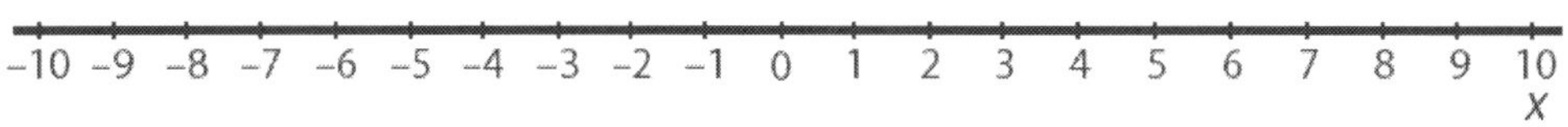

d. State their intersection: ______________________________.

5.

a. Solve the inequality $5x - 2 \leq -12$

b. Solve the inequality $-2x - 3 \leq -2$.

c. Represent both solutions on the real line:

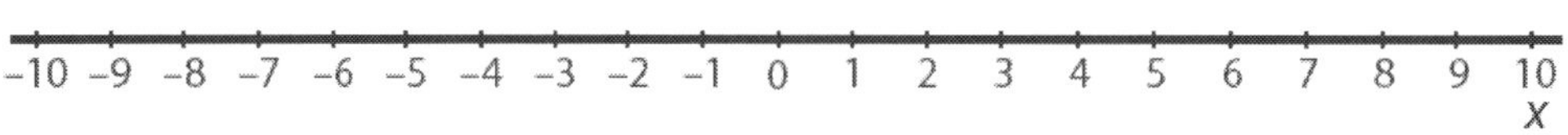

d. State their intersection: ______________________________

1.3. – RATIONALIZATION

1. Rationalize the denominator:

a. $\dfrac{2}{\sqrt{5}} =$

b. $\dfrac{3}{\sqrt{5}+1} =$

c. $\dfrac{-7}{\sqrt{5}-2} =$

d. $\dfrac{\sqrt{2}+3}{-5} =$

e. $\dfrac{\sqrt{2}+3}{\sqrt{6}-5} =$

f. $\dfrac{\sqrt{2}}{\sqrt{6}+\sqrt{3}} =$

g. $\dfrac{\sqrt{2}-1}{2\sqrt{5}-\sqrt{3}} =$

h. $\dfrac{-1}{2\sqrt{a}+b} =$

2. Rationalize the numerator:

a. $\dfrac{\sqrt{4}}{\sqrt{5}} =$

b. $\dfrac{3-\sqrt{2}}{\sqrt{5}+1} =$

c. $\dfrac{-7}{\sqrt{5}-2} =$

d. $\dfrac{\sqrt{2}+3}{\sqrt{6}-5} =$

e. $\dfrac{\sqrt{2}}{\sqrt{x}+\sqrt{3}} =$

f. $\dfrac{\sqrt{b}-a}{2\sqrt{a}-\sqrt{3}} =$

g. $\dfrac{-3\sqrt{7}+8}{2\sqrt{5}+7} =$

1.4. – EXPONENTS & LOGARITHMS

Product

$a^0 = \_\_$

$a^1 = \_\_$

$a^2 = \_\_ \times \_\_$

$a^3 = \_ \times \_ \times \_$

$\ldots$

$a^3 a^2 = \_\_\_\_\_\_\_\_\_\_ = \_\_\_$

$$a^m a^n = \_\_\_\_\_\_$$

Division

$\frac{a^5}{a^3} = \frac{\_\_\_\_\_\_\_\_\_\_}{\_\_\_\_\_\_\_\_} = \frac{\_\_\_\_}{\_\_\_} = \_\_\_$

$\frac{a^2}{a^5} = \frac{\_\_\_\_\_\_\_\_\_\_}{\_\_\_\_\_\_\_\_} = \frac{\_\_\_\_}{\_\_\_} = \_\_\_$

$$\frac{a^m}{a^n} = \_\_\_\_\_$$

Power

$(a^2)^3 = \_\_\_\_\_\_\_\_\_\_ = \_\_\_$

$\left(\frac{a^2}{b}\right)^3 = \frac{\_\_\_\_\_\_\_\_\_\_}{\_\_\_\_\_\_\_\_} = \frac{\_\_\_}{\_\_\_}$

$$(a^m)^n = \_\_\_$$

$$\left(\frac{a^m}{b^k}\right)^n = \frac{\_\_\_}{\_\_\_}$$

Radicals

$(a^3)^{\frac{1}{2}} = \_\_\_ = \_\_\_$

$(a^4)^{\frac{1}{7}} = \_\_\_ = \_\_\_$

$$(a^m)^{\frac{1}{n}} = \_\_\_ = \_\_\_$$

Exercises

Write in all possible forms and evaluate without using a calculator (follow example):

1. $4^{-1} = \frac{1}{4} = 0.25$
2. $10^0 =$
3. $10^1 =$
4. $10^3 =$
5. $10^{-1} =$
6. $10^{-2} =$
7. $10^{-3} =$
8. $10^{-4} =$
9. $2^0 =$
10. $2^1 =$
11. $2^{-1} =$
12. $2^{-2} =$
13. $2^{-3} =$
14. $2^{-4} =$
15. $(-1)^0 =$
16. $-1^0 =$
17. $(-1)^1 =$
18. $-1^1 =$
19. $(-1)^{-1} =$
20. $-1^2 =$
21. $(-1)^2 =$
22. $-1^2 =$
23. $(-1)^{-2} =$
24. $-1^{-2} =$
25. $(-3)^0 =$
26. $(-3)^1 =$
27. $-3^1 =$
28. $(-3)^2 =$
29. $-3^2 =$
30. $(-3)^{-1} =$

31. $-3^{-1} =$

32. $(-3)^{-2} =$

33. $-3^{-2} =$

34. $9^{\frac{1}{2}} =$

35. $16^{\frac{3}{4}} =$

36. $(3^{-1})^2 =$

37. $(-8^{-3})^{\frac{1}{2}} =$

38. $\left(\frac{1}{2}\right)^0 =$

39. $\left(\frac{1}{2}\right)^1 =$

40. $\left(\frac{1}{2}\right)^{-1} =$

41. $\left(\frac{1}{2}\right)^2 =$

42. $\left(\frac{1}{2}\right)^{-2} =$

43. $\left(\frac{3}{5}\right)^0 =$

44. $\left(\frac{3}{4}\right)^1 =$

45. $\left(\frac{2}{5}\right)^{-1} =$

46. $\left(\frac{5}{11}\right)^2 =$

47. $\left(\frac{-11}{2}\right)^{-2} =$

48. $\left(\frac{3}{-2}\right)^1 =$

49. $\left(\frac{-12}{\sqrt{2}}\right)^{-1} =$

50. $\left(\frac{5\sqrt{2}}{11}\right)^{2} =$

51. $\left(\frac{-2\sqrt{5}}{2}\right)^{-2} =$

52. $\left(\frac{3+5\sqrt{2}}{-2}\right)^{2} =$

53. $\left(\frac{-12}{2-\sqrt{2}}\right)^{-2} =$

54. $\left(\frac{5+\sqrt{2}}{11}\right)^{2} =$

55. $\left(\frac{-2-\sqrt{5}}{2+\sqrt{2}}\right)^{-2} =$

56. $\left(\frac{-27}{8}\right)^{\frac{2}{3}} =$

57. $\left(\frac{16}{9}\right)^{\frac{3}{4}} =$

58. $5^{27}5^{-29} =$

59. $4^{27}2^{-49} =$

60. $9^{12}3^{-20} =$

61. $(-125)^{\frac{2}{3}} =$

62. $\frac{5^{10}}{5^{2}} =$

63. $\frac{3^{10}}{9^{2}}3^{-2} =$

64. $\left(\frac{2}{5}\right)^{3} \times \left(\frac{5}{3}\right)^{3} =$

65. $\left(\frac{4}{7}\right)^{2} \div \left(\frac{9}{7}\right)^{2} =$

66. $\left(\frac{2}{5}\right)^{3} \times \left(\frac{3}{5}\right)^{-4} =$

67. $\left(\frac{3}{4}\right)^{5} \div \left(\frac{9}{64}\right)^{2} =$

68. $\left(\frac{7}{5}\right)^{7} \div \left(\frac{49}{125}\right)^{3} =$

69. $\left(\frac{2^{-3}}{3^{-2}}\right)^{3} \times \left(\frac{4}{27}\right)^{2} =$

70. $\left(\frac{4^{2}}{5^{-1}}\right)^{3} \times \left(\frac{25^{-1}}{64}\right)^{2} =$

71. $\left(\frac{3^{-5}}{4^{2}}\right)^{2} \div \left(\frac{9^{-2}}{2^{3}}\right)^{3} =$

72. $\left(\frac{5^{4}}{7^{-3}}\right)^{2} \div \left(\frac{25^{-1}}{49}\right)^{-3} =$

73. $\frac{3^{-2}}{9^{\frac{2}{3}}} 27^{\frac{5}{4}} =$

74. $\frac{4^{-4}\sqrt{2}}{8^{-\frac{2}{3}}} 16^{\frac{3}{4}} =$

75. $\sqrt{5}\,\frac{25^{2}5^{-1}}{25^{\frac{4}{3}}} 5^{\frac{1}{4}}\sqrt[3]{5} =$

76. $\frac{4^{-2}2^{-4}}{16^{2}(\sqrt[6]{16^{4}})}8^{\frac{1}{4}}2^{-1} =$

77. $x\sqrt{x}\sqrt{3} =$

78. $x\sqrt{x}+\sqrt{2x} =$

79. $\frac{1}{x\sqrt{x}} =$

80. $\frac{x\sqrt[3]{x}}{\sqrt{x}} =$

81. $s^{n}s^{2n}s^{2} =$

82. $a^{2k}ba^{3}b^{2k}a =$

83. $\frac{3^{n}}{9^{n}}27^{n} =$

84. $\frac{2^{n}}{8^{n+1}}16^{n-2} =$

85. $\frac{5^{-n}}{125^{2n-2}}5^{-n+2} =$

86. $\frac{x^{-n}}{x^{2n-2}}x^{-n+5} =$

87. $\frac{2x^{-n+1}}{2^{2}x^{3n+2}}x^{n+5} =$

88. $\dfrac{2yx^{-2n+3}}{2^5 y^{-1} x^{-4n+2}} x^{-2n+1} =$

89. $\dfrac{4^2 y^2 x^{-3} z}{2^2 xz^2 y^{-1} x} x^{-2} z^2 =$

90. $\dfrac{4^2 y^2 (x^{-2} z^2)^{-2}}{(2^2 x)^3 z^2 y^{-1} x} x^{-2} z^2 =$

91. $\dfrac{4^{-2} y^3 (x^{-2} z^3)^{-1}}{(2^{-3} x)^{-3} z^{-2} y^{-1} x} xz^2 =$

92. $\left(\dfrac{a}{b^2}\right)^2 \div \left(\dfrac{a^{-1}}{b^3}\right)^{-3} \times \left(\dfrac{1}{b}\right)^3 =$

93. $\left(\dfrac{ab}{b^2}\right)^{-2} \div \left(\dfrac{(2ba)^{-1}}{b^3}\right)^{-3} \times \left(\dfrac{2}{b}\right)^3 =$

94. $\dfrac{a^{-2} b^n (a^{-2n} b^3)^{-1}}{(b^{-3n} a)^3 a^{-2n} b^{-1}} =$

95. $\dfrac{a^{-2} b^n (a^{-2n} b^2)^n}{(b^{-3n} a)^n a^{-2n} b^n} =$

96. $\dfrac{3^n a^{-2} b^n (a^{-2n} b^3)^{n+1}}{(9^n b^{-2n} a)^n a^{-2n} b^{n+2}} =$

97. $\dfrac{3^n + 3^{n+1}}{3^{n-1}} =$

98. $\dfrac{4^n + 4^{n-1}}{4^{n-2}} =$

99. $\dfrac{7^{2n}+7^{2n-1}}{7^{2n-2}}=$

100. $\dfrac{7^{3n-1}-7^{3n}}{7^{2n-2}}=$

101. $2^{-1}+2=$

102. $3^{-1}-3^{-2}=$

103. $5^{-1}-5^{-2}=$

104. $3^{-3}+2^{-2}=$

105. $3^{-2}+4^{-2}=$

106. $7^{-2}+2^{-2}=$

107. $8^{-2}-3^{-2}=$

108. $7^{-2}-2^{-3}=$

109. $a^{-1}+a^{-1}=$

110. $ba^{-1}+a^{-1}=$

111. $a^{-1}-ba^{-1}=$

112. $(ba)^{-1}+a^{-1}=$

113. $ba^{-1}+(ba)^{-1}=$

LOGARITHMS

Definition of logarithms: $b^c = a \Leftrightarrow \log_b a = c \quad 1 \neq b > 0$

1. Complete the table and find x if possible:

Exponential Form	Logarithmic Form
$5^3 = 125$	
	$\log_6 36 = 2$
	$\log_x 64 = 2$
$x^3 = 27$	
	$\log_3(x+1) = 2$
$e^x = 9$	
	$\ln x = \log_e x = 2$
$e^{2x-1} = 17$	
	$\ln(3x+2) = \log_e(3x+2) = 2$
$4^x = 9$	
	$\log_6 x = 2$
$2^x = e$	
	$\ln(x^2) = \log_e(x^2) = 4$
	$\log 0.001 = x$
$10^x = 200$	
	$\log_3 \frac{1}{9} = -2$
	$\log_2 0.5 = x$

Logarithms were "invented" in order to solve equations in which: ________________

Properties of logarithms

I. **Product Rule:** $Log_b(MN) = Log_b(M) + Log_b(N)$, M, N, b positive, b≠1

II. **Quotient Rule:** $Log_b(\frac{M}{N}) = Log_b(M) - Log_b(N)$, M, N, b positive, b≠1

III. **Power Rule:** $Log_b(M^p) = pLog_b(M)$, M, b positive, b≠1

IV. $a^{\log_a(x)} = x$

Evaluate

1. $Log_2(32) =$
2. $Log_5(25) =$
3. $Log_5(125) =$
4. $Log_5(625) =$
5. $Log_3(3) =$
6. $Log_5(0) =$
7. $Log_5(1) =$
8. $Log_a(1) =$
9. $Log_2(-3) =$
10. $Log_2(\frac{1}{8}) =$
11. $Log_7(\frac{1}{49}) =$
12. $Log_4(32) =$
13. $Log_8(32) =$
14. $Log_{\frac{1}{2}}(4) =$
15. $Log_{\frac{1}{2}}(16) =$
16. $Log_{\frac{1}{3}}(81) =$
17. $Log_{\frac{1}{2}}(8) =$
18. $Log_{\frac{1}{2}}(-8) =$

19. $Log_{\frac{1}{3}}(\frac{1}{9}) =$

20. $Log_{\frac{1}{5}}(\frac{1}{125}) =$

21. $Log_1(8) =$

22. $Log_2(\frac{1}{\sqrt{8}}) =$

23. $Log_2(\sqrt[3]{32}) =$

24. $Log_3(\sqrt[3]{81}) =$

25. $Log_{\sqrt[5]{8}}(\sqrt[5]{8}) =$

26. $Log_{\frac{1}{2}}(\sqrt[5]{16}) =$

27. $Log_{17}(\frac{17}{17^{\frac{1}{3}}}\sqrt[5]{17}) =$

28. $Log(\sqrt{10}) =$

29. $Log(\sqrt[3]{10}) =$

30. $Log(\sqrt[7]{100}) =$

31. $Log(\sqrt[3]{10000}) =$

32. $Log(10^{-19}) =$

33. $Log(50) - Log(5) =$

34. $Log(25) + Log(4) =$

35. $Log_3(45) - Log_3(5) =$

36. $Log_6(18) + Log_6(2) =$

37. $Log_a(a^x) =$

38. $Log_a(a^{2x-3}) =$

39. $Log_e(e) =$

40. $Ln(e) =$

41. $Ln(e^2) =$

42. $Ln(e^{\frac{1}{2}}) =$

43. $Ln(e^{\frac{2}{5}}) =$

44. $Ln(e\sqrt[3]{e^4}) =$

45. $\dfrac{Ln(e^{-1})}{Log_{12}(\sqrt{12})} =$

46. $Ln(1) =$

47. $Ln(0) =$

48. $Ln(e^0) =$

49. $Ln(e^n) =$

50. $Ln(\frac{1}{\sqrt{e}}) =$

51. $Ln(\frac{1}{\sqrt[3]{e^2}}) =$

52. $Log_{\pi}(\frac{1}{\pi^4}) =$

53. $Log_{\pi}(\frac{1}{\sqrt{\pi^5}}) =$

54. $Log_a(\frac{1}{\sqrt[3]{a^2}}) =$

55. $10^{Log(100)} =$

56. $3^{Log_3(9)} =$

57. $3^{Log_3(\frac{1}{27})} =$

True or False

1. $Log(2x) - Log(3) = Log(2x+3)$ ______

2. $Log(x) - Log(9) = 2 \Leftrightarrow \frac{x}{9} = 100$

3. $Log(12) + Log(x) = 1 \Leftrightarrow 12x = 10$

4. $Log(2) + Log(5) = Log(7)$

5. $Log(10) - Log(5) = Log(2)$

6. $Log(20) + Log(2) = Log(22)$

7. $Log(15) - Log(3) = Log(5)$

8. $Log(A + B) = Log(A) + Log(B)$

Simplify

1. $Log_2(2^x 2^{x+y}) =$

2. $5^{Log_5(x+y)} =$

3. $Log_7(49^{xy}) =$

4. $Log_2(xy) - \frac{1}{3}Log_2(x^2) =$

5. $Log_2(\frac{8x^2}{y}) - 2Log_2(2x^2 y) =$

6. $\frac{1}{2}Log_3(\frac{9xy^2}{y}) - Log_3(27xy) =$

7. $3Log_4((xy)^3) - Log_4(xy) =$

8. $Log(2A) + Log(B) - 2Log(AB) =$

9. $Ln(ab^t) - Ln((ab)^t) - 2Ln(a) =$

10. If $Log_{10}(8) = x$ and $Log_{10}(3) = y$ express the following in terms of x and y only:

a. $Log_{10}(24) =$

b. $Log_{10}(\frac{8}{3}) =$

c. $Log_{10}(72) =$

d. $Log_{10}(\frac{9}{8}) =$

e. $Log_{10}(720) =$

Change of base

$$Log_b(M) = \frac{Log_c(M)}{Log_c(b)}$$

Change the following logarithms into a different base:

1. $Log_2(5) =$
2. $Log_3(-12) =$
3. $Log_{22}(51) =$
4. $Log_{2.3}(1) =$
5. $Log_{2.9}(2.9) =$
6. $Log_3(-5) =$
7. $Log_a(5) =$
8. $Log_{12}(5y) =$
9. $Log_e(2) =$
10. $Log(5) =$
11. $Ln(15) =$
12. $Log_{\sqrt{2}}(5) =$

13. $Log_3(\frac{2}{3}) =$

14. $Log_5(\frac{2}{\sqrt{5}}) =$

15. Simplify:

a. $\log_x b \cdot \log_b x =$ __

b. $\log_x q \cdot \log_q r \cdot \log_r x =$ __

Logarithmic Equations

1. $Log_4(x) = 2$

2. $Log_{\frac{1}{3}}(x) = 4$

3. $Log_{10}(2x+1) = 2$

4. $Log_2(64) = x$

5. $Ln(x) = 2.7$

6. $Ln(x+1) = 1.86$

7. $e^x = 6.27$

8. $Log_b(81) = 4$

9. $e^{-2x} = 4.12$

10. $Log_3(x) = Log_3(7) + Log_3(3)$

11. $5 \times 9^x = 10$

12. $10e^{4x+1} = 20$

13. $3^t = 2 \cdot 5^{2t}$

14. $3^{t+1} = 4 \cdot 6^{2t-3}$

15. $3 \cdot 2^t = 5 \cdot 6^{2t-3}$

16. $2 \cdot e^t = 8 \cdot 7^{2t-3}$

17. $b^t = c \cdot d^{2t}$

18. $a \cdot b^t = c \cdot d^{2t}$

19. $e^t + e^t = 2$

20. $e^{2t} + e^{2t} = 3$

21. $Ln(x) = 2$

22. $Ln(x^2) = 2$

23. $Ln(x^2 - 1) = 2$

24. $Ln(x+1) - Ln(2x) = -1$

25. $Ln(x^2 + 1) = 1$

26. $Log_{10}(x^2 + 2) = 2$

27. $Ln(x-2)+Ln(x+1)=0$

28. $Log_2(x)+Log_3(x)=1$

29. $Log_2(x)-Log_3(x)=1$

30. $Log_2(x)-2Log_3(x)=2$

31. $3Log_2(x)-2Log_3(x)=1$

32. $Log_2(x) - Log_3(x) = Log_3(x)$

33. $Log_2(x) - 2Log_x(2) = 0$

34. $Log_2(x) - 2Log_x(2) = 1$

35. $Log_2(x) - Log_x(3) = 0$

36. $Log_2(x) - 2Log_x(3) = 0$

1.5. – EQUATIONS

1st Degree (Linear Equations)

1. $\frac{x}{12} = 5$

2. $\frac{x}{7} + 2 = 5$

3. $\frac{2x}{7} + 2 = 5 - 3x$

4. $\frac{2x}{7} + \frac{2}{5} = -2x + 1$

5. $\frac{2x - 1}{x} = 3$

6. $\frac{x + 2}{2x} = 5$

7. $\frac{x - 2}{2x - 1} = 6$

8. $\frac{2x - 2}{x + 1} = -2$

9. $\frac{2x}{7} + 1 = \frac{-5x}{7}$

10. $\frac{2x}{7} + 4 = \frac{3x}{2}$

11. $\frac{2}{x} - 3 = \frac{3}{2x}$

12. $\frac{2}{x - 2} - 3 = \frac{3}{x - 2}$

13. $\frac{-2}{x} = \frac{3}{x - 2}$

14. $\frac{4}{x + 1} = \frac{4}{x + 2}$

15. $\frac{2}{x + 1} = \frac{4}{x + 2}$

16. $-\frac{2}{2x + 1} - 2 = \frac{4}{2x + 1}$

Isolate x

1. $\dfrac{4}{x} = \dfrac{a}{x+6}$

2. $\dfrac{14}{x+2} = \dfrac{a}{x+2} - a$

3. $\dfrac{2}{x+3} - a = \dfrac{a+b}{x+3}$

4. $\dfrac{5}{2x+1} - 3a = \dfrac{b}{2x+1}$

5. $\dfrac{-2x}{a+3} = \dfrac{x+2}{2a-1}$

6. $\dfrac{-5x+1}{2a} = \dfrac{bx}{3a+2}$

7. $\dfrac{a}{x+2} = \dfrac{b}{x+2} - b + 1$

8. $\dfrac{b}{2x-4} - 3 = \dfrac{b}{2x-4} - b + 1$

9. $\dfrac{1}{ax+2} = \dfrac{b}{x+a}$

10. $\dfrac{1}{ax+2} = \dfrac{b}{ax+2} - 3$

11. $3\dfrac{x}{ax+2} = 3$

12. $-3\dfrac{2x}{ax+3} = b$

13. $\dfrac{2x-3}{2ax+5} = -3b$

14. $\dfrac{x}{ax+2} = \dfrac{2}{a} - 3$

2nd degree (Quadratic equations)

a. Solve the following equations using the "complete the square method".
b. Check your answers using the quadratic formula.
c. Write the factorized expression.

1. $x^2 - 4x + 1 = 3$
2. $x^2 - 4x + 1 = -3$
3. $x^2 - 4x + 1 = -13$
4. $x^2 + 6x + 2 = 2$
5. $x^2 + 6x + 2 = -10$
6. $x^2 - 3x - 5 = 3$
7. $x^2 - 3x - 3 = -3$
8. $x^2 - 3x - 4 = -1$
9. $x^2 - 7x - 5 = 3$
10. $x^2 + x - 3 = 2$
11. $x^2 - 2x + 4 = 5$
12. $x^2 + 3x - 1 = 3$
13. $x^2 + 7x - 3 = 2$
14. $x^2 + 12x - 4 = -1$

Rational equations 2nd degree

1. $\frac{3}{x^2-4}=2$

2. $\frac{2}{x^2-2x+1}=1$

3. $-\frac{2}{x^2-2x+3}=1$

4. $\frac{x}{x^2-4}=2$

5. $\frac{x}{x-4}=5$

6. $\frac{x^2}{x^2-4x}=2$

7. $\frac{x^2-1}{x-5}=2$

8. $\frac{x}{x-4}+\frac{2}{x-4}=5$

9. $\frac{x}{x-4}+\frac{2}{x+3}=-2$

10. $\frac{x-1}{2x-2}-\frac{2x-1}{x+3}=3$

11. $\frac{x}{3x+2}-\frac{2x-1}{2x+3}=7$

12. $\frac{1}{x}+\frac{2}{x^2}=3$

13. $\frac{1}{x-1}+\frac{2}{x^2-1}=2$

14. $\frac{1}{x-3}-\frac{2}{x^2-9}=4$

Radical Equations

1. $\sqrt{8x+2} = 0$

2. $\sqrt{5x-2} = 6$

3. $\sqrt{5x^2-2} = 3$

4. $\sqrt{x^2+1} = -2$

5. $\sqrt{x^2-2} + 4 = -2$

6. $\sqrt{2x^2-2} + 4x = -2$

7. $\sqrt{2x-2} + 3x + 2 = -2$

8. $\sqrt{x+1} + \sqrt{x+3} = 2$

9. $\sqrt{x-1} + \sqrt{x+3} = 2$

10. $\sqrt{x-3} + \sqrt{x+3} = 3$

11. $\sqrt{5x+1} - \sqrt{3x-3} = 2$

12. $\sqrt{8x+2} - \sqrt{3x-3} = 0$

13. $\sqrt{x-1} + \sqrt{x+2} = -2$

14. $\frac{1}{\sqrt{-3x-1}} = \sqrt{-2+x}$

15. $-4\frac{1}{\sqrt{6x-2}} = \sqrt{2-5x}$

Higher degree simple equations

1. $x^4 - 2x^2 = 0$

2. $(2x - 3)(x^2 - 3)(x + 5)(x^3 + 2) = 0$

3. $(2x - 3)(x - 3) = 1$

4. $(6x - 7)(3x^2 - 5)(2x + 7)(2x^5 - 64)(4x^4 + 5) = 0$

5. $3x^5 - x^2 = 0$

6. $x^6 - 32x = 0$

7. $x^6 - 2x^5 + x^4 = 0$

8. $x^3 - 4x^2 + 3x = 0$

9. $2x^3 - 5x = 0$

10. $2x^3 - x^2 = 0$

11. $ax^4 - 3x = 0$

12. $ax^5 - x^2 = 0$

13. $x^4 - 5x^2 + 3 = -1$

17. $x^4 - 13x^2 + 36 = 0$

14. $x^4 - 10x^2 + 3 = -6$

18. $x^5 - 15x^3 + 54x = 0$

15. $x^6 + 3x^3 - 10 = 0$

19. $x^5 + x^3 - 6x = 0$

16. $x^8 = -2x^4 - 1$

20. $x^4 = 6x^2 - 5$

Rational exponent equations

1. $x^{\frac{1}{2}} = 2$

2. $2x^{\frac{2}{3}} = 3$

3. $3x^{-\frac{1}{2}} = 2$

4. $x + x^{\frac{1}{2}} = 0$

5. $2x - x^{\frac{2}{5}} = 0$

6. $x^{\frac{1}{3}} + 1 = 0$

7. $3x^{\frac{1}{2}} - x^{2} = 0$

8. $5x^{\frac{4}{3}} = -1$

9. $3x^{-\frac{3}{4}} = -2$

10. $x - 2x^{\frac{2}{3}} = 0$

11. $2x^{2} - x^{-\frac{3}{2}} = 0$

12. $x^{\frac{1}{2}} - 2x^{\frac{1}{6}} = 0$

Exponential equations

1. $2^x = 2$

2. $2^{x+2} = 2^2$

3. $\left(\frac{1}{32}\right)2^{3x+4} = 4$

4. $2^{-4x+1} = 8$

5. $3^{-5x+3} = 9$

6. $\left(\frac{1}{4}\right)^{x+2} = \frac{1}{16}$

7. $2^{x+2} = \frac{-1}{16}$

8. $2^{-2x+1} = 8^x$

9. $\left(\frac{1}{3}\right)^{4x^2-1} = 9^{2x}$

10. $\left(\frac{1}{125}\right)5^{x-1} = 1$

11. $3^{2x-5} = \frac{1}{3}$

12. $3^{2x^2-5} = \frac{1}{27}$

13. $\left(\frac{1}{5}\right)^{x-1} = -1$

14. $5^{x-1} = 5^{x(x-1)}$

15. $6^{x^2-8} = 6$

16. $5^{x-1} = \frac{1}{125}$

17. $\left(\frac{1}{36}\right)^{2x-3} = \frac{1}{6}$

18. $6^{2x-3} = -\frac{3}{4}$

19. $2^x = 3$

20. $5^x = 3$

21. $1^x = 2$

22. $2^x = -2$

23. $\frac{1}{5^x - 4} = 1$

24. $\frac{1}{5^x - 24} = 1$

25. $\frac{1}{5^{3x} - 24} = 1$

26. $\frac{2}{2^x - 7} = 2$

27. $\frac{125}{2^{\frac{x}{3}} - 7} = 5$

28. $6^x + 6^{x+1} = \frac{7}{6}$

29. $5^x + 5^{x+1} + 5^{x-1} = \frac{31}{5}$

30. $7^{x-1} + 7^{x-2} = \frac{8}{49}$

31. $7^{x-1} + 7^{x-2} = \frac{8}{7}$

32. $2^{x} + 2^{x-1} + 2^{x+2} = 11$

33. $2^{x} + 2^{x-1} + 2^{x+2} = 22$

34. $5^{2x} - 6 \times 5^{x} = -5$

35. $3^{2x} - 4 \times 3^{x} - 2 = -5$

36. $5^{2x} + 4 \times 5^{x} - 10 = -5$

37. $8^{2x} - 9 \times 8^{x} + 8 = 0$

38. $2 \times 8^{2x} - 18 \times 8^{x} + 10 = -6$

39. $3^{2x+1} - 3^{x+2} + 81 = 0$

40. $5^{2x-1} - 6 \times 5^{x-1} = -1$

41. $3^{2x+2} - 4 \times 3^{x+2} + 27 = 0$

System of equations

1. $\begin{array}{l} 5x+1=2y \\ 4y+x-3=0 \end{array}$

2. $\begin{array}{l} 5x+3y=2-2y \\ -y+2x-5=0 \end{array}$

3. $\begin{array}{l} 5x=2y \\ -y+2x=0 \end{array}$

4. $\begin{array}{l} x=2y-7 \\ 4y-2x=0 \end{array}$

5. $\begin{array}{l} -5x+1=2y \\ -4y+x-3=x \end{array}$

6. $\begin{array}{l} 5x+1=2y \\ 10y-25x=10 \end{array}$

7. $\begin{array}{l} 2x+1=2y \\ -4y+4x+2=0 \end{array}$

8. $\begin{array}{l} x=2y \\ -y+x^2-5=0 \end{array}$

9. $\begin{array}{l} x=1-y \\ -y+x^2-5=0 \end{array}$

10. $\begin{array}{l} x=1-y^2 \\ -y^2+x^2-5=0 \end{array}$

1.6. – EQUATIONS/INEQUALITIES WITH ABSOLUTE VALUE

I. $|x| = a$ $\quad x = a$ OR $x = -a$
II. $|x| > a$ $\quad x > a$ OR $x < -a$
III. $|x| < a$ $\quad -a < x < a$;($x > -a$ and $x < a$) ;($x \in (-a, a)$)

1. $|x| = 5$
2. $|x| = -5$
3. $|x| = 0$
4. $|x| = -1$
5. $|x| < 3$
6. $|x| > 2$
7. $|x| > -5$
8. $|x| < -5$
9. $|2x| = 1$
10. $|x| \geq 0$
11. $|x| \leq 0$
12. $|2x| = 1$
13. $|2x + 1| = 5$
14. $|7x + 21| - 5 = -5$
15. $2 - |5 - 8x| = 15$
16. $|4x + 2| = -5$

17. $|8x + 12| = 100$

25. $|18 - 6x| > 3$

18. $|2x + 1| < 2$

26. $|1 - 6x| < 7$

19. $|8 - 2x + 1| > 6$

27. $|8 - 5x| \leq 0$

20. $|5x - 21| > 0$

28. $|5x - 21| > 1$

21. $|5x - 21| \geq 0$

29. $|x + 11| = 5$

22. $|8x + 11| > -2$

30. $|x + 3| \leq 5$

23. $|91x + 61| < -2$

31. $|x + 11| = -15$

24. $|8 - 3x| > 8$

32. $|2x + 11| + 2 < 15$

1.7. – BINOMIAL THEOREM

1. 0! = ___   1! = ___   2! = ___   3! = ___   n! = ______________

2. Definition: $^{n}C_{k} = \binom{n}{k} = \dfrac{\_\_\_\_\_\_\_\_\_\_\_\_\_\_}{\_\_\_\_\_\_\_\_\_\_\_\_\_\_}$

3. Evaluate: $\binom{6}{2} =$ $\binom{9}{6} =$

   $\binom{4}{0} =$ $\binom{7}{1} =$

4. Show that $^{5}C_{2} = {}^{5}C_{3}$

5. Prove that $^{n}C_{k} = {}^{n}C_{n-k}$

6. $(a + b)^2 =$

7. $(a + b)^3 =$

8. $(a - b)^4 =$

9. $(a - b)^5 =$

10. $(a + b)^6 =$

11. Complete the ______________________ :

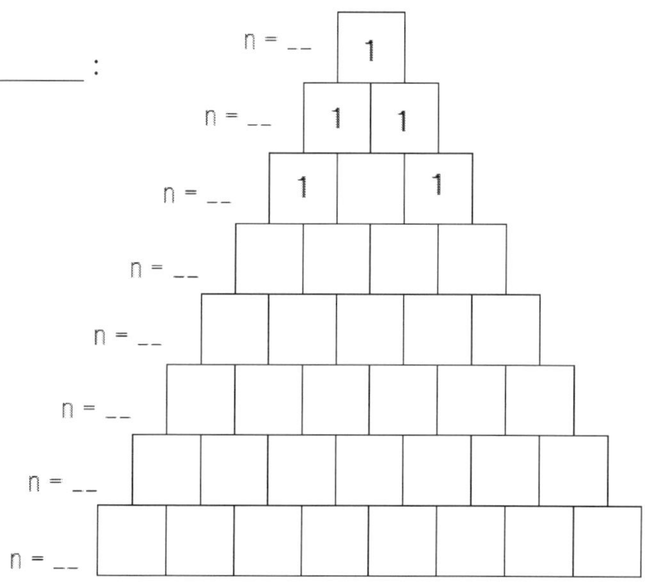

12. In conclusion: The coefficients of the binomial $(a+b)^n$ are given by the numbers in ____________________. The same numbers can be obtained by the expression________________.

13. The binomial theorem can be summarized by:

$$(a+b)^n = \sum_{k=0}^{n} \binom{n}{k} a^{n-k} b^k$$

$$t_{k+1} = \binom{n}{k} a^{n-k} b^k$$

14. $(2x+3)^5 =$

15. $(2x+3y)^4 =$

16. $(a+\frac{1}{a^2})^6 =$

17. $(\frac{a}{b}-\frac{b}{a})^7 =$

18. In each one of the questions 12 to 15 state the number of terms.

14. ___ 15.___ 16.___ 17. ___

19. Complete the sentence: a binomial of degree n has ________ terms.

20. Find and simplify the 8th term of the binomial $(3a^2 + \frac{2}{a})^{13}$

21. Find and simplify the 7th term of the binomial $(3x - 5y)^{11}$

22. Find and simplify the 5th term of the binomial $(3a^2 + y^4)^7$

23. Given the binomial $(\frac{x^2}{2} - \frac{3}{x^3})^{10}$

a. Write the first 3 terms and identify the pattern.

b. Find the coefficient of x^5.

c. Find the independent term.

d. Find the middle term; draw a conclusion about the existence of a middle term and how to find it.

24. Write 2 different binomials for which the first term of the expansion is $16x^{12}$.

25. Find the constant term in the following cases (identify the pattern first):

a. $(2x-\frac{3}{x^2})^9$

b. $(2x+\frac{1}{x^2})^4$

26. Given the binomial $(\frac{x}{2}-\frac{1}{x^2})^8$

a. Write the first 3 terms and identify the pattern.

b. Find the coefficient of x^3.

c. Find the independent term.

d. Find the middle term.

27. Given the binomial $(\frac{a}{x}-\frac{x^2}{a})^8$, it is known that the coefficient of the term in x^4 is 70. Find the possible values of a.

1.8. – SEQUENCES AND SERIES

Given The following sequences, write the first 3 terms and the term in the 20th position. If possible identify the pattern using text (follow example):

1. $a_n = 3n$ $a_1 = 3$ $a_2 = 6$ $a_3 = 9$ $a_{20} = 60$ Pattern: add 3
2. $a_n = 3n + 1$ $a_1 =$ $a_2 =$ $a_3 =$ $a_{20} =$ Pattern: ____________
3. $a_n = 3n - 5$ $a_1 =$ $a_2 =$ $a_3 =$ $a_{20} =$ Pattern: ____________
4. $a_n = 2n + 1$ $a_1 =$ $a_2 =$ $a_3 =$ $a_{20} =$ Pattern: ____________
5. $a_n = 2n$ $a_1 =$ $a_2 =$ $a_3 =$ $a_{20} =$ Pattern: ____________
6. $a_n = 2n - 4$ $a_1 =$ $a_2 =$ $a_3 =$ $a_{20} =$ Pattern: ____________
7. $a_n = -4n$ $a_1 =$ $a_2 =$ $a_3 =$ $a_{20} =$ Pattern: ____________
8. $a_n = -4n + 10$ $a_1 =$ $a_2 =$ $a_3 =$ $a_{20} =$ Pattern: ____________
9. $a_n = -4n - 6$ $a_1 =$ $a_2 =$ $a_3 =$ $a_{20} =$ Pattern: ____________
10. $a_n = \frac{n}{3}$ $a_1 =$ $a_2 =$ $a_3 =$ $a_{20} =$ Pattern: ____________
11. $a_n = \frac{n}{2}$ $a_1 =$ $a_2 =$ $a_3 =$ $a_{20} =$ Pattern: ____________
12. $a_n = \frac{2n}{5} + 1$ $a_1 =$ $a_2 =$ $a_3 =$ $a_{20} =$ Pattern: ____________
13. $a_n = \frac{-3n}{7} + 5$ $a_1 =$ $a_2 =$ $a_3 =$ $a_{20} =$ Pattern: ____________
14. $a_n = \frac{n}{9} - 5$ $a_1 =$ $a_2 =$ $a_3 =$ $a_{20} =$ Pattern: ____________
15. $a_n = \frac{n}{10} - 1$ $a_1 =$ $a_2 =$ $a_3 =$ $a_{20} =$ Pattern: ____________
16. $a_n = \frac{3n}{4} + 2$ $a_1 =$ $a_2 =$ $a_3 =$ $a_{20} =$ Pattern: ____________
17. $a_n = n^2$ $a_1 =$ $a_2 =$ $a_3 =$ $a_{20} =$ Pattern: ____________
18. $a_n = n^3$ $a_1 =$ $a_2 =$ $a_3 =$ $a_{20} =$ Pattern: ____________
19. $a_n = 2^n$ $a_1 =$ $a_2 =$ $a_3 =$ $a_{20} =$ Pattern: ____________
20. $a_n = -2^n$ $a_1 =$ $a_2 =$ $a_3 =$ $a_{20} =$ Pattern: ____________
21. $a_n = 2^{-n}$ $a_1 =$ $a_2 =$ $a_3 =$ $a_{20} =$ Pattern: ____________

22. $a_n = -2^{-n}$ $a_1 =$ $a_2 =$ $a_3 =$ $a_{20} =$ Pattern: ____________________

23. $a_n = (-2)^n$ $a_1 =$ $a_2 =$ $a_3 =$ $a_{20} =$ Pattern: ____________________

24. $a_n = 2^{n-1}$ $a_1 =$ $a_2 =$ $a_3 =$ $a_{20} =$ Pattern: ____________________

25. $a_n = 2^{n+2}$ $a_1 =$ $a_2 =$ $a_3 =$ $a_{20} =$ Pattern: ____________________

26. $a_n = 3 \times 2^n$ $a_1 =$ $a_2 =$ $a_3 =$ $a_{20} =$ Pattern: ____________________

27. $a_n = -5 \times 2^{n-1}$ $a_1 =$ $a_2 =$ $a_3 =$ $a_{20} =$ Pattern: ____________________

28. $a_n = 5 \times 2^{1-n}$ $a_1 =$ $a_2 =$ $a_3 =$ $a_{20} =$ Pattern: ____________________

29. $a_n = (-3)^{2-n}$ $a_1 =$ $a_2 =$ $a_3 =$ $a_{20} =$ Pattern: ____________________

30. $a_n = 2 \times (-3)^n$ $a_1 =$ $a_2 =$ $a_3 =$ $a_{20} =$ Pattern: ____________________

31. $a_n = 2 \times (-5)^{n-1}$ $a_1 =$ $a_2 =$ $a_3 =$ $a_{20} =$ Pattern: ____________________

32. $a_n = (-3)^{n+1}$ $a_1 =$ $a_2 =$ $a_3 =$ $a_{20} =$ Pattern: ____________________

33. $a_n = 1 + 5^{n-2}$ $a_1 =$ $a_2 =$ $a_3 =$ $a_{20} =$ Pattern: ____________________

34. $a_n = 3 \times 2^n$ $a_1 =$ $a_2 =$ $a_3 =$ $a_{20} =$ Pattern: ____________________

35. $a_n = -5 \times 2^{n-1}$ $a_1 =$ $a_2 =$ $a_3 =$ $a_{20} =$ Pattern: ____________________

36. $a_n = 2 \times 3^n$ $a_1 =$ $a_2 =$ $a_3 =$ $a_{20} =$ Pattern: ____________________

37. $a_n = 5^{n-2} + 3$ $a_1 =$ $a_2 =$ $a_3 =$ $a_{20} =$ Pattern: ____________________

38. $a_n = (-3)^n$ $a_1 =$ $a_2 =$ $a_3 =$ $a_{20} =$ Pattern: ____________________

39. $a_n = 2 \times (-3)^n$ $a_1 =$ $a_2 =$ $a_3 =$ $a_{20} =$ Pattern: ____________________

40. $a_n = 2 \times (-5)^{n-1}$ $a_1 =$ $a_2 =$ $a_3 =$ $a_{20} =$ Pattern: ____________________

41. $a_n = (-3)^{n+1}$ $a_1 =$ $a_2 =$ $a_3 =$ $a_{20} =$ Pattern: ____________________

42. $a_n = 1 + 5^{n-2}$ $a_1 =$ $a_2 =$ $a_3 =$ $a_{20} =$ Pattern: ____________________

43. The sequences in which the pattern is add/subtract a number are called ________

44. The sequences in which the pattern is multiply/divide (pay attention that dividing by a is the same as multiplying by _____) a number are called _________

45. $a_n = 2a_{n-1}$ $a_1 = 1$ $a_2 =$ $a_3 =$ $a_{20} =$ Pattern: ____________________

46. $a_{n+2} = a_n + a_{n+1}$ $a_1 = 1$ $a_2 = 1$ $a_3 =$ $a_{20} =$ Pattern: ____________________

47. In the last 2 sequences the terms are given in terms of ____________________

48. (T/F) Arithmetic and Geometric sequences are most of the sequences that exist.

49. The terms in a convergent geometric sequence tend to _______, in a none–convergent sequence the terms tend to _______ or _________.

50. Give an example of a convergent geometric sequence:

51. Give an example of a divergent geometric sequence:

52. Give an example of a alternating convergent geometric sequence:

53. Give an example of a none alternating divergent geometric sequence:

54. A convergent geometric sequence is a sequence in which r is _______________.

Arithmetic sequence (Pattern – Add a constant):

General term: $a_n = a_1 + (n-1)d$

Sum: $S_n = \frac{n}{2}(2a_1 + (n-1)d)$

Geometric Sequence (Pattern – multiply by a constant):

General term: $a_n = a_1 r^{n-1}$

Sum: $S_n = \frac{a(r^n - 1)}{r - 1}$

Convergent geometric sequence ($-1 < r < 1$): $S_\infty = \frac{a_1}{1-r}$

Example:

3, 7, 11, 15…
Arithmetic sequence.
Pattern: add 4.
General term: $a_n = 3 + (n-1)4$
General term can be written also like this: $a_n = -1 + 4n = 4n - 1$

Given the following sequences:

a. For each one write: arithmetic, geometric convergent, geometric divergent or neither, the next term and their general term (in case they are geometric or arithmetic only).

b. Try to write the general term of the other sequences as well.

55. 1, 2, 3, 4, ___…

56. 1, 2, 4, 8, ___…

57. 1, 3, 5, 7, ___…

58. 1, 3, 9, 27, ___…

59. 4, 6, 9, 13,5, ___…

60. 4, 1, –2, –5, ___…

61. 5, 0, –4, –7, ___…

62. 10, 1000, 100000, ___…

63. 30, 10, $\frac{10}{3}$, $\frac{10}{9}$, ___...

64. 2, 10, 50, 250, ___…

65. 2, 102, 202, 302, ___...

66. 1, –1, 1, –1, ____

67. –2, 2, –2, 2, ___...

68. 3, –6, 12, –24, ___...

69. –8, 4, –2, 1, ___…

70. 5, 1, $\frac{1}{5}$, $\frac{1}{25}$, ___...

71. 100, 10, 1, $\frac{1}{10}$, ___..

72. $\frac{3}{4}$, $\frac{3}{8}$, $\frac{3}{16}$, ___...

73. 12, 11, 10, 9, ___...

74. $\frac{4}{9}$, $\frac{5}{9}$, $\frac{6}{9}$, ___…

75. 9, 8, 6, 5, 3, 2, ___...

76. 5, 9, 13, ___...

77. 1, $\frac{3}{2}$, $\frac{9}{4}$, $\frac{27}{8}$, ___…

78. 5, $-\frac{5}{3}$, $\frac{5}{9}$, $-\frac{5}{27}$, ___…

79. $-1, -2, -3,$ ____…

80. $-2, 4, -8,$ ____…

81. $70, 20, \frac{40}{7},$ ____…

82. $100, 10, 1,$ ____…

83. $100, -10, 1, \frac{-1}{10},$ ____...

84. $3, 24, 192,$ ____...

85. $90, 9, \frac{9}{10},$ ____...

86. $\frac{3}{2}, \frac{4}{3}, \frac{5}{4},$ ____…

87. $\frac{40}{3}, \frac{20}{6}, \frac{10}{12}, \frac{5}{24},$ ____...

88. $\frac{2}{3}, -\frac{4}{9}, \frac{8}{27}, -\frac{16}{81},$ ____...

89. $-\frac{1}{2}, -\frac{1}{4}, -\frac{1}{8}, -\frac{1}{16},$ ____...

90. $\frac{1}{7}, -\frac{1}{14}, \frac{1}{21}, -\frac{1}{28},$ ____...

91. 8, 5, 3, 0, ___...

92. $3, \frac{3}{4}, \frac{3}{16}$, ___...

93. 81, –9, 1, $-\frac{1}{9}$, ___...

94. 2, –10, 50, ___...

In each one of the following sequences find the term indicated:

95. 1, 4 , 7... (a_{31})

96. –8, –5, –2... (a_{37})

97. 4, –8, 16... (a_{15})

98. 32, –8, 2... (a_{11})

99. 68, –34, 17... (a_9)

100. The 4th term of a geometric sequence is 3, the 6th term is $\frac{27}{4}$.

a. Find the ratio of the sequence.
b. Is this sequence convergent? Explain
c. Find a_1
d. Find a_{12}
e. Sum the first 15 terms.

101. The 2nd term of a arithmetic sequence is –2, the 6th term is –4.

a. Find the difference of the sequence.
b. Find a_1
c. Find a_{12}
d. Sum the first 50 terms.

102. The 10th term of a geometric sequence is 5, the 14th term is $\frac{80}{81}$

a. Find the ratio of the sequence.
b. Is this sequence convergent? Explain
c. Find a_1
d. Find a_7
e. Sum the first 10 terms.
f. Sum all the terms of the sequence.

103. The 7th term of a arithmetic sequence is 120, the 16th term is 201.

a. Find the difference of the sequence.
b. Find a_1
c. Find a_{12}
d. Sum the first 50 terms.

104. All the terms in a geometric sequence are positive. The first term is 7 and the 3rd term is 28.

a. Find the common ratio.
b. Find the sum of the first 14 terms.

105. The fifth term of an arithmetic sequence is –20 and the twelfth term is –44.

a. Find the common difference.
b. Find the first term of the sequence.
c. Calculate the eighty–seventh term.
d. Calculate the sum of the first 150 terms.

106. Sum the following sequences:

a. $3 + 6 + 9 + 12 + \ldots + 69 =$

b. $6 + 14 + 22 + 30 + \ldots + 54 =$

c. $5 + \frac{5}{3} + \frac{5}{9} + \ldots =$

d. $1 + 2 + 3 + 4 + \ldots + 158 =$

e. $9 + 18 + 27 + 36 + \ldots + 900 =$

f. $80 + 20 + 5 + \ldots$

107. Consider the arithmetic series $-6 + 1 + 8 + 15 + \ldots$

Find the least number of terms so that the sum of the series is greater than 10000.

108. In a theatre there are 20 seats in the first row, 23 in the 2nd, 26 in the 3rd etc. There are 40 rows in the theatre. Find the total number of seats available.

109. A ball bounces on the floor. It is released from a height of 160 cm. After the 1st bounce it reaches a height of 120 cm and 90 cm after the 2nd. If the patterns continue find:

a. The height the ball will reach after the 6th bounce.
b. The total distance the ball passed after a long period o time.

110. In a certain forest the current population of rabbits is 200 objects. It is know that the population increases by 20% every year.

a. Find the population of rabbits after a year.
b. Find the population of rabbits after 2 years.
c. What kind of a sequence is it? State the expression for the population after n years.
d. Find the total number of rabbits after 10 years (assuming none has died).

111. In a research it was observed that the number of defective products produced by a machine per year decreases by 10% every year (due to technological improvements). In a certain year the machine made 300 products.

a. Find the number of defective products produced a year later.
b. Find the number of defective products produced 2 years later.
c. What kind of a sequence is it? State the expression for the number of errors committed after n years.
d. Find the total number of bad products produced in the first 8 years.

112. In a certain company the pay scale follows a pattern of an arithmetic sequence (every year). This means:

a. The salary increases by a certain % every year (True/False), explain.

b. The salary increases by a certain amount every year (True/False), explain

COMPOUND INTEREST

1. 1200$ are put in account that gives 2% per year. Calculate the amount of money in the account after:

    a. 1 year.

    b. 2 years.

2. To increase an amount A by 5% it should be multiplied by ______.
3. To increase an amount A by 56% it should be multiplied by ______.
4. To decrease an amount A by 5% it should be multiplied by ______.
5. To increase an amount A by 15% it should be multiplied by ______.
6. To decrease an amount A by 12% it should be multiplied by ______.
7. To increase an amount A by 230% it should be multiplied by ______.
8. 1000$ are put in account that takes 5% commission per year. Calculate the amount of money in the account after:

    a. 1 year.

    b. 2 years.

9. 2000$ are being put in a deposit that pays 5% (per year).

   a. Fill the table:

Number of Years	Interest earned at the end of the year	Amount in deposit ($)
0		2000
1	$\frac{5}{100}2000 = 100$	2100
2	$\frac{5}{100}2100 = 105$	2205
3	$\frac{5}{100}2205 = 110.25$	
4		
5		

   b. Observe the numbers in the compound interest column: 2000, 2100, 2205… What kind of a sequence is that? Write its general term.

   c. How much money will be in the account after 20 years?

   d. Discuss the meaning of writing $a_n = a_1 r^{n-1}$ or writing $a_n = a_0 r^n$. Use the exercise as an example.

10. A loan of 1200$ is made at 12% per year compounded semiannually, over 5 years the debt will grow to:

   a. $\$1200(1 + 0.12)^5$
   b. $\$1200(1 + 0.06)^{10}$
   c. $\$1200(1 + 0.6)^{10}$
   d. $\$1200(1 + 0.06)^5$
   e. $\$1200(1 + 0.12)^{10}$

11. A loan of 23200$ is made at 8% per year compounded quarterly, over 6 years the debt will grow to:

   a. $\$23200(1 + 0.08)^{24}$
   b. $\$23200(1 + 0.02)^6$
   c. $\$23200(1 + 0.8)^{24}$
   d. $\$23200(1 + 0.02)^{24}$
   e. $\$23200(1 + 0.2)^{24}$

12. A loan of 20$ is made at 6% per year compounded monthly, over 8 years the debt will grow to:

   a. $\$20(1 + 0.005)^{96}$
   b. $\$20(1 + 0.06)^{96}$
   c. $\$20(1 + 0.05)^{96}$
   d. $\$20(1 + 0.006)^{12}$
   e. $\$20(1 + 0.006)^{96}$

13. A loan of X$ is made at 9% per year compounded every 4 months, over 5 years the debt will grow to:

   a. $\$X(1 + 0.09)^{15}$
   b. $\$X(1 + 0.9)^{15}$
   c. $\$X(1 + 0.3)^{15}$
   d. $\$X(1 + 0.03)^{15}$
   e. $\$X(1 + 0.003)^{15}$

14. A loan of X$ is made at i% per year compounded every m months, over n years the debt will grow to:

$$Debt = \_\_(1 + -)^{-}$$

15. Calculate the total amount owing after two years on a loan of 1500$ if the interest rate is 11% compounded

    a. Annually

    b. Semiannually

    c. Quarterly

    d. Monthly

16. How much will a client have to repay on a loan of 800$ after 2 years, if the 12% interest is compounded annually.

17. Find the compound interest **earned** by the deposit. Round to the nearest cent. $3000 at 12% compounded semiannually for 10 years

18. How many years will it take to a 100$ to double assuming interest rate is 6%. Compounded semiannually.

19. How many years will it take to a X$ to triple assuming interest rate is 7%. Compounded quarterly

20. Find the interest rate given to a certain person in case he made a deposit of 1000$ and obtained 1200$ after 3 years, compounded monthly.

21. Find the interest rate given to a certain person in case he made a deposit of 2500$ and obtained 3000$ after 10 years, compounded yearly.

SIGMA NOTATION

1. The sum $\sum_{k=2}^{4} 2^k$ is equal to which of the following?
   a. $2^1 + 2^2 + 2^3 + 2^4$
   b. $2^2 + 2^4$
   c. $2^2 + 3^3 + 4^4$
   d. $2^2 + 2^3 + 2^4$

2. The sum $\frac{1}{4}\sum_{m=2}^{4} x_m$ is equal to which of the following?
   a. $\frac{1}{4}x_2 + \frac{1}{4}x_3 + \frac{1}{4}x_4$
   b. $\frac{1}{4}x_2 + x_3 + x_4$
   c. $\frac{1}{2}x_2 + \frac{1}{3}x_3 + \frac{1}{4}x_4$
   d. $\frac{1}{4}(2+3+4)$

3. The sum $\sum_{j=4}^{n} \frac{j}{j+1}$ is equal to which of the following?
   a. $\frac{1}{2}+\frac{3}{4}+\frac{5}{6}+...+\frac{n}{n+1}$
   b. $\frac{1}{2}+\frac{2}{3}+\frac{3}{4}+...+\frac{n}{n+1}$
   c. $\frac{4}{5}+\frac{5}{6}+\frac{6}{7}+...+\frac{n}{n+1}$
   d. $\frac{4}{5}+\frac{5}{6}+\frac{6}{7}+...+\frac{n+4}{n+5}$

4. Write out fully what is meant by
   a. $\sum_{i=4}^{i=6} 2i-1=$
   b. $\sum_{i=2}^{i=5} \frac{i}{i^2+1}=$
   c. $\sum_{i=4}^{i=6} (2i-3)^2=$
   d. $\sum_{k=3}^{i=7} (2^k+\sqrt{k})=$
   e. $\sum_{i=1}^{i=4} (-1)^i \times 3^{2i}$

5. Write each series using sigma notation:

a. $4 + 9 + 16 + 25 + 36 + 49 + 64 + 81 = \sum_{i=\_}^{i=\_}$ ____________

b. $5 + 9 + 13 + 17 + 21 + 25 + 29 + 33\ldots = \sum_{i=\_}^{i=\_}$ ____________

c. $1 - \frac{1}{3} + \frac{1}{9} - \frac{1}{27} + \frac{1}{81} - \frac{1}{243} = \sum_{i=\_}^{i=\_}$ ____________

6. Use sigma notation to represent 3 + 6 + 9 + 12 + ... for 28 terms. Sum the terms.

$\sum_{i=\_}^{i=\_}$ ____________

7. Use sigma notation to represent –3 + 6 – 12 + 24 – 48 + ... for 35 terms. Sum the terms.

$\sum_{i=\_}^{i=\_}$ ____________

8. Use sigma notation to represent: 8.3 + 8.1 + 7.9 + 7.7 +…. for 100 terms. Sum the terms

$\sum_{i=\_}^{i=\_}$ ____________

9. An infinite geometric series is given by $\sum_{i=1}^{\infty} 2(1-x)^i$

a. Find the value of x for which the series has a finite sum

b. When x = 0.5, find the minimum number of terms needed to give a sum which is greater than 1.9

CHAPTER 2 – FUNCTIONS

2.1. – INTRODUCTION

1. Write the definition of a function in your own words:

2. Write 2 examples of relations that are functions:

   $f(x) = x^2$

   $f(x) = 2x + 3$

3. Draw a sketch of the functions that describe those relations. Can you write the mathematical expression to describe them?

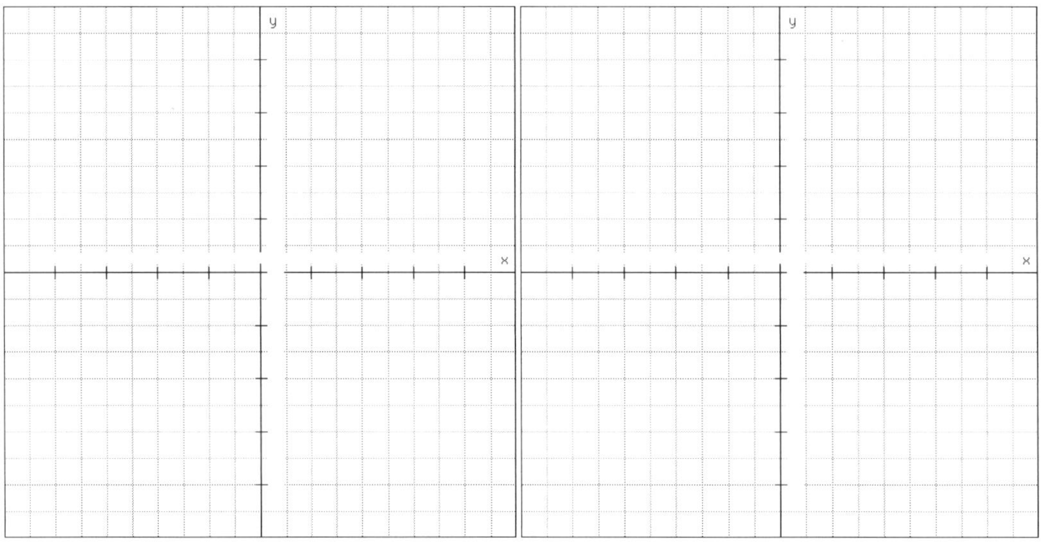

4. Write 2 examples of relations that are not functions:

   $f(x) = 2 + 3$

   $f(x) = 0$

5. Which one of the following graphs cannot represent function:

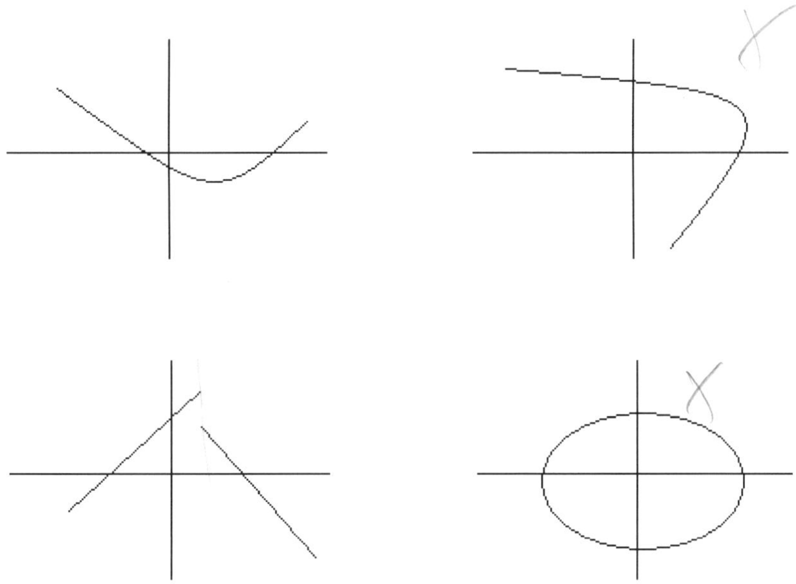

6. Draw an example of a curve that is not a function:

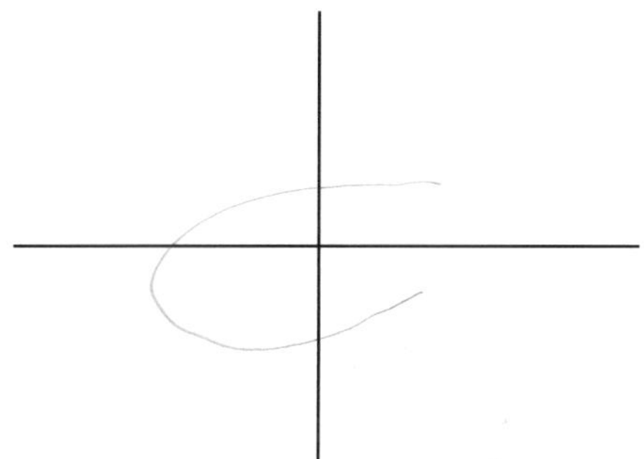

7. Draw an example of a curve that is a function:

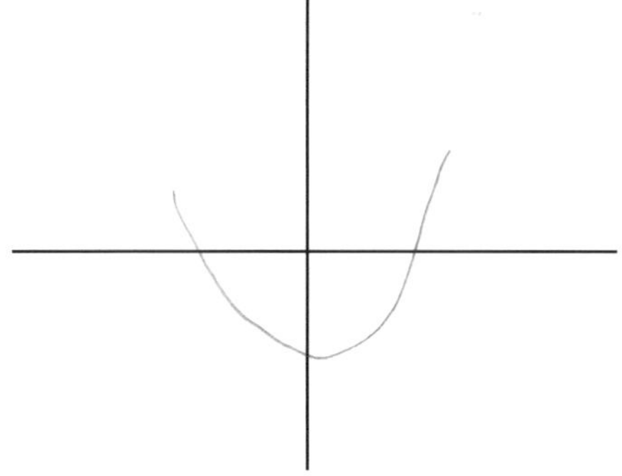

8. The domain of a function is the: x ______________________________

9. The Range of a function is the: y ______________________________

10. Given the Height – age curve for a human.

a. Sketch an approximate graph:

b. In your sketch Height(0) = _______, it is the height of ________________

c. In your sketch Height(t) = 100cm. Then t is: _____________

d. State its domain: _______________________

e. State its range: _______________________

11. Out of the following relations circle the ones that are functions:

a. Person's name → Person's age
b. City → Number of habitants
c. City → Names of habitants
d. Family → Home Address
e. Satellite's name → Position of satellite
f. Time → Position of object
g. One → One
h. One → Many
i. Many → One

12. Given the function:

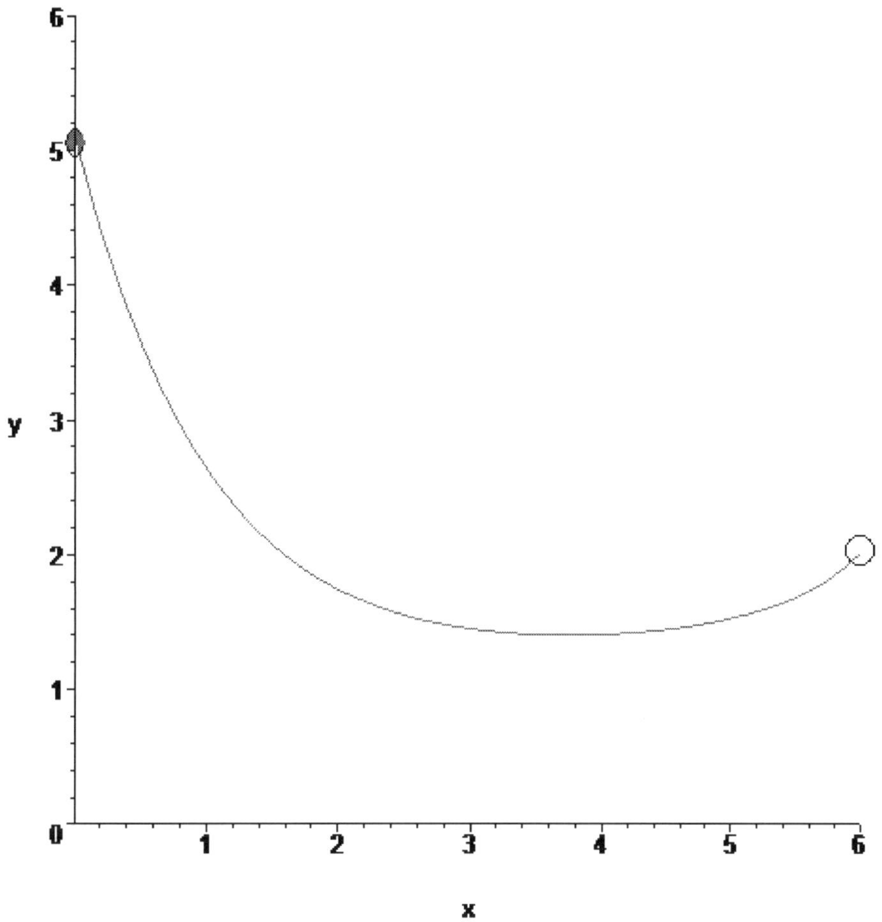

a. f(0) = __________

b. f(2) = _________ = f(__)

c. f(7) = _________

d. f(x) = 3, __x = ____________________

e. f(x) = 2, _x = _____________________

f. State its domain: _______________________

g. State its range: _______________________

h. Is this function one to one? One to many? Explain.

13. Given the function:

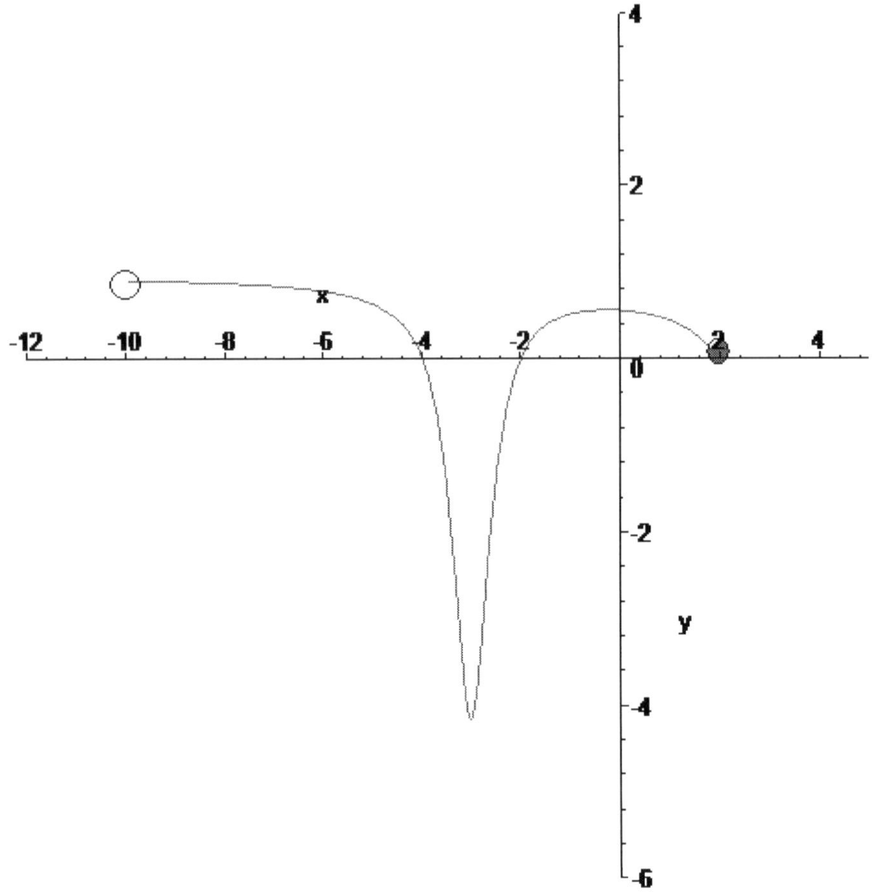

a. f(x) = 0, ____________________________

b. f(0) = ___________ =f(__)

c. f(–8) = __________

d. f(–3) = __________

e. f(–4) = ___________ =f(__)

f. f(3) = __________

g. State its domain: __________________________

h. State its range: __________________________

i. Is this function one to one? One to many? Explain.

14. Given the following function:

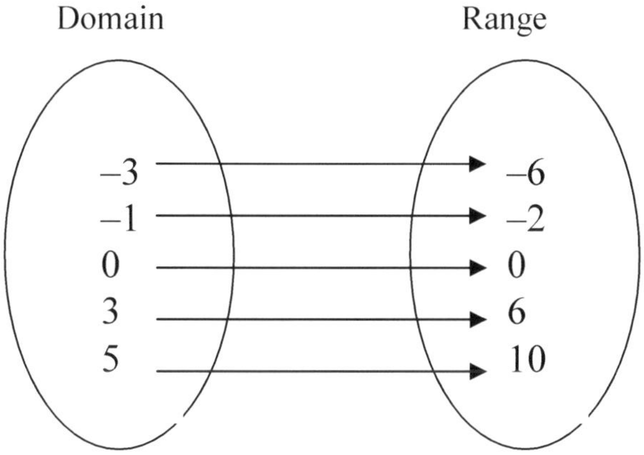

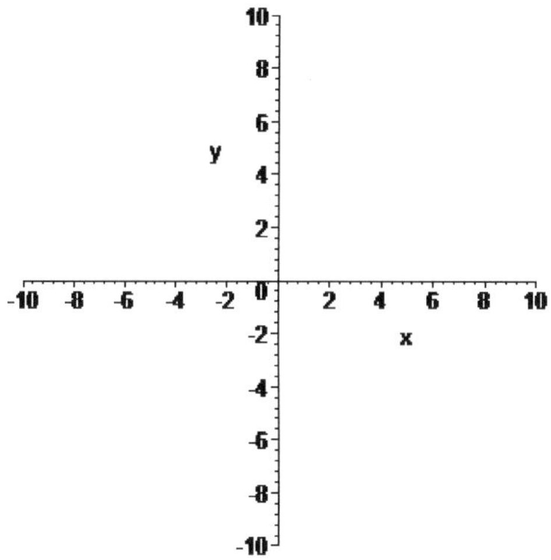

a. What are the allowed values for the independent variable (The domain)?

b. What are the allowed values for the dependent variable (The range)?

c. Sketch the function on the graph.

d. Can you write a mathematical expression to express this function?

15. Given the following function:

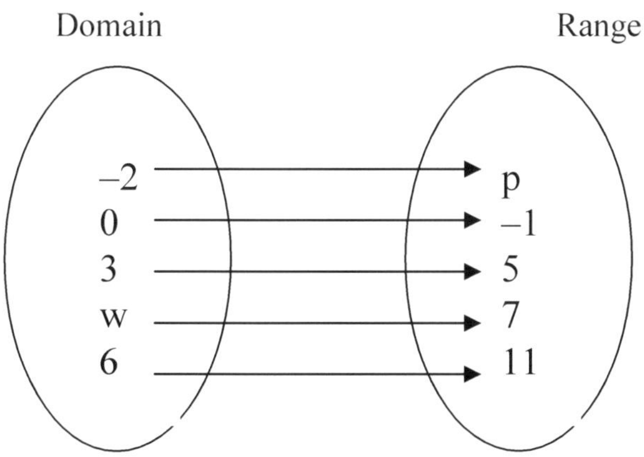

a. Can you write a mathematical expression to express this function?

b. Find p. Find w.

16. Use the graph below to answer the following:

a. $f(0)$ = ___

b. $f(7)$ = ___

c. $f(2)$ = ___

d. Is $f\left(-1/2\right)$ positive or negative?

e. For what values of x is $f(x)=0$

f. Is $f(1) > f(7)$?

g. For what values of x is $f(x) > 0$?

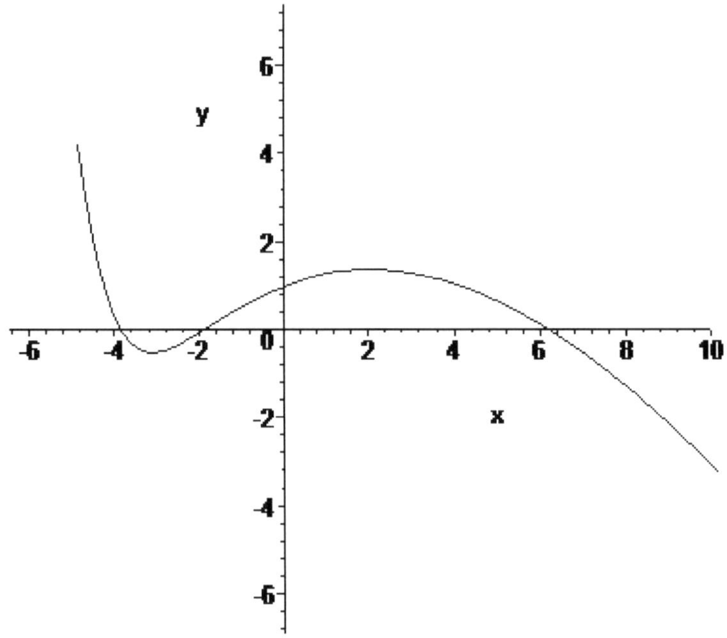

17. Functions can be represented using: _______________ or __________________.

18. The following graph describes the concentration of a drug injected into the blood as a function of the time (in minutes) since the injection. $t = 0$ corresponds to the time of injection.

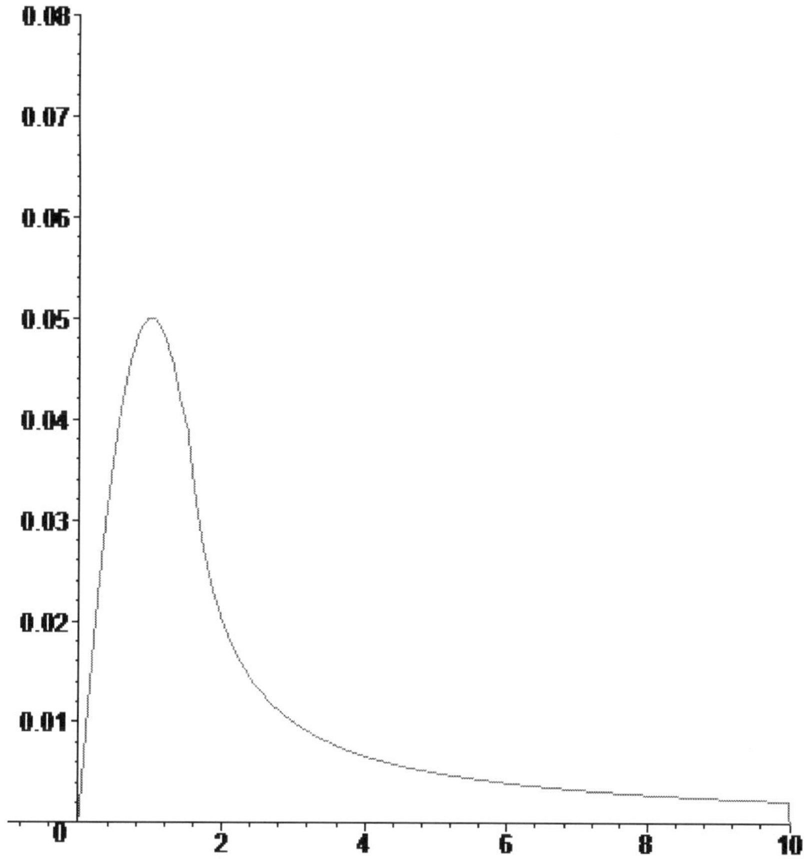

a. What is the concentration of the drug 4 hours after the injection?

b. During what period of time is the concentration increasing?

c. After how long is the concentration maximum?

d. When is the concentration greater than 0.02?

e. State the domain and range of the function.

19. The graph below shows the temperature in C° on a particular day as a function of time since midnight.

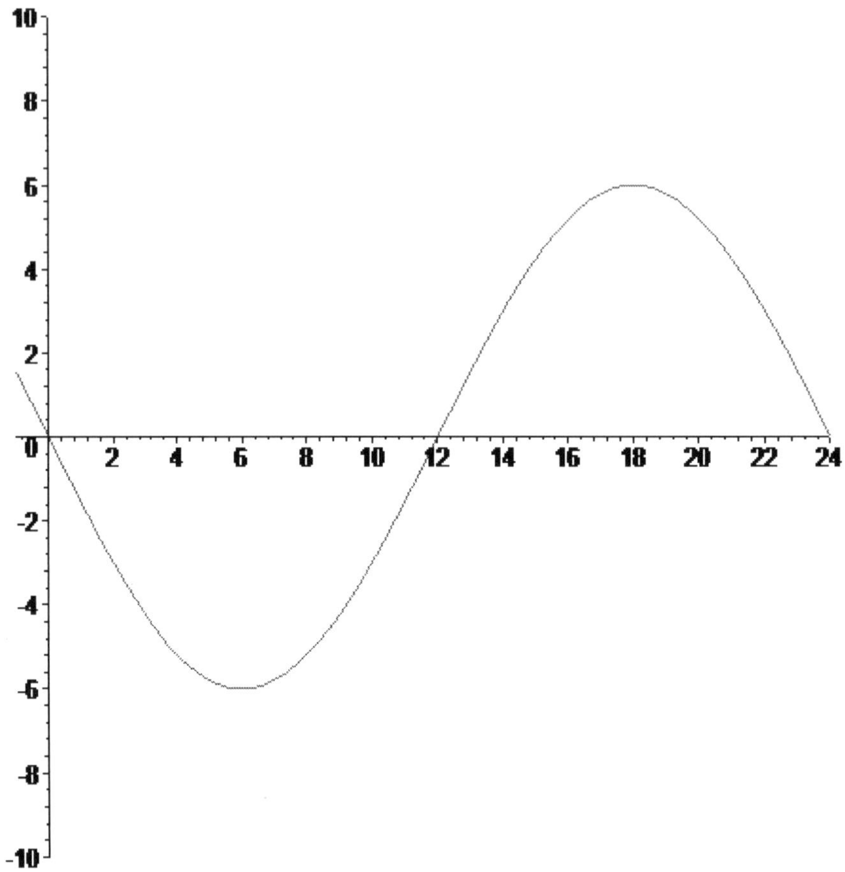

a. What was the temperature at 4:00 a.m.?

b. When was the temperature 4 degrees?

c. When was the temperature below freezing? (less than 0 degrees)

d. When was the temperature increasing?

f. State the domain and range of the function.

2.2. – LINEAR FUNCTIONS

1. Given the function: $f(x) = -5$

- Complete the following table:

X	–5	–4	–3	–2	–1	0	1	2	3	4	5
f(x)											

- Sketch the points of the chart on a graph (use a ruler).
- State the domain of the function: ________________
- State the *y* intercept (sketched on the graph: (____, ____)
- State the *x* intercept: (____, ____)
- The function is increasing on the interval: ________
- The function is decreasing on the interval: ________
- Sketch the function of the graph used for the points initially drawn
- State the range of the function: ________

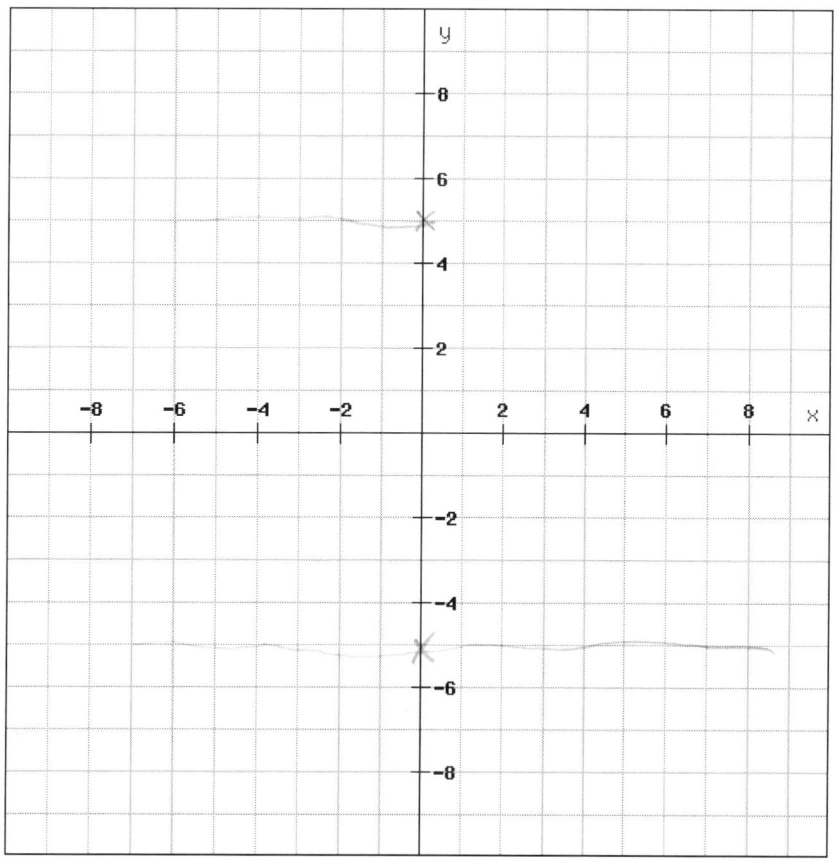

2. Given the function: f(x) = x + 3

- Complete the following table:

x	–5	–4	–3	–2	–1	0	1	2	3	4	5
f(x)	-2	-1	0	1							

- Sketch the points of the chart on a graph (use a ruler).
- State the domain of the function: ________________
- State the *y* intercept (sketched on the graph: (____, ____)
- State the *x* intercept: (____, ____)
- The function is increasing on the interval: ________
- The function is decreasing on the interval: ________
- Sketch the function of the graph used for the points initially drawn
- State the range of the function: ________

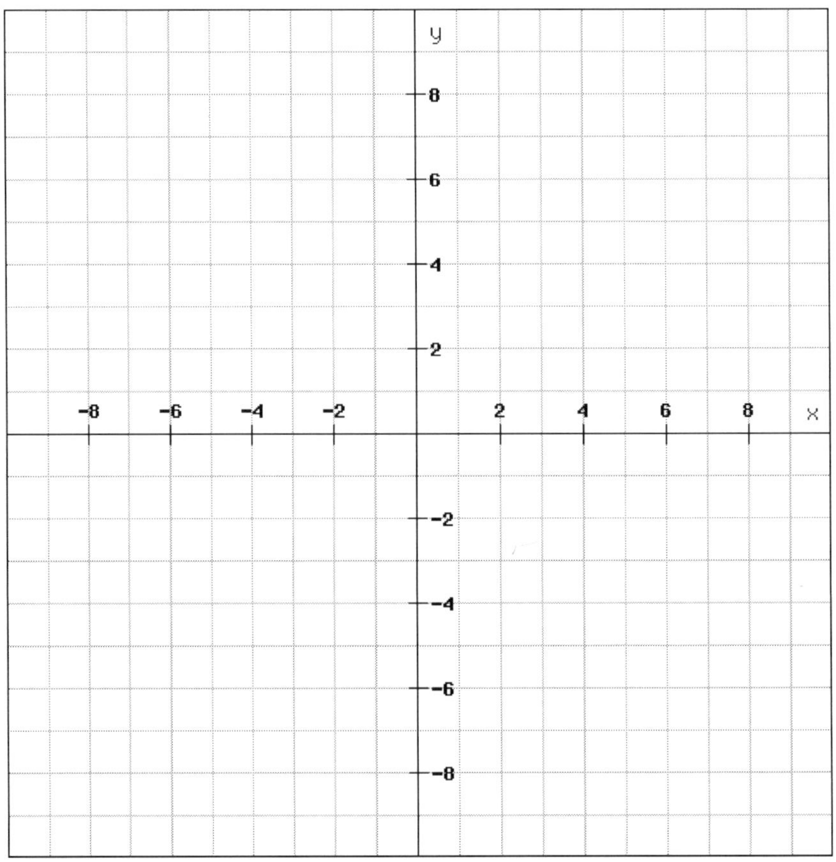

3. Given the function: f(x) = –2x – 5

- Complete the following table:

x	–5	–4	–3	–2	–1	0	1	2	3	4	5
f(x)											

- Sketch the points of the chart on a graph (use a ruler).
- State the domain of the function: ________________
- State the *y* intercept (sketched on the graph: (____, ____)
- State the *x* intercept: (____, ____)
- The function is increasing on the interval: ________
- The function is decreasing on the interval: ________
- Sketch the function of the graph used for the points initially drawn
- State the range of the function: ________

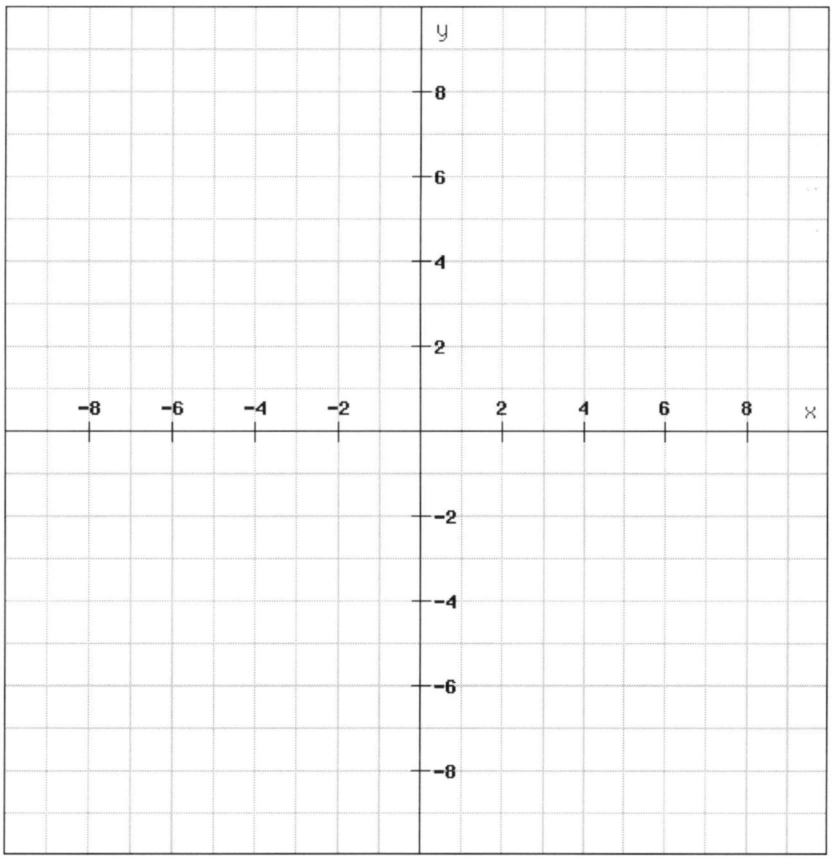

4. Given the function: f(x) = 4x – 3

- Complete the following table:

x	–5	–4	–3	–2	–1	0	1	2	3	4	5
f(x)											

- Sketch the points of the chart on a graph (use a ruler).
- State the domain of the function: ________________
- State the *y* intercept (sketched on the graph: (____, ____)
- State the *x* intercept: (____, ____)
- The function is increasing on the interval: ________
- The function is decreasing on the interval: ________
- Sketch the function of the graph used for the points initially drawn
- State the range of the function: ________

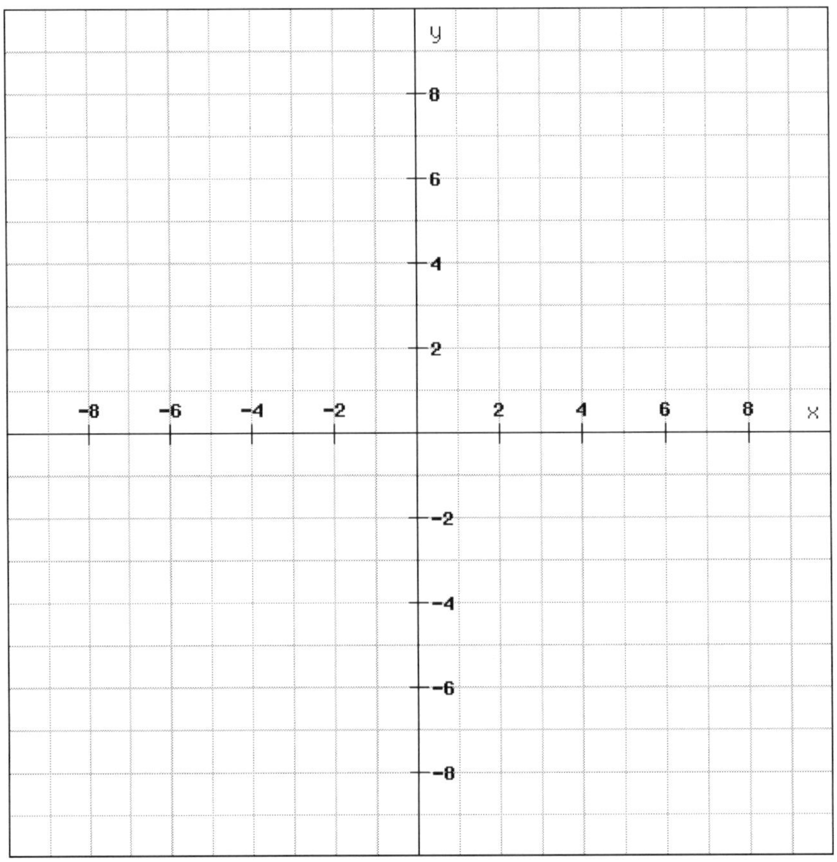

5. Given below are the equations for five different lines. Match the function with its graph.

Function	On the graph
$f(x) = 20 + 2x$	
$g(x) = 4x + 20$	
$s(x) = -30 + 2x$	
$a(x) = 60 - x$	
$b(x) = -2x + 60$	

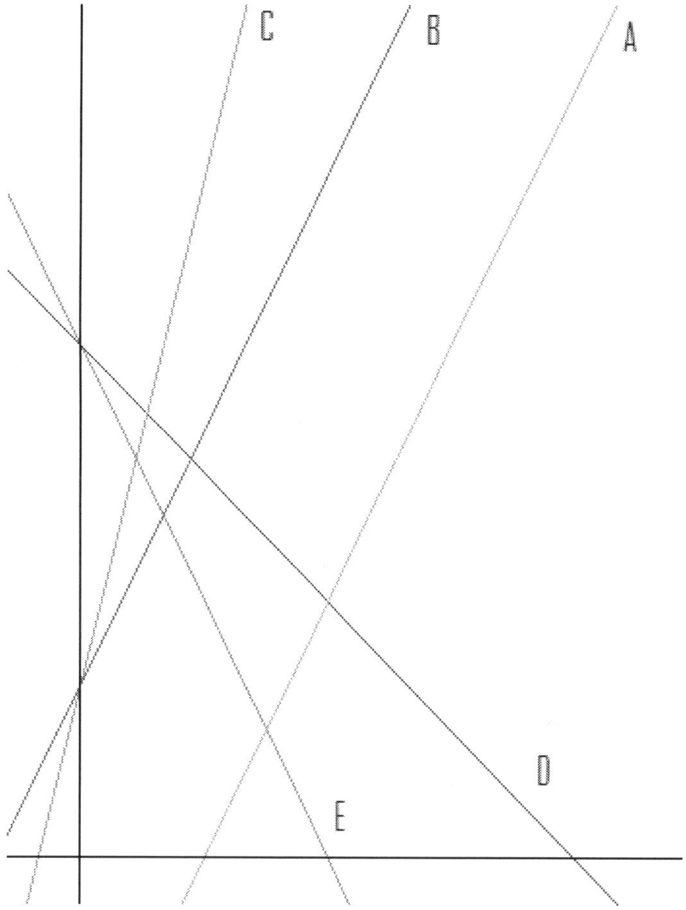

6. The general functions that describes a straight line is ___________________

7. We know a function is a straight line because __________________________

8. The y–intercept (also called vertical intercept), tells us where the line crosses the ____________. The corresponding point is of the form (,).

9. The x–intercept (also called horizontal intercept), tells us where the line crosses the ____________. The corresponding point is of the form (,).

10. If $m > 0$, the line ________ left to right. If ________ the line decreases left to right.

11. In case the line is horizontal m is _________ and the line is of the form ________.

12. The larger the value of m is, the _____________ the graph of the line is.

13. Given the graph, write, the slope (m), b and the equation of the line:

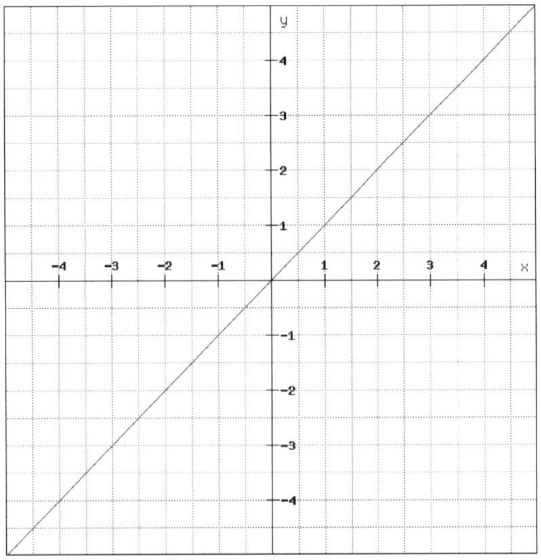

m = __1__ b = __0__ f(x) = __x__

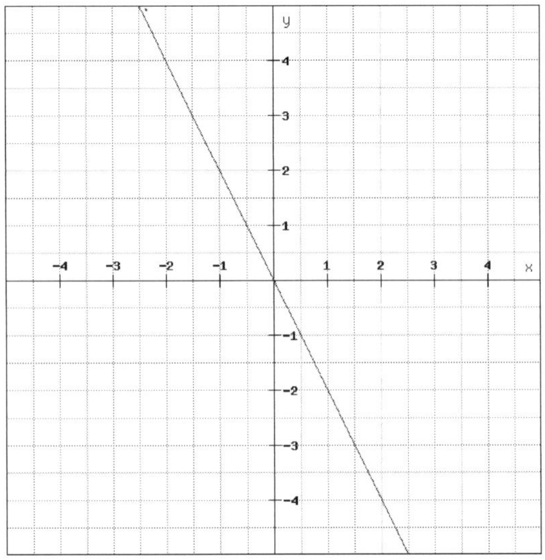

m = __-1__ b = __0__ f(x) = __-x__

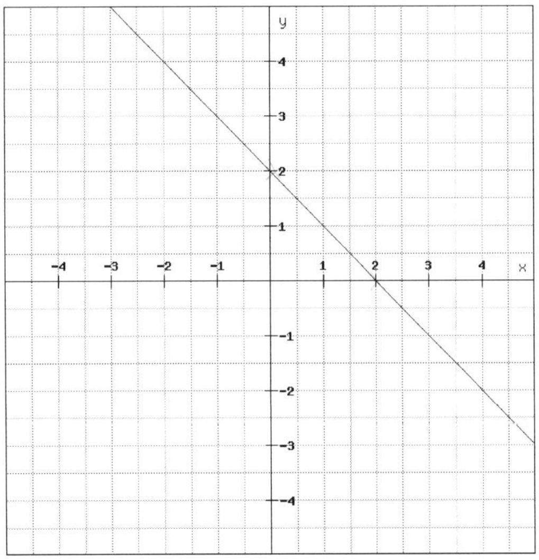

m = __-1__ b = __2__ f(x) = __-x+2__

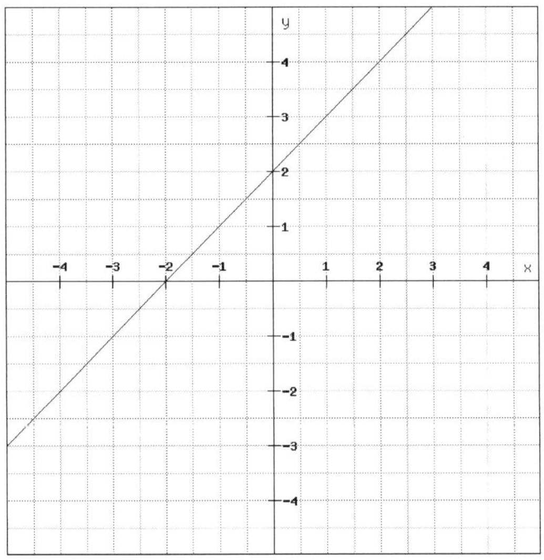

m = __1__ b = __2__ f(x) = __x+2__

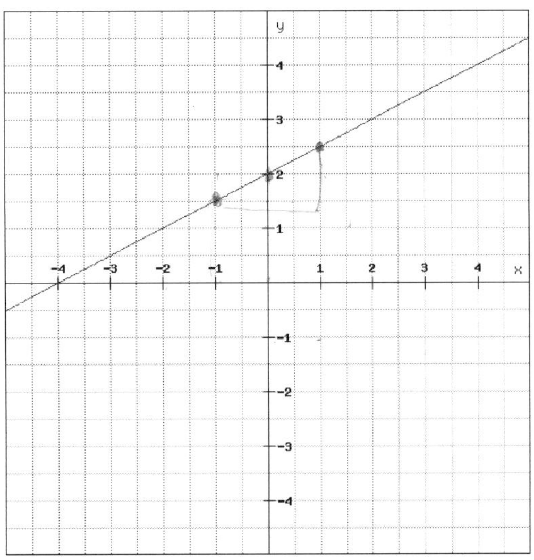

m = ____ b = _____ f(x) = $\frac{1}{2}x+2$

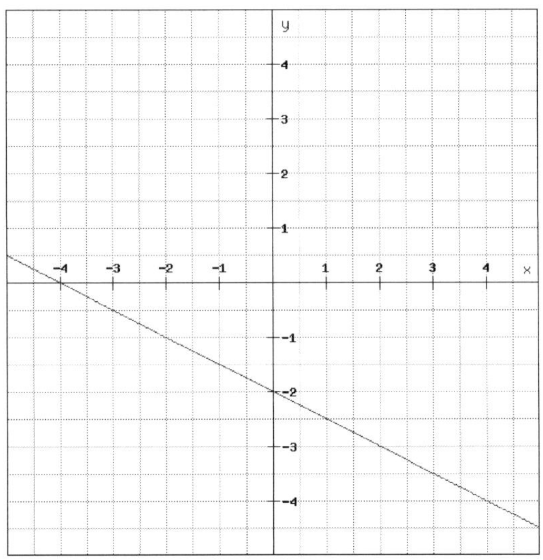

m = ____ b = _____ f(x) = $-\frac{1}{2}x-2$

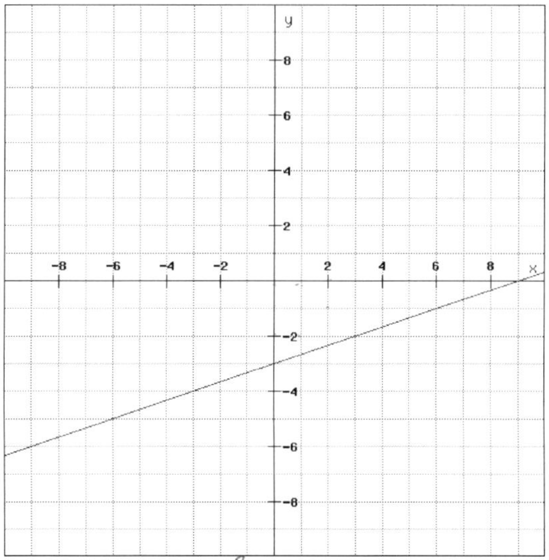

m = ____ b = ____ f(x) = ____________

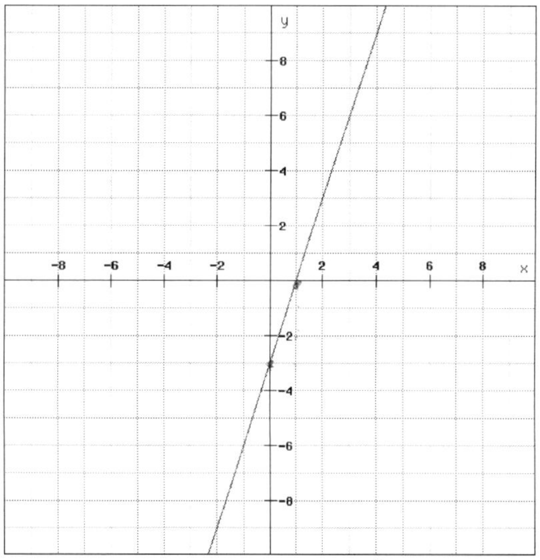

m = ____ b = ____ f(x) = ____________

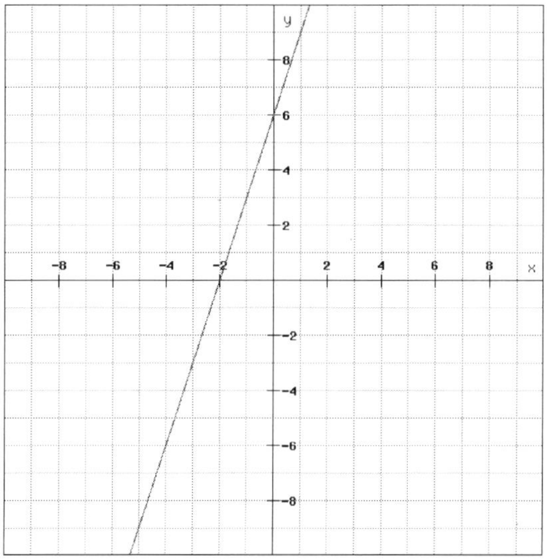

m = ____ b = ____ f(x) = ____________

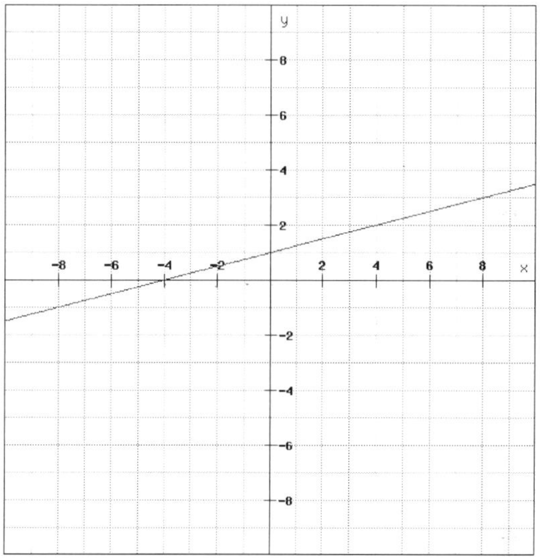

m = ____ b = ____ f(x) = ____________

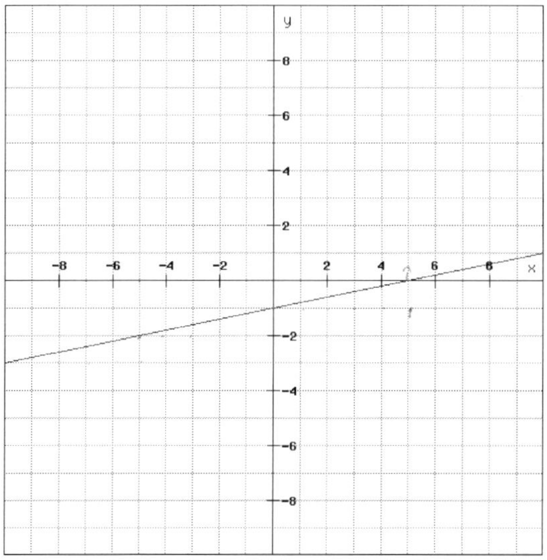

m = ____ b = ____ f(x) = ____________

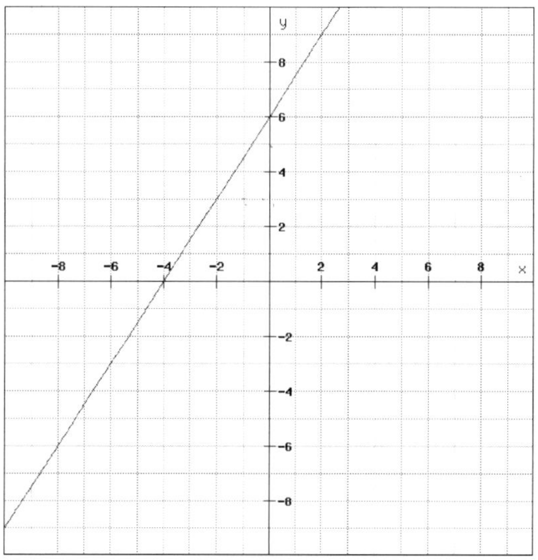

m = ____ b = ____ f(x) = ____________

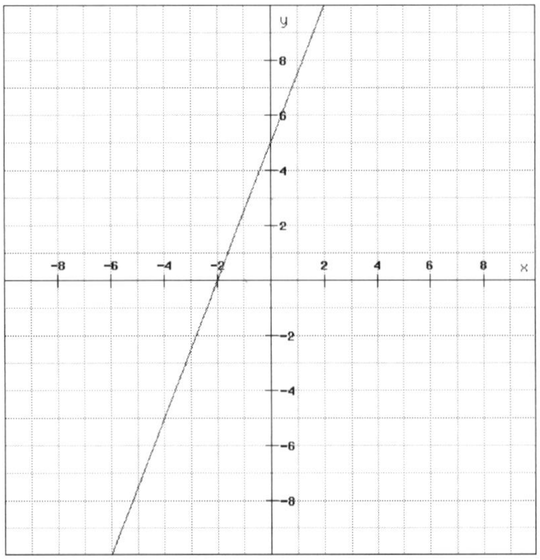

m = ____ b = 5 f(x) = $\frac{5}{2}x+5$

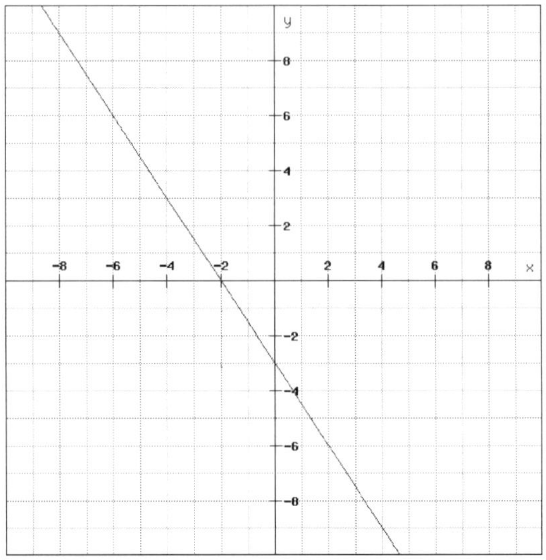

m = ____ b = -3 f(x) = $\frac{3}{2}x-3$

Analyze the following functions:

1. f(x) = 1

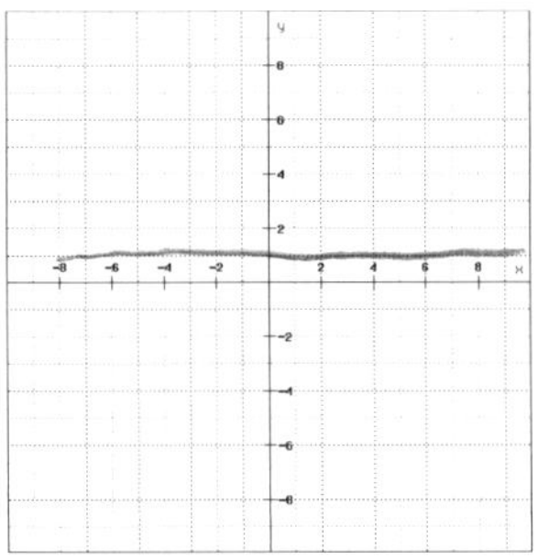

Domain: x ∈ IR

Range: only 1

Increase: x

Decrease: x

y intercept: (,)

x intercept: (,)

2. f(x) = 2

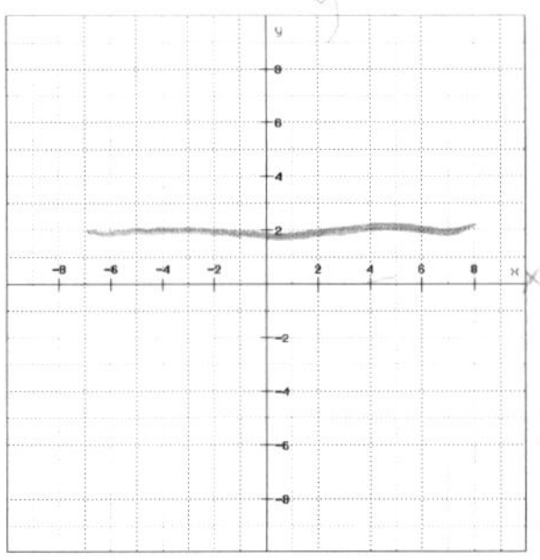

Domain: x ∈ IR

Range: y[2]

Increase: /

Decrease: /

y intercept: (0,2)

x intercept: (,)

3. f(x) = –1

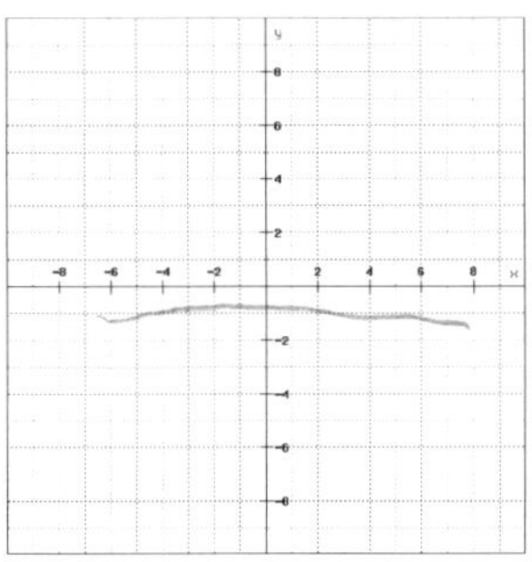

Domain: x ∈ IR

Range: y[-1]

Increase: /

Decrease: ____

y intercept: (,)

x intercept: (,)

4. f(x) = 0

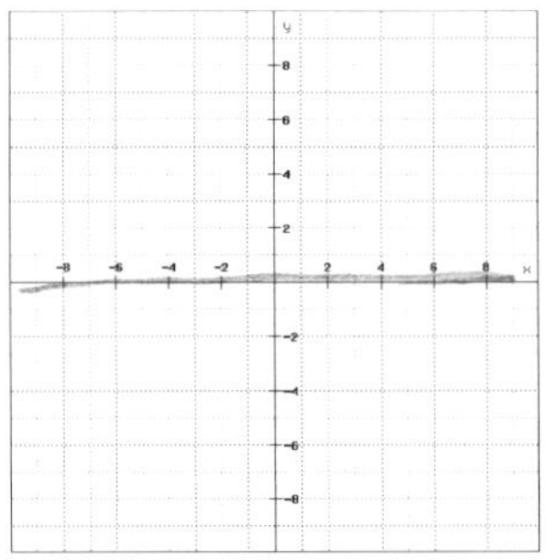

Domain: x ∈ IR

Range: R [0]

Increase: /

Decrease: /

y intercept: (,)

x intercept: (,)

5. f(x) = x

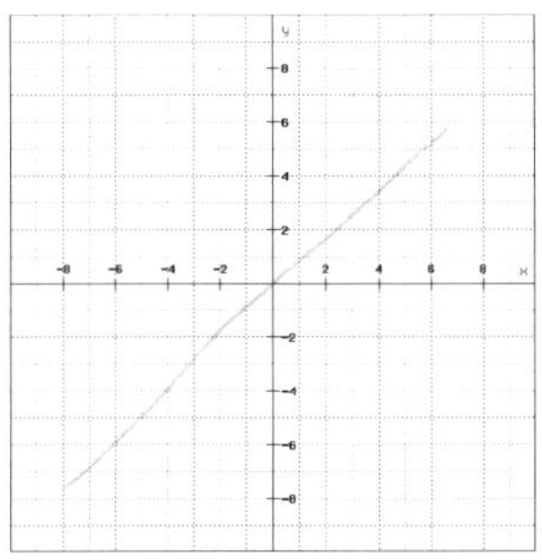

Domain: x ∈ R

Range: y ∈ R

Increase: ____

Decrease: ____

y intercept: (,)

x intercept: (,)

6. f(x) = x + 1

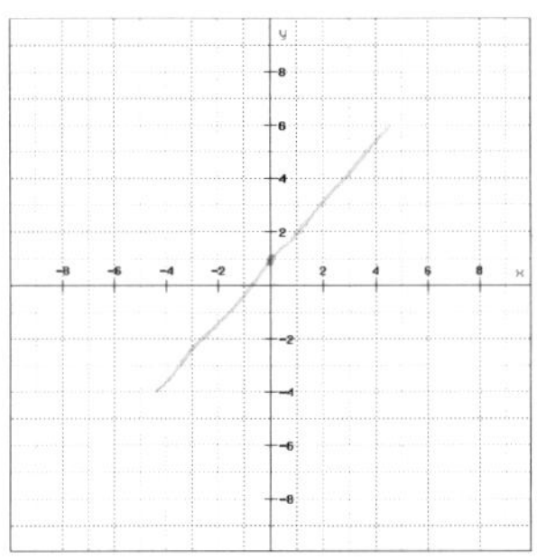

Domain: x ∈ IR

Range: y ∈ IR

Increase: /

Decrease: /

y intercept: (,)

x intercept: (,)

7. f(x) = – x

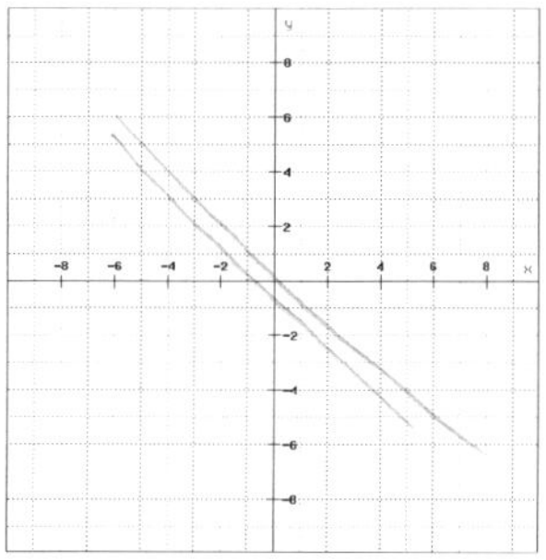

Domain: $x \in \mathbb{R}$

Range: $y \in \mathbb{R}$

Increase:__________

Decrease:__________

y intercept: (,)

x intercept: (,)

8. f(x) = – x – 2

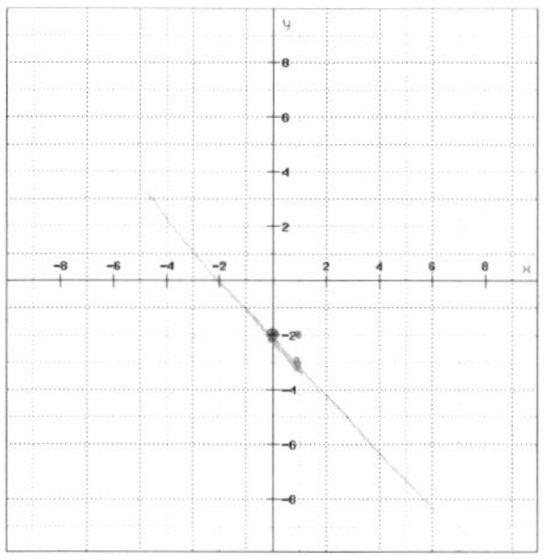

Domain:__________

Range:__________

Increase:__________

Decrease:__________

y intercept: (,)

x intercept: (,)

9. f(x) = 2x

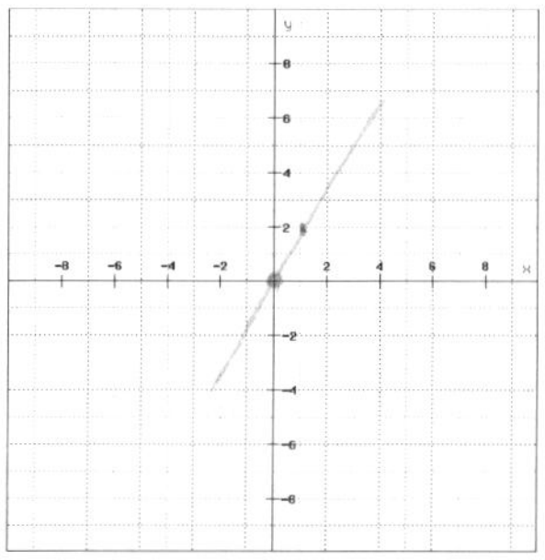

Domain:__________

Range:__________

Increase:__________

Decrease:__________

y intercept: (,)

x intercept: (,)

10. f(x) = 3x – 5

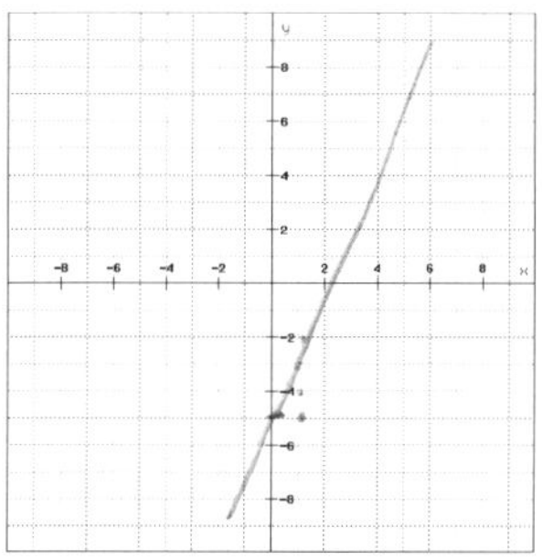

Domain:__________

Range:__________

Increase:__________

Decrease:__________

y intercept: (,)

x intercept: (,)

11. f(x) = 3 – 2x

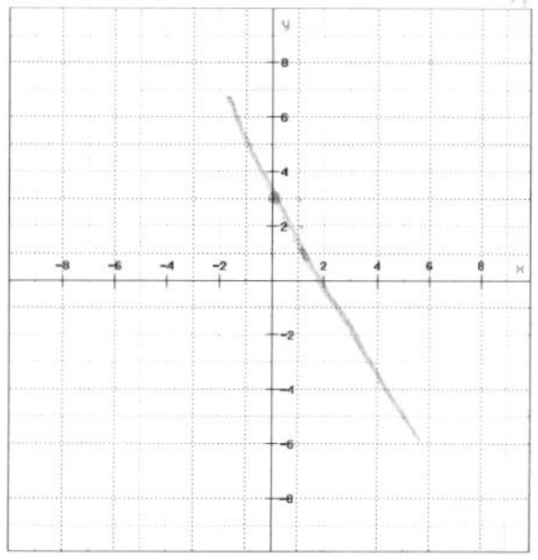

Domain: $x \in \mathbb{R}$

Range: $y \in \mathbb{R}$

Increase:__________

Decrease:__________

y intercept: (,)

x intercept: (,)

12. f(x) = $\frac{x}{3}$

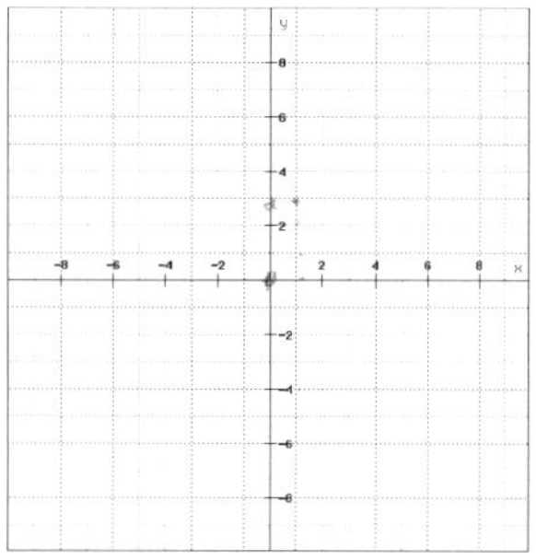

Domain:__________

Range:__________

Increase:__________

Decrease:__________

y intercept: (,)

x intercept: (,)

13. f(x) = 2x + 1

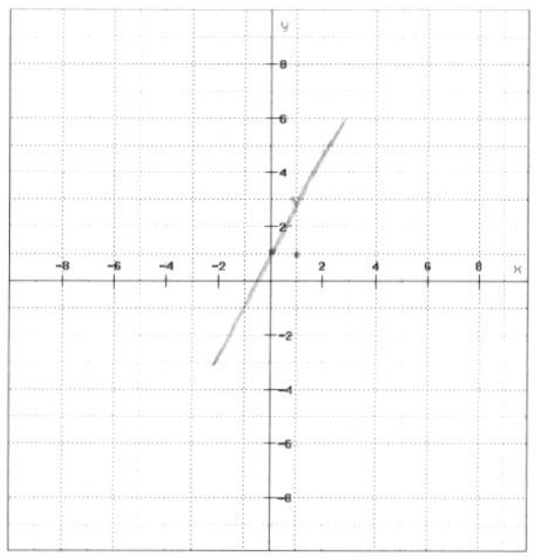

Domain:__________

Range:__________

Increase:__________

Decrease:__________

y intercept: (,)

x intercept: (,)

14. f(x) = 2x – 2

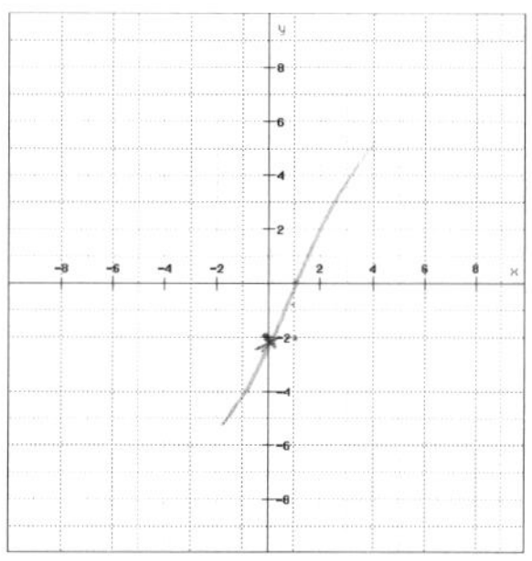

Domain:__________

Range:__________

Increase:__________

Decrease:__________

y intercept: (,)

x intercept: (,)

15. $f(x) = 3x + 5$

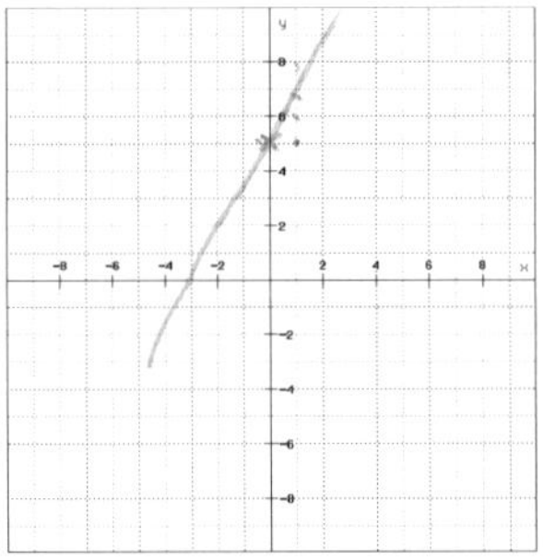

Domain: ____________

Range: ____________

Increase: ____________

Decrease: ____________

y intercept: (,)

x intercept: (,)

16. $f(x) = \dfrac{x}{2} - 5$

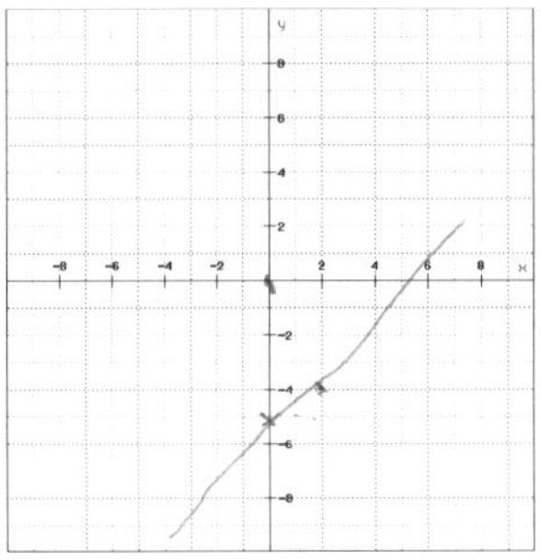

Domain: ____________

Range: ____________

Increase: ____________

Decrease: ____________

y intercept: (,)

x intercept: (,)

17. $f(x) = \dfrac{x}{4} + 6$

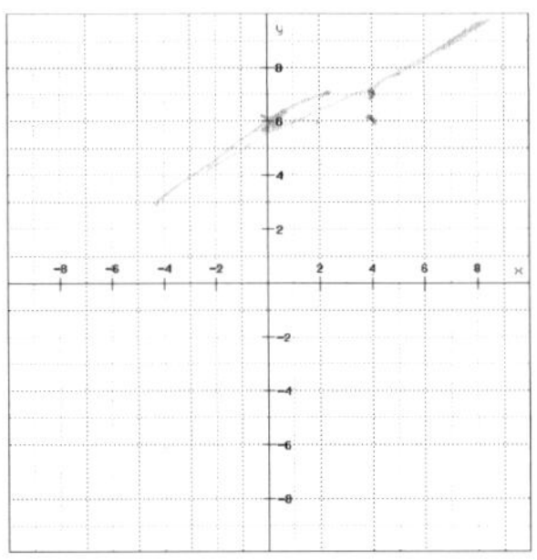

Domain: ____________

Range: ____________

Increase: ____________

Decrease: ____________

y intercept: (,)

x intercept: (,)

18. $f(x) = \dfrac{3}{2}x - 5$

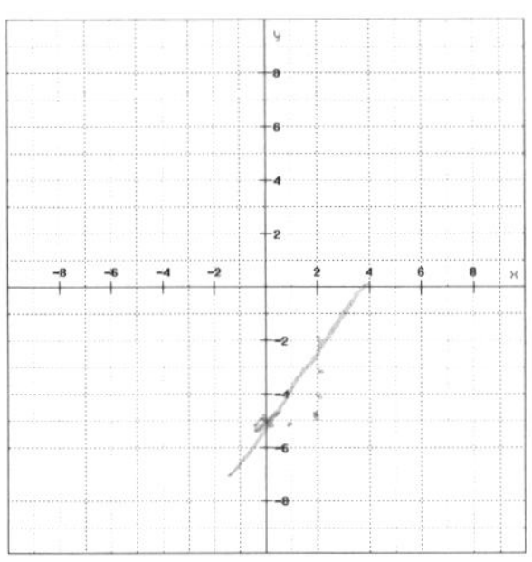

Domain: ____________

Range: ____________

Increase: ____________

Decrease: ____________

y intercept: (,)

x intercept: (,)

19. $f(x) = -\dfrac{3}{2}x - \dfrac{3}{2}$

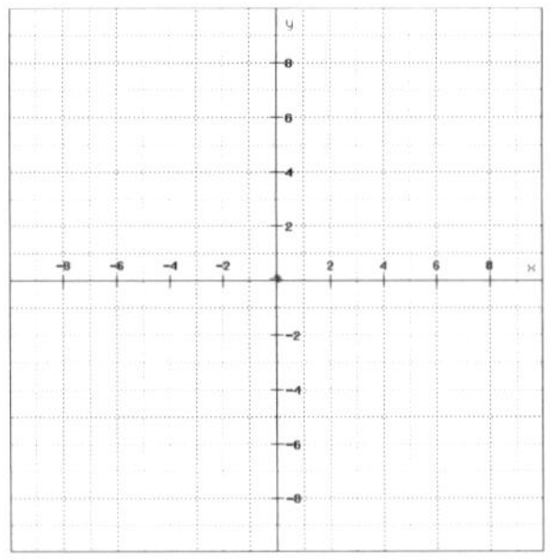

Domain: ____________

Range: ____________

Increase: ____________

Decrease: ____________

y intercept: (,)

x intercept: (,)

20. $f(x) = -\dfrac{1}{2}x - \dfrac{3}{2}$

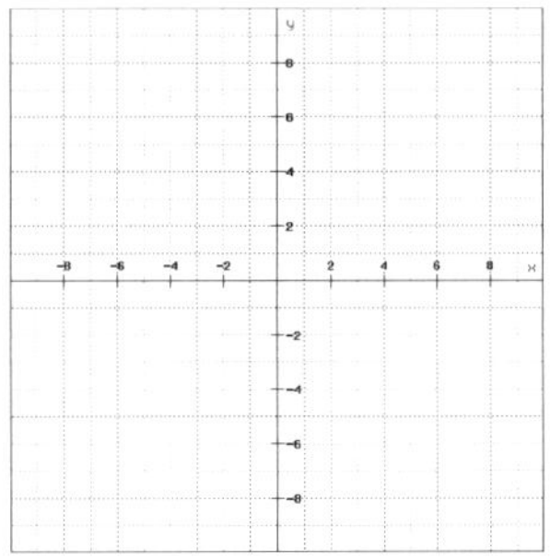

Domain: ____________

Range: ____________

Increase: ____________

Decrease: ____________

y intercept: (,)

x intercept: (,)

21. $f(x) = \dfrac{7}{2}x - \dfrac{1}{4}$

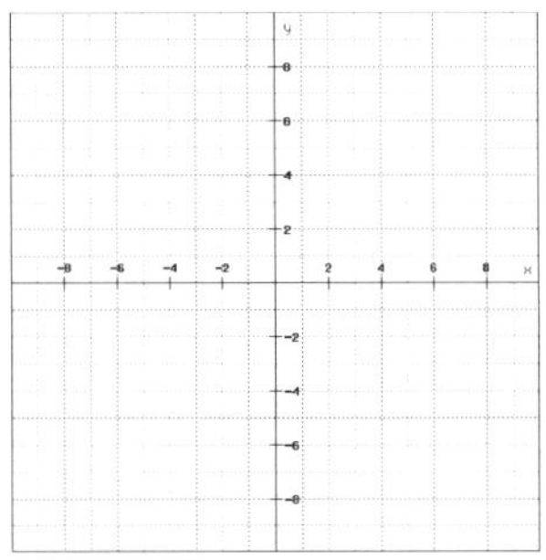

Domain: ____________

Range: ____________

Increase: ____________

Decrease: ____________

y intercept: (,)

x intercept: (,)

22. $f(x) = -\dfrac{9}{5}x + \dfrac{8}{3}$

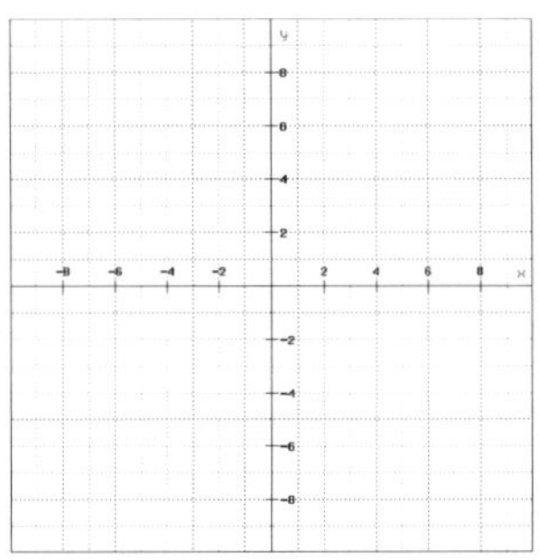

Domain: ____________

Range: ____________

Increase: ____________

Decrease: ____________

y intercept: (,)

x intercept: (,)

23. $3x + 2y = 2$

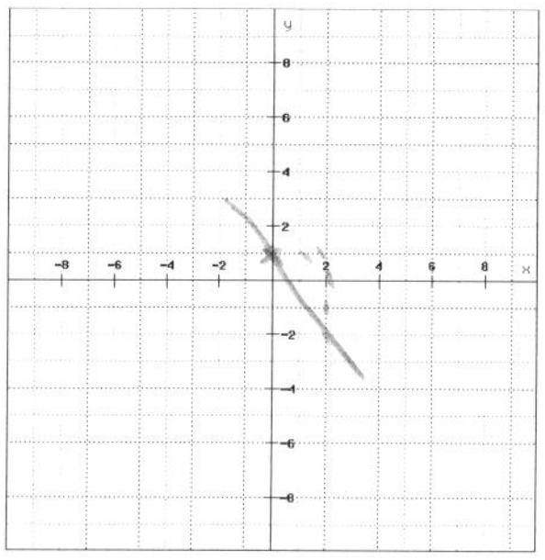

Domain: ____________

Range: ____________

Increase: ____________

Decrease: ____________

y intercept: (,)

x intercept: (,)

24. $4x - 2y - 3 = 1$

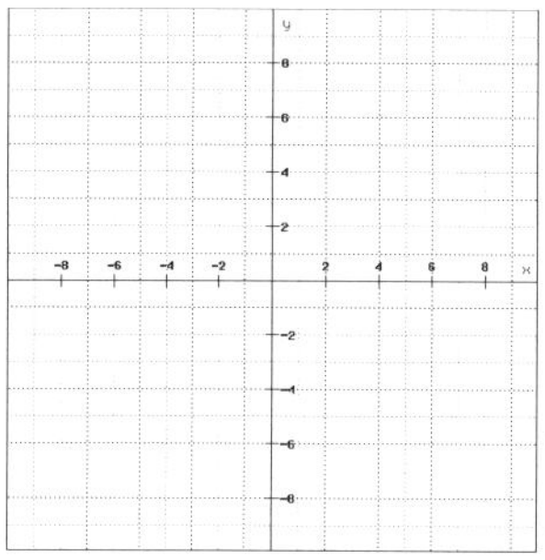

Domain: ____________

Range: ____________

Increase: ____________

Decrease: ____________

y intercept: (,)

x intercept: (,)

25. $-2y + 3x = -5$

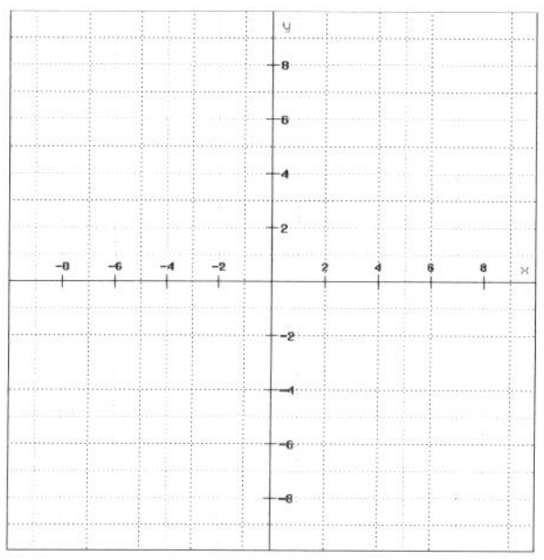

Domain: ____________

Range: ____________

Increase: ____________

Decrease: ____________

y intercept: (,)

x intercept: (,)

26. $y - x = 2$

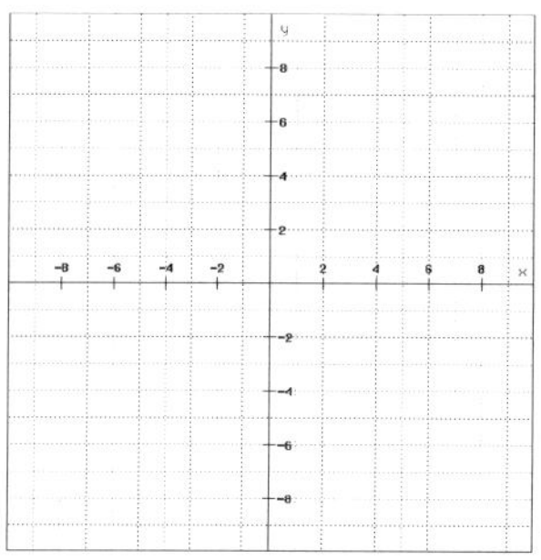

Domain: ____________

Range: ____________

Increase: ____________

Decrease: ____________

y intercept: (,)

x intercept: (,)

27. $y + 2x - 3 = 1$

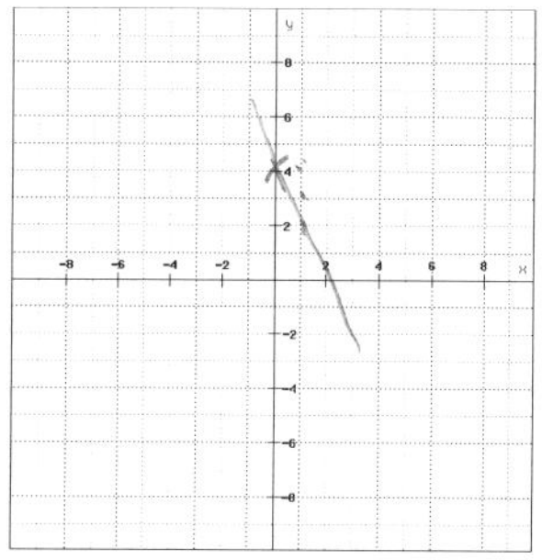

Domain: ____________

Range: ____________

Increase: ____________

Decrease: ____________

y intercept: (,)

x intercept: (,)

28. $5y + 5x = 5$

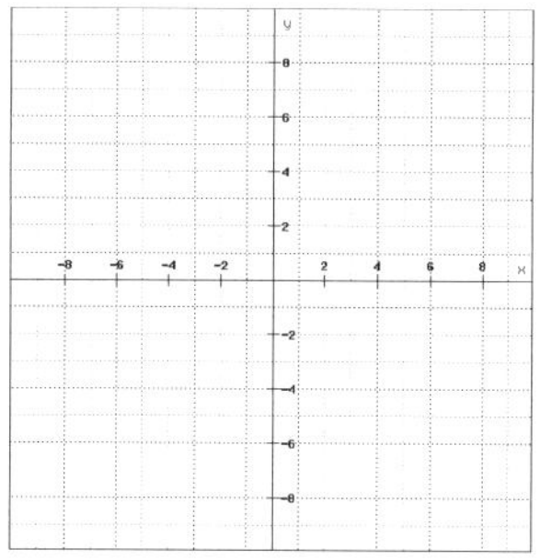

Domain: ____________

Range: ____________

Increase: ____________

Decrease: ____________

y intercept: (,)

x intercept: (,)

29. $2x - 2y - 3 = 1$

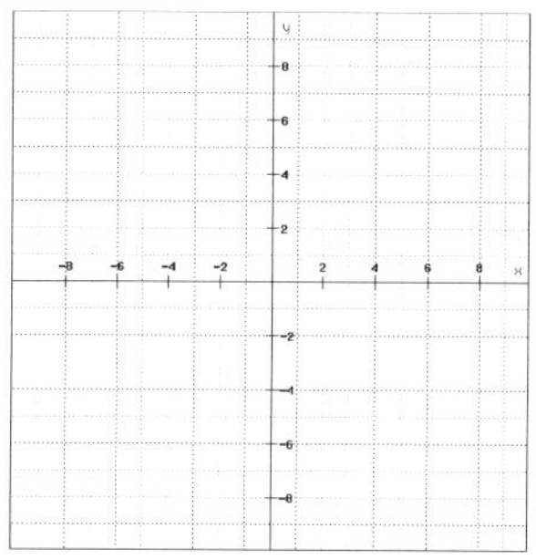

Domain: ____________

Range: ____________

Increase: ____________

Decrease: ____________

y intercept: (,)

x intercept: (,)

30. $x - 2y - 150 = 0$

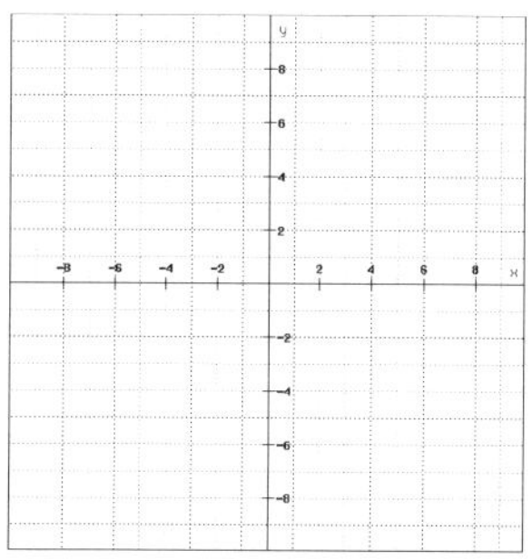

Domain: ____________

Range: ____________

Increase: ____________

Decrease: ____________

y intercept: (,)

x intercept: (,)

31. Write the equation of the line that has a slope of 2 and passes through the point (2, 4) in the forms: y = mx + b and ax + by + c = 0, (a, b $\in Z$)

$m = 2$

$y - y_1 = m(x - x_1)$

$y - 4 = 2(x - 2)$

$y - 4 = 2x - 4 \quad | + 4$

$y = 2x$

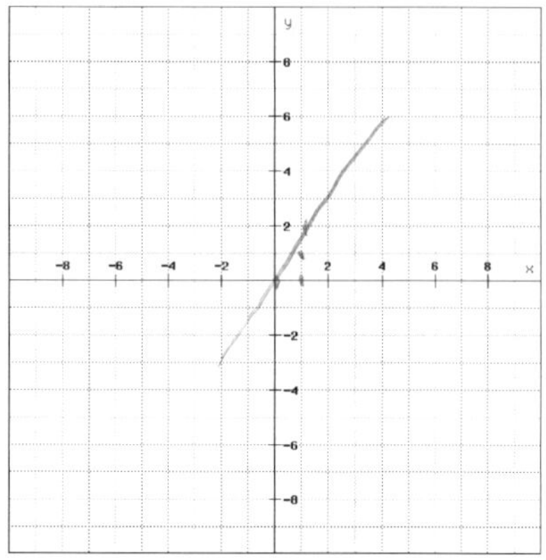

32. Write the equation of the line that has a slope of $-\frac{1}{2}$ and passes through the point (–2, –3) in the forms: y = mx + b and ax + by + c = 0, (a, b $\in Z$)

$m = -\frac{1}{2} \quad (-2, -3)$

$y - y_1 = m(x - x_1)$

$y + 3 = -\frac{1}{2}(x + 2)$

$y + 3 = -\frac{1}{2}x - 2$

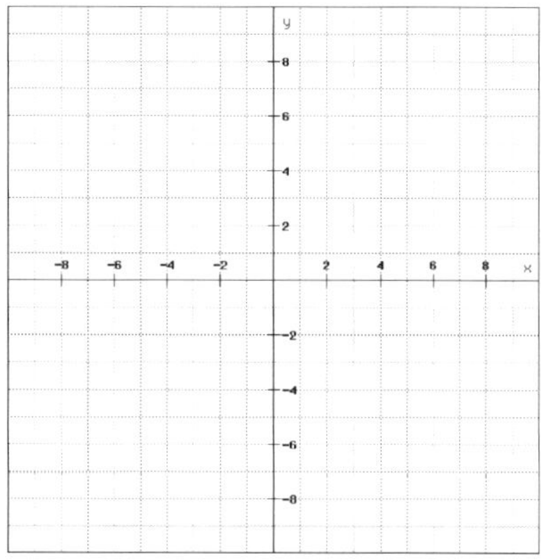

33. Write the equation of the line that has a slope of $-\frac{5}{2}$ and passes through the point (–1, 2) in the forms: y = mx + b and ax + by + c = 0, (a, b $\in Z$)

$m = \frac{-5}{2}$

$(-1, 2)$

$y - y_1 = m(x - x_1)$

$y - 2 = \frac{-5}{2}(x + 1)$

$y - 2 = \frac{-5}{2}x - 3{,}5 \quad | + 2$

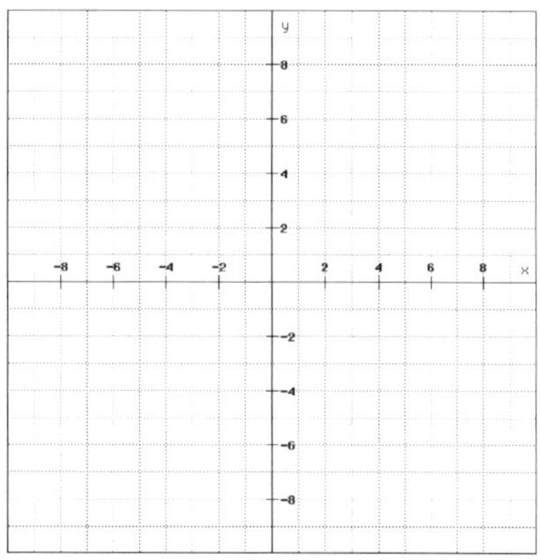

$y - y_1 = m(x - x_1)$

$y - 2 = \frac{-5}{2}(x + 1)$

$y - 2 = \frac{-5}{2}x - \frac{5}{2} \quad | + 2$

$y = \frac{-5}{2}x - 0.5$

34. Find the equation of the line that passes through the points (1, 1), (2, 4), indicate its y and x intercepts and sketch it. Write its equation in the forms: y = mx + b and ax + by + c = 0, (a, b $\in Z$)

(1,1) (2,4)

$m = \frac{y_2 - y_1}{x_2 - x_1} \quad \frac{4-1}{2-1} = 3$

$y - y_1 = m(x - x_1)$

$y - 1 = 3(x - 1)$

$y - 1 = 3x - 3 \quad | +1$

$y = 3x - 2$

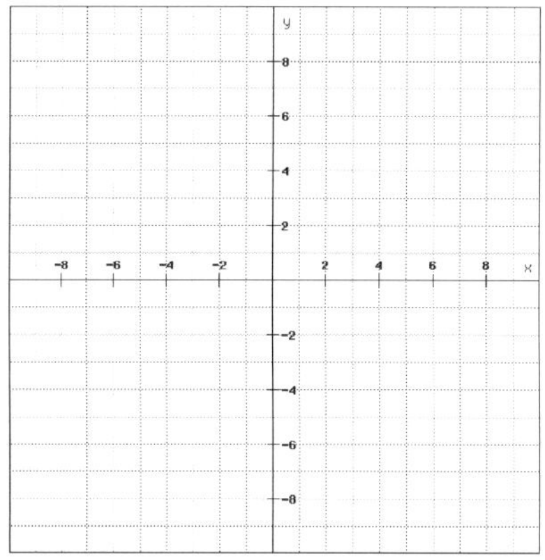

35. Find the equation of the line that passes through the points (–1, –5), (4, 3), indicate its y and x intercepts and sketch it. Write its equation in the forms: y = mx + b and ax + by + c = 0, (a, b $\in Z$)

(-1, -5) (4, 3)

$m = \frac{3+5}{4+1} = \frac{8}{5}$

$y - 3 = \frac{8}{5}(x - 4)$

$y - 3 = \frac{8}{5}x - \frac{32}{5} \quad | +3$

$y = \frac{8}{5}x - \frac{17}{5}$

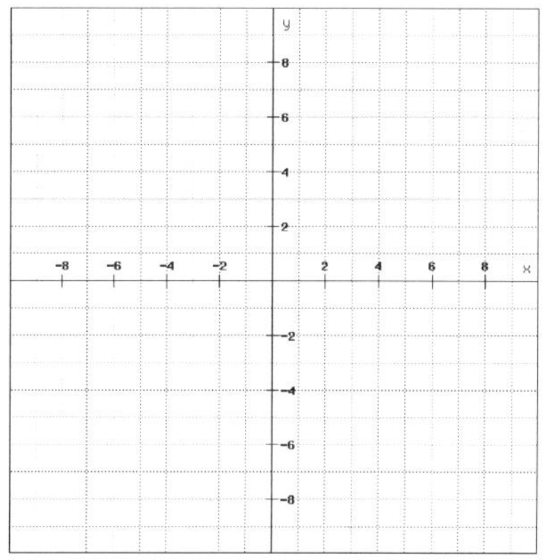

36. Find the equation of the line that passes through the points (–5, 1), (–2, 4), indicate its y and x intercepts, sketch it and write it in both formas y = mx + b and ax + by + c = 0, (a, b $\in Z$)

$m = \frac{4-1}{-2+5} = \frac{3}{3} = 1$

$y - 1 = 1(x + 5)$

$y - 1 = x + 5 \quad | +1$

$y = x + 6$

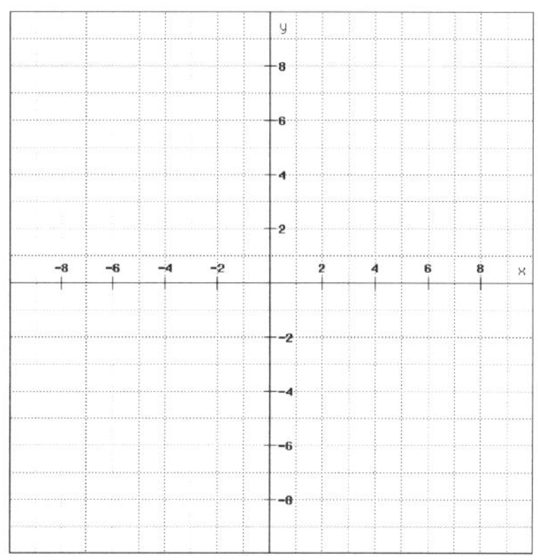

37. Write the equation of the line that is parallel to the line y = 5x – 2 and passes through the point (–2, –1). Write its equation in the forms: y = mx + b and ax + by + c = 0, (a, b $\in Z$)

parallel to $y = 5x - 2$

$m = 5$

$(-2, -1)$

$y + 1 = 5(x + 2)$

$y + 1 = 5x + 10$

$y = 5x + 9$

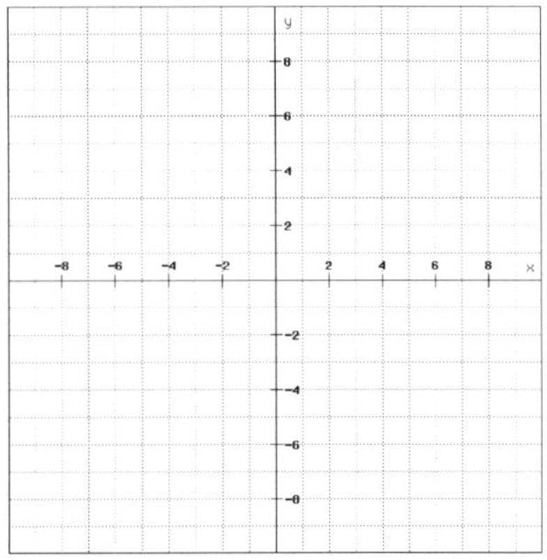

38. Write the equation of the line that is parallel to the line y = –0.5x – 1 and passes through the point (–3, 6). Write its equation in the forms: y = mx + b and ax + by + c = 0, (a, b $\in Z$)

$m = -0.5$ $(-3, 6)$

$y - 6 = -0.5(x + 3)$

$y - 6 = -0.5x - 1.5$ | +6

$y = -0.5x + 4.5$

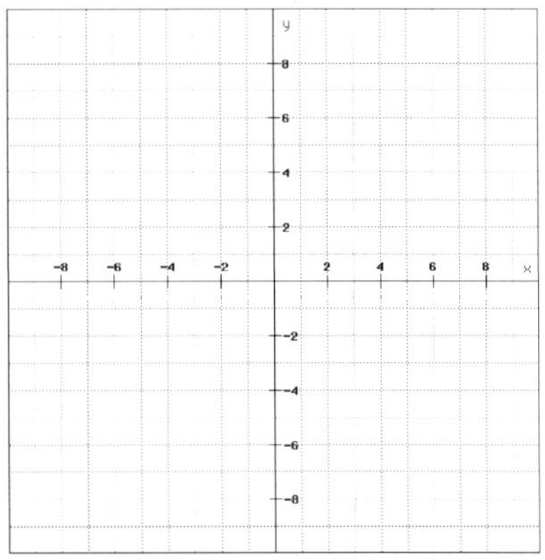

39. Sketch and write the equation of the line with a slope of $-\frac{1}{5}$ that passes through the point (0,2).

$-\frac{1}{5}$, (0, 2)

~~y−2 = 0(x~~

~~y =~~

$y - 2 = -\frac{1}{5}(x - 0)$

$y - 2 = -\frac{1}{5}x$ | +2

$y = -\frac{1}{5}x + 2$

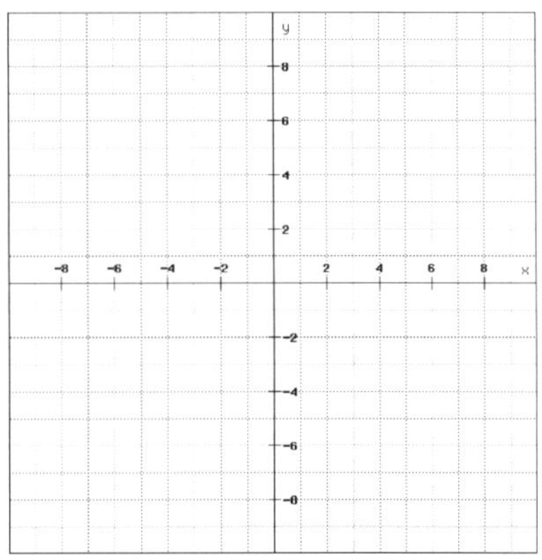

40. Sketch and write the equation of the lines with a slope: 1, 2, –3, –1, $-\frac{1}{2}$, $-\frac{1}{3}$, that passes through the point (0,0).

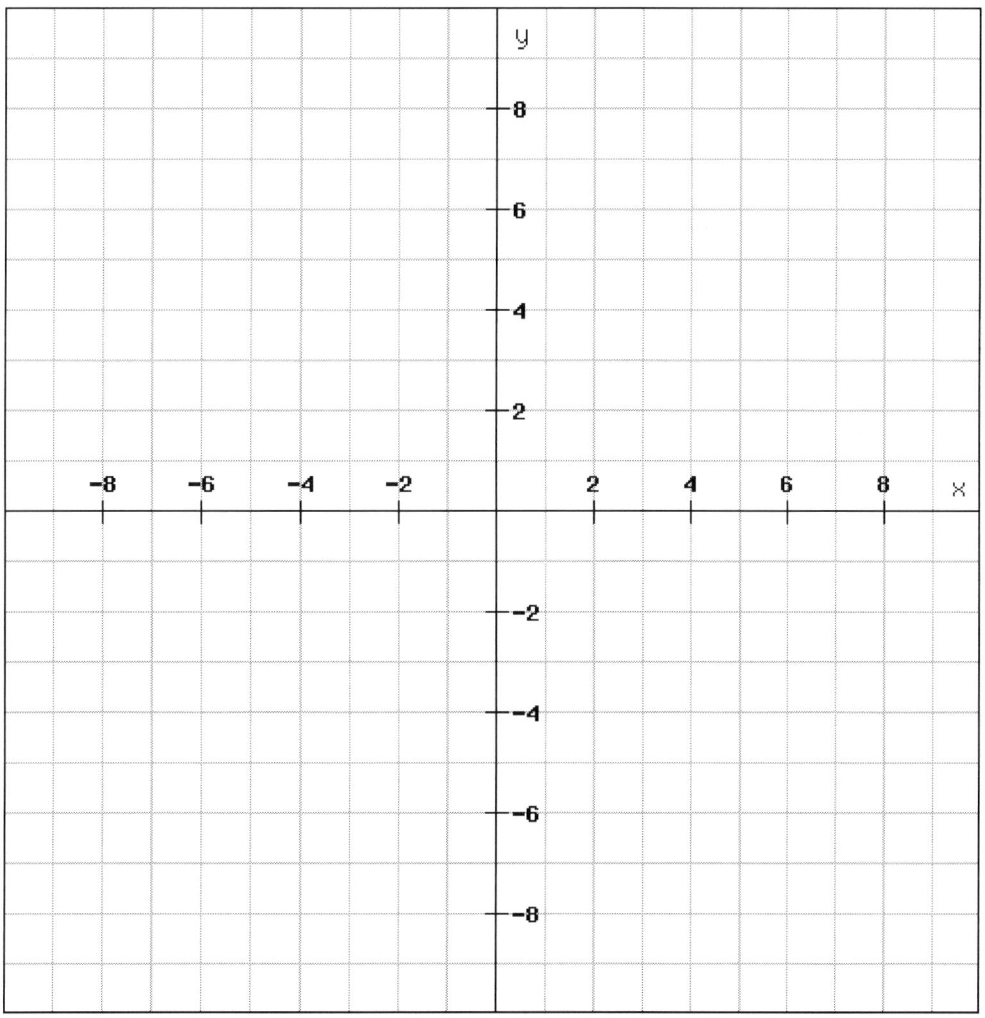

41. Sketch and write the equation of the line with a slope of –3 that passes through the point (0,–3).

$m = -3 \quad (0,-3)$

$y + 3 = -3(x) \mid -3$

$y = -3x - 3$

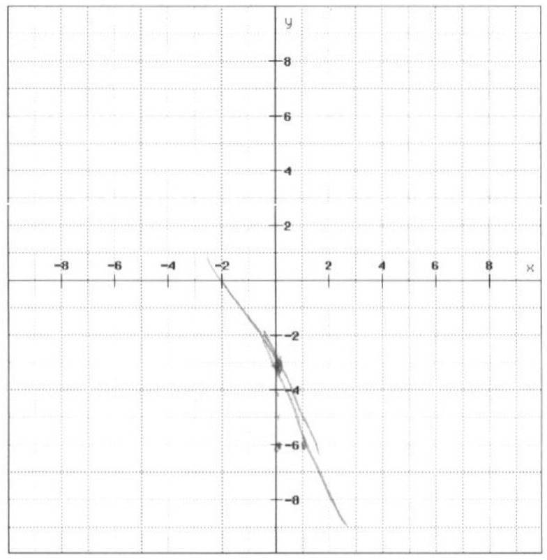

42. Sketch and write the equation of the line with a slope of 2 that passes through the point (2,0)

$m = 2 \quad (2,0)$

$y = 2(x - 2)$

$y = 2x - 4$

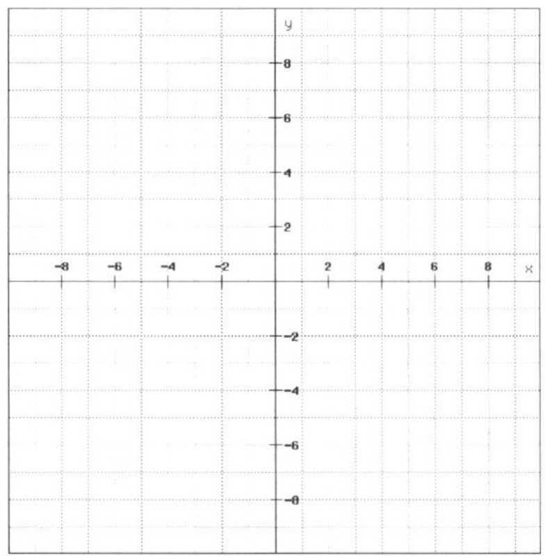

43. Sketch and write the equation of the line with a slope of $-\frac{1}{2}$ that passes through the point (–2,0)

$m = -\frac{1}{2} \quad (-2,0)$

$y = -\frac{1}{2}(x + 2)$

y = [illegible]

$y = -\frac{1}{2}x - 1$

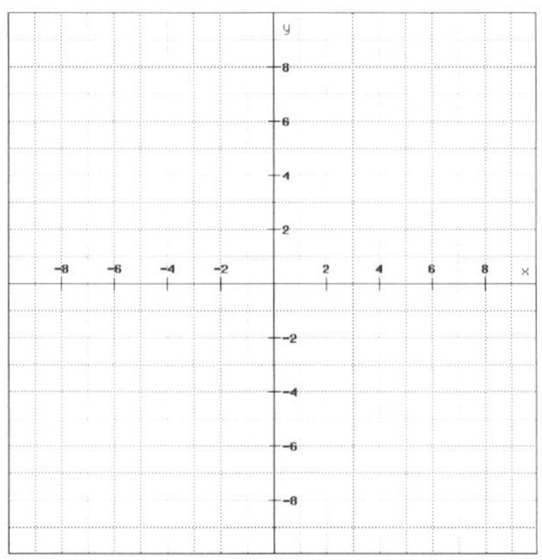

44. Sketch and write the equation of the line with a slope of 2 that passes through the point (–4,2)

$m = 2$, $(-4,2)$

$y - 2 = 2(x + 4)$ | $+2$

$y = 2x + 10$

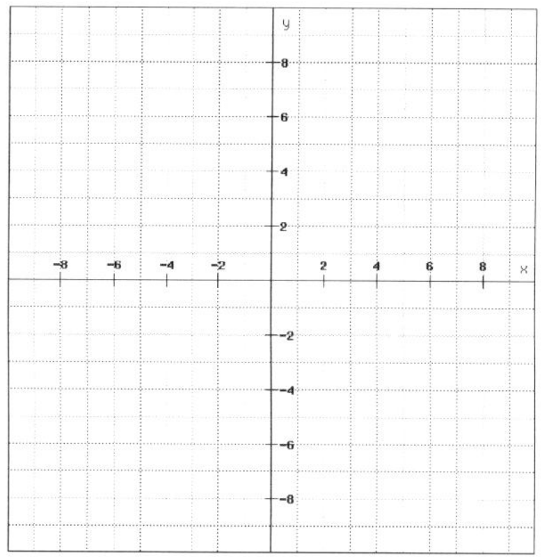

45. Find the intersection between the lines f(x) = 2x – 3 and f(x) = –5x – 2

$2x - 3 = -5x - 2$ | $+5x$

$7x - 3 = -2$ | $+3$

$7x = 1$ | $:7$

$x = \frac{1}{7}$?

46. Find the intersection between the lines f(x) = –12x – 13 and f(x) = 15x + 20.

DISTANCE AND MIDPOINT BETWEEN 2 POINTS

47. Given the points (1, 2) and (5, 8). Find the distance between them. Find the midpoint. Sketch to illustrate your answer.

(1,2) (5,8)

$d = \sqrt{(x_1 - x_2)^2 + (y_1 - y_2)^2}$

$d = \sqrt{(1-5)^2 + (2-8)^2}$

$= \sqrt{16 + 36}$

$= \sqrt{52}$

$m = \frac{x_1 + x_2}{2} \quad \frac{y_1 + y_2}{2}$

$= \frac{1+5}{2} = 3 \quad \frac{2+8}{2} = 5$

(3,5)

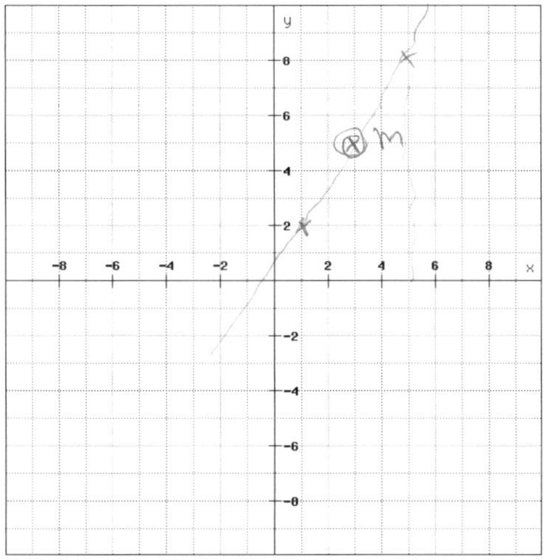

48. Given the points (–3, 2) and (5, –6). Find the distance between them. Find the midpoint. Sketch to illustrate your answer.

$d = \sqrt{(-3-5)^2 + (2+6)^2}$

$d = \sqrt{64 + 64}$

$d = \sqrt{128}$

$m = \frac{-3+5}{2} = 1$

$= \frac{2-6}{2} = -2$

(1, -2)

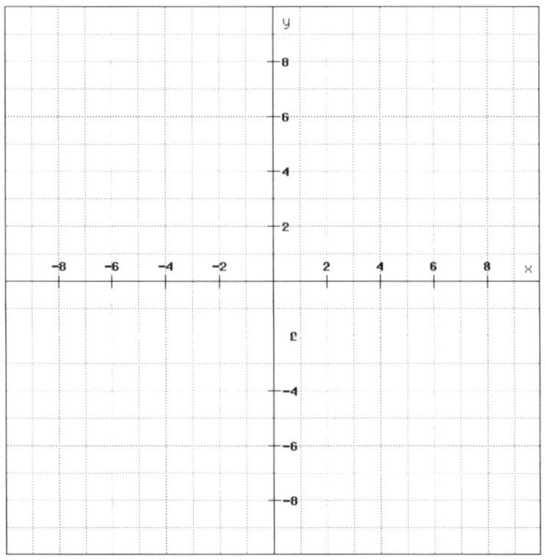

49. Given the points (–1, –6) and (–5, –1). Find the distance between them. Find the midpoint. Sketch to illustrate your answer.

(-1,-6) (-5,-1)

$d = \sqrt{(-1+5)^2 + (-6+1)^2}$

$= \sqrt{16 + 25}$

$d = \sqrt{41}$

$m = \frac{-1-5}{2} = -3$

$\frac{-6-1}{2} = -3.5$

(-3, -3.5)

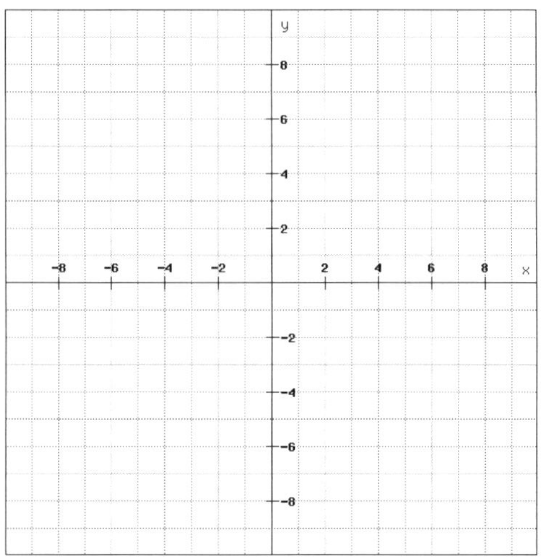

PERPENDICULAR LINES ($m\,m_{\perp} = -1$)

50. Find the equation of a line perpendicular to the line y = 3x – 2 that passes through the point (3, 12). Sketch to illustrate your answer.

$y = 3 \quad m = 3$

$\Rightarrow m = -\frac{1}{3}$

$y - 12 = -\frac{1}{3}(x - 3)$

$y - 12 = -\frac{1}{3}x + 1 \quad | + 12$

$y = \frac{1}{3}x + 13$

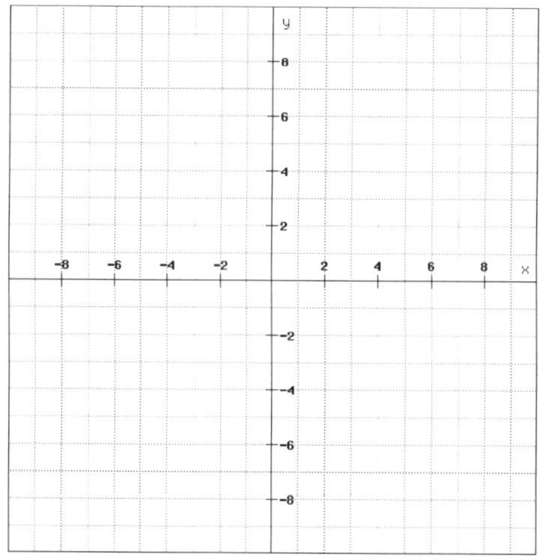

51. Find all the lines perpendicular to the line y = –3x + 4. Fin the ones that passes through the point (–3, 1). Sketch to illustrate your answer.

$m = \frac{1}{3} \quad (-3, 1)$

$y - 1 = \frac{1}{3}(x + 3)$

$= \frac{1}{3}x + 1 \quad | + 1$

$y = \frac{1}{3}x + 2$

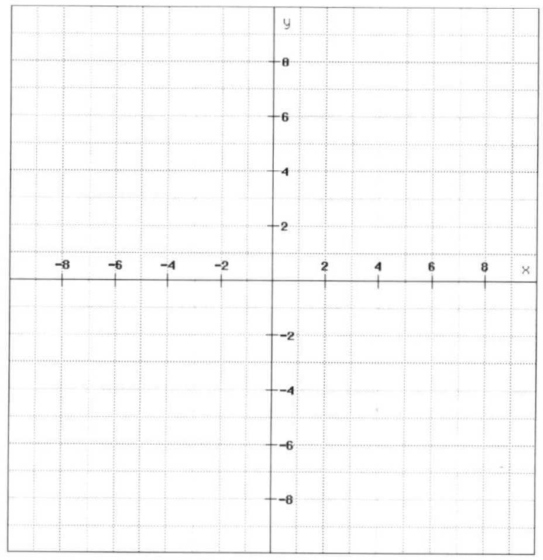

52. Find a line perpendicular to the line $y = -\frac{2}{5}x + 1$ that passes through the point (–1, –7). Sketch to illustrate your answer.

$m = \frac{5}{2}$

$y + 7 = \frac{5}{2}(x + 1)$

$= \frac{5}{2}x + 3.5 \quad | - 7$

$y = \frac{5}{2}x - 4.5$

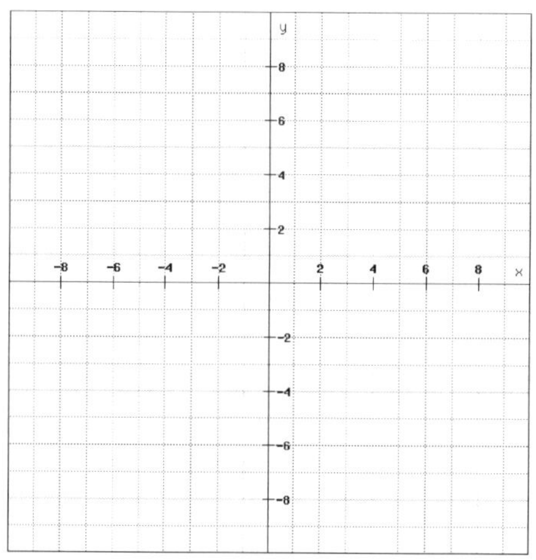

53. Given that the slope of one of the lines is 3 and that the lines are perpendicular, find the **exact** coordinates of the point of intersection of the two lines.

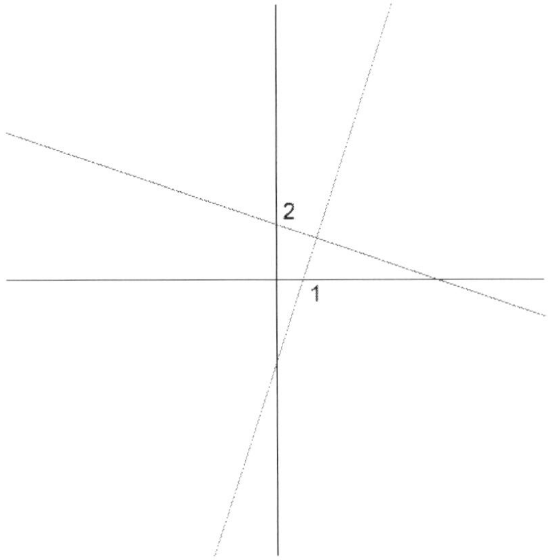

m=3

Application

1. The price of a new toy (in US$) is C(t) = 20 – 0.5t, t given in days.
   a. Sketch the corresponding graph.

f(x) = −0.5x + 20

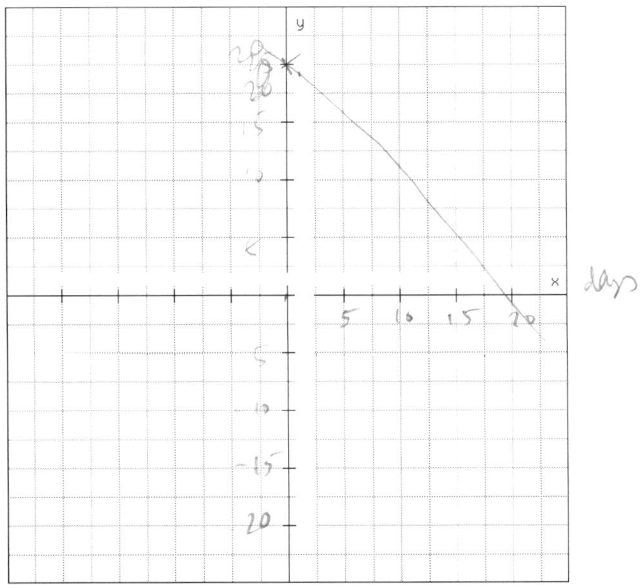

   b. What was the initial price of the toy? 20

   c. Find the price of the toy after 10 days

   d. What is the domain of the function, argument the answer, D [0, 40]

   e. What is the range of the function. [0, 20]

   f. What is the meaning of 0.5? Does it have units? What are they?

2. You need to rent a car for one day and to compare the charges of 3 different companies. Company I charges 20$ per day with additional cost of 0.20$ per mile. Company II charges 30$ per day with additional cost of 0.10$ per mile. Company III charges 70$ per day with no additional mileage charge.

   a. Write the cost function for each one of the companies.

1) 20 + 0.2x ⇒ 0.2x + 20$

2) 0.10x + 30$

3) 70$

f(x) = 70

   b. Sketch all 3 graphs on the same axes system.

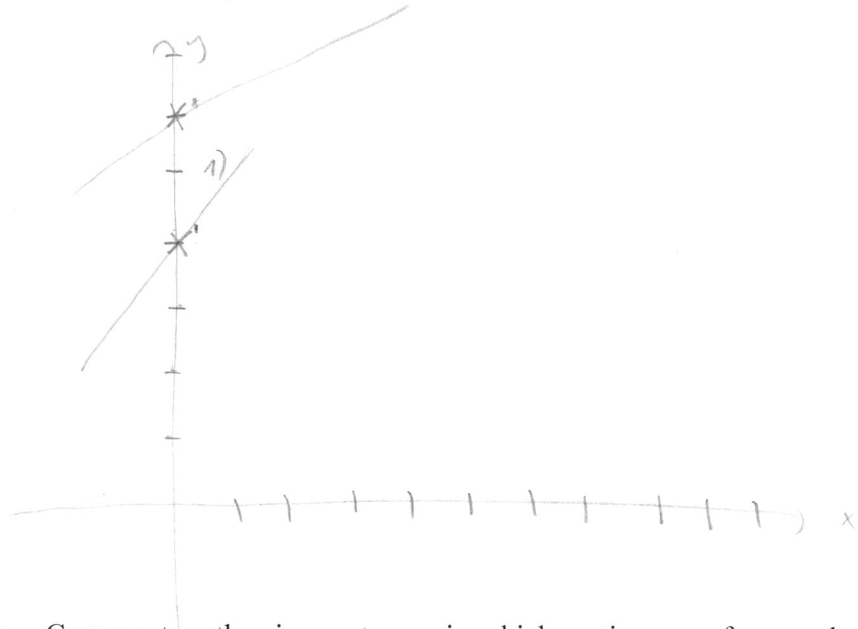

   c. Comment on the circumstances in which renting a car from each one of the companies is best.

1 & 2) ⇒ 0.2x + 20 = 0.10x + 30 | −0.1x

100 für x einsetzen

0.1x + 20 = 30 | −20

0.1x = 10 | :(0.1)

x = 100

(100, 40)

0.2 · 100 + 20

2, 3

⇒ 400

0.10x + 30 = 70 | −30

0.1x = 40 | : 0.1

x = 400

0.1 · 400 + 30 = 70

(400, 70)

2.3. – QUADRATIC FUNCTIONS

Introduction:

1. Given the functions: $f(x) = x^2$, $g(x) = x^2 - 2$. Complete the following table:

x	–5	–4	–3	–2	–1	0	1	2	3	4	5	6
f(x)	25	16	9	4	1	0	1	4	9	16	25	36
g(x)	23	14	7	2	-1	-2	-1	2				

- Sketch the points of the chart on a graph (use a ruler).
- State the domain of the function: ________________
- State the *y* intercept (sketched on the graph: (____, ____)
- State the *x* intercept(s): (____, ____), (____, ____)
- Write in all possible forms:

- Find the max/min point(s): (____, ____)
- The function is increasing on the interval: ________
- The function is decreasing on the interval: ________
- Sketch the function of the graph used for the points initially drawn
- State the range of the function: ________

f(x)

range ⇒ R [0, ∞)

g(x) [-2, ∞)

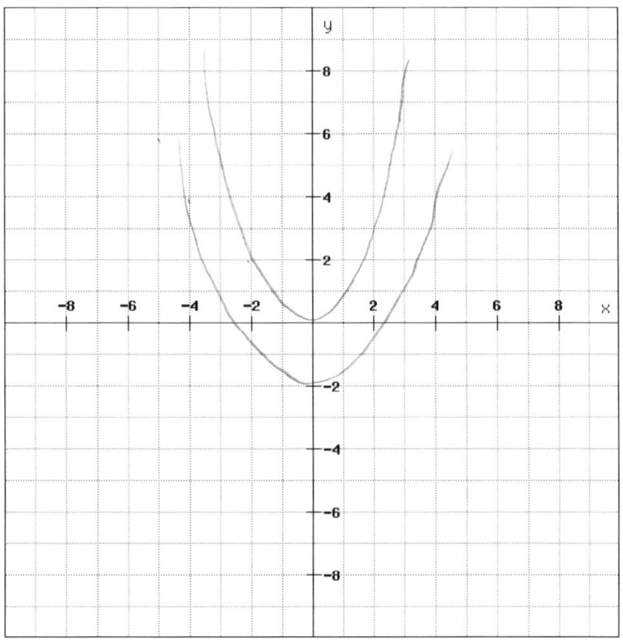

2. Given the functions: $f(x) = (x - 2)^2$, $g(x) = (x + 3)^2 - 2$. Complete the following chart:

x	–5	–4	–3	–2	–1	0	1	2	3	4	5	6
f(x)												
g(x)												

- Sketch the points of the chart on a graph (use a ruler).
- State the domain of the function: ________________
- State the *y* intercept (sketched on the graph: (____, ____)
- State the *x* intercept(s): (____, ____), (____, ____)
- Write in all possible forms:

- Find the max/min point(s): (____, ____)
- The function is increasing on the interval: ________
- The function is decreasing on the interval: ________
- Sketch the function of the graph used for the points initially drawn
- State the range of the function: ________
- State its axes of symmetry:

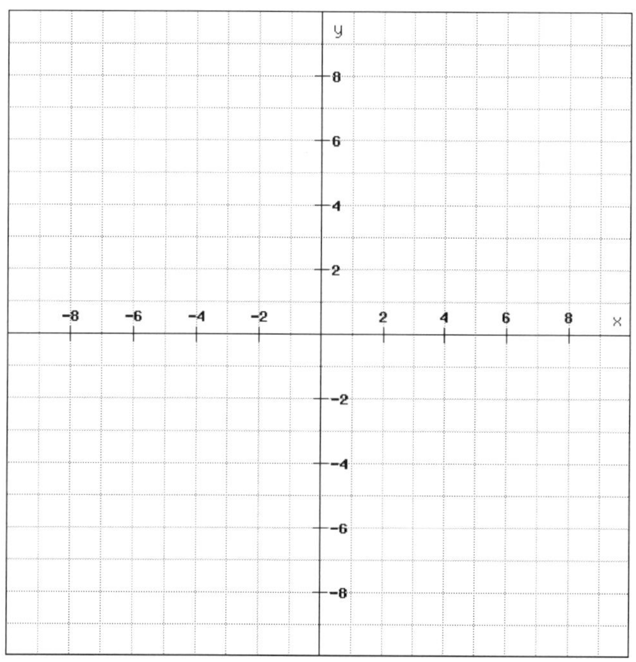

3. Given the functions: $f(x) = (x + 2)(x - 4)$, $g(x) = 2x^2 - x - 3$ Complete the following chart:

x	–5	–4	–3	–2	–1	0	1	2	3	4	5	6
f(x)												
g(x)												

- Sketch the points of the chart on a graph (use a ruler).
- State the domain of the function: ________________
- State the *y* intercept (sketched on the graph: (____, ____)
- State the *x* intercept(s): (____, ____), (____, ____)
- Write in all possible forms:
- Find the max/min point(s): (____, ____)
- The function is increasing on the interval: ________
- The function is decreasing on the interval: ________
- Sketch the function of the graph used for the points initially drawn
- State the range of the function: ________
- State its axes of symmetry:

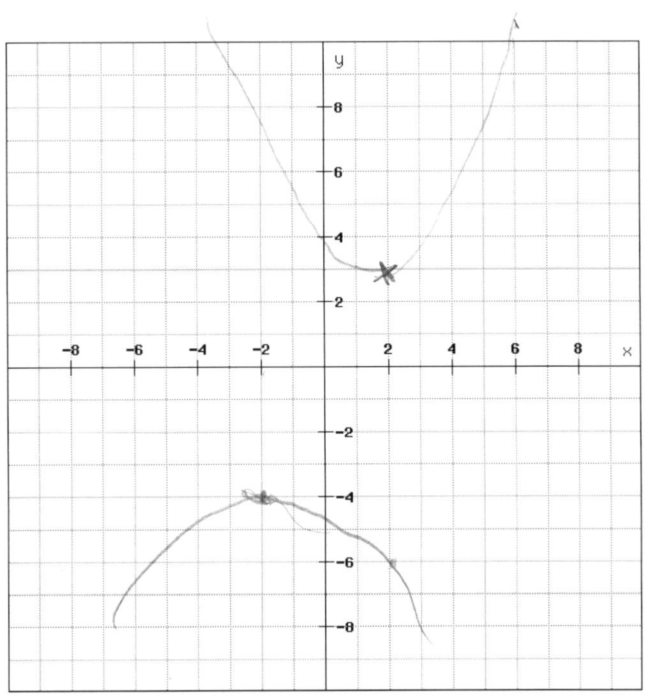

In general, a quadratic function f can be written in several different ways:

a. $f(x) = ax^2 + bx + c$ **standard form**, where a, b and c are constants

b. $f(x) = a(x - r)(x - s)$ **factored form**, where a, r and s are constants

c. $f(x) = a(x - h)^2 + k$ **vertex form**, where a, h and k are constants

Example:

Vertex form:	$f(x) = 3(x - 2)^2 - 3$
Partial factored form:	$f(x) = 3(x - 1)(x - 3)$
Standard form:	$f(x) = 3x^2 + 12x + 9$

<u>Complete the sentences:</u>

1. The graph of a quadratic function is called a ____________________.
2. In factored form, the numbers r and s represent the ________________ of f.
3. In vertex form, the point (h, k) is called the _____________ of the parabola. The axis of symmetry of the parabola is the line _______________.
4. The graph of the parabola opens upwards if ___________________ and downwards if ______________.
5. In case $f(x) = x^2 + 1$, the function can be written in ____ form(s) only. Why?
6. In case $f(x) = x^2 - 1$, the function can be written in ____ form(s) only. Show your answer:
7. A parabola has its vertex at the point (2, 3) and goes through the point (6, 11). Find the expression of the function.

   $f(x) = (x-2)^2 + 3$ $\quad \frac{-4}{-8} = \frac{1}{2}$ $\quad y = \frac{1}{2}(x-2)^2 + 3$

8. A parabola has its vertex at the point (– 2, 4) and passes through the point (2, – 6). Find the expression of the function.

   (-2, 4) (2, -6) $\quad m = \frac{-6-4}{2+2} = \frac{-10}{4} = \frac{-5}{2}$

9. Write the analytical expression that corresponds the following functions in all possible forms, assume $a = 1$ or -1 in all cases:

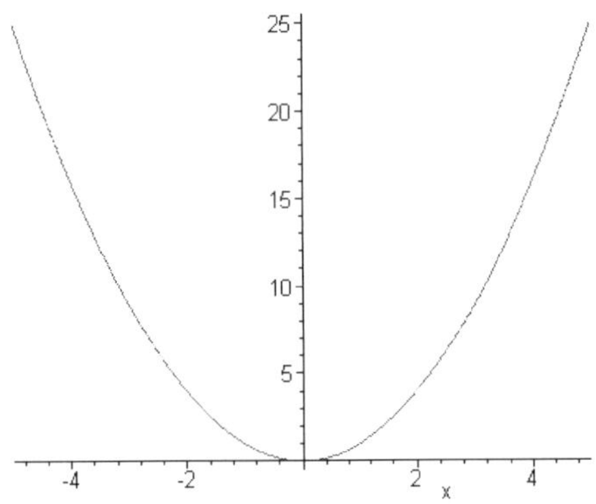

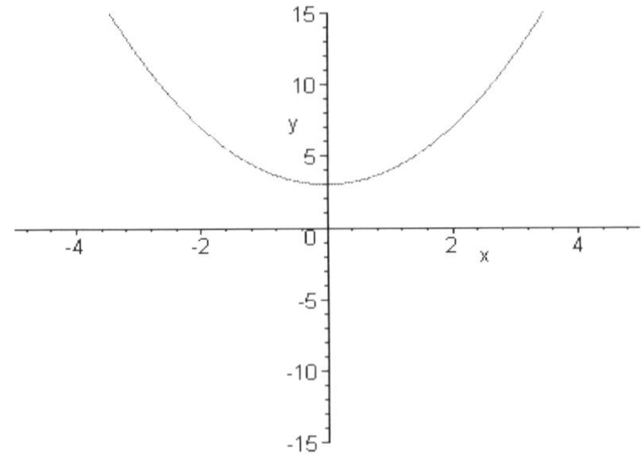

vertex form

Range: y[0,∞) ________ Range: y R y[3,∞) ________

Vertex form: ________ Vertex form: ________

Factorized form: ________ Factorized form: ________

Standard form: f(x) = x² ________ Standard form: f(x) = x² + 3 ________

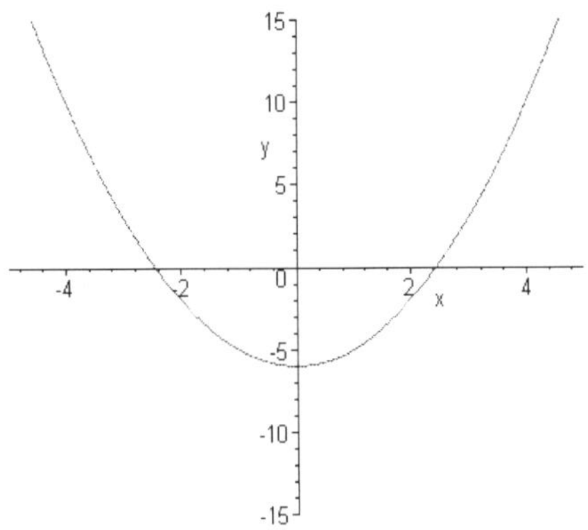

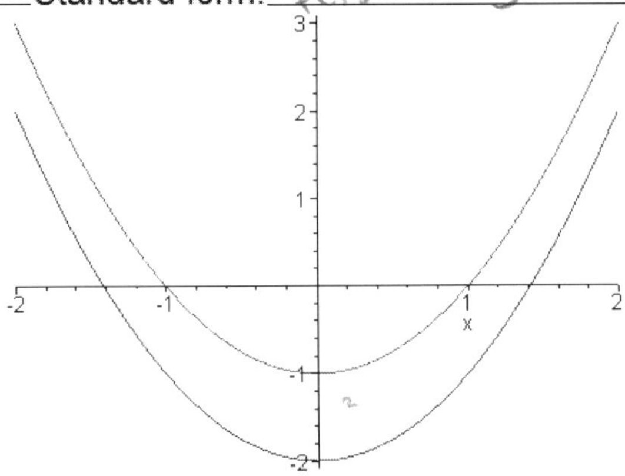

Range: y[-6,∞) ________ Range: 1) y[-2,∞) 2 [-1,∞) ________

Vertex form: ________ Vertex form: ________

Factorized form: ________ Factorized form: (x-1) ________

Standard form: f(x) = x² - 6 ________ Standard form: f(x) = x² - 2 , x² - 1 ________

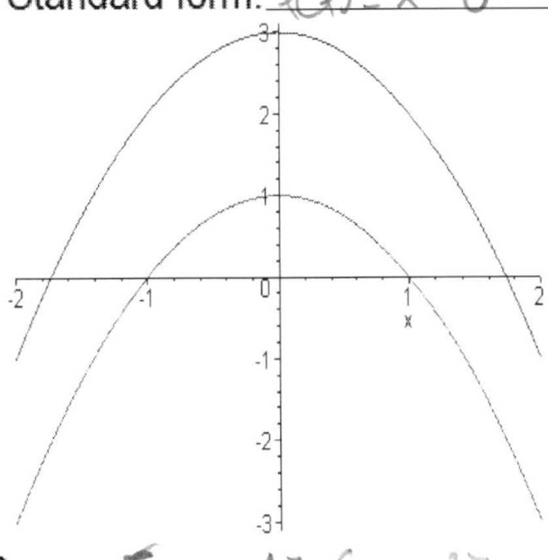

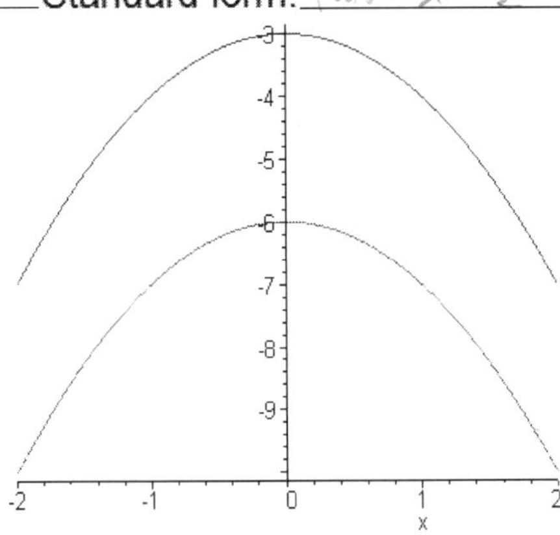

Range: [-∞, 1] (-∞, 3] ________ Range: ________

Vertex form: ________ Vertex form: ________

Factorized form: ________ Factorized form: ________

Standard form: f(x) = -x² + 3 ________ Standard form: ________

10. Complete the tables:

Function	On the graph
$f(x) = x^2$	~~A~~ b
$f(x) = \dfrac{x^2}{2}$	C
$f(x) = \dfrac{x^2}{3}$	D
$f(x) = 2x^2$	A

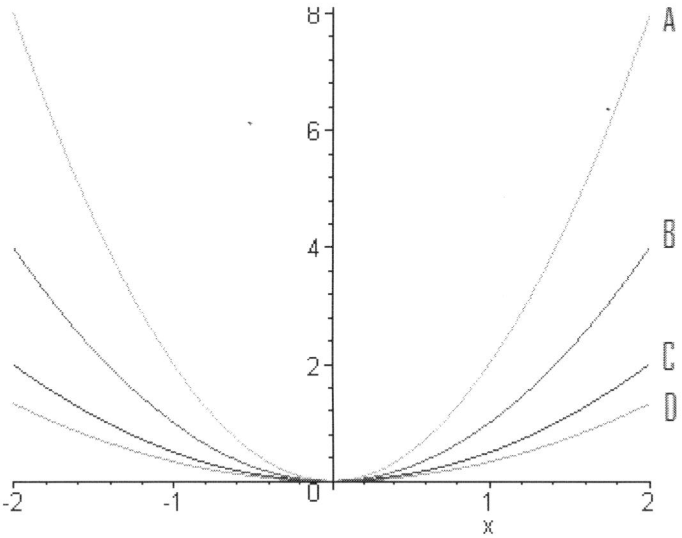

11. Complete the table:

Function	On the graph
$f(x) = x^2 + 2$	b
$f(x) = x^2 - 2$	C
$f(x) = x^2 - 3$	D
$f(x) = 2x^2 + 2$	A

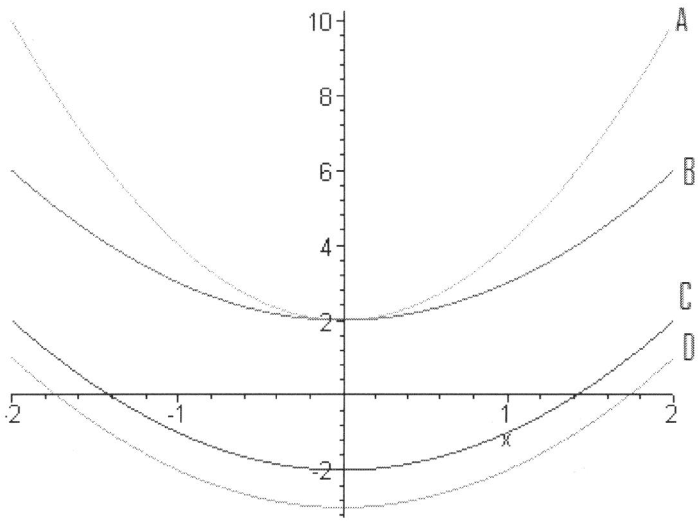

12. Complete the table:

Function	On the graph
$f(x) = -x^2 + 2$	C
$f(x) = x^2 - 4$	D
$f(x) = -x^2 + 3$	B
$f(x) = 2x^2 + 2$	A

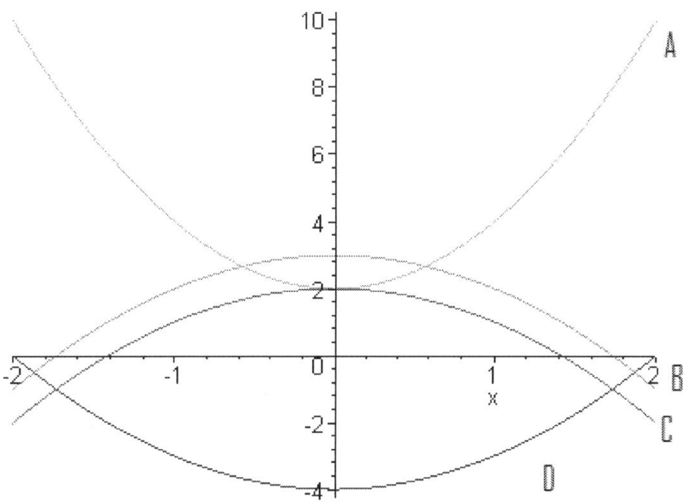

13. Write the expression of the function in all possible forms, indicate the range assume $a = 1$ or -1 in all cases:

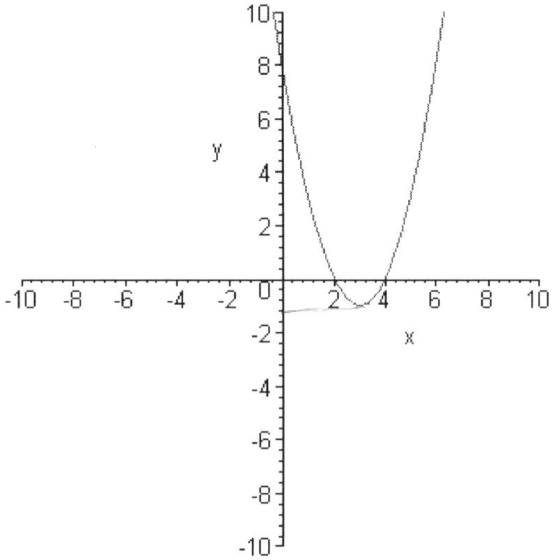

Range: [-1,∞)
Vertex form: ________
Factorized form: ________
Standard form: f(x)=x^2

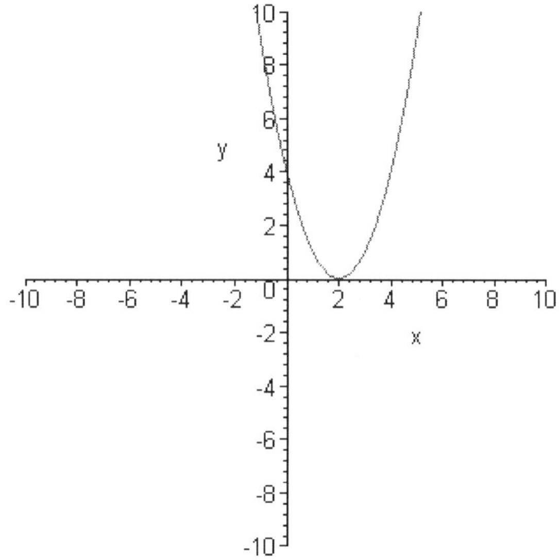

Range: ________
Vertex form: ________
Factorized form: ________
Standard form: ________

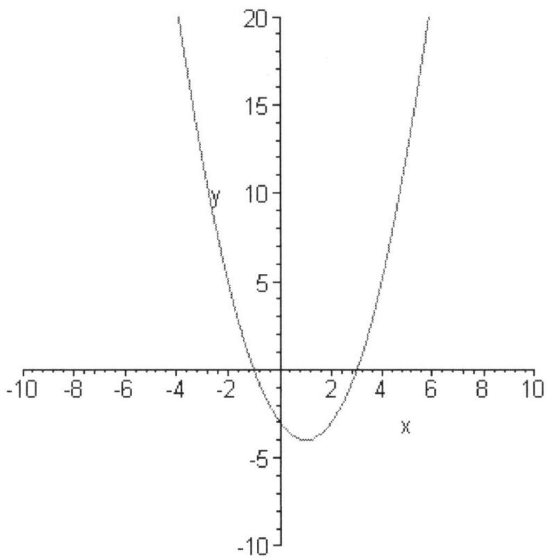

Range: ________
Vertex form: ________
Factorized form: ________
Standard form: ________

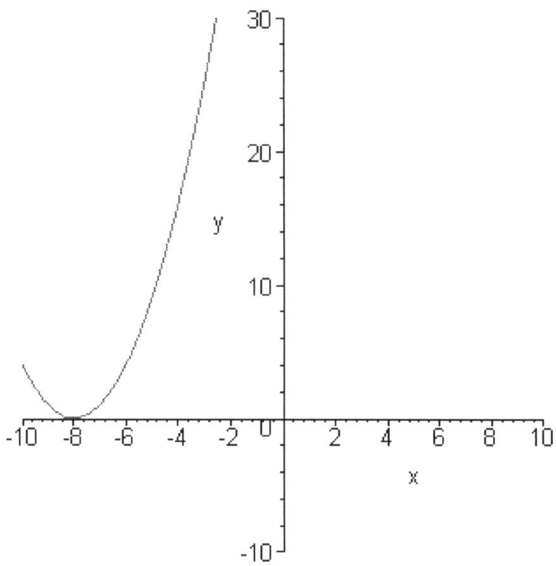

Range: ________
Vertex form: ________
Factorized form: ________
Standard form: ________

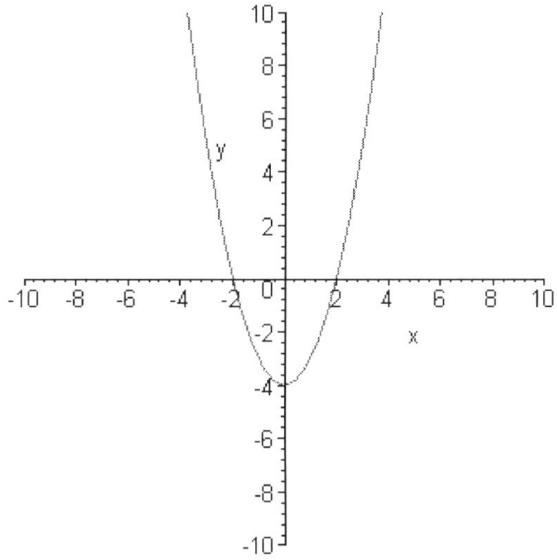

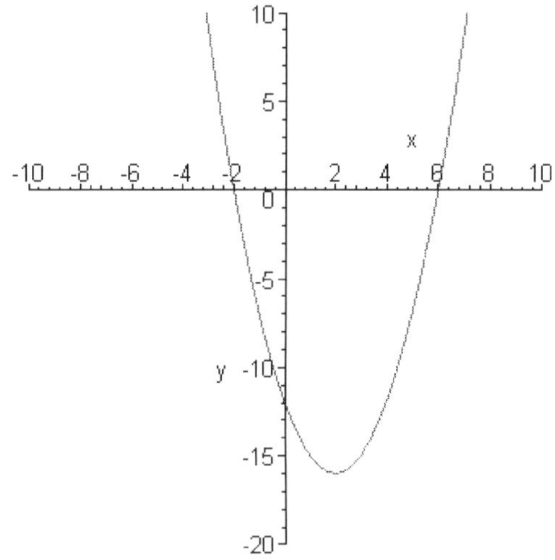

Range: ______________________
Vertex form: __________________
Factorized form:_______________
Standard form:________________

Range: ________________________
Vertex form: ___________________
Factorized form:_________________
Standard form:__________________

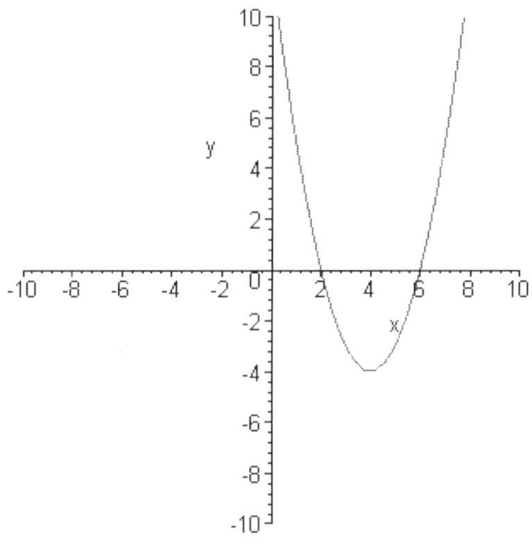

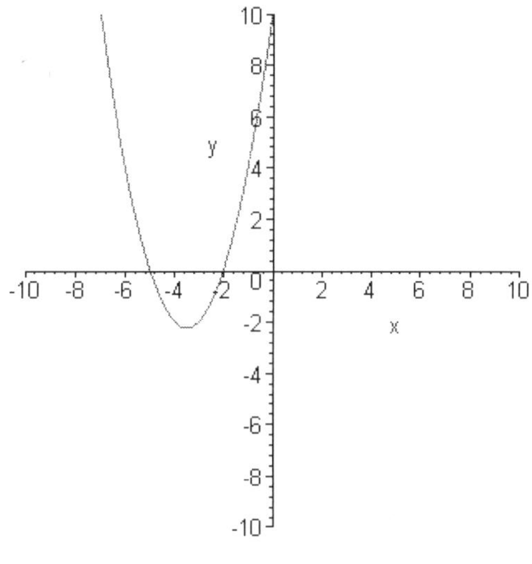

Range: ______________________
Vertex form: __________________
Factorized form:_______________
Standard form:________________

Range: ________________________
Vertex form: ___________________
Factorized form:_________________
Standard form:__________________

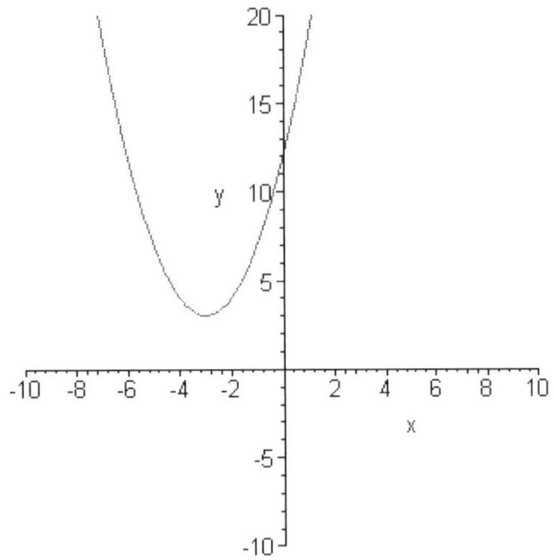

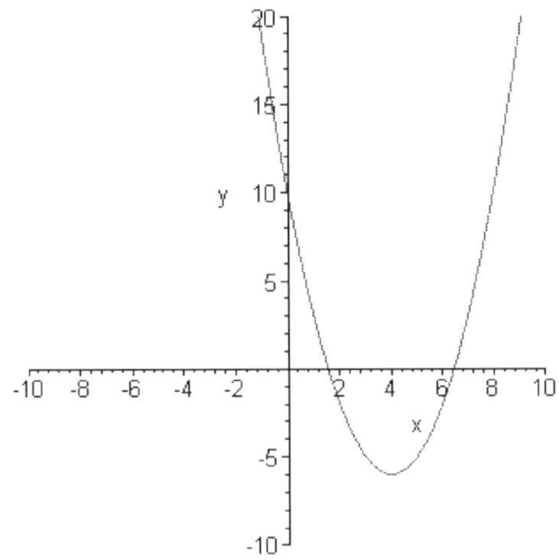

Range: ______________________ Range: ______________________

Vertex form: __________________ Vertex form: __________________

Factorized form: ______________ Factorized form: ______________

Standard form: ________________ Standard form: ________________

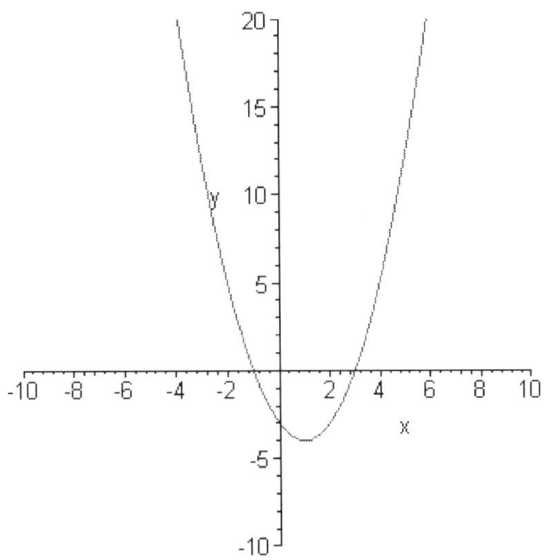

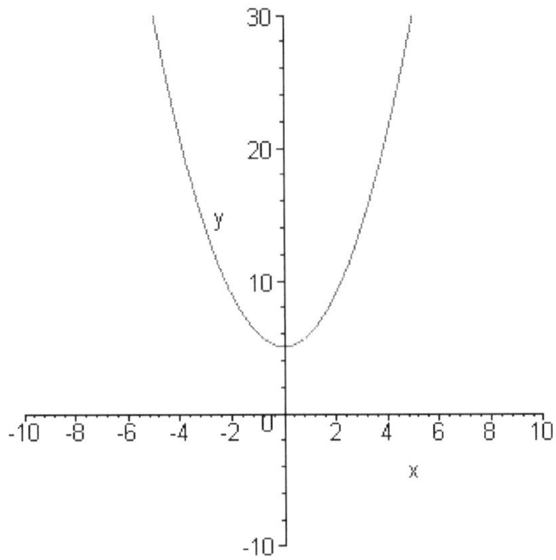

Range: ______________________ Range: ______________________

Vertex form: __________________ Vertex form: __________________

Factorized form: ______________ Factorized form: ______________

Standard form: ________________ Standard form: ________________

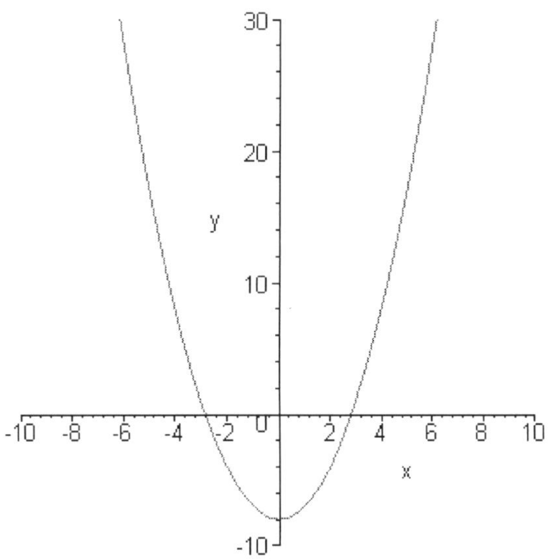

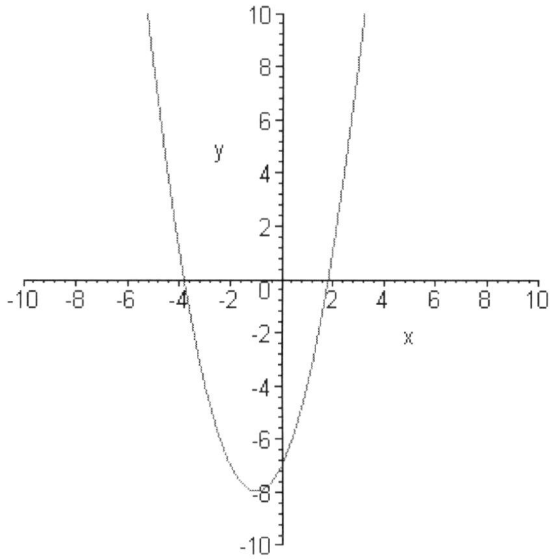

Range: ______________________ Range: ______________________

Vertex form: ________________ Vertex form: ________________

Factorized form: ____________ Factorized form: ____________

Standard form: ______________ Standard form: ______________

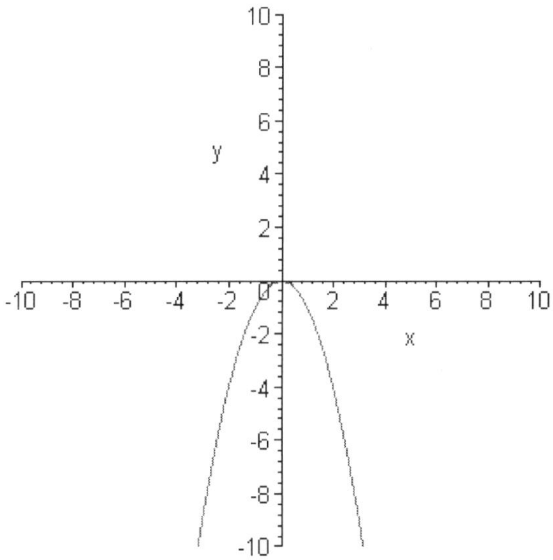

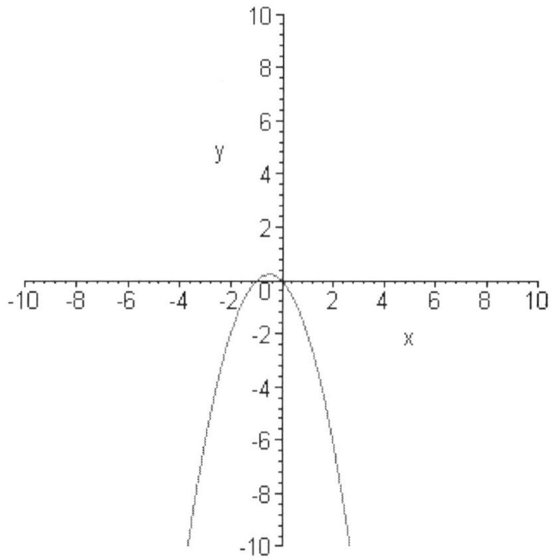

Range: ______________________ Range: ______________________

Vertex form: ________________ Vertex form: ________________

Factorized form: ____________ Factorized form: ____________

Standard form: ______________ Standard form: ______________

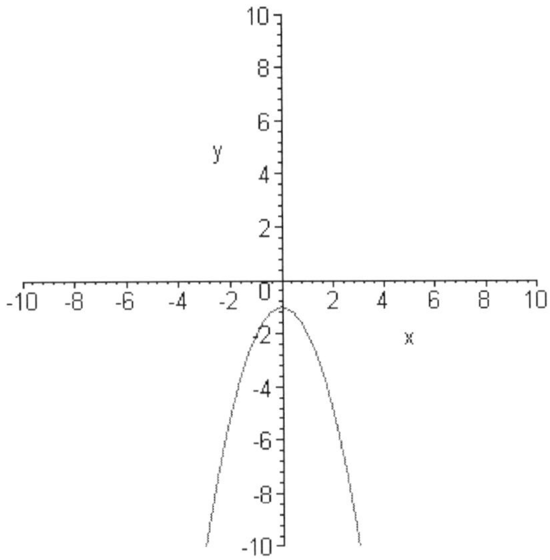

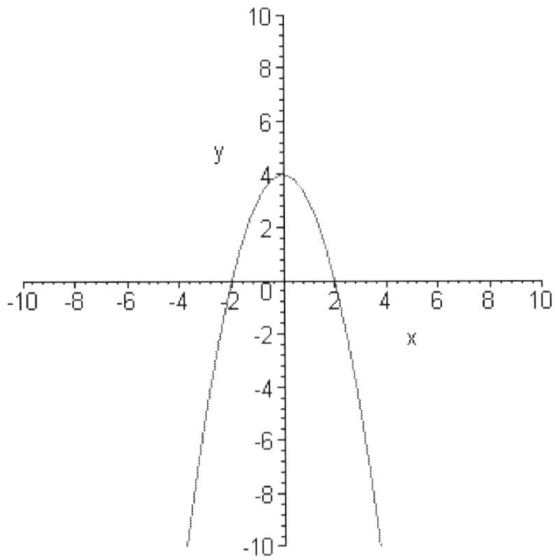

Range: ______________________ Range: ______________________
Vertex form: ______________________ Vertex form: ______________________
Factorized form: ______________________ Factorized form: ______________________
Standard form: ______________________ Standard form: ______________________

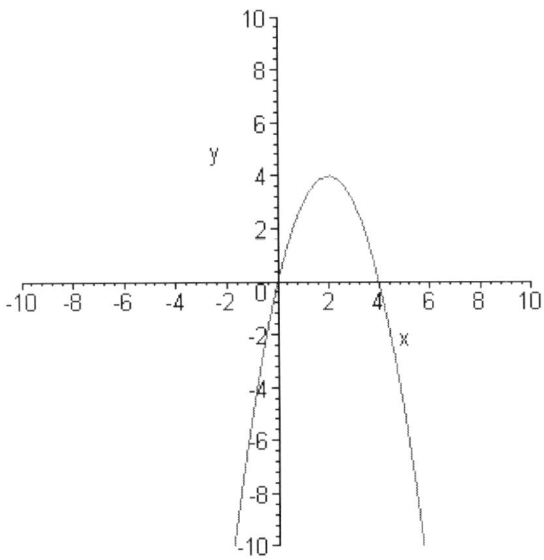

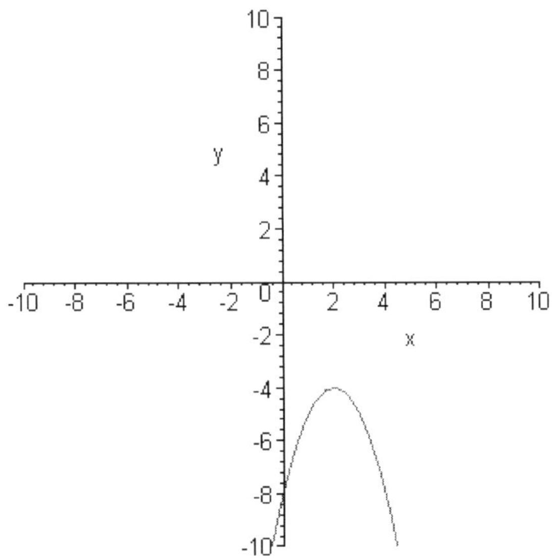

Range: ______________________ Range: ______________________
Vertex form: ______________________ Vertex form: ______________________
Factorized form: ______________________ Factorized form: ______________________
Standard form: ______________________ Standard form: ______________________

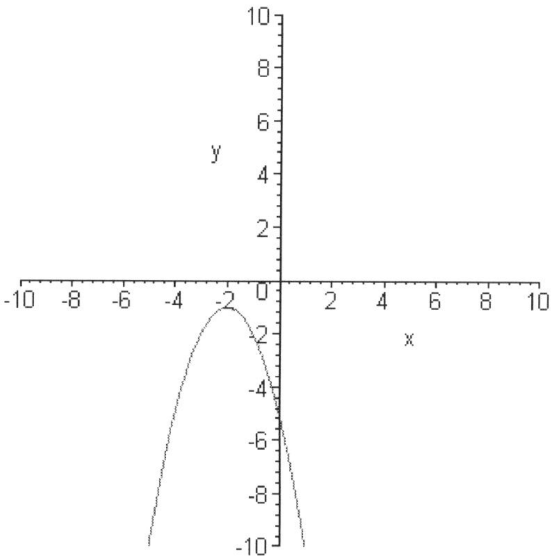

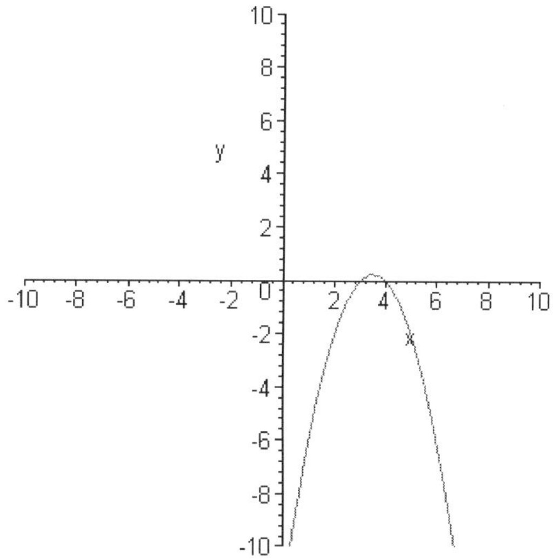

Range: ____________________ Range: ____________________

Vertex form: ________________ Vertex form: ________________

Factorized form:______________ Factorized form:______________

Standard form:_______________ Standard form:_______________

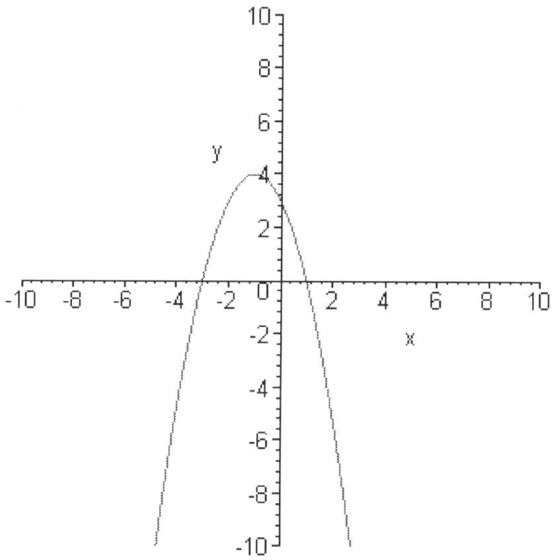

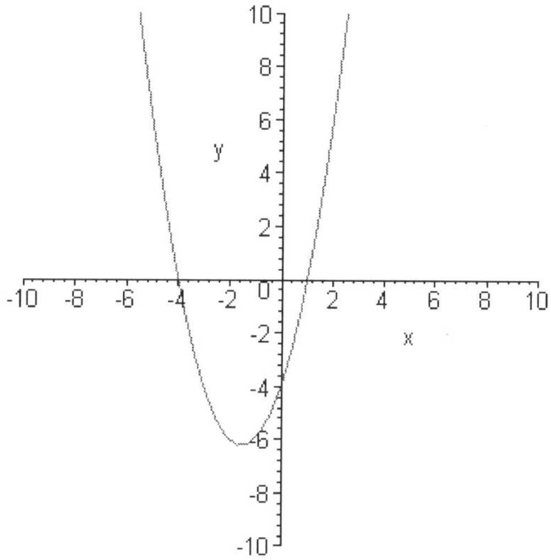

Range: ____________________ Range: ____________________

Vertex form: ________________ Vertex form: ________________

Factorized form:______________ Factorized form:______________

Standard form:_______________ Standard form:_______________

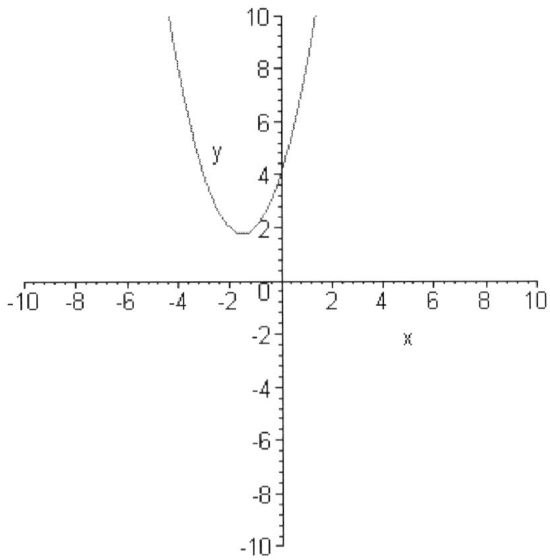

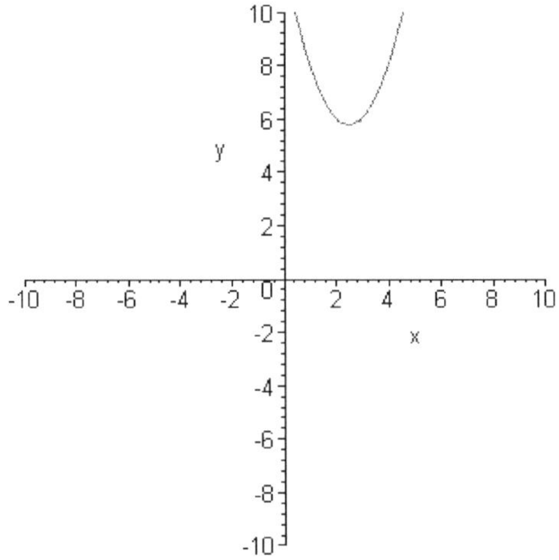

Range: ____________________ Range: ____________________
Vertex form: ____________________ Vertex form: ____________________
Factorized form: ____________________ Factorized form: ____________________
Standard form: ____________________ Standard form: ____________________

14. Analyze the following functions:

1. $f(x) = -3$

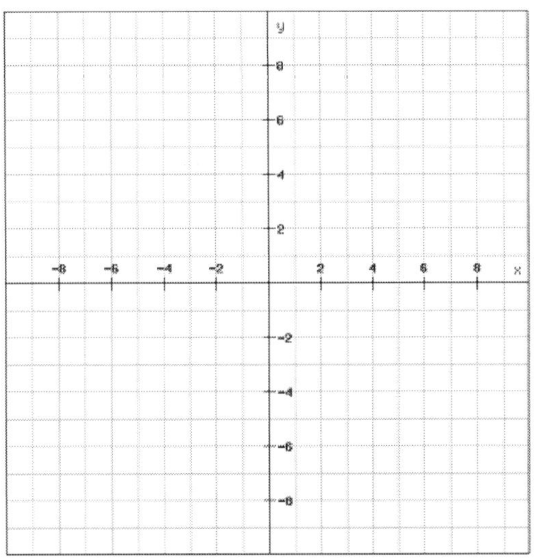

Vertex form: ____________________

Factorized form: ____________________

Domain: ________ Range: ________

y intercept:(__, __)

x intercept(s):(___, ___), (___, ___)

Increases: _______ Decreases: _______

2. $f(x) = 5x$

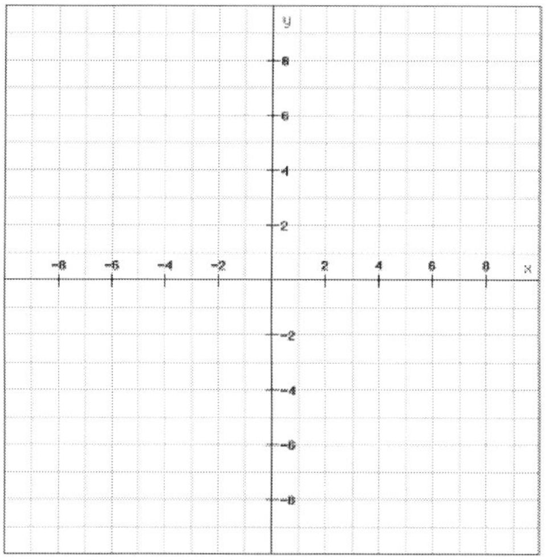

Vertex form: ____________________

Factorized form: ____________________

Domain: ________ Range: ________

y intercept:(__, __) Vertex:(__, __)Max/Min

x intercept(s):(___, ___), (___, ___)

Increases: _______Decreases: _______

3. $f(x) = x^2 + 8x + 19$

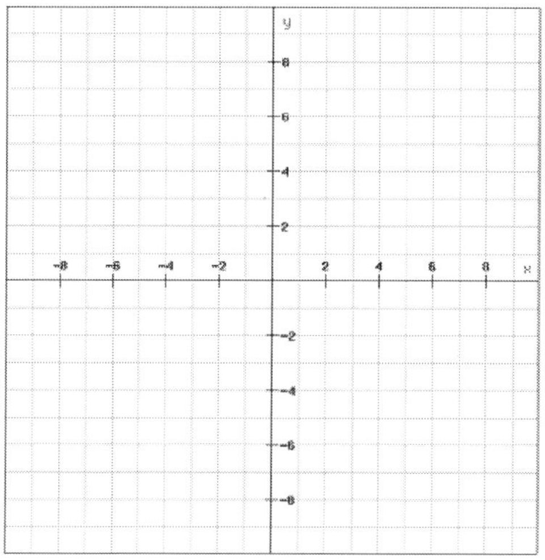

Vertex form: ____________________

Factorized form: ____________________

Domain: ________ Range: ________

y intercept:(__, __) Vertex:(__, __)Max/Min

x intercept(s):(___, ___), (___, ___)

Increases: _______Decreases: _______

4. $f(x) = 10x^2 - 8x - 2$

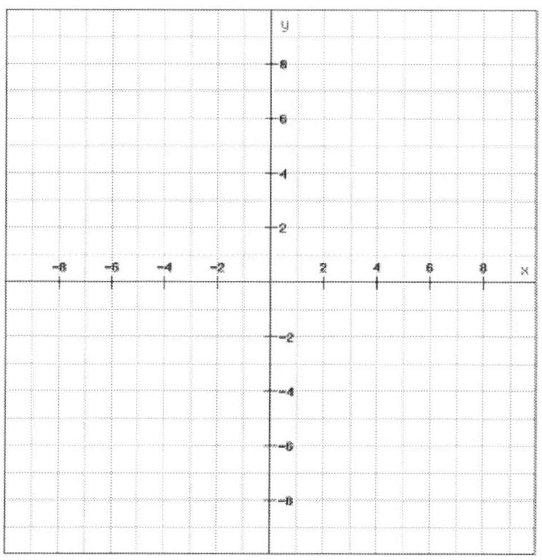

Vertex form: ____________________

Factorized form: ____________________

Domain: ________ Range: ________

y intercept:(__, __) Vertex:(__, __)Max/Min

x intercept(s):(___, ___), (___, ___)

Increases: _______Decreases: _______

5. $f(x) = x^2 + 4x + 1$

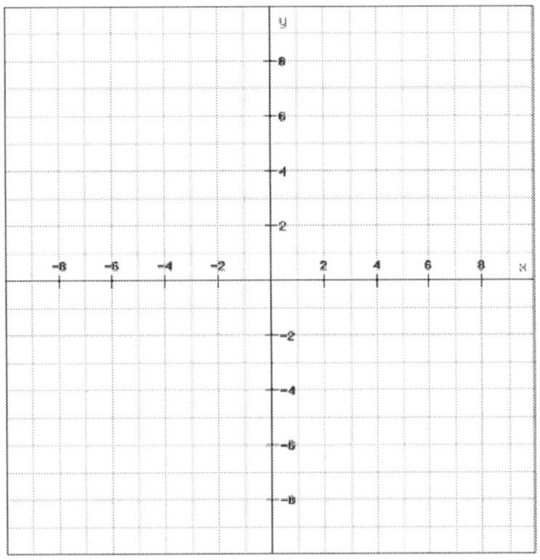

Vertex form: ________________________

Factorized form: ____________________

Domain: ________ Range: ________

y intercept:(__, __) Vertex:(__, __)Max/Min

x intercept(s):(___, ___), (___, ___)

Increases: _______ Decreases: _______

6. $f(x) = 4x^2 - 14x + 6$

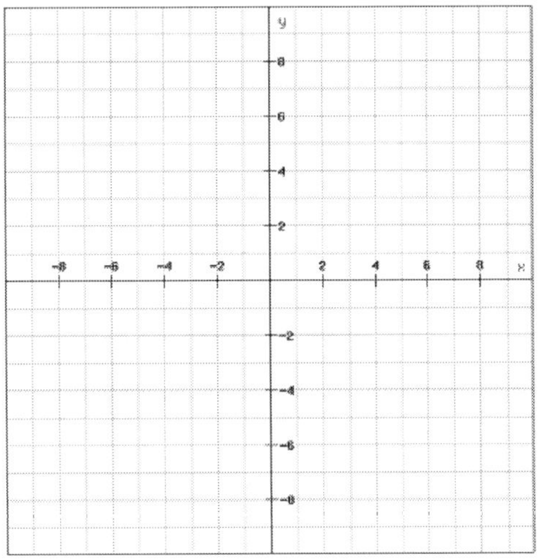

Vertex form: ________________________

Factorized form: ____________________

Domain: ________ Range: ________

y intercept:(__, __) Vertex:(__, __)Max/Min

x intercept(s):(___, ___), (___, ___)

Increases: _______ Decreases: _______

7. $f(x) = 2x^2 - 3x - 5$

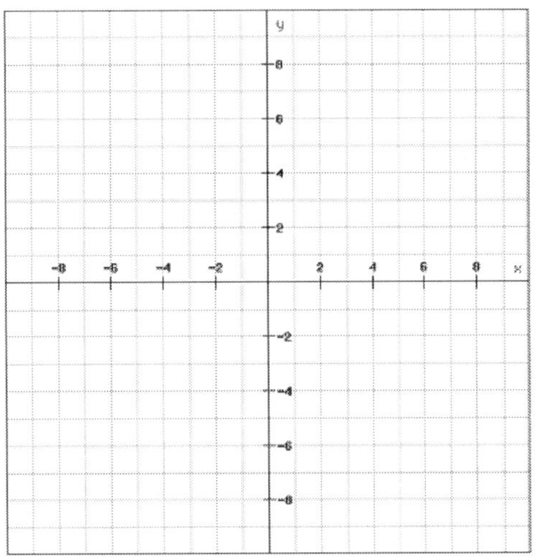

Vertex form: ________________________

Factorized form: ____________________

Domain: ________ Range: ________

y intercept:(__, __) Vertex:(__, __)Max/Min

x intercept(s):(___, ___), (___, ___)

Increases: _______ Decreases: _______

8. $f(x) = x^2 + 3x - 10$

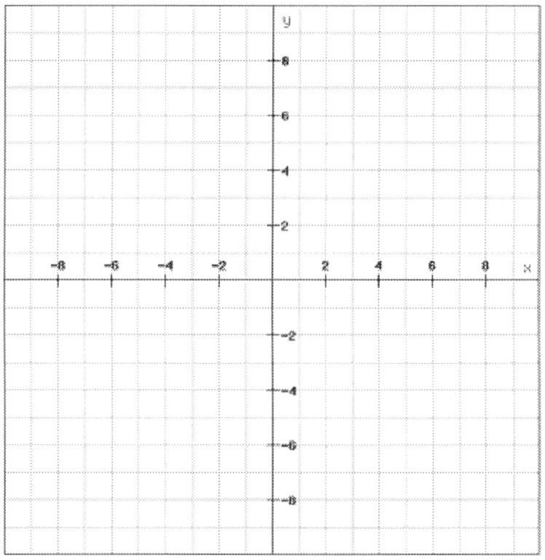

Vertex form: ______________________

Factorized form: ______________________

Domain: ________ Range: ________

y intercept:(__, __) Vertex:(__, __)Max/Min

x intercept(s):(___, ___), (___, ___)

Increases: _______Decreases: _______

9. $f(x) = x^2 + 7x - 1$

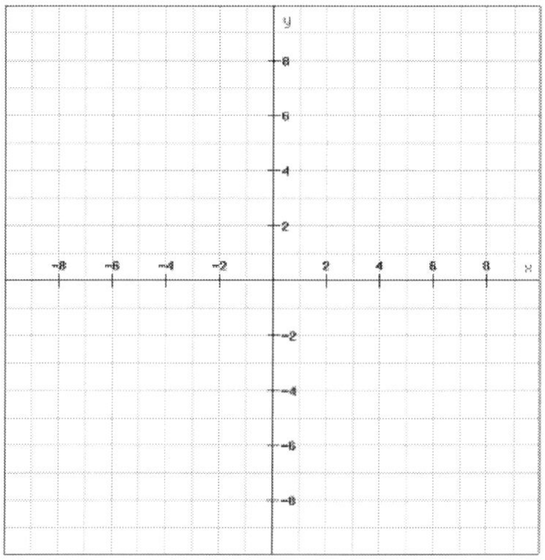

Vertex form: ______________________

Factorized form: ______________________

Domain: ________ Range: ________

y intercept:(__, __) Vertex:(__, __)Max/Min

x intercept(s):(___, ___), (___, ___)

Increases: _______Decreases: _______

10. $f(x) = x^2 + 2x + 7$

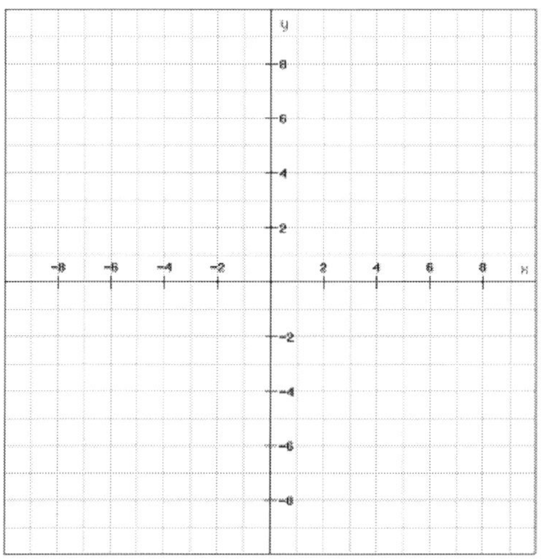

Vertex form: ______________________

Factorized form: ______________________

Domain: ________ Range: ________

y intercept:(__, __) Vertex:(__, __)Max/Min

x intercept(s):(___, ___), (___, ___)

Increases: _______Decreases: _______

11. $f(x) = x^2 + x - 1$

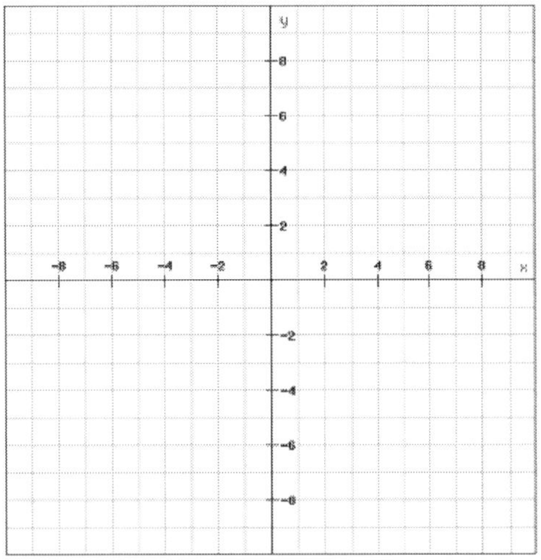

Vertex form: ______________________

Factorized form: ____________________

Domain: ________ Range: ________

y intercept:(__, __) Vertex:(__, __)Max/Min

x intercept(s):(___, ___), (___, ___)

Increases: _______Decreases: _______

12. $f(x) = x^2 + 2x + 1$

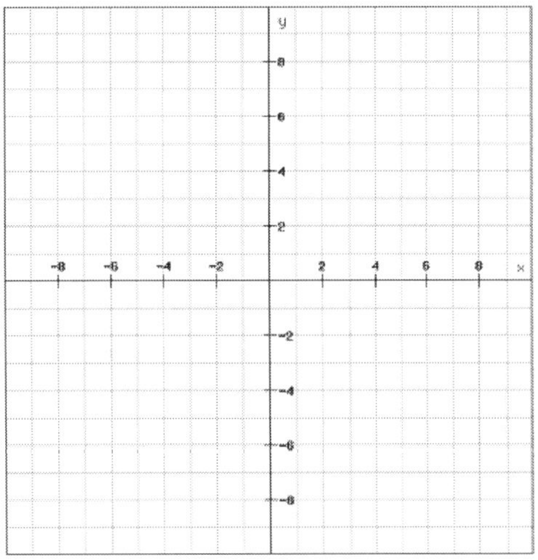

Vertex form: ______________________

Factorized form: ____________________

Domain: ________ Range: ________

y intercept:(__, __) Vertex:(__, __)Max/Min

x intercept(s):(___, ___), (___, ___)

Increases: _______Decreases: _______

13. $f(x) = x^2 + 1$

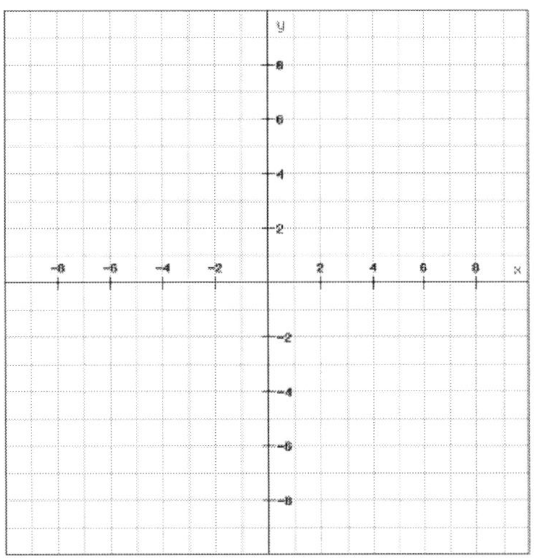

Vertex form: ______________________

Factorized form: ____________________

Domain: ________ Range: ________

y intercept:(__, __) Vertex:(__, __)Max/Min

x intercept(s):(___, ___), (___, ___)

Increases: _______Decreases: _______

14. $f(x) = x^2 - 1$

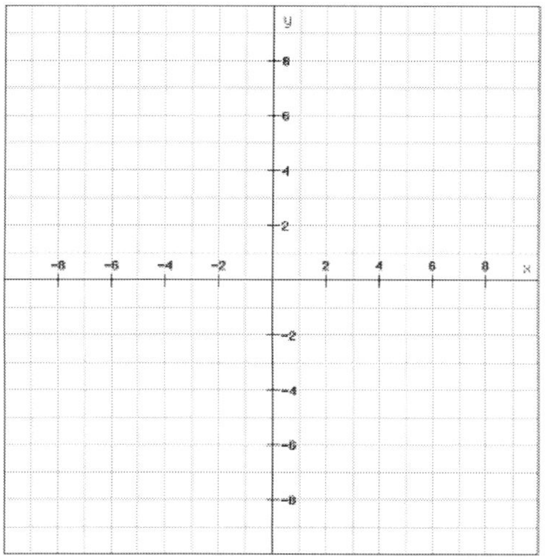

Vertex form: ____________________________

Factorized form:________________________

Domain: ________ Range: _________

y intercept:(__, __) Vertex:(__, __)Max/Min

x intercept(s):(___, ___), (___, ___)

Increases: _______Decreases: _______

15. $f(x) = x^2 + 3x$

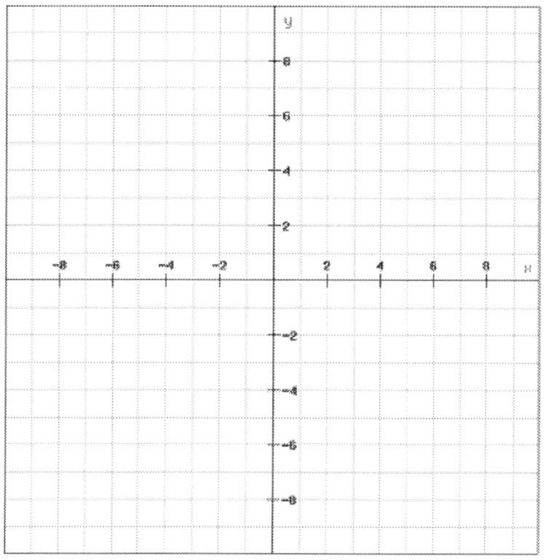

Vertex form: ____________________________

Factorized form:________________________

Domain: ________ Range: _________

y intercept:(__, __) Vertex:(__, __)Max/Min

x intercept(s):(___, ___), (___, ___)

Increases: _______Decreases: _______

16. $f(x) = x^2 + 5x$

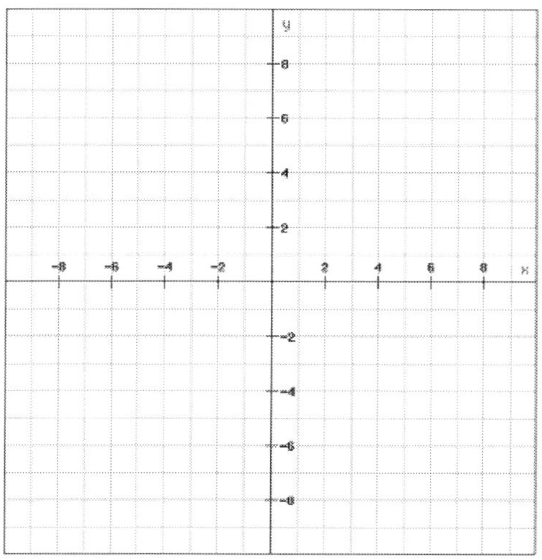

Vertex form: ____________________________

Factorized form:________________________

Domain: ________ Range: _________

y intercept:(__, __) Vertex:(__, __)Max/Min

x intercept(s):(___, ___), (___, ___)

Increases: _______Decreases: _______

17. $f(x) = x^2 - 3x$

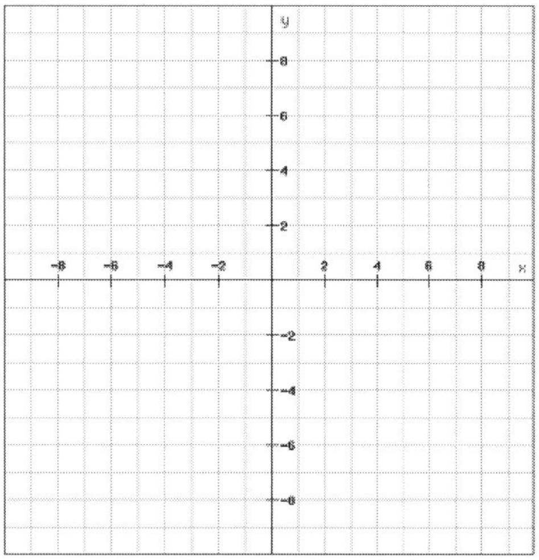

Vertex form: ______________________

Factorized form:___________________

Domain: ________ Range: ________

y intercept:(__, __) Vertex:(__, __)Max/Min

x intercept(s):(___, ___), (___, ___)

Increases: _______Decreases: _______

18. $f(x) = x^2 - 7x$

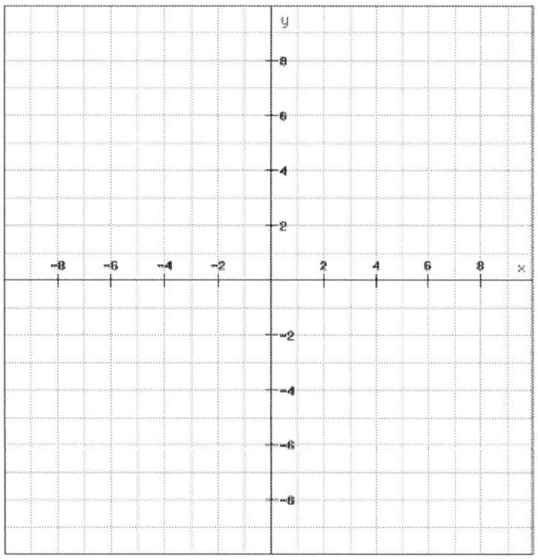

Vertex form: ______________________

Factorized form:___________________

Domain: ________ Range: ________

y intercept:(__, __) Vertex:(__, __)Max/Min

x intercept(s):(___, ___), (___, ___)

Increases: _______Decreases: _______

19. $f(x) = x^2 + 4x + 6$

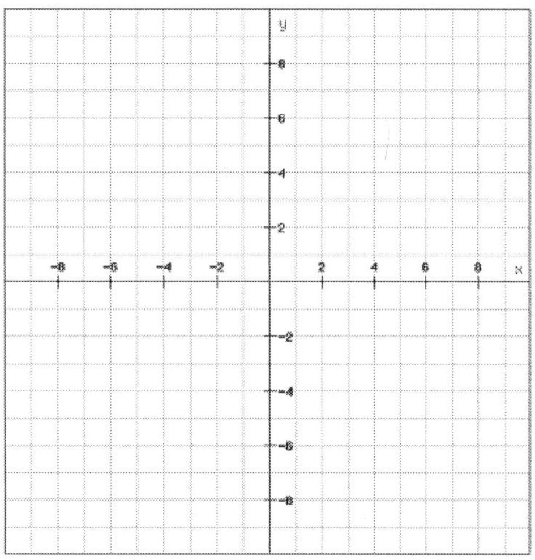

Vertex form: ______________________

Factorized form:___________________

Domain: ________ Range: ________

y intercept:(__, __) Vertex:(__, __)Max/Min

x intercept(s):(___, ___), (___, ___)

Increases: _______Decreases: _______

20. $f(x) = -2x^2 - 16x - 29$

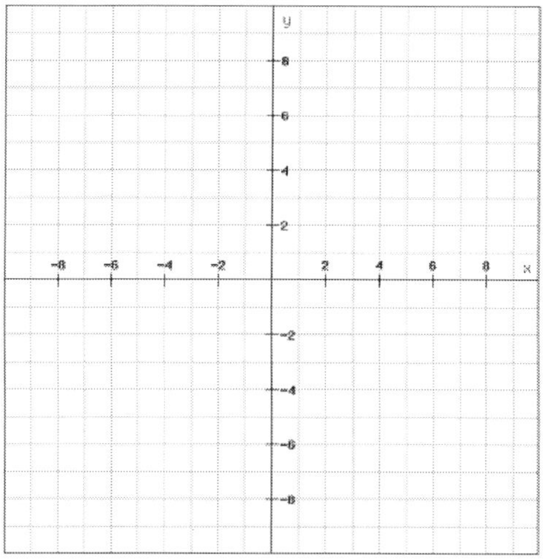

Vertex form: ____________________

Factorized form:__________________

Domain: ________ Range: ________

y intercept:(__, __) Vertex:(__, __)Max/Min

x intercept(s):(___, ___), (___, ___)

Increases: _______Decreases: _______

21. $f(x) = x^2 - 6x + 4$

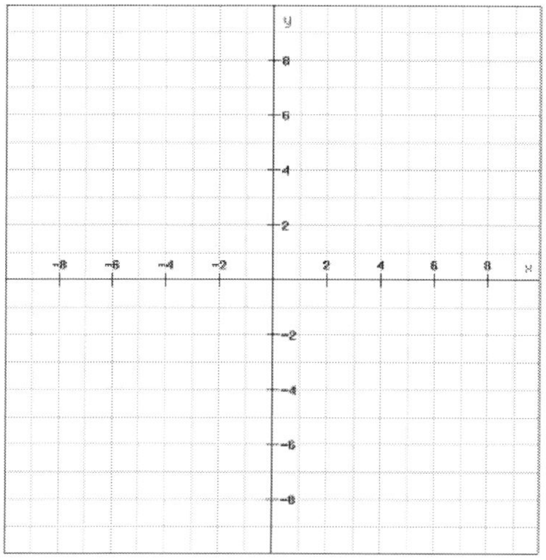

Vertex form: ____________________

Factorized form:__________________

Domain: ________ Range: ________

y intercept:(__, __) Vertex:(__, __)Max/Min

x intercept(s):(___, ___), (___, ___)

Increases: _______Decreases: _______

22. $f(x) = x^2 - 7x + 2$

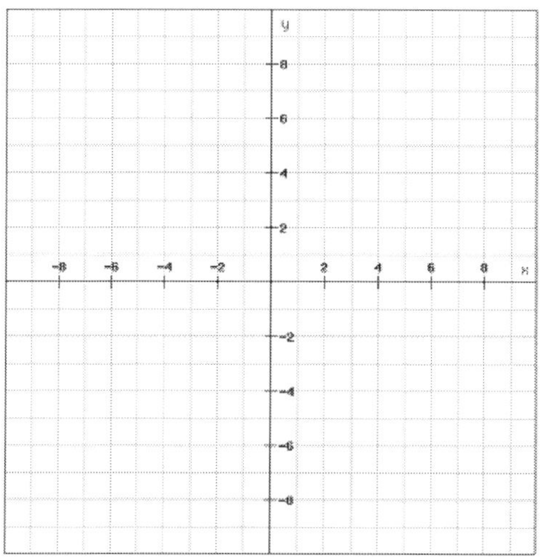

Vertex form: ____________________

Factorized form:__________________

Domain: ________ Range: ________

y intercept:(__, __) Vertex:(__, __)Max/Min

x intercept(s):(___, ___), (___, ___)

Increases: _______Decreases: _______

23. $f(x) = x^2 + 3x + 10$

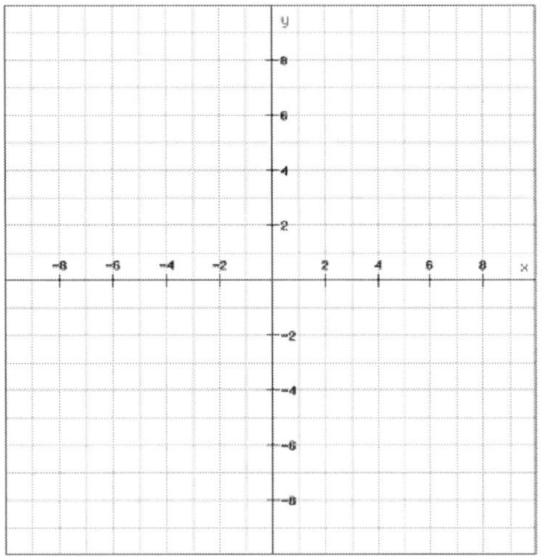

Vertex form: ______________________

Factorized form:____________________

Domain: ________ Range: ________

y intercept:(__, __) Vertex:(__, __)Max/Min

x intercept(s):(___, ___), (___, ___)

Increases: _______Decreases: _______

24. $f(x) = x^2 + 5$

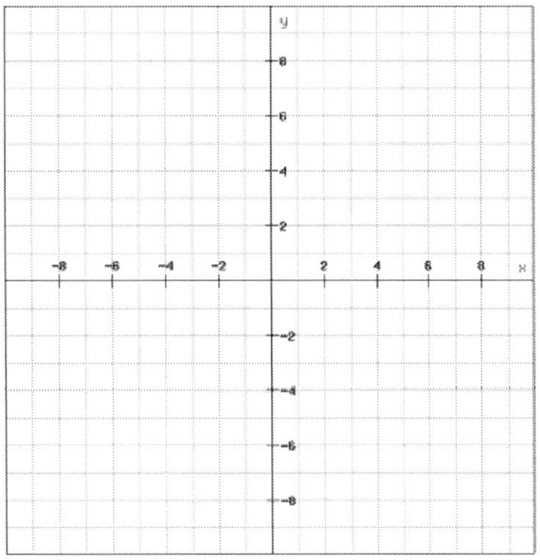

Vertex form: ______________________

Factorized form:____________________

Domain: ________ Range: ________

y intercept:(__, __) Vertex:(__, __)Max/Min

x intercept(s):(___, ___), (___, ___)

Increases: _______Decreases: _______

25. $f(x) = x^2 - 3$

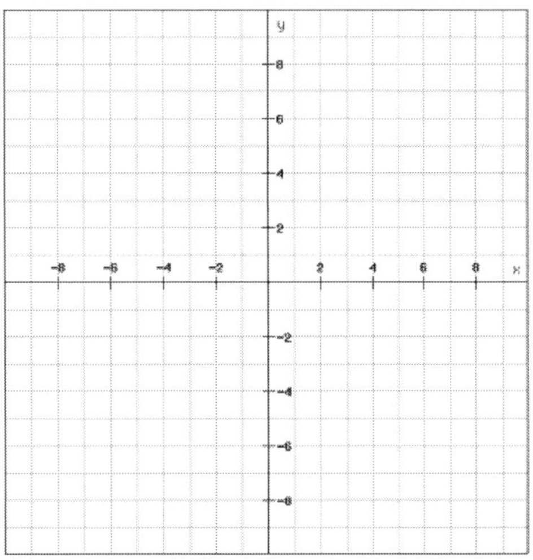

Vertex form: ______________________

Factorized form:____________________

Domain: ________ Range: ________

y intercept:(__, __) Vertex:(__, __)Max/Min

x intercept(s):(___, ___), (___, ___)

Increases: _______Decreases: _______

26. $f(x) = x^2 - 7x$

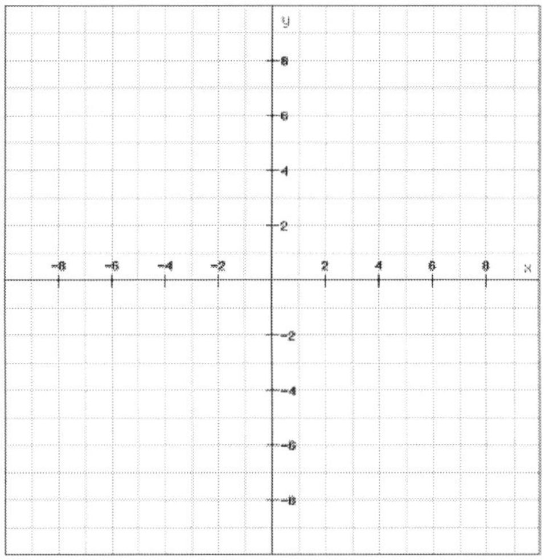

Vertex form: ______________________

Factorized form: ______________________

Domain: ________ Range: ________

y intercept:(__, __) Vertex:(__, __)Max/Min

x intercept(s):(___, ___), (___, ___)

Increases: _______ Decreases: _______

27. $f(x) = x^2 + 3x - 5$

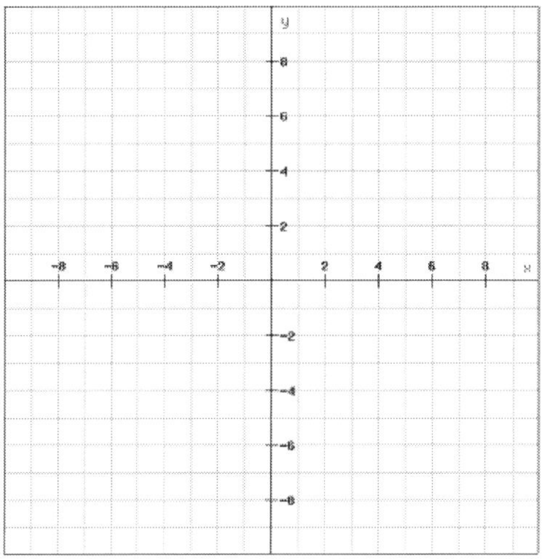

Vertex form: ______________________

Factorized form: ______________________

Domain: ________ Range: ________

y intercept:(__, __) Vertex:(__, __)Max/Min

x intercept(s):(___, ___), (___, ___)

Increases: _______ Decreases: _______

28. $f(x) = 5x^2 - 3$

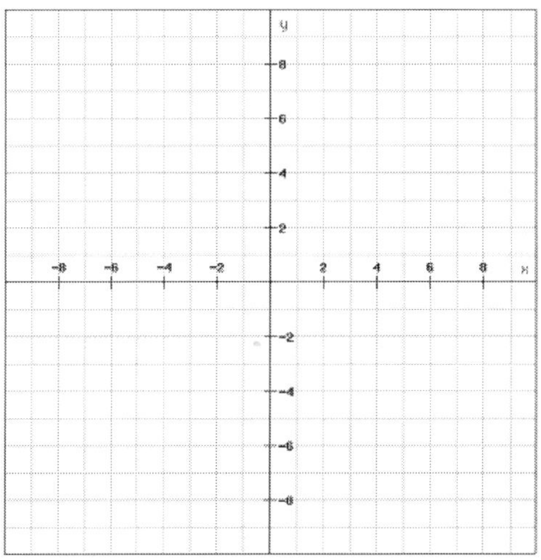

Vertex form: ______________________

Factorized form: ______________________

Domain: ________ Range: ________

y intercept:(__, __) Vertex:(__, __)Max/Min

x intercept(s):(___, ___), (___, ___)

Increases: _______ Decreases: _______

29. $f(x) = 5x^2 - 10x$

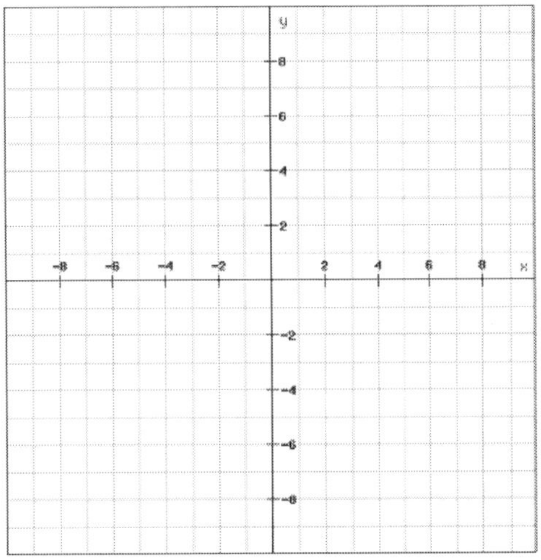

Vertex form: ______________________

Factorized form: ____________________

Domain: ________ Range: ________

y intercept:(__, __) Vertex:(__, __)Max/Min

x intercept(s):(___, ___), (___, ___)

Increases: _______Decreases: _______

30. $f(x) = -5x^2$

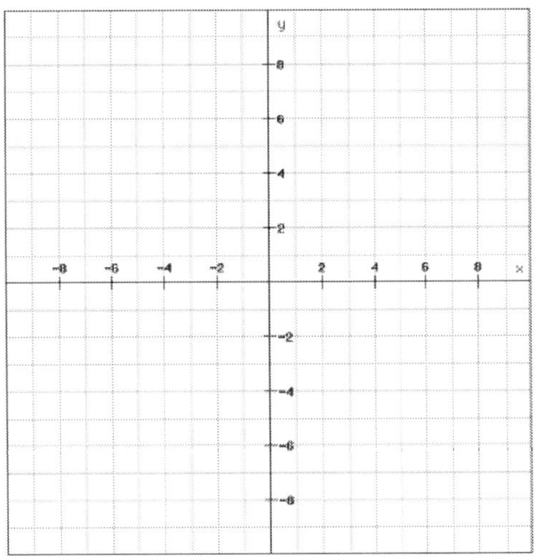

Vertex form: ______________________

Factorized form: ____________________

Domain: ________ Range: ________

y intercept:(__, __) Vertex:(__, __)Max/Min

x intercept(s):(___, ___), (___, ___)

Increases: _______Decreases: _______

31. $f(x) = -x^2 + 6x - 8$

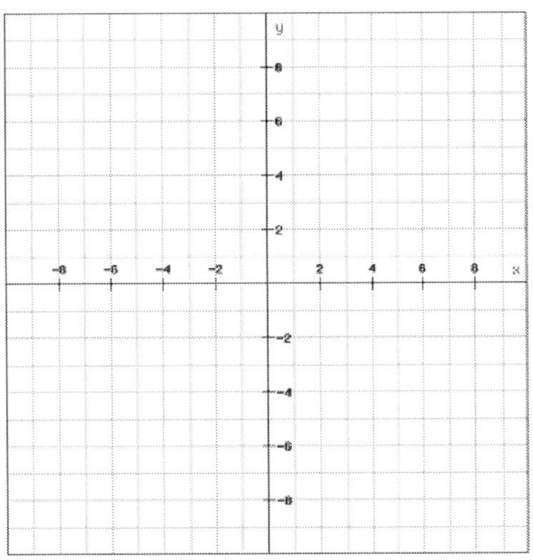

Vertex form: ______________________

Factorized form: ____________________

Domain: ________ Range: ________

y intercept:(__, __) Vertex:(__, __)Max/Min

x intercept(s):(___, ___), (___, ___)

Increases: _______Decreases: _______

32. $f(x) = -x^2 - 6x + 2$

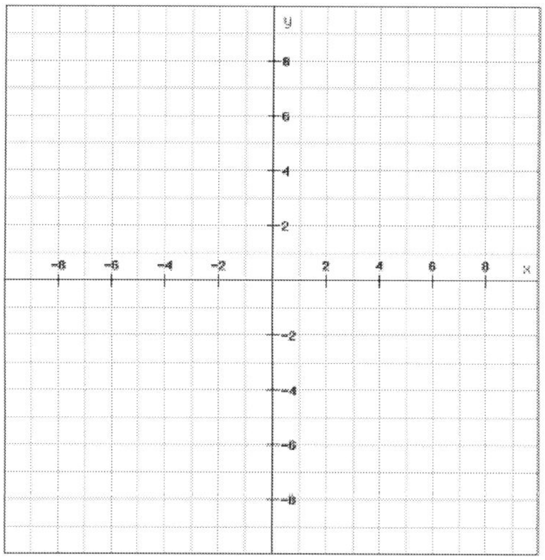

Vertex form: ____________________

Factorized form: ____________________

Domain: ________ Range: ________

y intercept:(__, __) Vertex:(__, __)Max/Min

x intercept(s):(___, ___), (___, ___)

Increases: _______ Decreases: _______

33. $f(x) = -x^2 + x - 5$

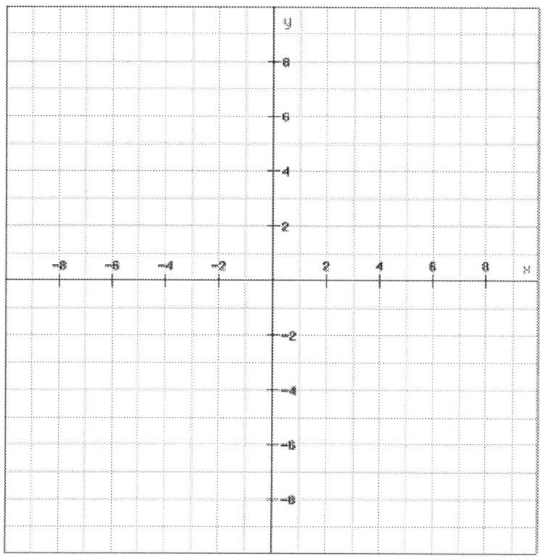

Vertex form: ____________________

Factorized form: ____________________

Domain: ________ Range: ________

y intercept:(__, __) Vertex:(__, __)Max/Min

x intercept(s):(___, ___), (___, ___)

Increases: _______ Decreases: _______

34. $f(x) = -x^2 - 4x - 4$

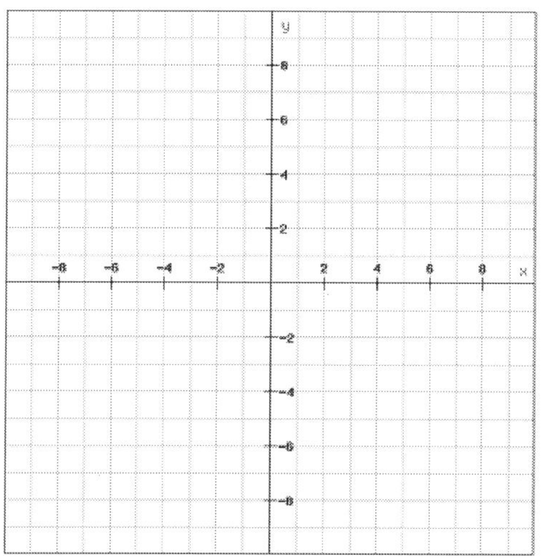

Vertex form: ____________________

Factorized form: ____________________

Domain: ________ Range: ________

y intercept:(__, __) Vertex:(__, __)Max/Min

x intercept(s):(___, ___), (___, ___)

Increases: _______ Decreases: _______

35. $f(x) = -x^2 + 3$

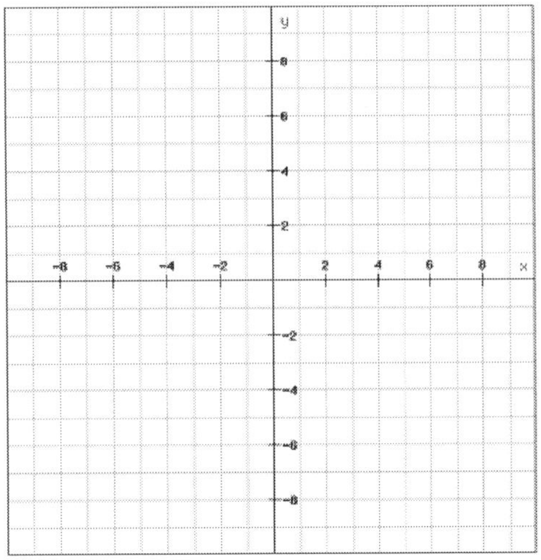

Vertex form: ______________________

Factorized form: ____________________

Domain: ________ Range: ________

y intercept:(__, __) Vertex:(__, __)Max/Min

x intercept(s):(___, ___), (___, ___)

Increases: _______Decreases: _______

36. $f(x) = 3x^2$

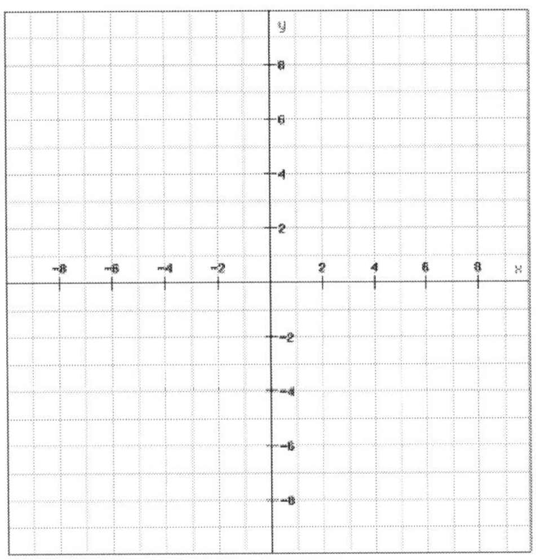

Vertex form: ______________________

Factorized form: ____________________

Domain: ________ Range: ________

y intercept:(__, __) Vertex:(__, __)Max/Min

x intercept(s):(___, ___), (___, ___)

Increases: _______Decreases: _______

37. $f(x) = x^2 + 3x + 4$

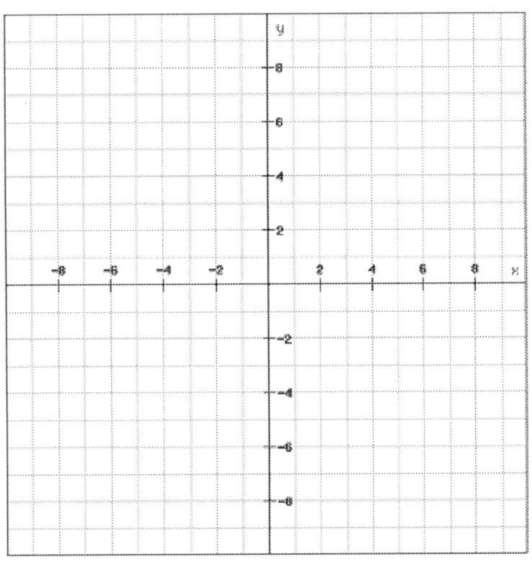

Vertex form: ______________________

Factorized form: ____________________

Domain: ________ Range: ________

y intercept:(__, __) Vertex:(__, __)Max/Min

x intercept(s):(___, ___), (___, ___)

Increases: _______Decreases: _______

38. $f(x) = -4x + 3$

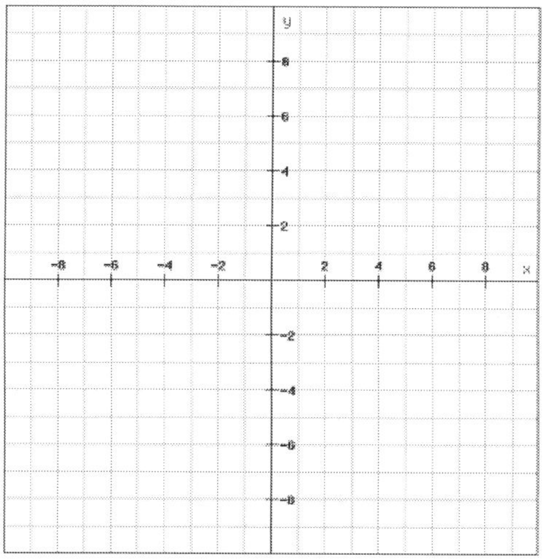

Vertex form: ____________________

Factorized form: ____________________

Domain: ________ Range: ________

y intercept:(__, __) Vertex:(__, __)Max/Min

x intercept(s):(___, ___), (___, ___)

Increases: _______ Decreases: _______

39. $f(x) = x^2 - 2$

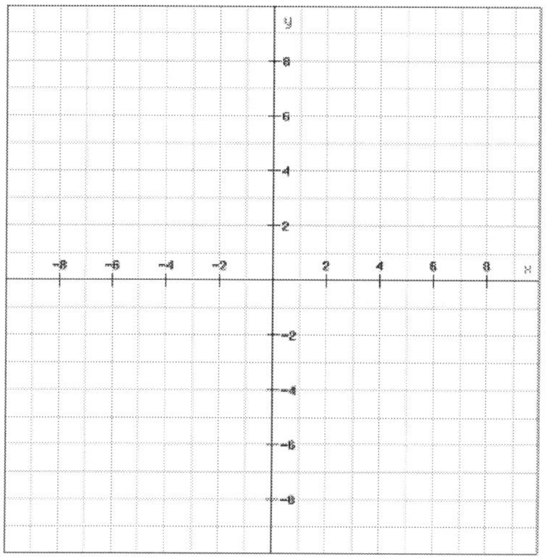

Vertex form: ____________________

Factorized form: ____________________

Domain: ________ Range: ________

y intercept:(__, __) Vertex:(__, __)Max/Min

x intercept(s):(___, ___), (___, ___)

Increases: _______ Decreases: _______

40. $f(x) = x^2 - 2x$

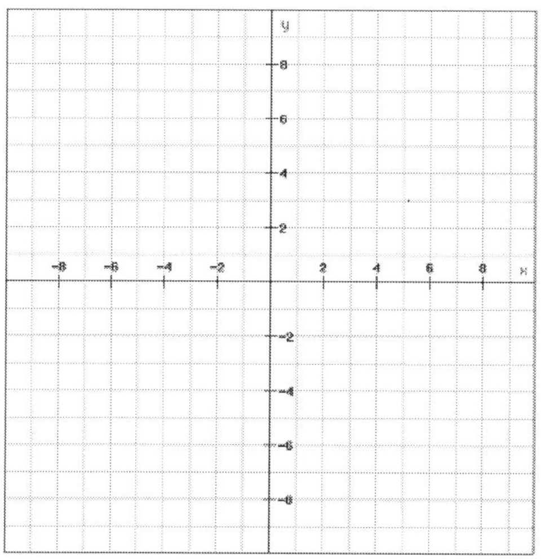

Vertex form: ____________________

Factorized form: ____________________

Domain: ________ Range: ________

y intercept:(__, __) Vertex:(__, __)Max/Min

x intercept(s):(___, ___), (___, ___)

Increases: _______ Decreases: _______

41. What are the coordinates of the vertex of $y = 7(x + 3)^2 + 4$? (___, ___) and its axis of symmetry?

42. What are the coordinates of the vertex of $y = -2(x - 4)^2 + 2$? (___, ___) and its axis of symmetry?

43. The graph of the relation $x = -5(y + 2)^2 + 6$ is a parabola. Which way does this parabola open? (up, down, left or right).

44. What value of b makes the expression $x^2 + 8x + b$ a perfect square?

45. When a quadratic function can be written as a perfect square on the graph it means that ____.

46. what are the zeros of the quadratic relation $y = 10x^2 - 20x$, and its axis of symmetry?

47. Find the roots (zeros) of the equation $20(6 + 5x)(12 - x) = 0$ and its axis of symmetry.

48. The quadratic equation is used to find the _________ of the quadratic function. In case this equation has _______________ it means the quadratic function is completely _________ or __________ the x axis and the value of $b^2 - 4ac$ ____________. In case $b^2 - 4ac$ is __________ the quadratic function will have _______________ and lastly if $b^2 - 4ac$ is __________ the quadratic function will have _______________.

If $b^2 - 4ac$ __ 0 there are _______________Example: _______________

If $b^2 - 4ac$ __ 0 there are _______________Example: _______________

If $b^2 - 4ac$ __ 0 there are _______________Example: _______________

49. What values of b make the relation $y = 6x^2 + bx + 5$ have no zeros?

50. Under what conditions will the parabola with equation $y = a(x - h)^2 + k$ have two x–intercepts?

51. How many zeros does the quadratic relation $y = -1.7(x + 13.2)^2 - 3.1$ have?

52. A parabola has its vertex in the third quadrant and opens down. A possible value for $b^2 - 4ac$ can be __________

53. Write the equation, in vertex form, of a parabola that has its vertex in the second quadrant, contains two zeros, and is narrower than $y = x^2$

54. Write the equation, in vertex form, of a parabola that has its vertex in the third quadrant, contains two zeros, and is wider than $y = x^2$

55. W rite the relation $y = -4(x - 2)^2 + 7$ in standard form and find its axis of symmetry

56. Determine the value of the vertex of the relation $y = -(x - 3)(x + 1)$. Is the vertex a maximum or a minimum?

57. T he parabola $y = -4(x - 2)^2 + 7$ is reflected about the x–axis. Write the equation of the image parabola.

Inequalities of the 2nd degree – use a graph to solve

1. $x^2 > 0$ $\qquad$ $x^2 < 0$

2. $x^2 + 1 > 0$ $\qquad$ $x^2 + 1 < 0$

3. $x^2 - 1 > 0$ $\qquad$ $x^2 - 1 < 0$

4. $x^2 - 3 \geq 0$ $x^2 - 3 \leq 0$

5. $x^2 - 3x > 0$ $x^2 - 3x < 0$

6. $2x^2 + 4 > 0$ $2x^2 + 4 < 0$

7. $x^2 - 3x + 2 > 0$ $x^2 - 3x + 2 < 0$

8. $x^2 + 2x - 3 > 0$ $x^2 + 2x - 3 < 0$

9. $2x^2 + 8x - 10 > 0$ $2x^2 + 8x - 10 < 0$

10. $x^2 - 2x + 1 > 0$ $2x^2 + 2x \leq 0$

11. $x^2 + 11x + 10 > 0$ $2x^2 + 3x + 1 < 0$

Application:

1. The height of a ball kicked upwards is given by $h(t) = 40t - 16t^2$ meters, where t is measured in seconds.

   a. Sketch the corresponding function, label the axes.

   b. Calculate h(1) and give a practical interpretation to your answer.

   c. Calculate the zeros of h(t) and explain the meaning in the context of the problem.

   d. Solve the equation $h(t) = 10$ and explain the meaning of the solutions in the context of the problem.

   e. Obtain the maximum height of the ball and the instant in which it reaches it.

2. The width of a rectangle is three times is length, its area is 243 m^2. Find its perimeter.

3. Find 2 consecutive even numbers that when their sum is squared 100 is obtained.

4. The efficiency of an engine as a function of the concentration of a certain chemical component is given by $f(x) = -0.5x^2 + x$, $0 \le x \le 2$.

   a. Sketch the function in its domain.

   b. Find the concentration of the chemical for which the efficiency is maximized. What is the efficiency in this case?

5. A hundred meters of fencing is available to enclose a rectangular field along side of a River, What dimensions will produce the maximum area that can be enclosed?

2.4. – TRANSLATIONS AND REFLECTIONS

Vertical translation: $f(x) \rightarrow f(x) + a$

1. Given the function $f(x) = x^2$, write the expression for $f(x) + 1$. Sketch the functions. What kind of translation is that?

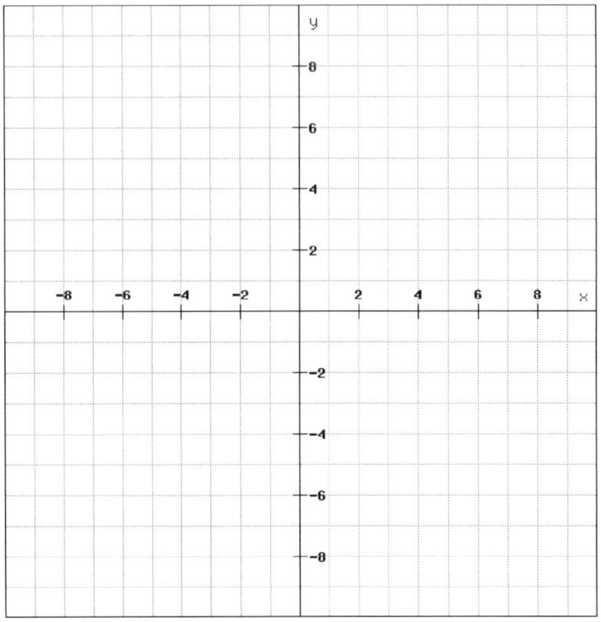

2. Given the function $f(x) = (x+1)^2$, write the expression for $f(x) - 3$. Sketch the functions. What kind of translation is that?

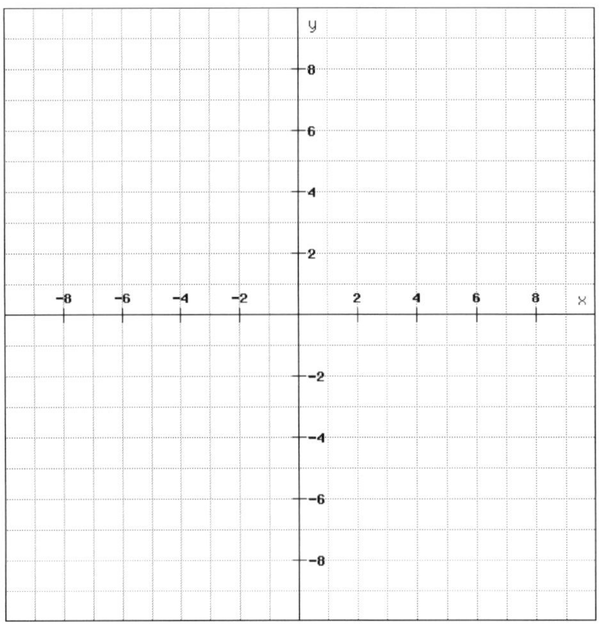

Horizontal Translation ($f(x) \rightarrow f(x+b)$):

3. Given the function $f(x) = x^2$, write the expression for $f(x - 3)$. Sketch the function. What kind of translation is that?

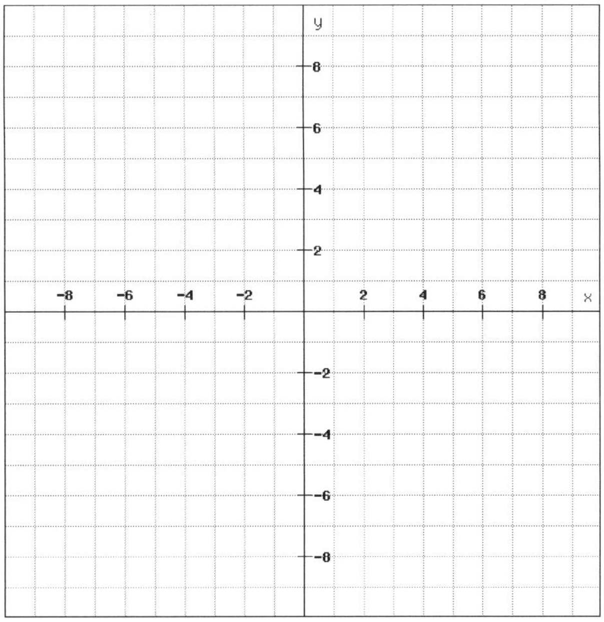

4. Given the function $f(x) = 2 - x^2$, write the expression for $f(x + 1)$. Sketch the function. What kind of translation is that?

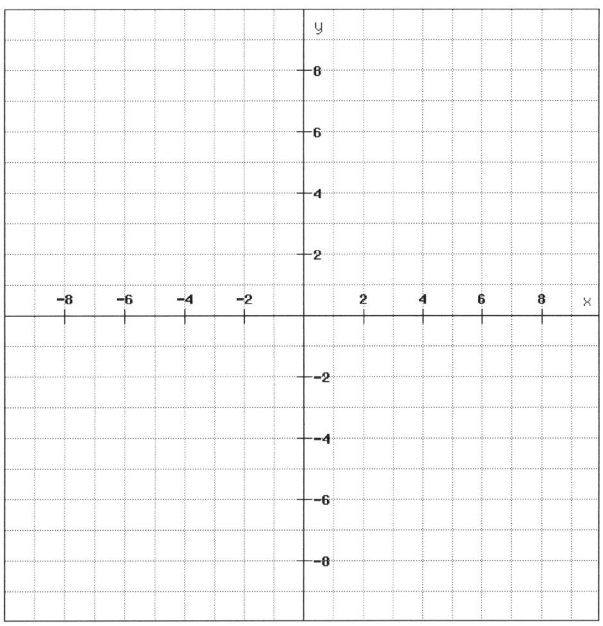

5. Given the function $f(x) = x^2$, write the expression for $f(x - 3)$. Sketch the function. What kind of translation is that?

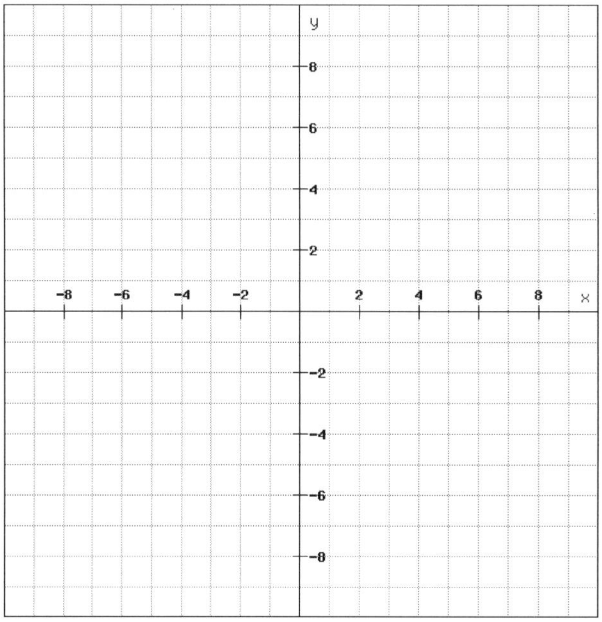

6. Given the function $f(x) = (x+2)^2 - 1$, write the expression for $f(x - 3) + 5$. Sketch the function. What kind of translation is that?

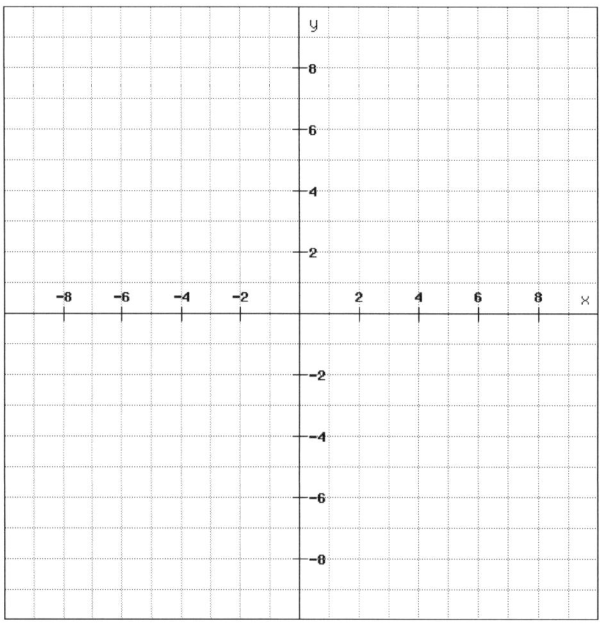

Horizontal and Vertical translation: $f(x) \rightarrow f(x + b) + a$

7. Given the function $f(x) = x^2$, write the expression for $f(x - 3) + 1$. Sketch the function. What kind of translation is that?

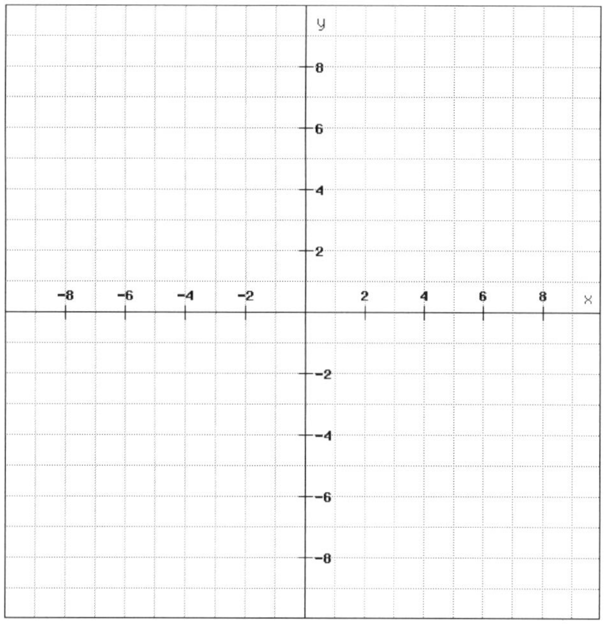

8. Given the function $f(x) = 1 - x^2$, write the expression for $f(x + 2) - 3$ .Sketch the function. What kind of translation is that?

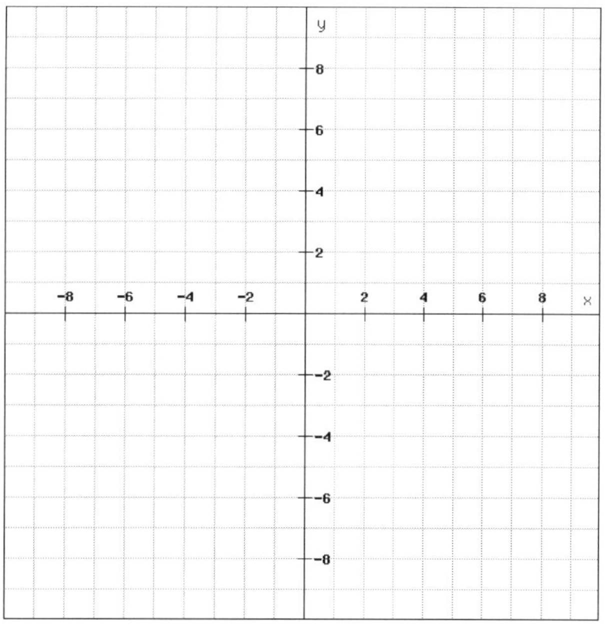

Vertical Dilation (change of amplitude): $f(x) \rightarrow pf(x)$

9. Given the function $f(x) = x^2$, write the expression for $2f(x)$. Sketch the function. What kind of Dilation is that?

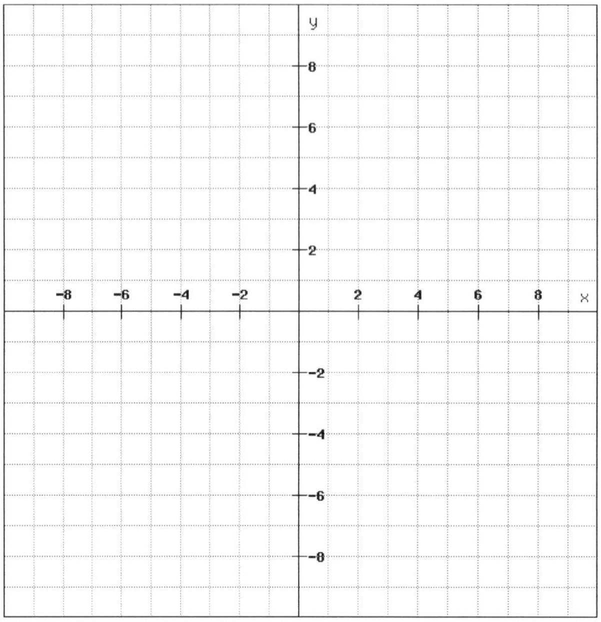

10. Given the function $f(x) = 6 - x^2$, write the expression for $\frac{1}{3}f(x)$. Sketch the function. What kind of Dilation is that?

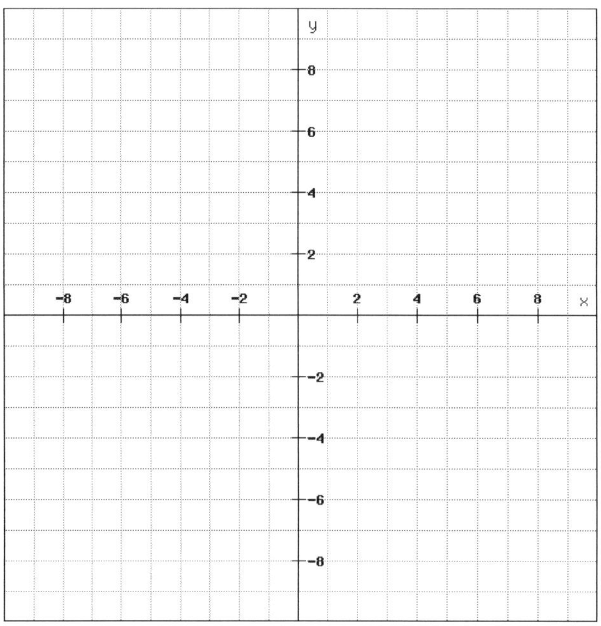

11. Given the function $f(x) = x^2$, write the expression for $3f(x - 3) - 4$. Sketch the function. Describe the sequence of transformations applied, pay attention to order.

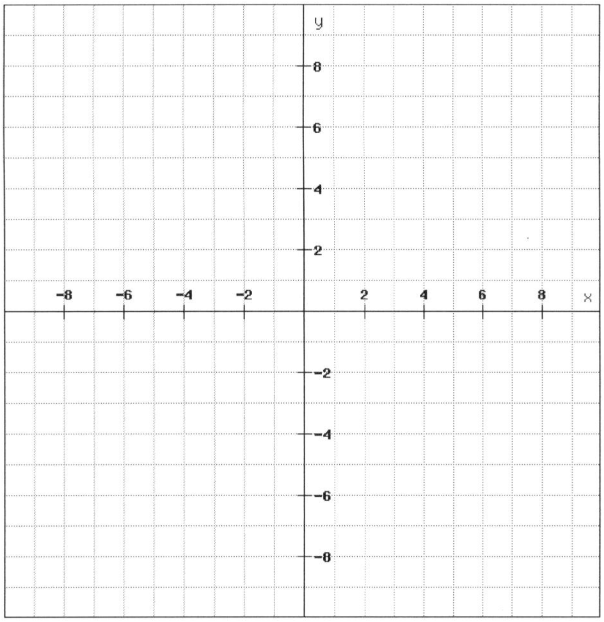

Horizontal Dilation (change of scale): $f(x) \rightarrow f(px)$

12. Given the function $f(x) = x^2$, write the expression for $f(2x)$. Sketch the function. What kind of Dilation is that?

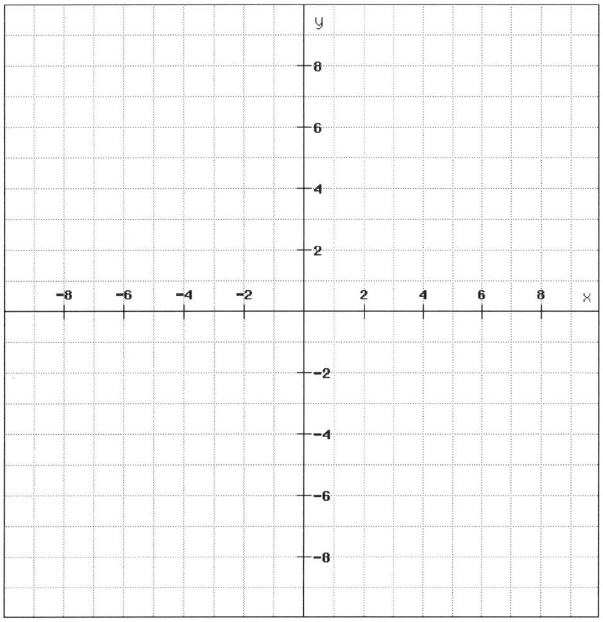

13. Given the function $f(x) = (x + 1)^2$, write the expression for $f(\frac{1}{3}x)$. Sketch the function. What kind of Dilation is that?

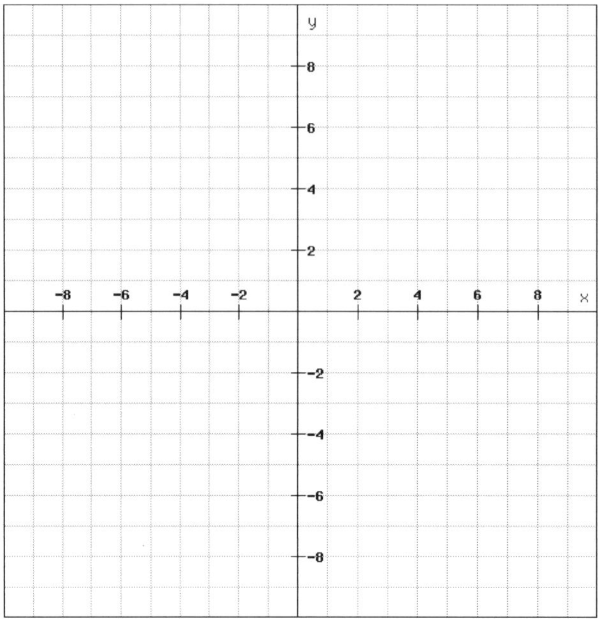

14. Given the function $f(x) = 6 + x^2$, write the expression for $\frac{1}{3}f(2x)$. Sketch the function. What kinds of Dilations/Translations are applied?

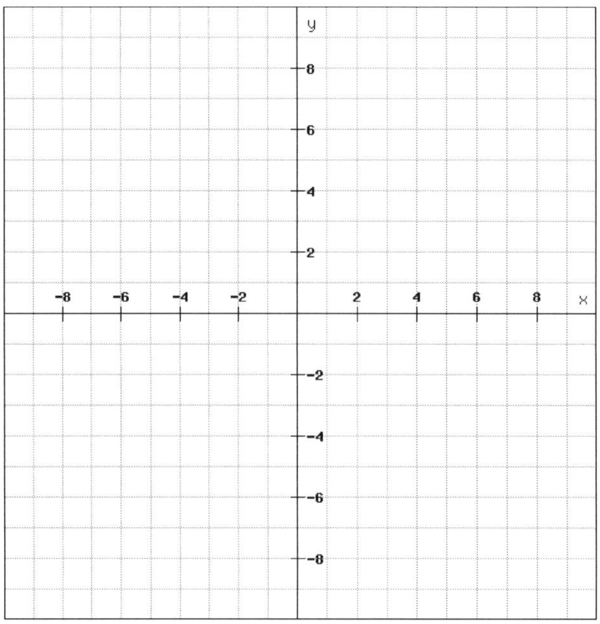

Reflections about x axis: $f(x) \rightarrow -f(x)$

15. Given the function $f(x) = (x - 2)^2$, write the expression for $-f(x)$. Sketch the function. What kind of Reflection is that?

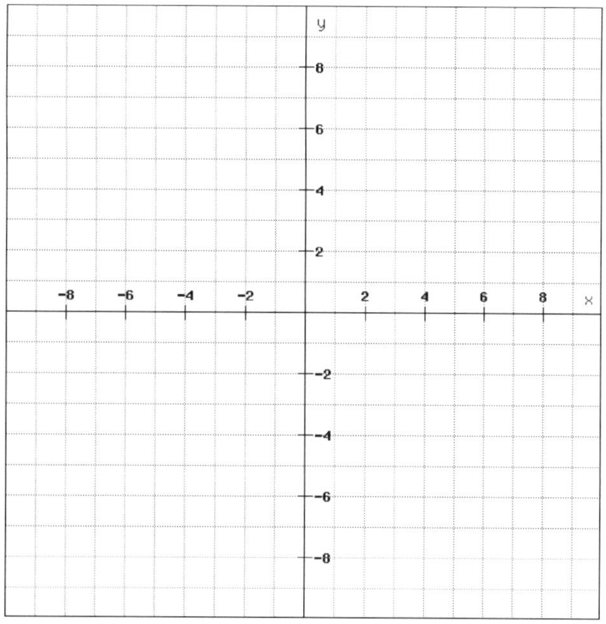

16. Given the function $f(x) = (x - 4)^2$, write the expression for $-f(3x)$. Sketch the function. What kinds of Transformations/Reflections are applied?

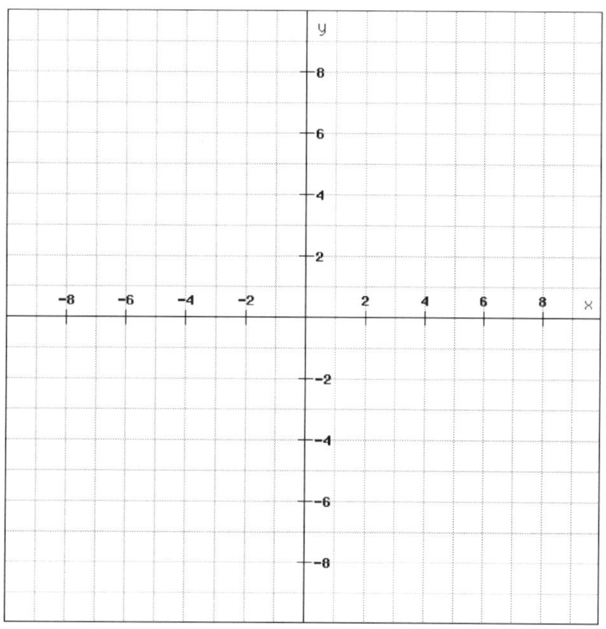

Reflections about y axis: $f(x) \rightarrow f(-x)$

17. Given the function $f(x) = 2x - 4$, write the expression for $f(-x)$. Sketch the function. What kind of Reflection is that?

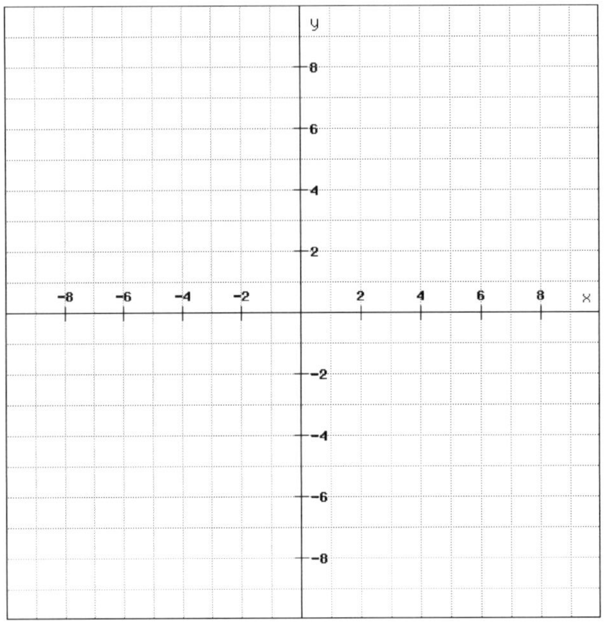

18. Given the function $f(x) = (x + 2)^2 - 7$, write the expression for $-2f(-x)$. Sketch the function. What kind of Transformation is that?

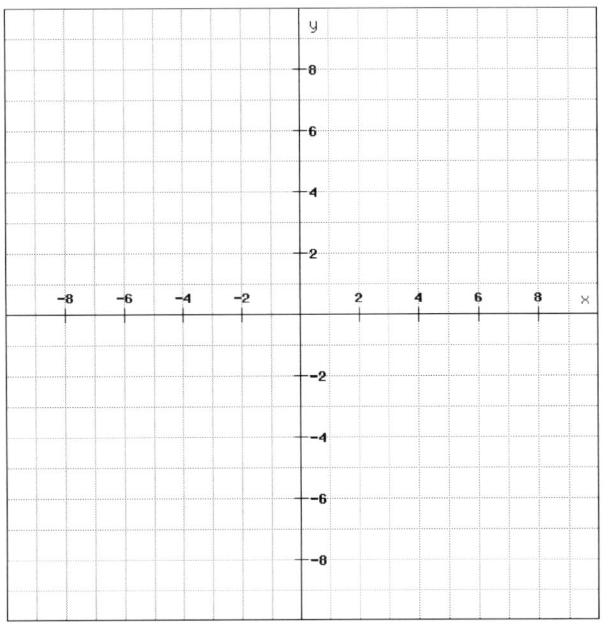

<u>Summarizing:</u>

<u>Vertical Translations:</u> $g(x) = f(x) + k$. The graph is translated k units upward if $k > 0$ and k units downward if $k < 0$.

<u>Horizontal translations:</u> $g(x) = f(x + c)$. The graph is translated c units to the left if $c > 0$ and c units to the right if $c < 0$.

<u>Vertical Dilation (Change of amplitude and/or reflection about the x axis):</u>

$g(x) = Af(x)$.

The amplitude of the graph is increased by a factor of A if $|A| > 1$ and decreased by a factor of A if $|A| < 1$. In addition, if $A < 0$ the graph is inverted (Reflection about x axis)

<u>Horizontal Dilation (Change of scale and/or reflection about the y axis):</u>

$g(x) = f(ax)$.

The graph is "compressed" if $|a| > 1$ and "stretched out" if $|a| < 1$. In addition, if $a < 0$ the graph is reflected about the y–axis.

Exercises:

1. Consider the function $f(x) = x^2$

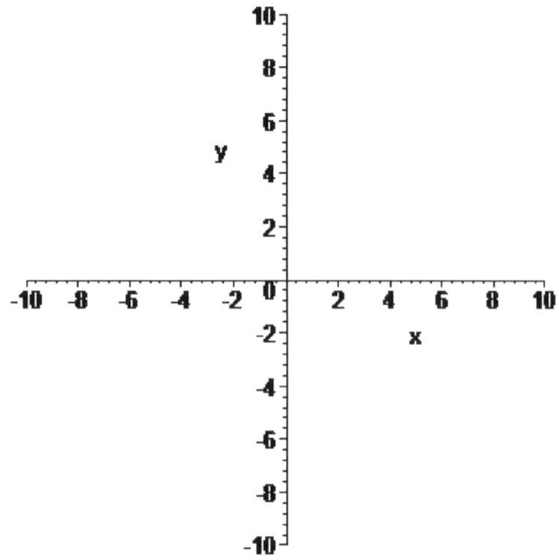

   a. Write the expression of the function

      $g(x) = f(x) + 2 =$ _______________

   b. This is a ______________ translation.

   c. Sketch both functions on the same graph.

2. Consider the function $f(x) = (x - 2)(x + 3)$

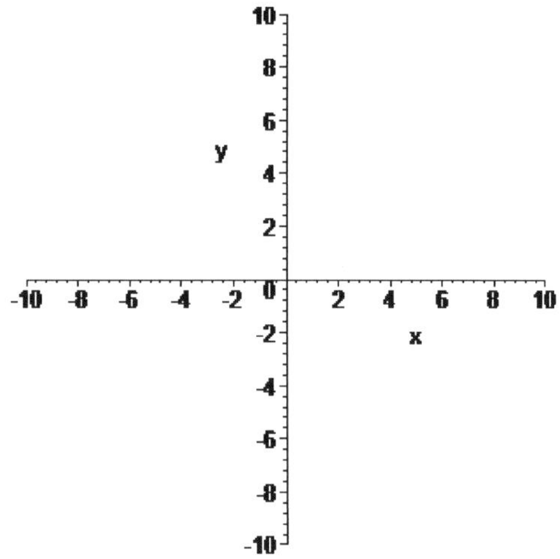

   a. Write the expression of the function

      $g(x) = f(x) - 3 =$ _______________

   b. This is a ______________ translation.

   c. Sketch both functions on the same graph.

3. Consider the function $f(x) = -2x^2$

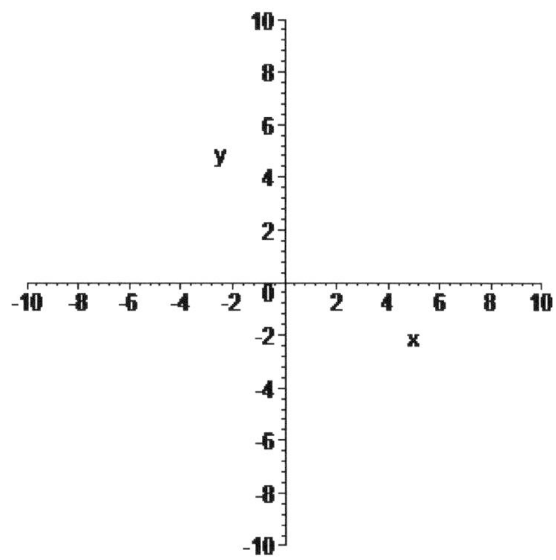

   a. Write the expression of the function

      $g(x) = f(x+1) - 5 =$ _______________

b. This is a ______________ translation and a

   ___________ translation.

c. Sketch both functions on the same graph.

4. Consider the function $f(x) = 2(x - 3)^2$

   a. Write the expression of the function

      $g(x) = -f(x) =$ ________________

   b. This is a ________________ about the

      ____

   c. Sketch both functions on the same graph.

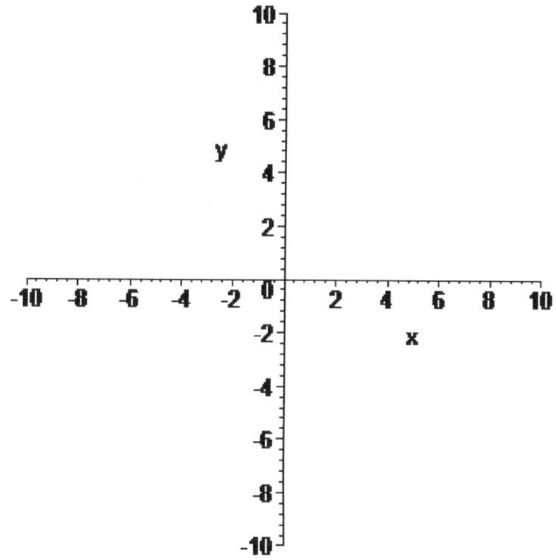

5. Consider the function $f(x) = (x + 2)^2 - 1$

   a. Write the expression of the function

      $g(x) = f(-x) =$ ________________

   b. This is a ________________ about the

      ____

   c. Sketch both functions on the same graph.

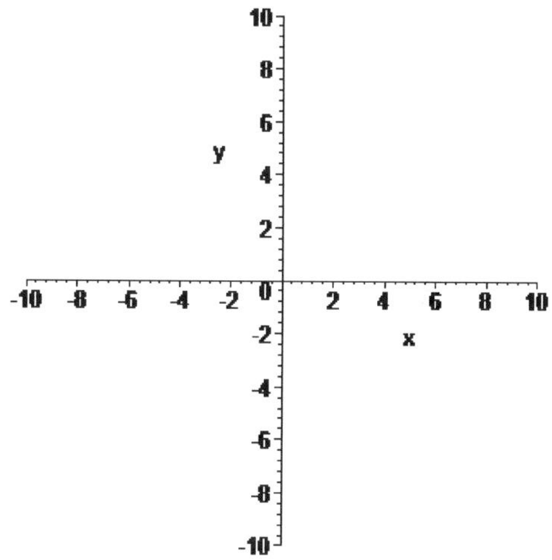

6. Consider the function $f(x) = -(x - 2)^2 + 5$

   a. Write the expression of the function

      $g(x) = 3f(x) =$ ________________

   b. This is a ____________________________

      with scale factor ______________

   c. Sketch both functions on the same graph.

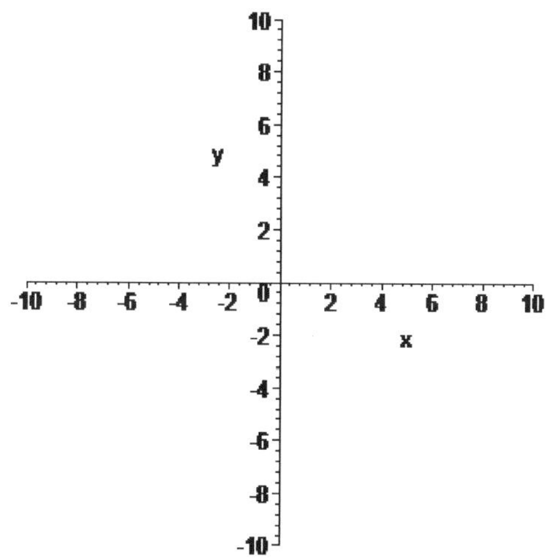

7. Consider the function $f(x) = (x - 5)^2 + 2$

   a. Write the expression of the function

      $g(x) = f(\frac{x}{2}) =$ ________________

   b. This is a ___________________________

      with scale factor ______________

   c. Sketch both functions on the same graph.

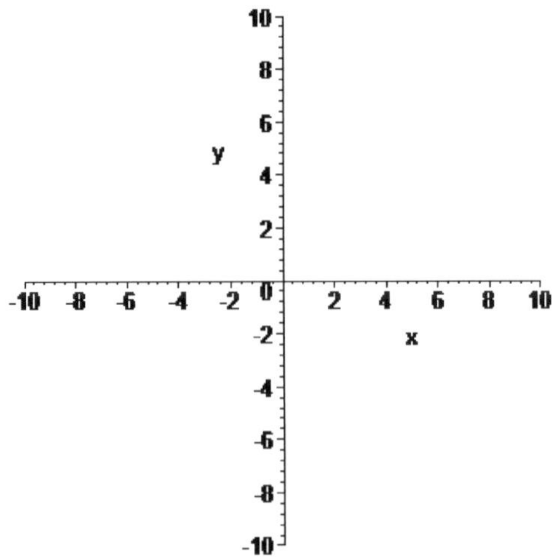

8. Consider the function $f(x) = x^2 - 6$

   a. Write the expression of the function

      $g(x) = -f(3x) =$ ________________

   b. This is a ________________________

      and a ___________________________

   c. Sketch both functions on the same graph.

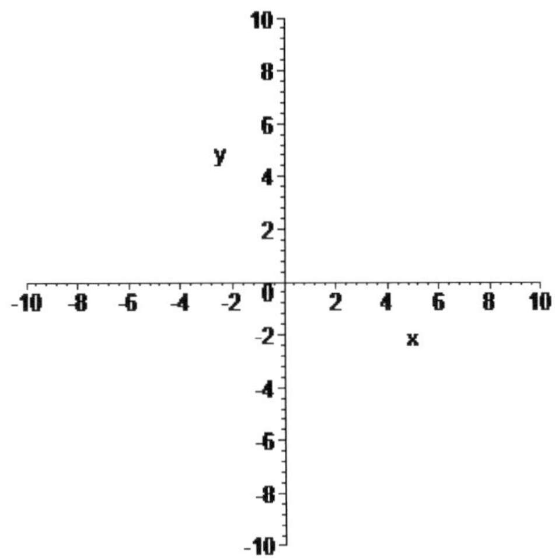

9. Write the expression for the function $f(x) = \frac{x}{x^2+1}$ shifted 2 positions up and 3 left.

10. Write the expression for the function $f(x) = \frac{x-1}{x^3+1}$ shifted 5 positions down and 4 right.

11. Write the expression for the function $f(x) = \dfrac{x}{x^2+1}$ dilated vertically 3 times.

12. Write the expression for the function $f(x) = \dfrac{x+1}{x^2+1}$ dilated horizontally 3 times, shifted 2 positions to the right and 1 up.

13. The function $f(x) = x^2$ is transformed to $g(x) = (x - 2)^2 + 5$. Write the sequence of transformations applied.

14. The function $f(x) = x^2$ is transformed to $g(x) = 2(x + 1)^2 + 5$. Write the sequence of transformations applied.

15. The function $f(x) = -x^2$ is transformed to $g(x) = (x - 1)^2 - 5$. Write the sequence of transformations applied.

16. The function $f(x) = (x - 7)^2$ is transformed to $g(x) = -6(x + 3)^2 - 2$. Write the sequence of transformations applied.

17. Given f(x) = x^2, f(–x) = _______. Is it true that f(x) = f(–x) in this case? _____

18. Given f(x) = x^3, f(–x) = _______. Is it true that f(x) = f(–x) in this case? _____

19. Given f(x) = x^3, f(–x) = _______. Is it true that f(x) = –f(–x) in this case? _____

20. Given f(x) = $\frac{1-x^2}{x^2+1}$, f(–x) = ______. Is it true that f(x) = f(–x) in this case? ___

21. Given f(x) = $\frac{x^3}{x^2+1}$, f(–x) = ______. Is it true that f(x) = –f(–x) in this case? ___

22. Given f(x) = $(x-3)^2$, f(–x) = ______. Is it true that f(x) = f(–x) in this case?

___, is it true that f(x) = –f(–x) in this case? _____

23. Functions in which f(x) = f(–x) are called ______________. The graphical

meaning is that ____

24. Functions in which f(x) = –f(–x) are called ______________. The graphical

meaning is that ____

2.5. – RATIONAL FUNCTIONS

1. Given the functions: $f(x) = \frac{1}{x}$, $g(x) = \frac{2}{x}$, Complete the following table:

x	–10	–2	–1	–0.5	–0.1	–0.01	0	0.01	0.1	1	2	10
f(x)												
g(x)												

- Sketch the points of the table on a graph (use a ruler).
- State the domain of the function: ________________
- State the *y* intercept (sketched on the graph: (____, ____)
- State the *x* intercept(s): (____, ____), (____, ____)
- Write the corresponding limits and the equation of the vertical asymptote: _____
- Write the corresponding limits and the equation of the horizontal asymptote: ___
- Function is increasing on the interval: _____, decreasing on the interval:______
- Find the max/min point(s): (____, ____)
- State the range of the function: ________

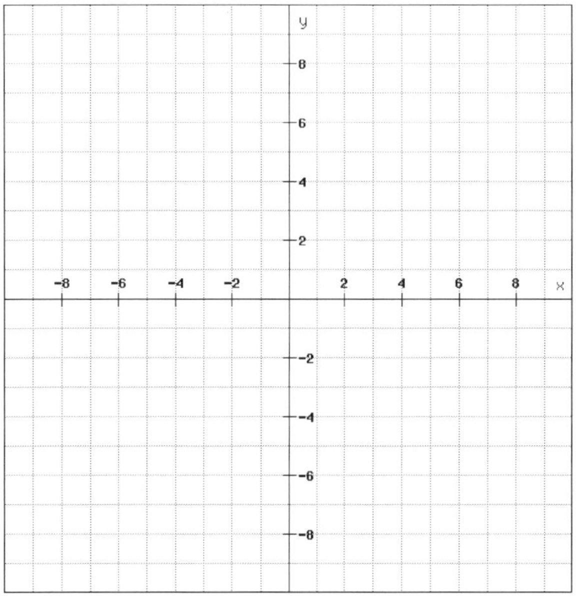

2. Given the functions: $f(x) = -3\frac{1}{x}$, $g(x) = \frac{-2}{x}$, Complete the following table:

x	–10	–2	–1	–0.5	–0.1	–0.01	0	0.01	0.1	1	2	10
f(x)												
g(x)												

- Sketch the points of the table on a graph (use a ruler).
- State the domain of the function: ________________
- State the *y* intercept (sketched on the graph: (____, ____)
- State the *x* intercept(s): (____, ____), (____, ____)
- Write the corresponding limits and the equation of the vertical asymptote: _____
- Write the corresponding limits and the equation of the horizontal asymptote: ___
- Function is increasing on the interval: _____, decreasing on the interval:______
- Find the max/min point(s): (____, ____)
- State the range of the function: ________

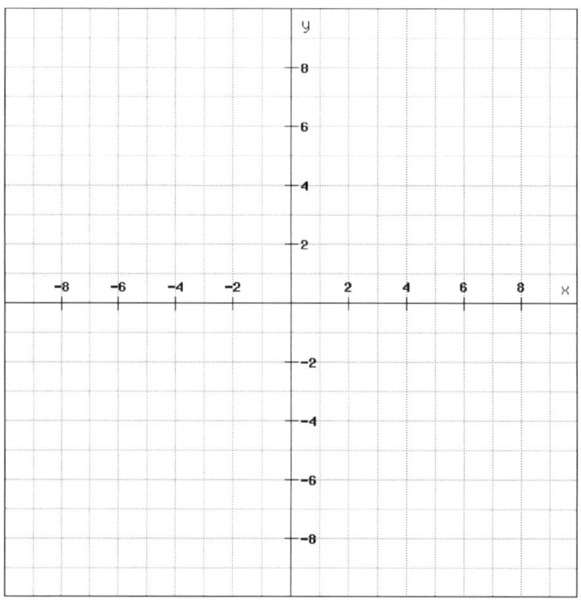

3. Given the functions: $f(x) = \frac{1}{x} + 2$, $g(x) = \frac{2}{x} - 3$, Complete the following table:

x	–10	–2	–1	–0.5	–0.1	–0.01	0	0.01	0.1	1	2	10
f(x)												
g(x)												

- Sketch the points of the table on a graph (use a ruler).
- State the domain of the function: ________________
- State the y intercept (sketched on the graph: (____, ____)
- State the x intercept(s): (____, ____), (____, ____)
- Write the corresponding limits and the equation of the vertical asymptote: ______
- Write the corresponding limits and the equation of the horizontal asymptote: ___
- Function is increasing on the interval: ______, decreasing on the interval:______
- Find the max/min point(s): (____, ____)
- State the range of the function: ________

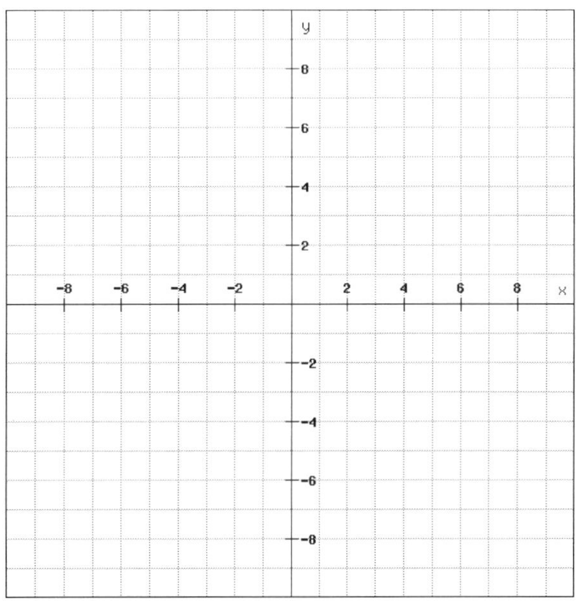

4. Given the functions: $f(x) = \dfrac{1}{x+2}$, $g(x) = \dfrac{-2}{x-4}$, Complete the following table values:

x												
f(x)												
g(x)												

- Sketch the points of the table on a graph (use a ruler).
- State the domain of the function: ________________
- State the *y* intercept (sketched on the graph: (____, ____)
- State the *x* intercept(s): (____, ____), (____, ____)
- Write the corresponding limits and the equation of the vertical asymptote: _____
- Write the corresponding limits and the equation of the horizontal asymptote: ___
- Function is increasing on the interval: _____, decreasing on the interval:______
- Find the max/min point(s): (____, ____)
- State the range of the function: ________

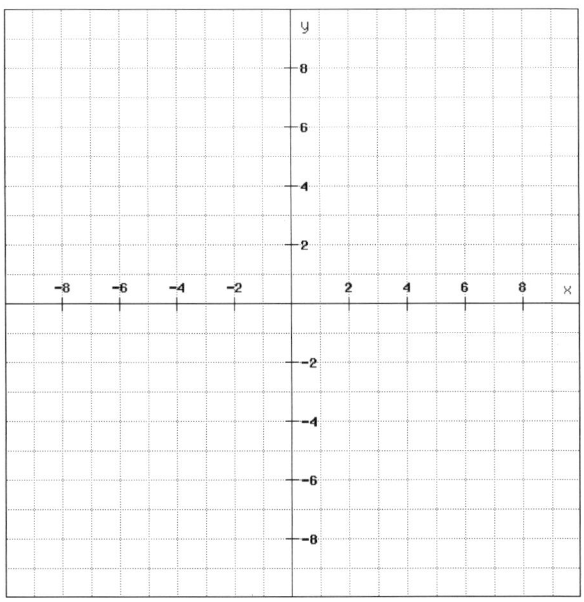

5. Given the functions: $f(x) = \frac{1}{x-3} + 2$, $g(x) = \frac{4}{x-5} - 2$, Complete the following table:

x												
f(x)												
g(x)												

- Sketch the points of the table on a graph (use a ruler).
- State the domain of the function: ________________
- State the *y* intercept (sketched on the graph: (____, ____)
- State the *x* intercept(s): (____, ____), (____, ____)
- Write the corresponding limits and the equation of the vertical asymptote: ______
- Write the corresponding limits and the equation of the horizontal asymptote: ___
- Function is increasing on the interval: _____, decreasing on the interval:______
- Find the max/min point(s): (____, ____)
- State the range of the function: ________

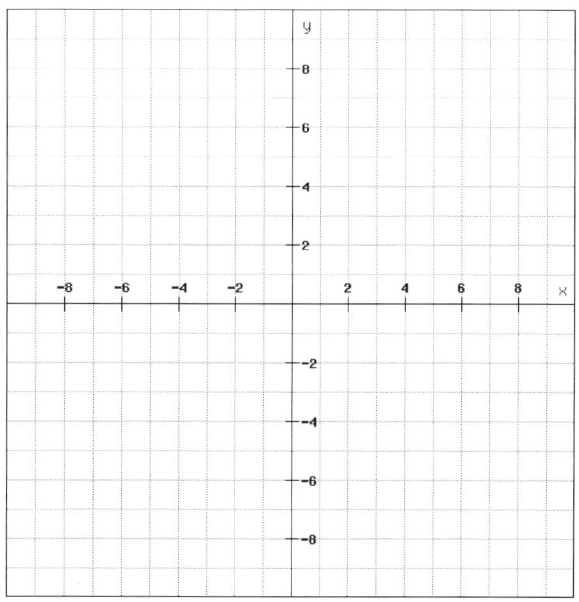

6. Given the function $f(x) = \frac{1}{x}$ Write the same function translated:

a. 2 positions up: ______________ 2 positions left: ______________

b. 4 positions up and 3 right: ______________________________

7. Given the function $f(x) = \frac{3}{x}$

a. 3 positions down: ______________ 5 positions right: ______________

b. 0.5 positions up and $\frac{3}{7}$ right: ______________________________

8. Given the function $f(x) = \frac{-3}{x} + 1$

a. 6 positions down: ______________ 5 positions left: ______________

b. 12 positions up and 10 right: ______________________________

c. Write in different forms: ______________________________

9. Given the function $f(x) = \frac{7}{2x} + 5$

a. 1 positions down: ______________ 7 positions right: ______________

b. 2 positions up and 1 left: ______________________________

c. Write in different forms: ____________________

10. Given the function $f(x) = \frac{2x+3}{2x+6}$

a. State its domain: ____________

b. Write in different forms: ____________________

c. Sketch the function. Is this a Rational function? Explain

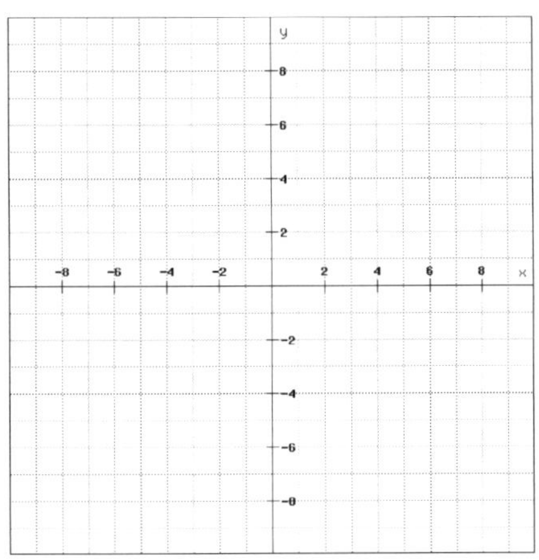

Analyze the following functions:

1. $f(x) = \frac{1}{2x}$

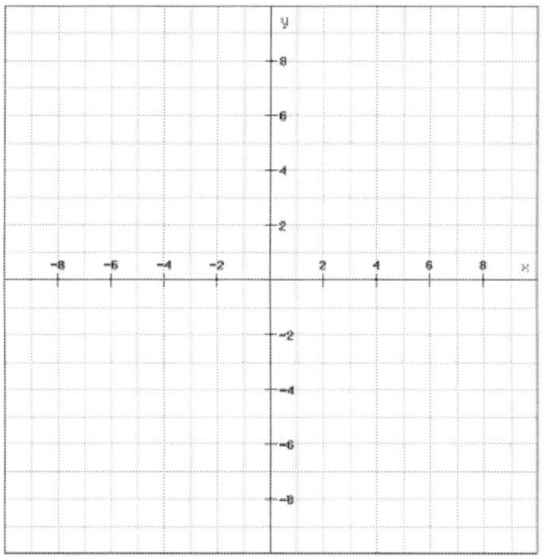

Horizontal asymptote:______ Domain: __________

Lim

Range: ___________

Lim

Increases: ________

Vertical asymptote: ________ Decreases: ________

Lim

y intercept:(___, ___)

Lim

x intercept:(___, ___)

2. $f(x) = -2\frac{1}{x}$

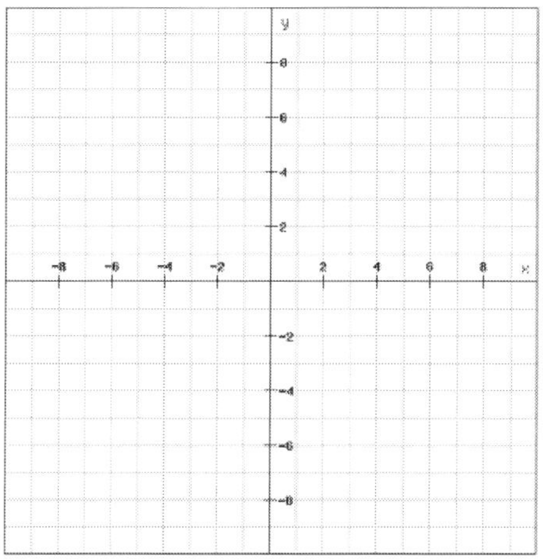

Horizontal asymptote:______ Domain: __________

Lim

Range: ___________

Lim

Increases: ________

Vertical asymptote: ________ Decreases: ________

Lim

y intercept:(___, ___)

Lim

x intercept:(___, ___)

3. $f(x) = \frac{1}{2+x}$

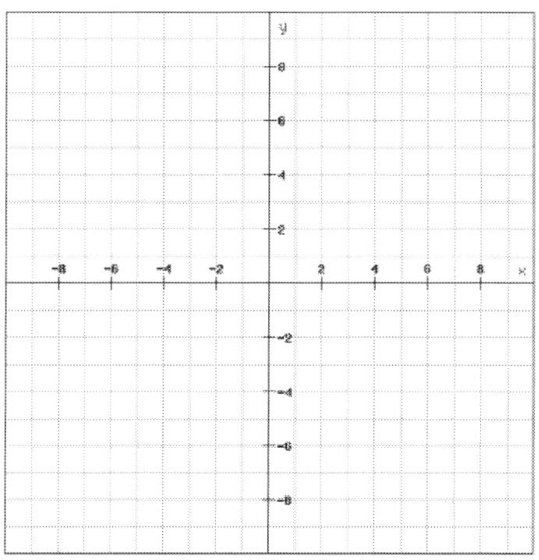

Horizontal asymptote:______ Domain: __________

Lim

Range: ___________

Lim

Increases: ________

Vertical asymptote: ________ Decreases: ________

Lim

y intercept:(___, ___)

Lim

x intercept:(___, ___)

4. $f(x) = \dfrac{1}{1-x}$

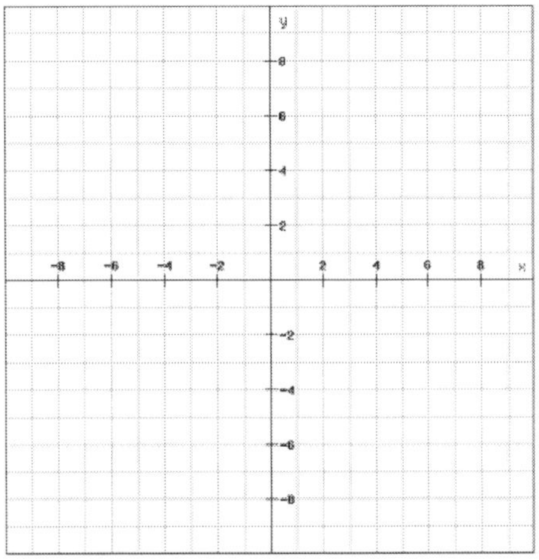

Horizontal asymptote:______ Domain: __________

Lim

Range: ___________

Lim

Increases: ________

Vertical asymptote: ________ Decreases: ________

Lim

y intercept:(___, ___)

Lim

x intercept:(___, ___)

5. $f(x) = -\dfrac{2}{x+1}$

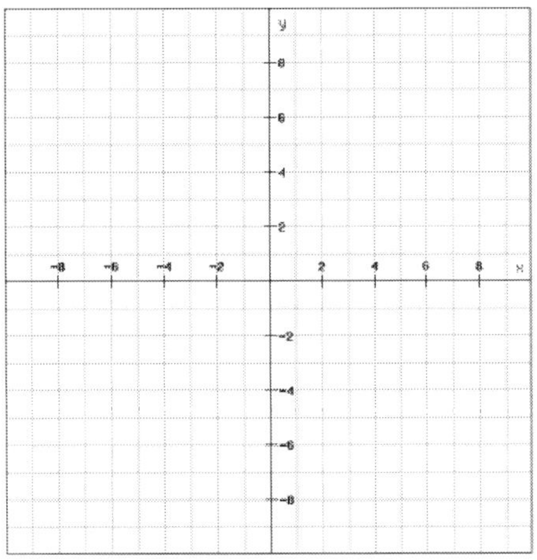

Horizontal asymptote:______ Domain: __________

Lim

Range: ___________

Lim

Increases: ________

Vertical asymptote: ________ Decreases: ________

Lim

y intercept:(, ___)

Lim

x intercept:(___, ___)

6. $f(x) = \dfrac{5}{2x} + 1$

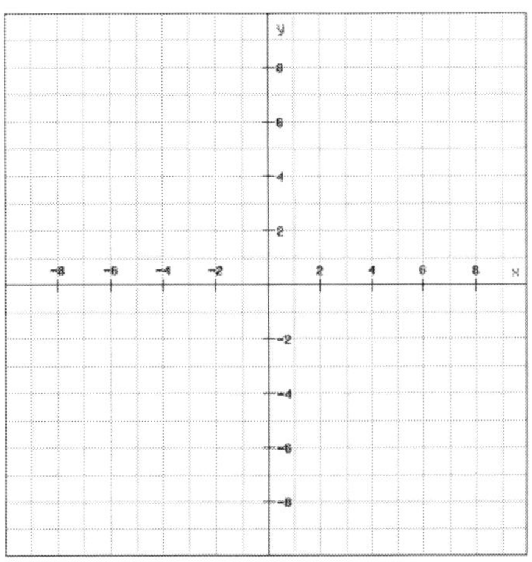

Horizontal asymptote:______ Domain: __________

Lim

Range: ___________

Lim

Increases: ________

Vertical asymptote: ________ Decreases: ________

Lim

y intercept:(___, ___)

Lim

x intercept:(___, ___)

7. $f(x) = -\frac{2}{x} + 1$

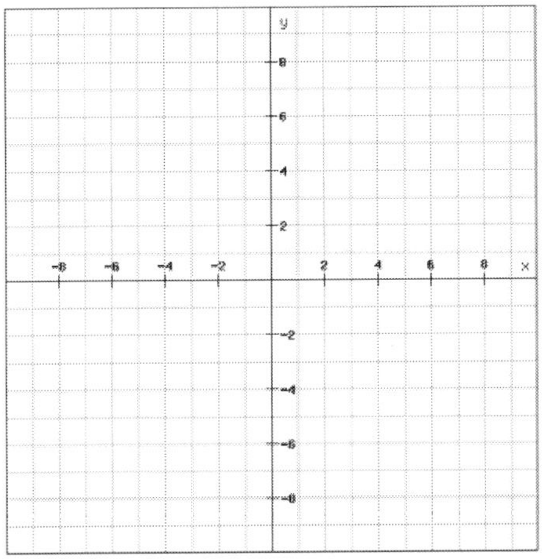

Horizontal asymptote:______ Domain: __________

Lim

Range: ___________

Lim

Increases: ________

Vertical asymptote: ________ Decreases: ________

Lim

y intercept:(___, ___)

Lim

x intercept:(___, ___)

8. $f(x) = \frac{2}{x+3} - 4$

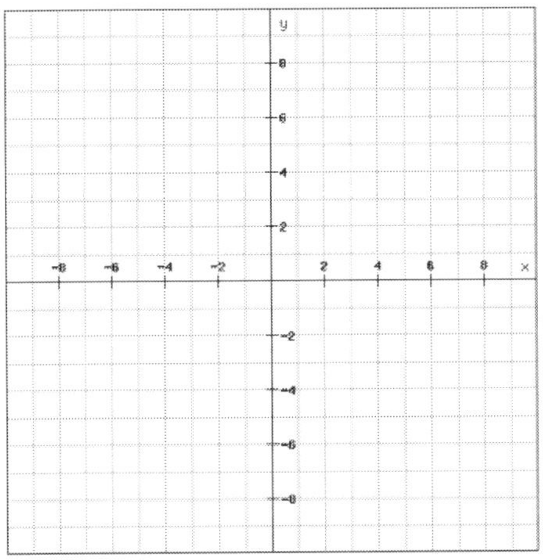

Horizontal asymptote:______ Domain: __________

Lim

Range: ___________

Lim

Increases: ________

Vertical asymptote: ________ Decreases: ________

Lim

y intercept:(___, ___)

Lim

x intercept:(___, ___)

9. $f(x) = \frac{2}{7-x} + 4$

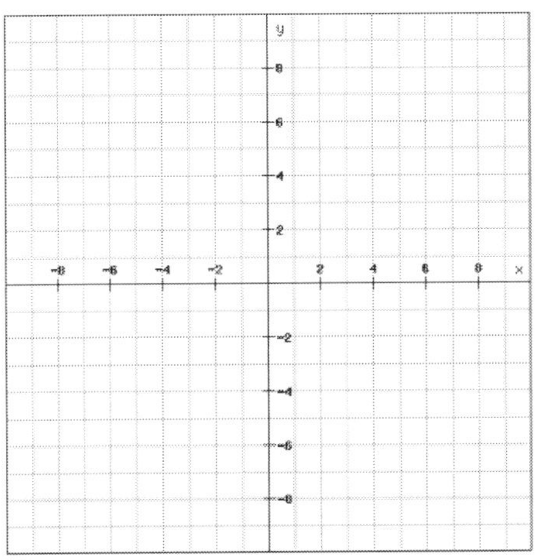

Horizontal asymptote:______ Domain: __________

Lim

Range: ___________

Lim

Increases: ________

Vertical asymptote: ________ Decreases: ________

Lim

y intercept:(___, ___)

Lim

x intercept:(___, ___)

10. $f(x)=\dfrac{-2}{x-1}-4$

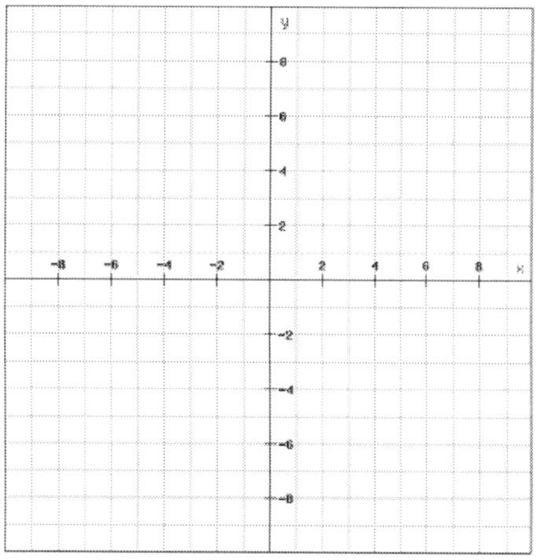

Horizontal asymptote:______ Domain: __________

Lim

Range: ___________

Lim

Increases: ________

Vertical asymptote: ________ Decreases: ________

Lim

y intercept:(___, ___)

Lim

x intercept:(___, ___)

11. $f(x)=-\dfrac{4}{x+4}-2$

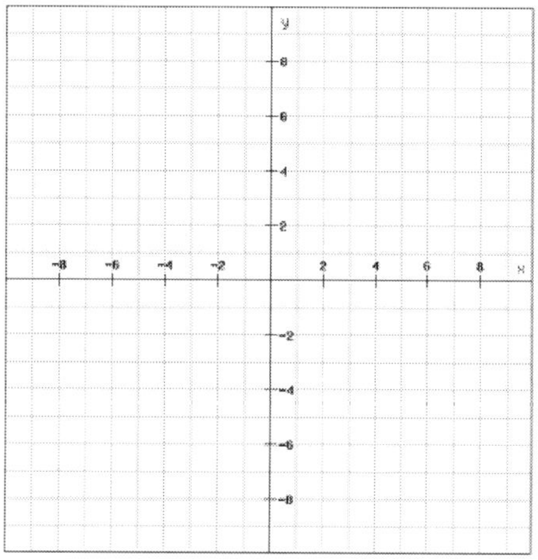

Horizontal asymptote:______ Domain: __________

Lim

Range: ___________

Lim

Increases: ________

Vertical asymptote: ________ Decreases: ________

Lim

y intercept:(___, ___)

Lim

x intercept:(___, ___)

12. $f(x)=\dfrac{1-2x}{x-2}$

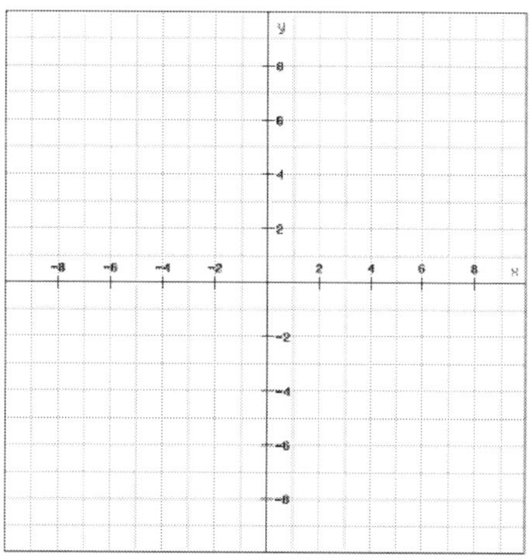

Horizontal asymptote:______ Domain: __________

Lim

Range: ___________

Lim

Increases: ________

Vertical asymptote: ________ Decreases: ________

Lim

y intercept:(___, ___)

Lim

x intercept:(___, ___)

13. $f(x) = \dfrac{8x+3}{4x-2}$

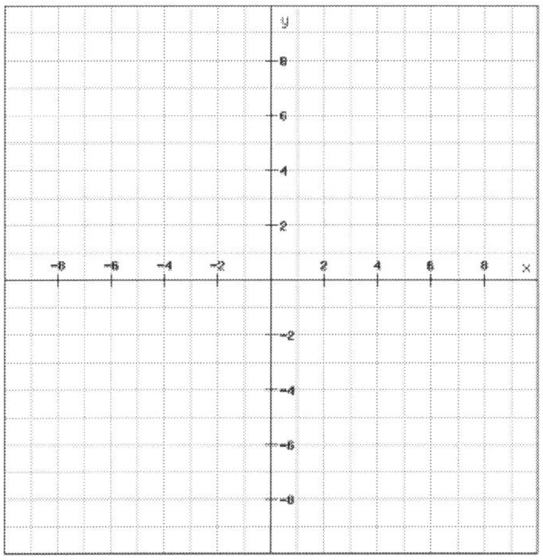

Horizontal asymptote:______ Domain: __________

Lim

Range: ___________

Lim

Increases: ________

Vertical asymptote: ________ Decreases: ________

Lim

y intercept:(___, ___)

Lim

x intercept:(___, ___)

14. $f(x) = \dfrac{x-2}{x-3}$

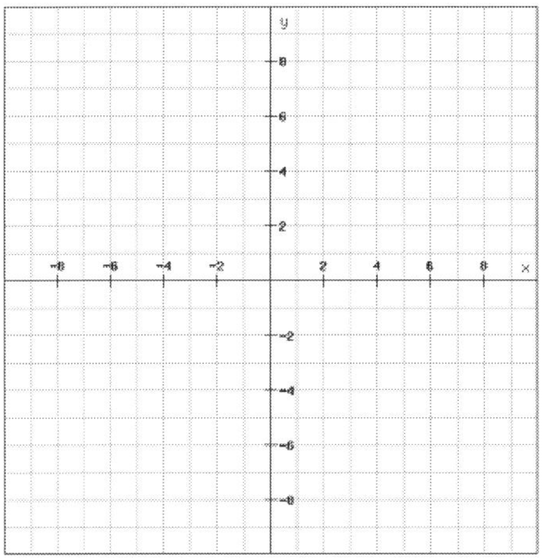

Horizontal asymptote:______ Domain: __________

Lim

Range: ___________

Lim

Increases: ________

Vertical asymptote: ________ Decreases: ________

Lim

y intercept:(___, ___)

Lim

x intercept:(___, ___)

15. $f(x) = \dfrac{3x-5}{4x+3}$

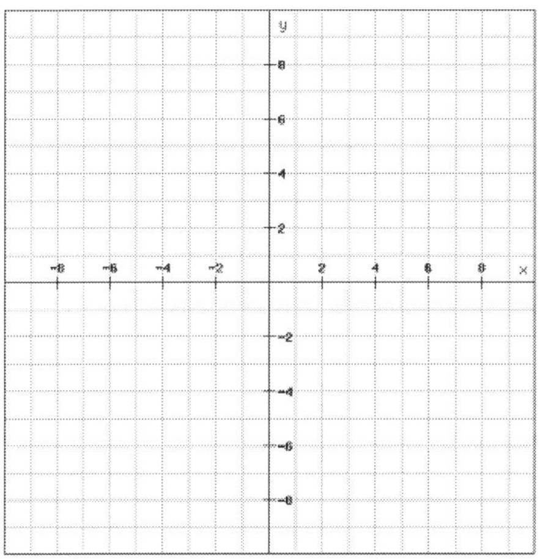

Horizontal asymptote:______ Domain: __________

Lim

Range: ___________

Lim

Increases: ________

Vertical asymptote: ________ Decreases: ________

Lim

y intercept:(___, ___)

Lim

x intercept:(___, ___)

16. $f(x) = \dfrac{6}{4x+3} - 5$

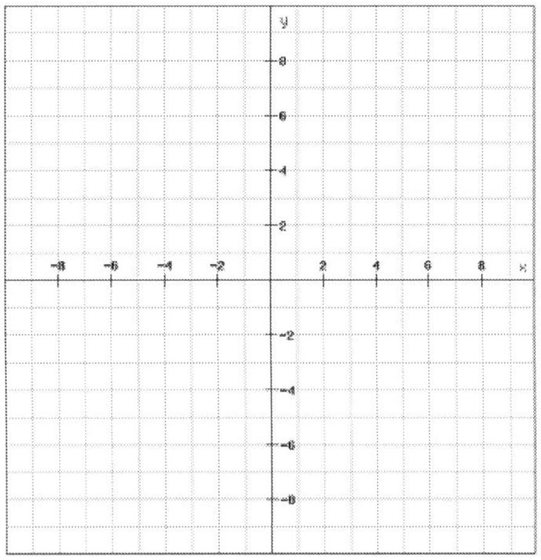

Horizontal asymptote:______ Domain: __________

Lim

Range: ___________

Lim

Increases: ________

Vertical asymptote: ________ Decreases: ________

Lim

y intercept:(___, ___)

Lim

x intercept:(___, ___)

17. $f(x) = \dfrac{3x-2}{x-3}$

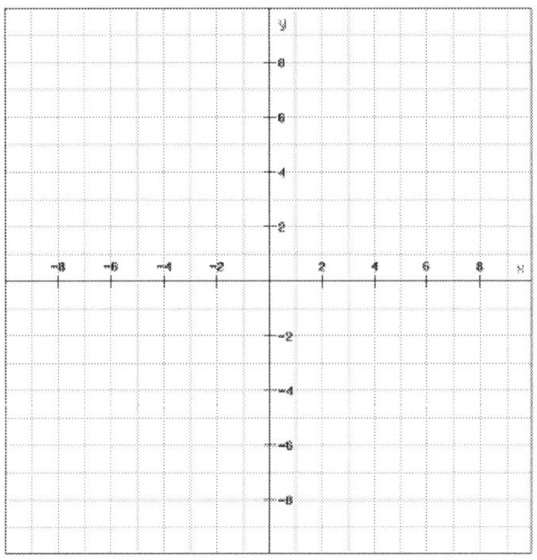

Horizontal asymptote:______ Domain: __________

Lim

Range: ___________

Lim

Increases: ________

Vertical asymptote: ________ Decreases: ________

Lim

y intercept:(___, ___)

Lim

x intercept:(___, ___)

18. $f(x) = \dfrac{4x-1}{-2x-3}$

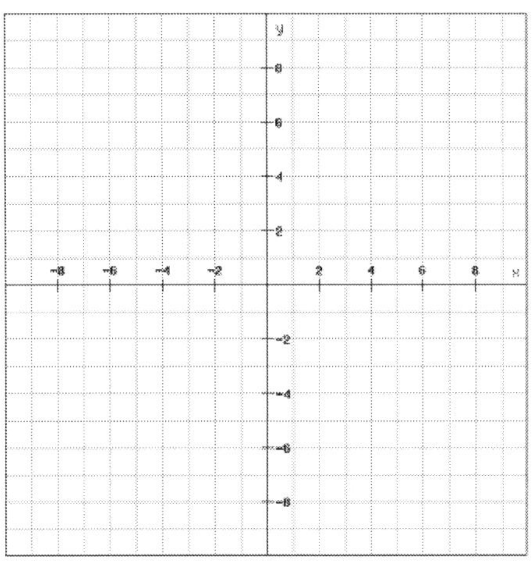

Horizontal asymptote:______ Domain: __________

Lim

Range: ___________

Lim

Increases: ________

Vertical asymptote: ________ Decreases: ________

Lim

y intercept:(___, ___)

Lim

x intercept:(___, ___)

19. $f(x)=\dfrac{4x}{8x-5}$

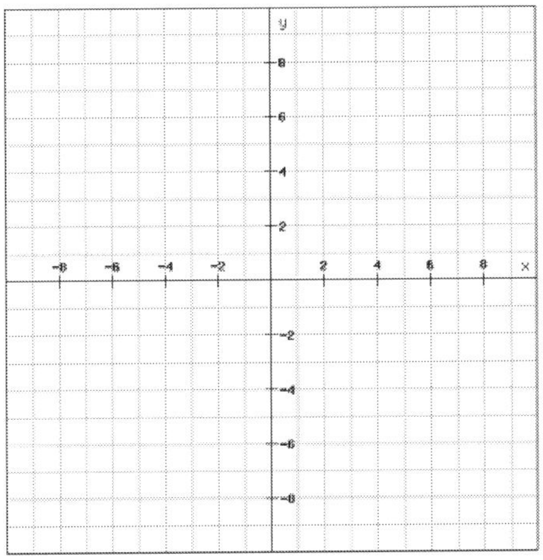

Horizontal asymptote:______ Domain: __________

Lim

Range: ___________

Lim

Increases: ________

Vertical asymptote: _______ Decreases: ________

Lim

y intercept:(___, ___)

Lim

x intercept:(___, ___)

20. $f(x)=\dfrac{1}{-5x-3}$

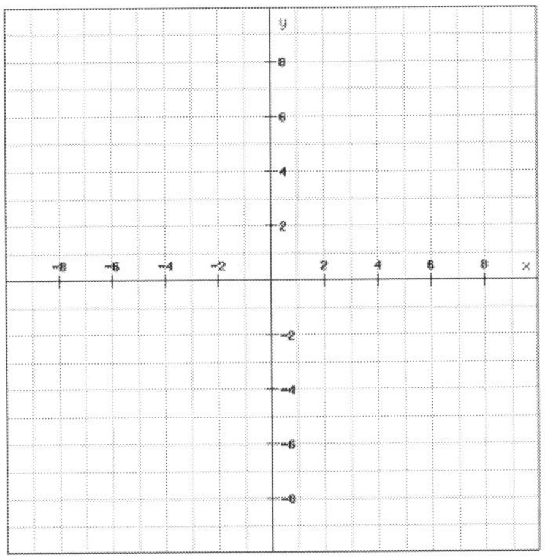

Horizontal asymptote:______ Domain: __________

Lim

Range: ___________

Lim

Increases: ________

Vertical asymptote: _______ Decreases: ________

Lim

y intercept:(___, ___)

Lim

x intercept:(___, ___)

21. $f(x)=\dfrac{4x+3}{x+1}$

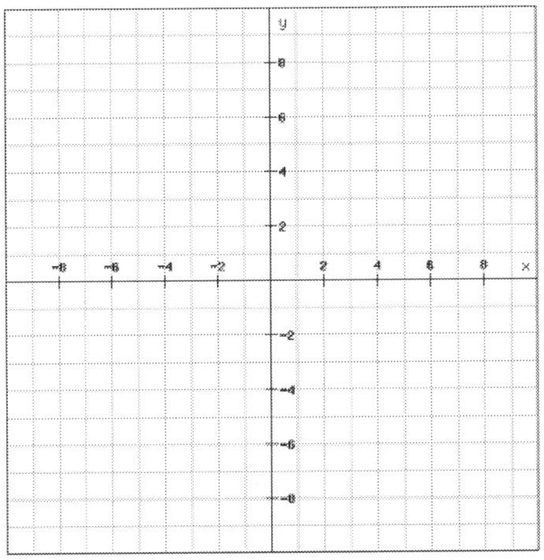

Horizontal asymptote:______ Domain: __________

Lim

Range: ___________

Lim

Increases: ________

Vertical asymptote: _______ Decreases: ________

Lim

y intercept:(___, ___)

Lim

x intercept:(___, ___)

22. $f(x) = \dfrac{4x+3}{5x+3}$

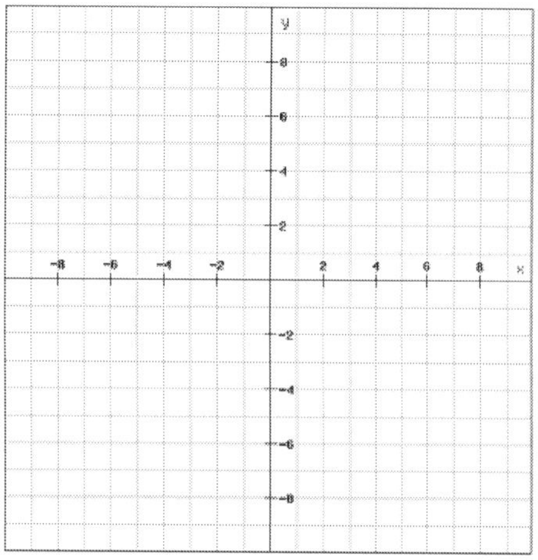

Horizontal asymptote:______ Domain: __________

Lim

Range: __________

Lim

Increases: __________

Vertical asymptote: ________ Decreases: ________

Lim

y intercept:(___, ___)

Lim

x intercept:(___, ___)

23. On making a certain product there is a fixed cost of 2 Euros and a variable cost per product. The variable cost is 60 Euros for 1 product, 30 Euros for 2 products, 20 Euros for 3 products etc.

a. What is the total cost of making a product in case 4 products are made?

b. Write a function for the cost of a product.

c. Sketch the function obtained on a graph, label the graph.

d. What is the cost of a product in case a large number of products is made.

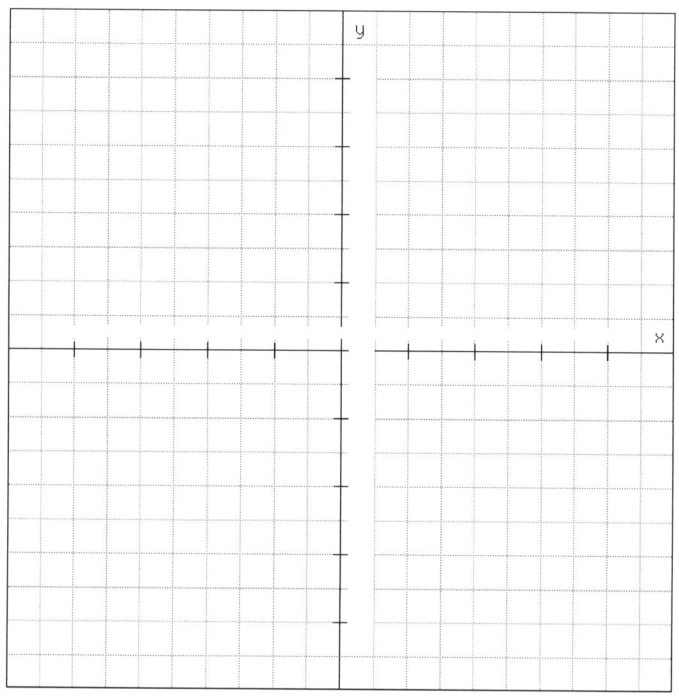

24. The cost per unit C(x) to produce x units of a product is given by $C(x) = \frac{300}{x+10}$

a. What is the cost per unit when 180 units are produced?

b. If the cost per unit is $1.50, how many units have been produced?

25. In the following formula, S(x) is the minimum number of hours of studying required to attain a test score of x $C(x) = \frac{0.32x}{100.5 - x}$

a. How many hours of study are needed to score 85?

b. What score can you get if you study 8 hours?

c. How many hours of study are needed to score 100?

d. State the domain of the function: ______________________________

e. Sketch the function in the domain found.

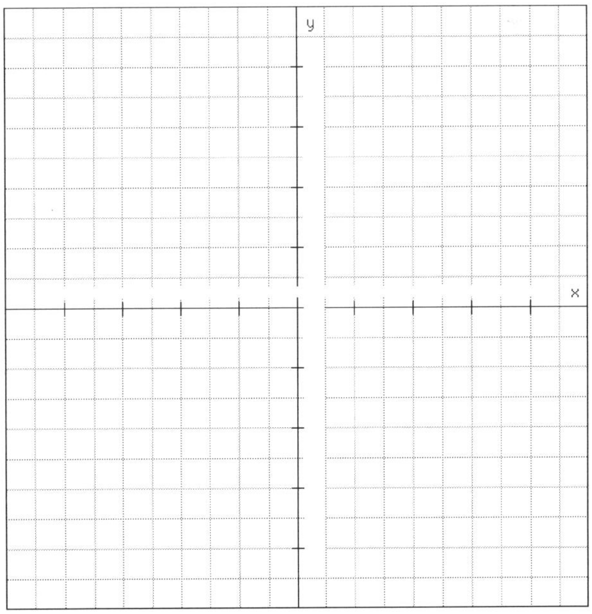

2.6. – EXPONENTIAL FUNCTIONS

1. Given the functions: $f(x) = 2^x$, $g(x) = 3^x$, Complete the following chart:

x	–5	–4	–3	–2	–1	0	1	2	3	4	5	6
f(x)												
g(x)												

- Sketch the points of the table on a graph.
- State the domain of the function: ________________
- State the *y* intercept (sketched on the graph: (_____, _____)
- State the *x* intercept(s): (_____, _____), (_____, _____)
- Write the corresponding limits and the equation of the vertical asymptote: ______
- Write the corresponding limits and the equation of the horizontal asymptote: ___
- Function is increasing on the interval: _____, decreasing on the interval:______
- Find the max/min point(s): (_____, _____)
- State the range of the function: ________

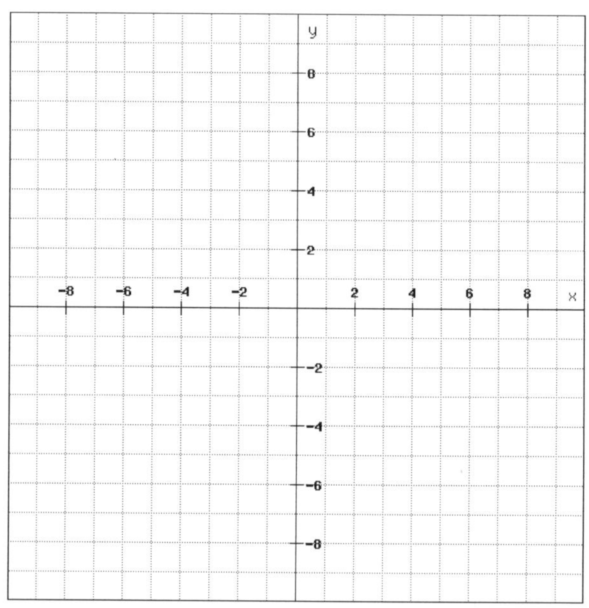

2. Given the functions: $f(x) = 2^{-x}$, $g(x) = 3^{-x}$, Complete the following chart:

x	–5	–4	–3	–2	–1	0	1	2	3	4	5	6
f(x)												
g(x)												

- Sketch the points of the table on a graph.
- State the domain of the function: ________________
- State the *y* intercept (sketched on the graph: (____, ____)
- State the *x* intercept(s): (____, ____), (____, ____)
- Write the corresponding limits and the equation of the vertical asymptote: _____
- Write the corresponding limits and the equation of the horizontal asymptote: ___
- Function is increasing on the interval: _____, decreasing on the interval:______
- Find the max/min point(s): (____, ____)
- State the range of the function: ________
- Write in more forms: ________________

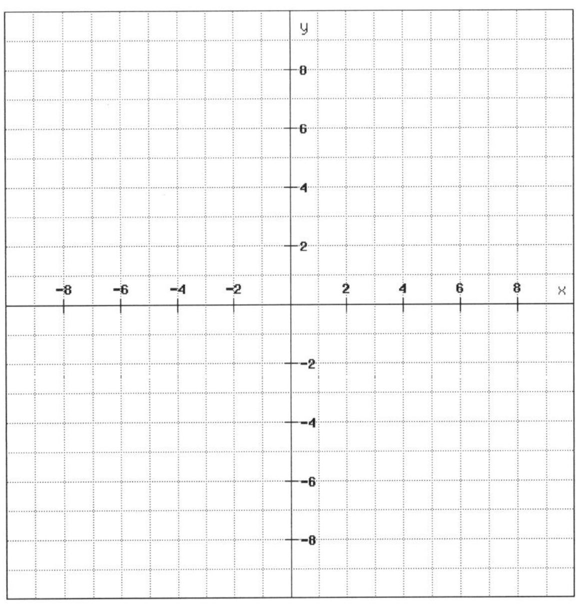

3. Given the functions: $f(x) = -2^x$, $g(x) = -3^x$, Complete the following chart:

x	–5	–4	–3	–2	–1	0	1	2	3	4	5	6
f(x)												
g(x)												

- Sketch the points of the table on a graph.
- State the domain of the function: ________________
- State the *y* intercept (sketched on the graph: (____, ____)
- State the *x* intercept(s): (____, ____), (____, ____)
- Write the corresponding limits and the equation of the vertical asymptote: _____
- Write the corresponding limits and the equation of the horizontal asymptote: ___
- Function is increasing on the interval: _____, decreasing on the interval:______
- Find the max/min point(s): (____, ____)
- State the range of the function: ________
- Write in more forms: ________________

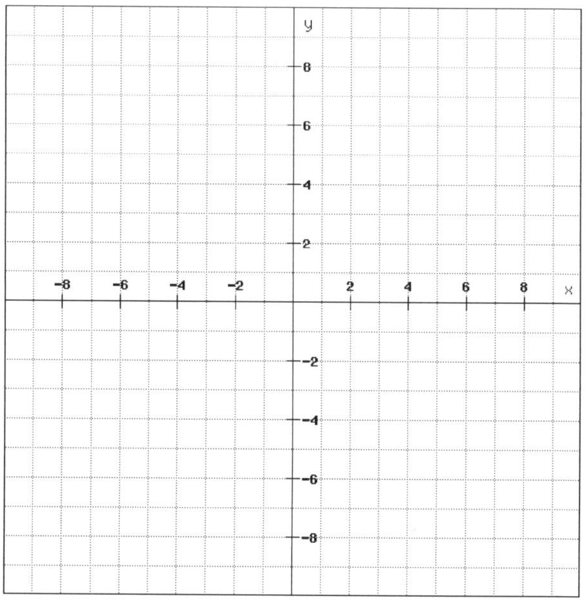

4. Given the functions: $f(x) = -2^{-x}$, $g(x) = -3^{-x}$, Complete the following chart:

x	–5	–4	–3	–2	–1	0	1	2	3	4	5	6
f(x)												
g(x)												

- Sketch the points of the table on a graph.
- State the domain of the function: ________________
- State the *y* intercept (sketched on the graph: (____, ____)
- State the *x* intercept(s): (____, ____), (____, ____)
- Write the corresponding limits and the equation of the vertical asymptote: _____
- Write the corresponding limits and the equation of the horizontal asymptote: ___
- Function is increasing on the interval: _____, decreasing on the interval:______
- Find the max/min point(s): (____, ____)
- State the range of the function: ________
- Write in more forms: ________________

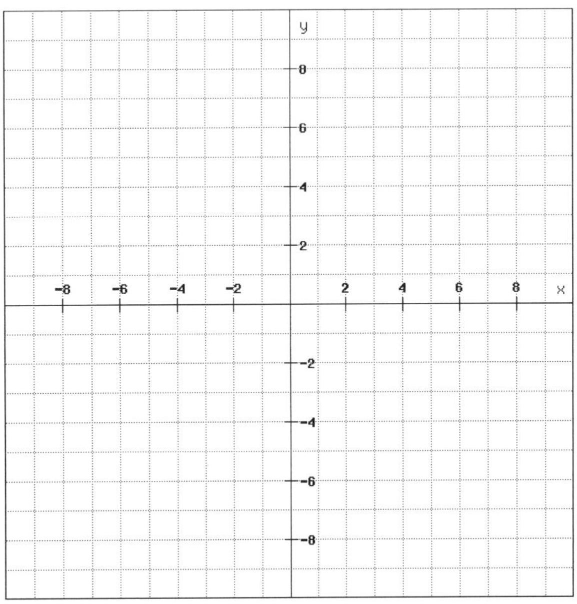

5. Given the functions: $f(x) = -5 \times 4^{-2x} + 1$, Complete the following chart:

x	–5	–4	–3	–2	–1	0	1	2	3	4	5	6
f(x)												
g(x)												

- Sketch the points of the table on a graph.
- State the domain of the function: ________________
- State the y intercept (sketched on the graph: (____, ____)
- State the x intercept(s): (____, ____), (____, ____)
- Write the corresponding limits and the equation of the vertical asymptote: _____
- Write the corresponding limits and the equation of the horizontal asymptote: ___
- Function is increasing on the interval: _____, decreasing on the interval:______
- Find the max/min point(s): (____, ____)
- State the range of the function: ________
- Write in more forms: ________________

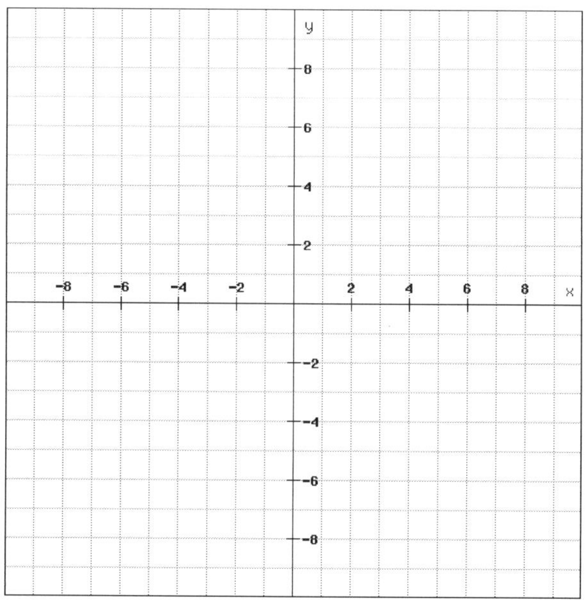

6. Given the graph of the function $f(x) = \left(\frac{1}{2}\right)^x = (\_\_)^x =$ ___ sketch, on the same set of axes, the graphs of the functions:

$g(x) = \left(\frac{1}{2}\right)^{x-2} = (\_\_)^{x-2} =$ ___ $=$ ___

$d(x) = \left(\frac{1}{2}\right)^x - 2 =$ _________

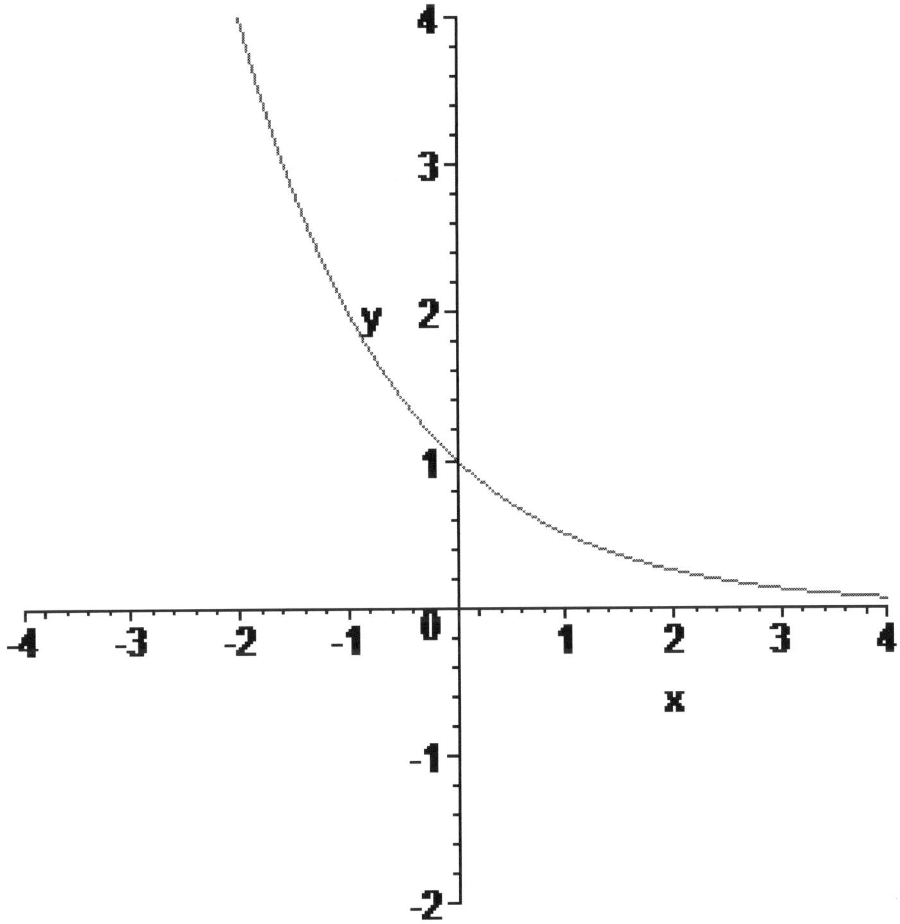

7. Given the graph, complete the table below:

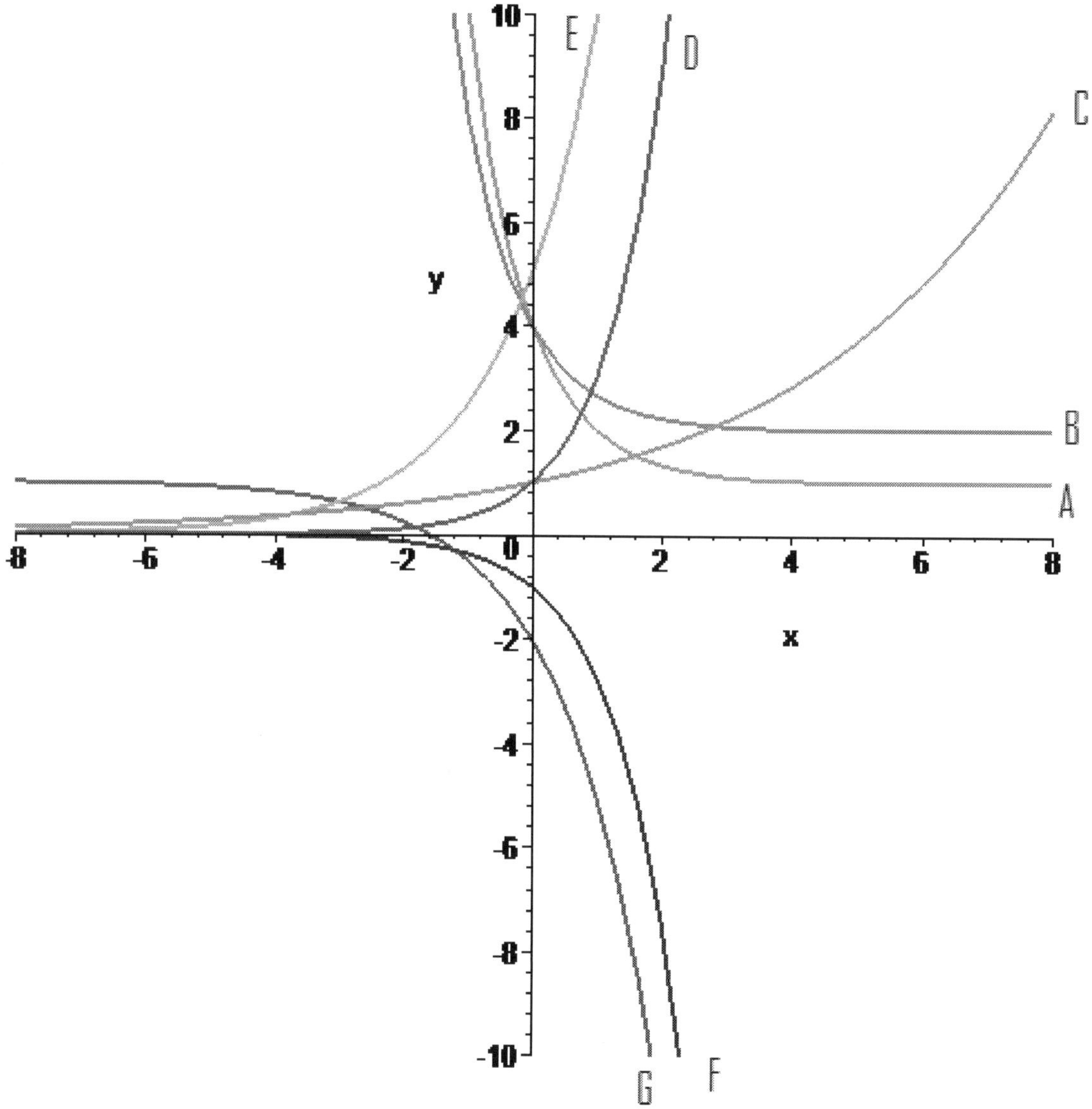

Function	On the graph
$f(x) = 5 \times 2^x$	
$f(x) = 2 + 2 \times 3^{-x}$	
$f(x) = 3 \times 3^{-x} + 1$	
$f(x) = (1.3)^x$	
$f(x) = -e^x$	
$f(x) = 3^x$	
$f(x) = -3 \times 2^x + 1$	

8. Given the function $f(x) = e^x$

a. Write the same function translated 2 positions up.

b. Write the same function translated 2 positions left.

c. Write the same function translated 4 positions up and 3 right.

d. Sketch all three functions:

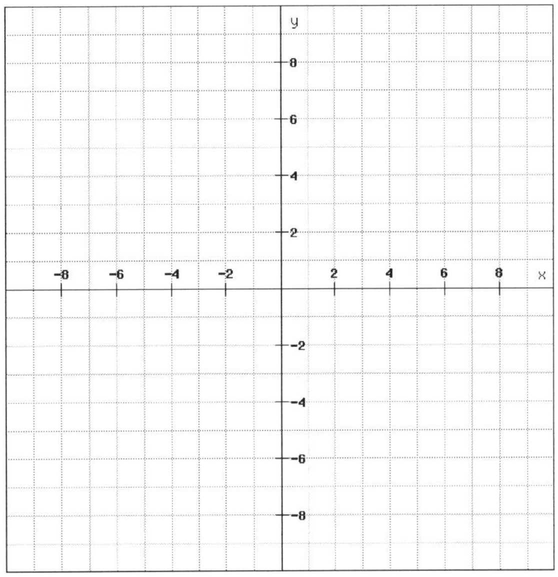

9. Given the function $f(x) = -3 \times 6^{-2x} + 1$

a. Write the same function translated 2 positions up.

b. Write the same function translated 2 positions left.

c. Write the same function translated 4 positions up and 3 right.

d. Sketch all three functions:

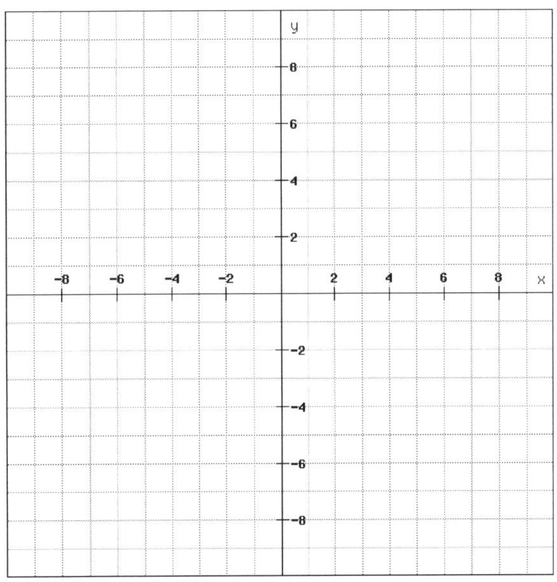

Analyze the functions:

1. $f(x) = 4^x$

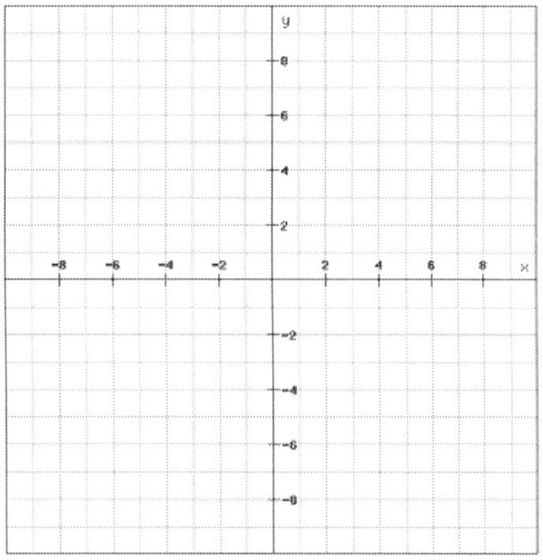

Horizontal asymptote:______ Domain: __________

Lim

Range: ___________

Lim

Increases: _________

Vertical asymptote: _______ Decreases: ________

Lim

y intercept:(___, ___)

Lim

x intercept:(___, ___)

2. $f(x) = -3^x$

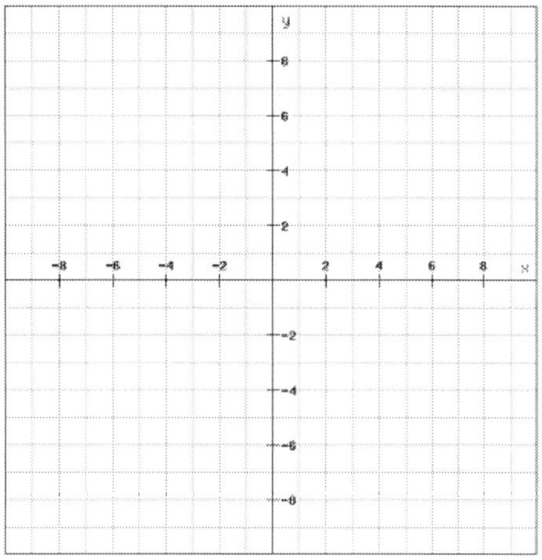

Horizontal asymptote:______ Domain: __________

Lim

Range: ___________

Lim

Increases: _________

Vertical asymptote: _______ Decreases: ________

Lim

y intercept:(___, ___)

Lim

x intercept:(___, ___)

3. $f(x) = 2^{-x}$

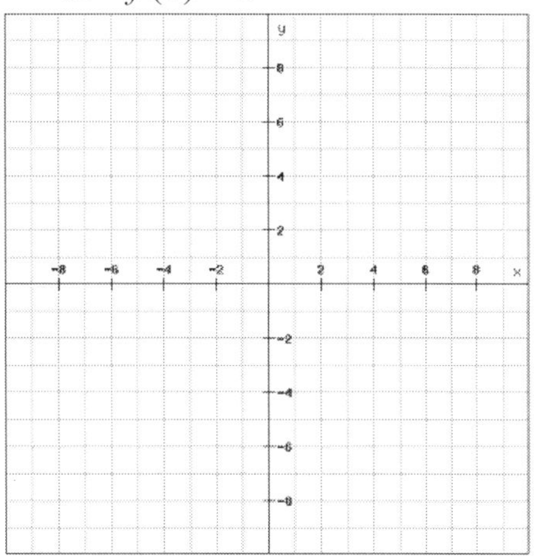

Horizontal asymptote:______ Domain: __________

Lim

Range: ___________

Lim

Increases: _________

Vertical asymptote: _______ Decreases: ________

Lim

y intercept:(___, ___)

Lim

x intercept:(___, ___)

4. $f(x) = -2^{-x}$

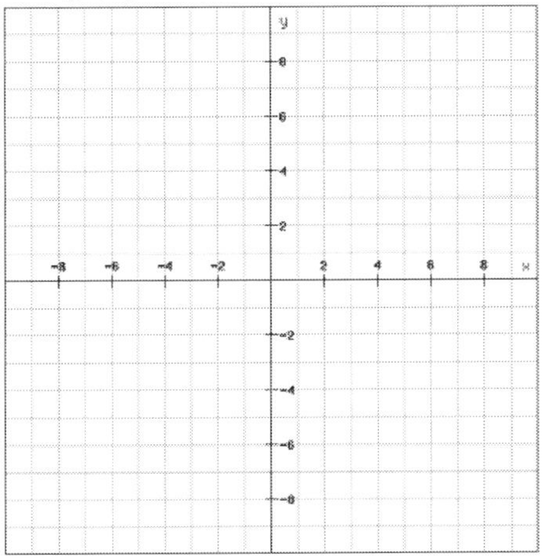

Horizontal asymptote:______ Domain: __________

Lim

Range: ___________

Lim

Increases: ________

Vertical asymptote: ________ Decreases: ________

Lim

y intercept:(___, ___)

Lim

x intercept:(___, ___)

5. $f(x) = \left(\frac{1}{4}\right)^x$

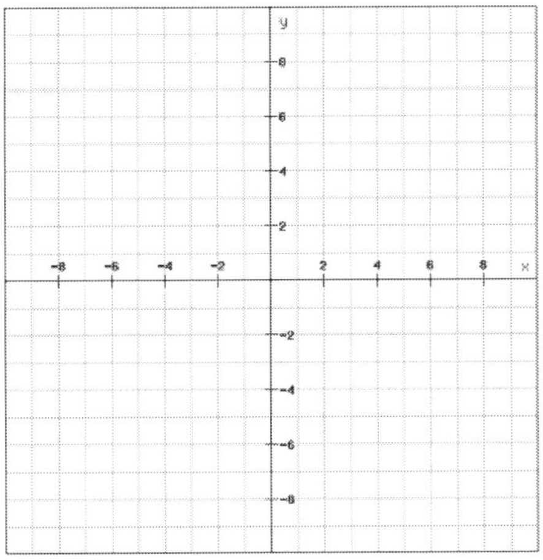

Horizontal asymptote:______ Domain: __________

Lim

Range: ___________

Lim

Increases: ________

Vertical asymptote: ________ Decreases: ________

Lim

y intercept:(___, ___)

Lim

x intercept:(___, ___)

6. $f(x) = 3\left(\frac{2}{7}\right)^x$

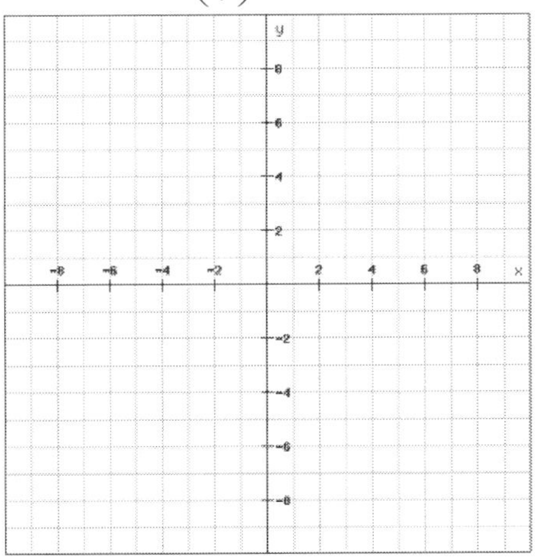

Horizontal asymptote:______ Domain: __________

Lim

Range: ___________

Lim

Increases: ________

Vertical asymptote: ________ Decreases: ________

Lim

y intercept:(___, ___)

Lim

x intercept:(___, ___)

7. $f(x) = -2^{x+5}$

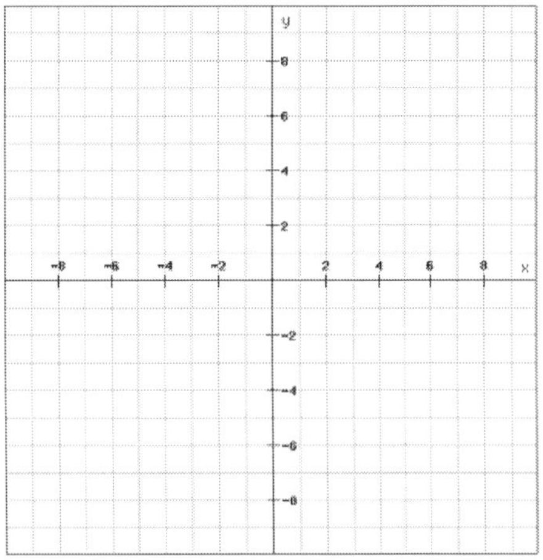

Horizontal asymptote:______ Domain: __________

Lim

Range: ___________

Lim

Increases: _________

Vertical asymptote: ________ Decreases: ________

Lim

y intercept:(___, ___)

Lim

x intercept:(___, ___)

8. $f(x) = \left(\frac{2}{3}\right)^x$

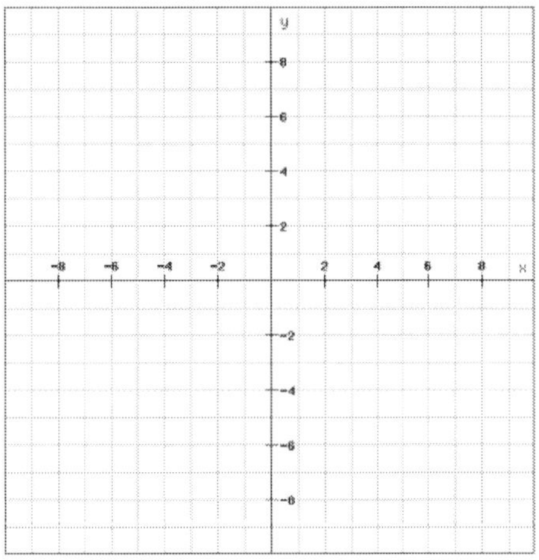

Horizontal asymptote:______ Domain: __________

Lim

Range: ___________

Lim

Increases: _________

Vertical asymptote: ________ Decreases: ________

Lim

y intercept:(___, ___)

Lim

x intercept:(___, ___)

9. $f(x) = 3 \cdot 7^{x-4}$

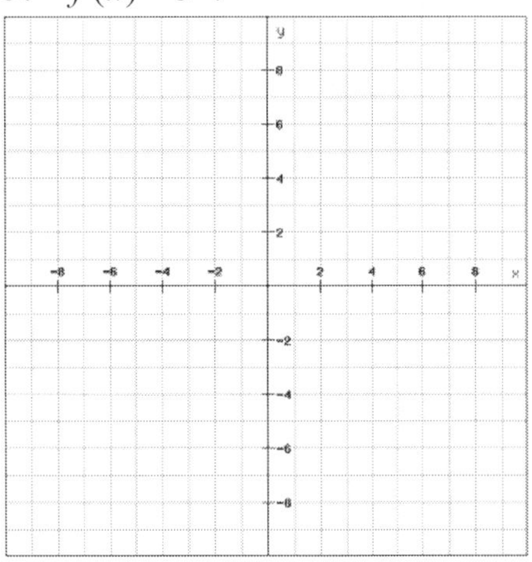

Horizontal asymptote:______ Domain: __________

Lim

Range: ___________

Lim

Increases: _________

Vertical asymptote: ________ Decreases: ________

Lim

y intercept:(___, ___)

Lim

x intercept:(___, ___)

10. $f(x) = -7^{x-2} + 2$

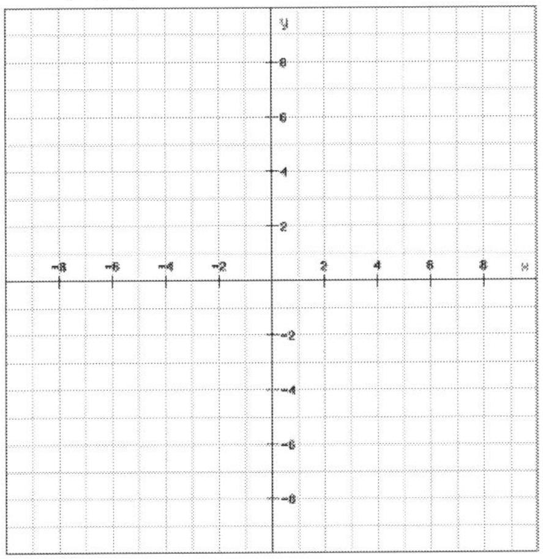

Horizontal asymptote:______ Domain: __________

Lim

Range: ___________

Lim

Increases: ________

Vertical asymptote: ________ Decreases: ________

Lim

y intercept:(___, ___)

Lim

x intercept:(___, ___)

11. $f(x) = 2 \cdot 5^{-x-2} - 5$

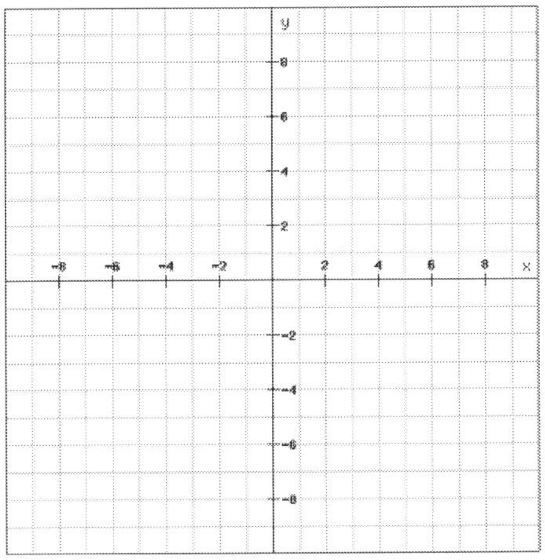

Horizontal asymptote:______ Domain: __________

Lim

Range: ___________

Lim

Increases: ________

Vertical asymptote: ________ Decreases: ________

Lim

y intercept:(___, ___)

Lim

x intercept:(___, ___)

12. $f(x) = -3^{-x-3} + 4$

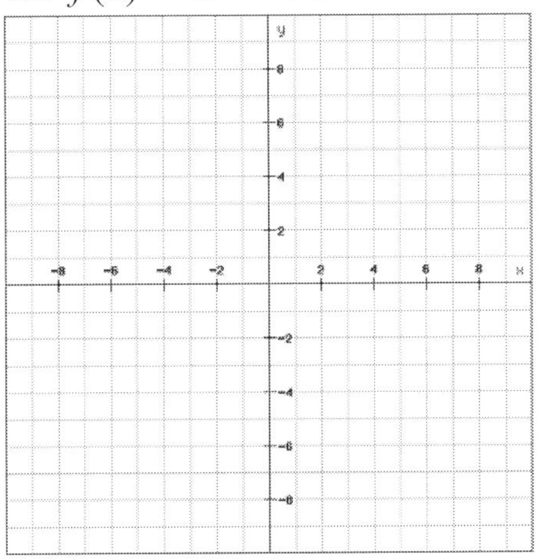

Horizontal asymptote:______ Domain: __________

Lim

Range: ___________

Lim

Increases: ________

Vertical asymptote: ________ Decreases: ________

Lim

y intercept:(___, ___)

Lim

x intercept:(___, ___)

13. $f(x) = -e^{x}$

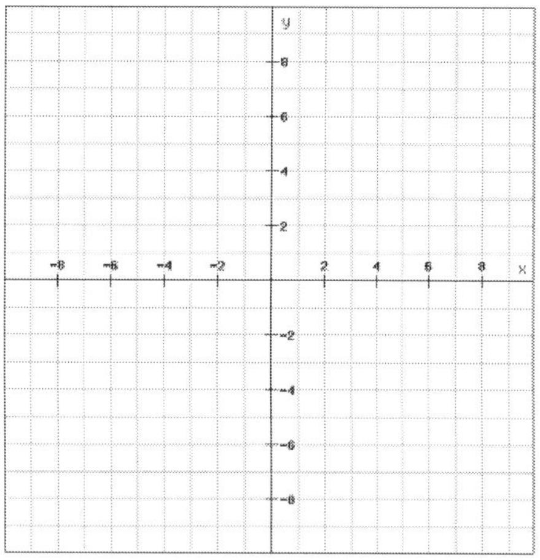

Horizontal asymptote:______ Domain: __________

Lim

Range: ___________

Lim

Increases: _________

Vertical asymptote: ________ Decreases: ________

Lim

y intercept:(___, ___)

Lim

x intercept:(___, ___)

14. $f(x) = e^{x+2}$

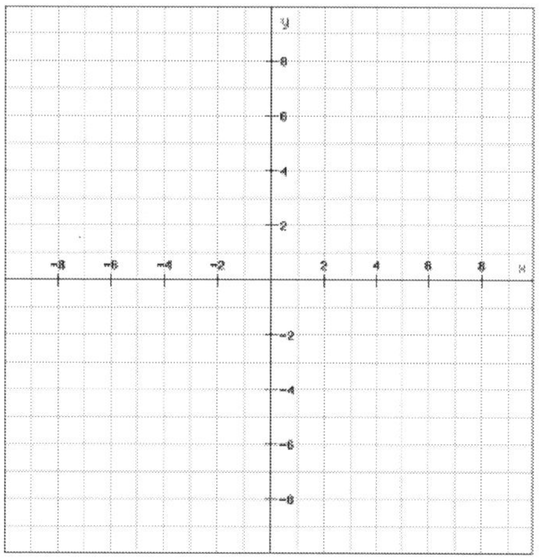

Horizontal asymptote:______ Domain: __________

Lim

Range: ___________

Lim

Increases: _________

Vertical asymptote: ________ Decreases: ________

Lim

y intercept:(___, ___)

Lim

x intercept:(___, ___)

15. $f(x) = -e^{x} + 4$

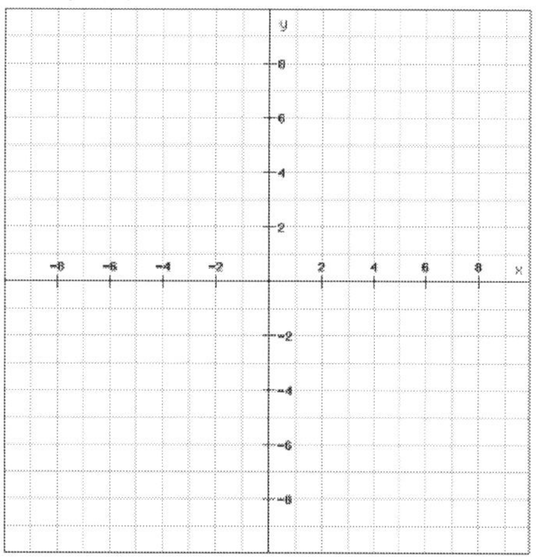

Horizontal asymptote:______ Domain: __________

Lim

Range: ___________

Lim

Increases: _________

Vertical asymptote: ________ Decreases: ________

Lim

y intercept:(___, ___)

Lim

x intercept:(___, ___)

16. $f(x) = 0.1e^{x+1} + 2$

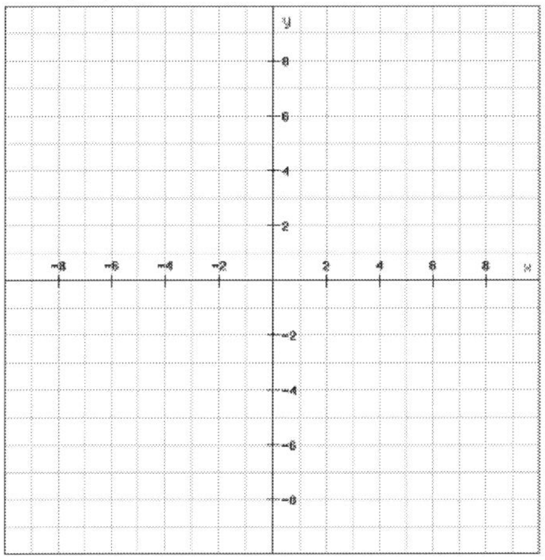

Horizontal asymptote:______ Domain: __________

Lim

Range: ___________

Lim

Increases: _________

Vertical asymptote: ________ Decreases: ________

Lim

y intercept:(___, ___)

Lim

x intercept:(___, ___)

17. $f(x) = 2e^{2x+1} - 4$

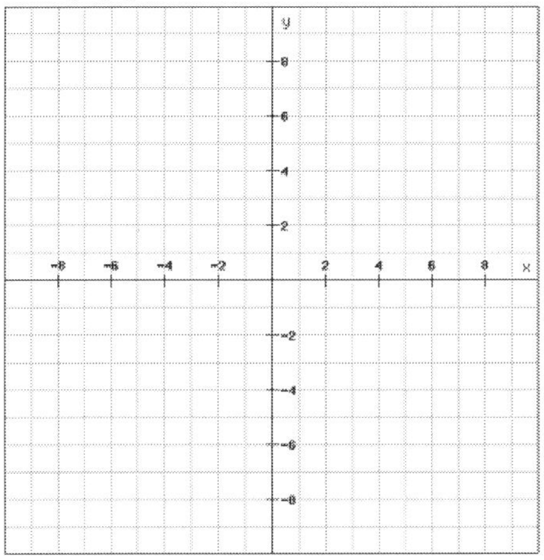

Horizontal asymptote:______ Domain: __________

Lim

Range: ___________

Lim

Increases: _________

Vertical asymptote: ________ Decreases: ________

Lim

y intercept:(___, ___)

Lim

x intercept:(___, ___)

18. $f(x) = -2 \cdot 6^{x-2} - 1$

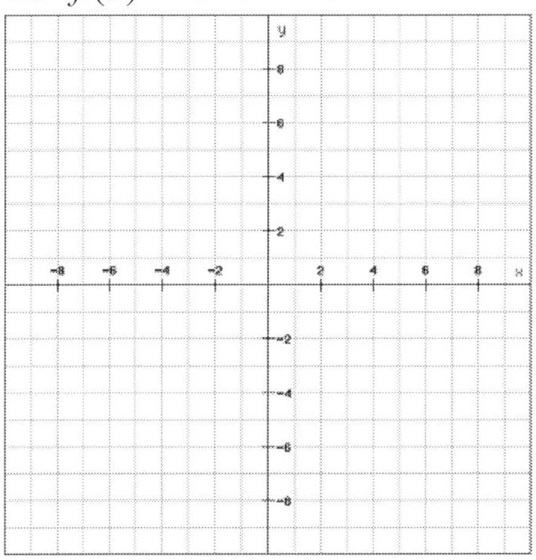

Horizontal asymptote:______ Domain: __________

Lim

Range: ___________

Lim

Increases: _________

Vertical asymptote: ________ Decreases: ________

Lim

y intercept:(___, ___)

Lim

x intercept:(___, ___)

19. $f(x) = 2 \cdot 3^{x-2} - 5$

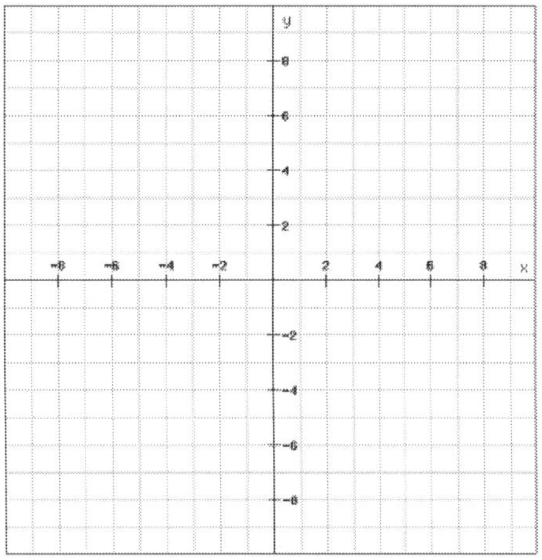

Horizontal asymptote:______ Domain: __________

Lim

Range: ____________

Lim

Increases: _________

Vertical asymptote: ________ Decreases: ________

Lim

y intercept:(___, ___)

Lim

x intercept:(___, ___)

20. $f(x) = 7 \cdot 5^{x-2} + 2$

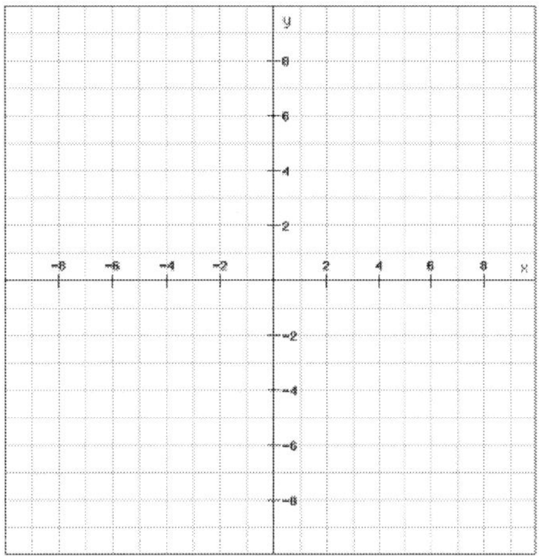

Horizontal asymptote:______ Domain: __________

Lim

Range: ____________

Lim

Increases: _________

Vertical asymptote: ________ Decreases: ________

Lim

y intercept:(___, ___)

Lim

x intercept:(___, ___)

21. $f(x) = -2 \cdot 3^{-2x+1} + 4$

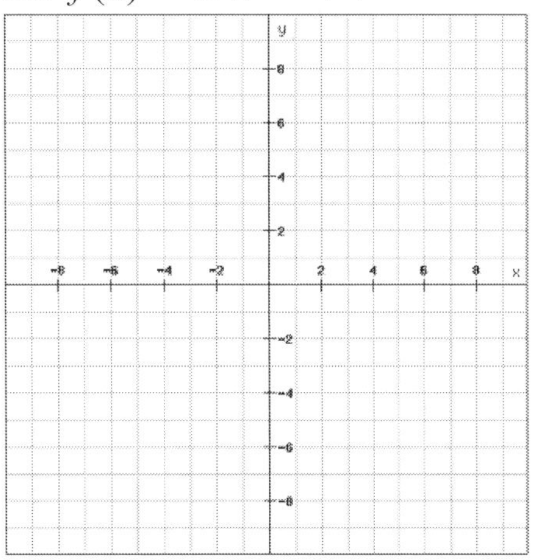

Horizontal asymptote:______ Domain: __________

Lim

Range: ____________

Lim

Increases: _________

Vertical asymptote: ________ Decreases: ________

Lim

y intercept:(___, ___)

Lim

x intercept:(___, ___)

Application

1. The population of a rapidly–growing country starts at 4 million and increases by 10% each year.
   a. Complete the table below:

t(years)	P, population (in millions)	ΔP, increase in population (in millions)
0		
1		
2		
3		
4		

   b. Do you identify a pattern? Can you write a general expression of the population (P) as a function of the time (t)?

   c. Sketch its graph:

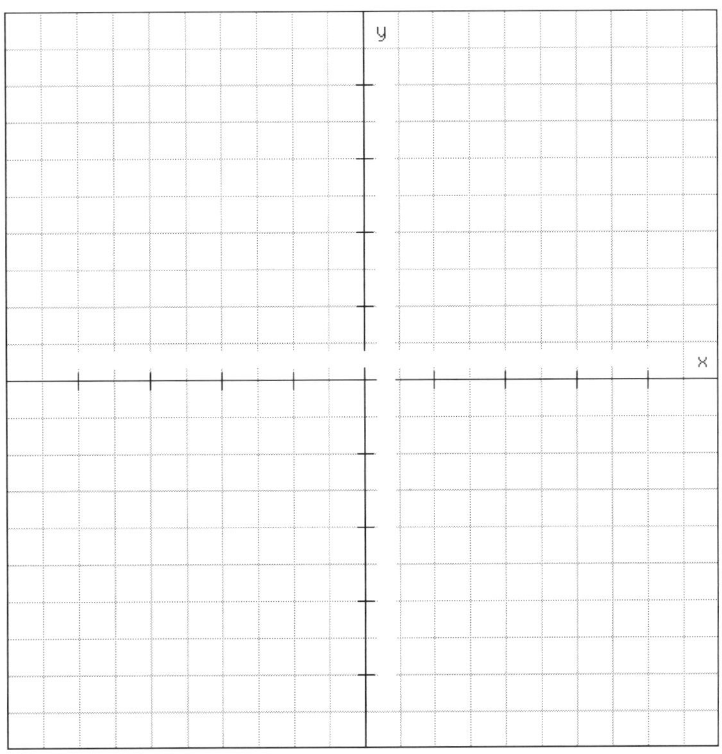

2. Suppose we start with 200 grams of radioactive substance that decays by 20% per year.

    a. First, complete the table below.

t (years)	0	1	2	3	4
Q (grams)					

    b. Find the expression of the function A(t), A the amount of substance and t the time in years.

    c. Sketch its graph.

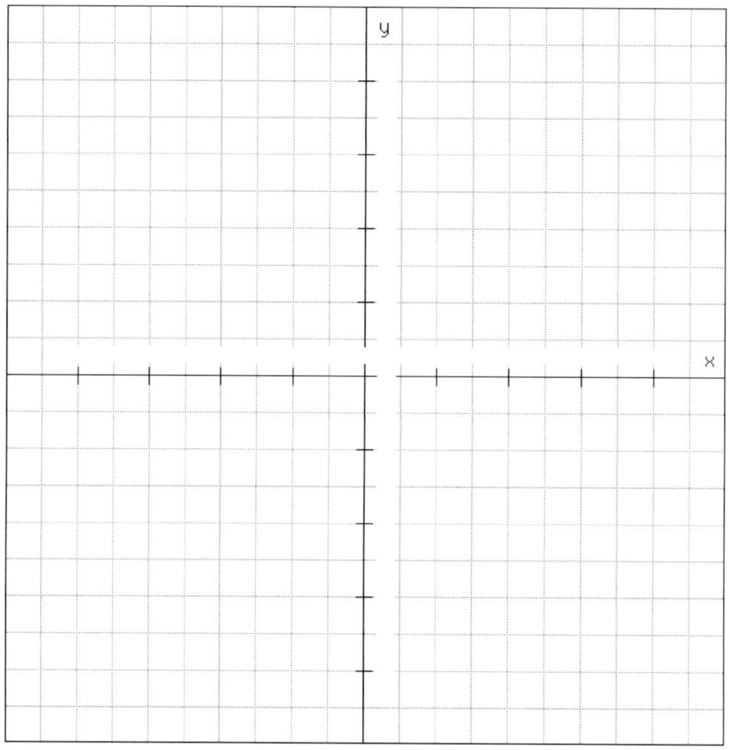

3. Suppose you invest 10000$ in the year 2000 and the investment earns 5.5% annually.

    a. a. Find the expression of the function A(t), A the amount of money and t the time in years.

    b. What will be the investment worth in 2010, 2020, 2030?

2.7. – LOGARITHMIC FUNCTIONS

1. Given the functions: $f(x) = \log_2(x)$, $g(x) = \log_3(x)$, Complete the following table:

x	–5	–1	–0.1	0	0.0001	0.001	0.1	1	2	16	81	1024
f(x)												
g(x)												

- Sketch the points of the table on a graph.
- State the domain of the function: ________________
- State the *y* intercept (sketched on the graph: (____, ____)
- State the *x* intercept(s): (____, ____), (____, ____)
- Write the corresponding limits and the equation of the vertical asymptote: _____
- Write the corresponding limits and the equation of the horizontal asymptote: ___
- Function is increasing on the interval: _____, decreasing on the interval:______
- Find the max/min point(s): (____, ____)
- State the range of the function: ________

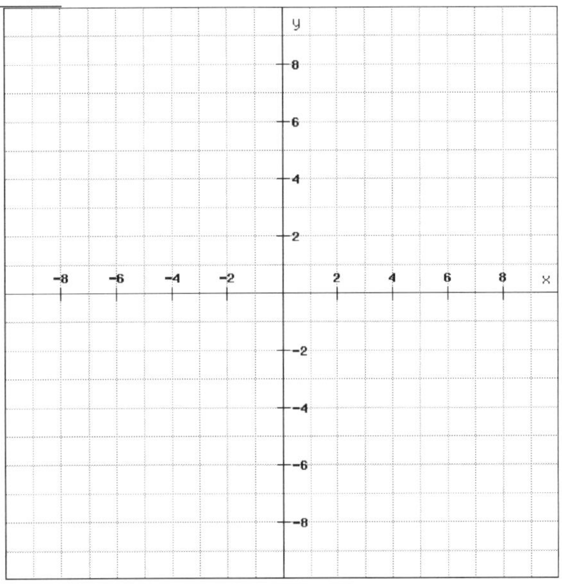

2. Given the functions: $f(x) = \log_1(x)$, $g(x) = \log_{-2}(x)$, Complete the following table:

x	−5	−1	−0.1	0	0.0001	0.001	0.1	1	2	16	81	1024
f(x)												
g(x)												

Conclusion:

3. Given the functions: $f(x) = \log_e(x)$, $g(x) = \log(x)$, Complete the following table:

x	–5	–1	–0.1	0	0.0001	0.001	0.1	1	2	16	81	1024
f(x)												
g(x)												

- Sketch the points of the table on a graph.
- State the domain of the function: ________________
- State the *y* intercept (sketched on the graph: (____, ____)
- State the *x* intercept(s): (____, ____), (____, ____)
- Write the corresponding limits and the equation of the vertical asymptote: _____
- Write the corresponding limits and the equation of the horizontal asymptote: ___
- Function is increasing on the interval: _____, decreasing on the interval:______
- Find the max/min point(s): (____, ____)
- State the range of the function: ________

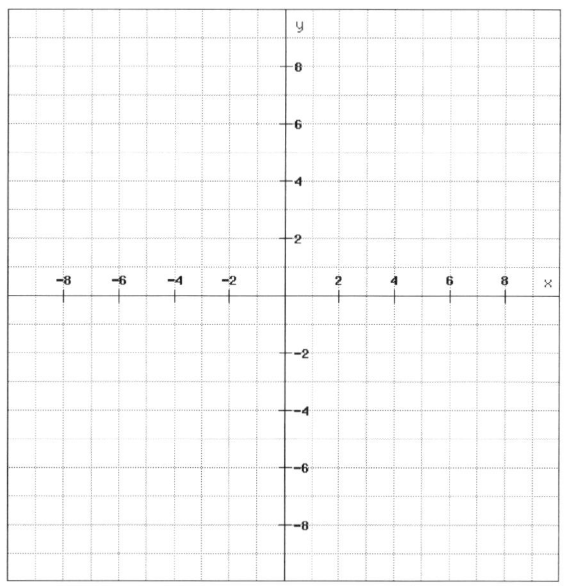

4. Given the functions: $f(x) = \log_4(x) + 4$, $g(x) = \log_3(x) - 3$, Complete the following table:

x	–5	–1	–0.1	0	0.0001	0.001	0.1	1	2	16	81	1024
f(x)												
g(x)												

- Sketch the points of the table on a graph.
- State the domain of the function: ________________
- State the *y* intercept (sketched on the graph: (____, ____)
- State the *x* intercept(s): (____, ____), (____, ____)
- Write the corresponding limits and the equation of the vertical asymptote: _____
- Write the corresponding limits and the equation of the horizontal asymptote: ___
- Function is increasing on the interval: _____, decreasing on the interval:______
- Find the max/min point(s): (____, ____)
- State the range of the function: ________

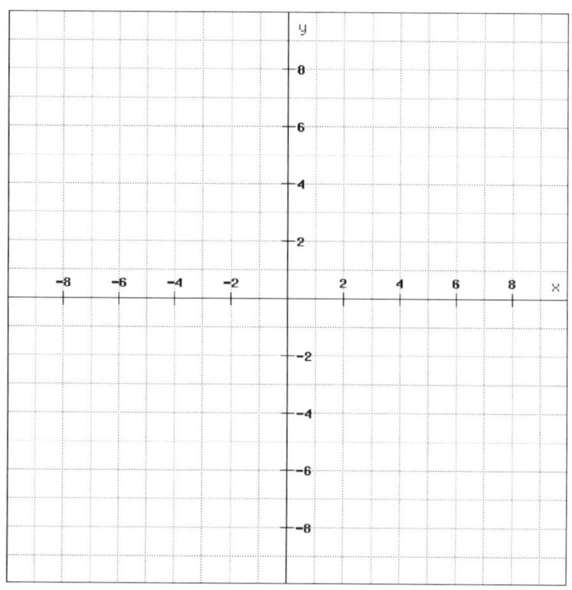

5. Given the functions: $f(x) = \log_2(x - 2)$, $g(x) = \log_3(x + 4)$, Complete the following table:

x	–5	–1	–0.1	0	0.0001	0.001	0.1	1	2	16	81	1024
f(x)												
g(x)												

- Sketch the points of the table on a graph.
- State the domain of the function: ________________
- State the *y* intercept (sketched on the graph: (____, ____)
- State the *x* intercept(s): (____, ____), (____, ____)
- Write the corresponding limits and the equation of the vertical asymptote: _____
- Write the corresponding limits and the equation of the horizontal asymptote: ___
- Function is increasing on the interval: _____, decreasing on the interval:______
- Find the max/min point(s): (____, ____)
- State the range of the function: ________

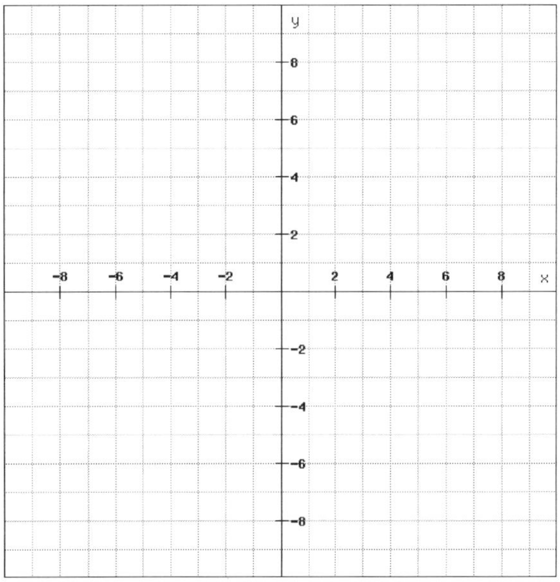

6. Given the functions: $f(x) = \log_2(2x - 5) + 1$, $g(x) = \log_3(3x + 2) - 5$, Complete the following table:

x	–5	–1	–0.1	0	0.0001	0.001	0.1	1	2	16	81	1024
f(x)												
g(x)												

- Sketch the points of the table on a graph.
- State the domain of the function: ________________
- State the y intercept (sketched on the graph: (____, ____)
- State the x intercept(s): (____, ____), (____, ____)
- Write the corresponding limits and the equation of the vertical asymptote: _____
- Write the corresponding limits and the equation of the horizontal asymptote: ___
- Function is increasing on the interval: _____, decreasing on the interval:______
- Find the max/min point(s): (,)
- State the range of the function: ________

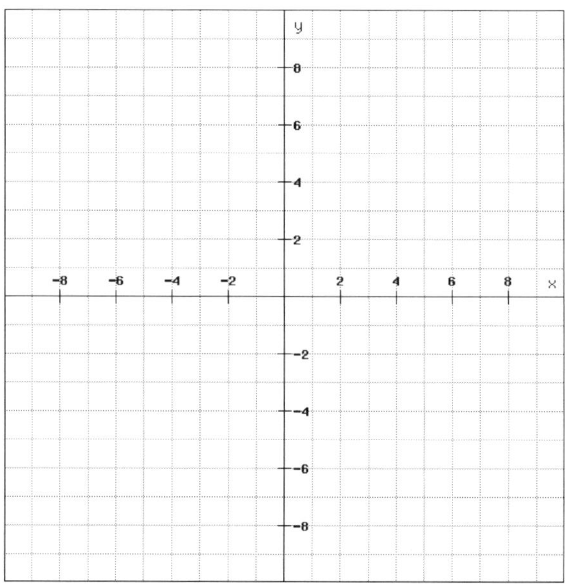

7. Given the graph, complete the table below:

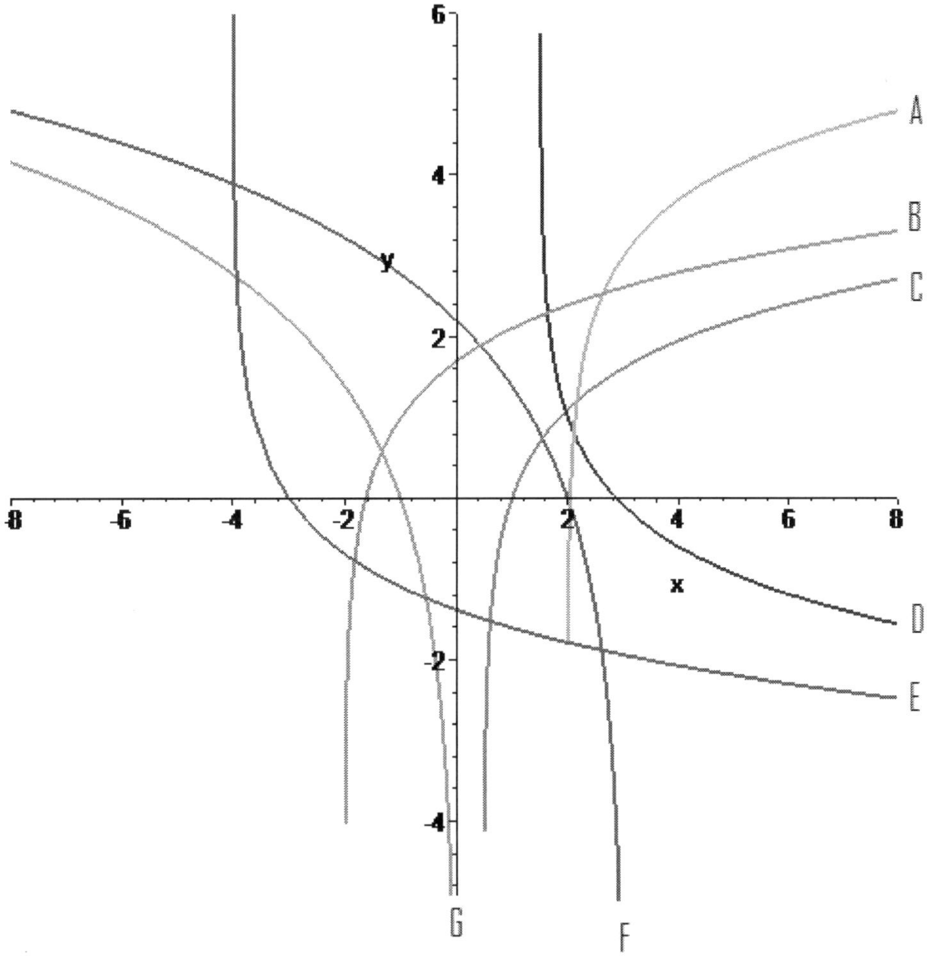

Function	On the graph
$f(x) = 2\ln(-x)$	
$f(x) = \ln(x+2)+1$	
$f(x) = 2\ln(3-x)$	
$f(x) = \ln(2x-1)$	
$f(x) = -\ln(x+4)$	
$f(x) = -\ln(2x-3)$	
$f(x) = \ln(x-2)+3$	

8. Given the function $f(x) = Ln(x)$

a. Write the same function translated 2 positions up.

b. Write the same function translated 2 positions left.

c. Write the same function translated 4 positions up and 3 right.

d. Sketch all 3 functions

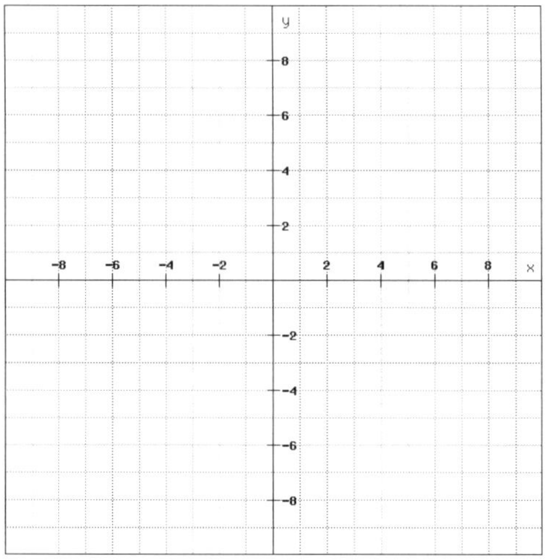

9. Given the function $f(x) = -Log_3(-2x)$

a. Write the same function translated 2 positions up.

b. Write the same function translated 2 positions left.

c. Write the same function translated 4 positions up and 3 right.

d. Sketch all 3 functions

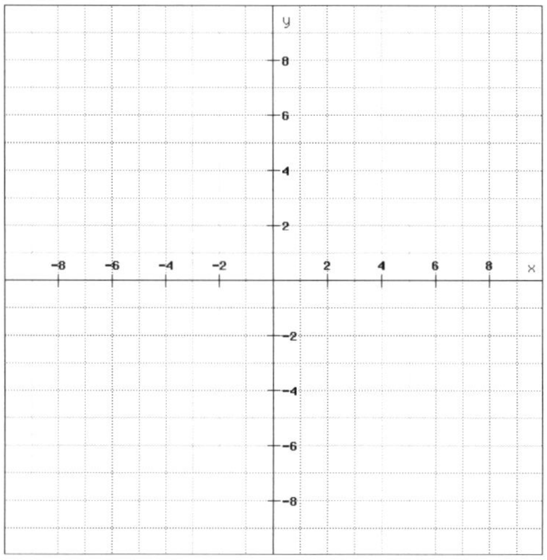

Analyze the following functions:

1. f(x) = log(x) – 2

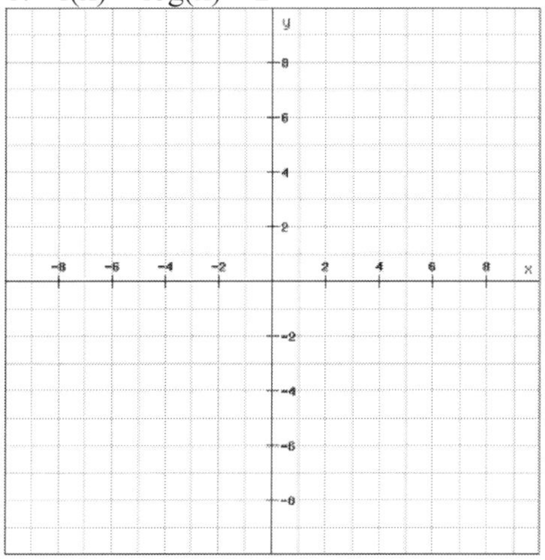

Horizontal asymptote:______ Domain: __________

Lim

Range: ___________

Lim

Increases: ________

Vertical asymptote: _______ Decreases: _______

Lim

y intercept:(___, ___)

Lim

x intercept:(___, ___)

2. f(x) = log(x–1)

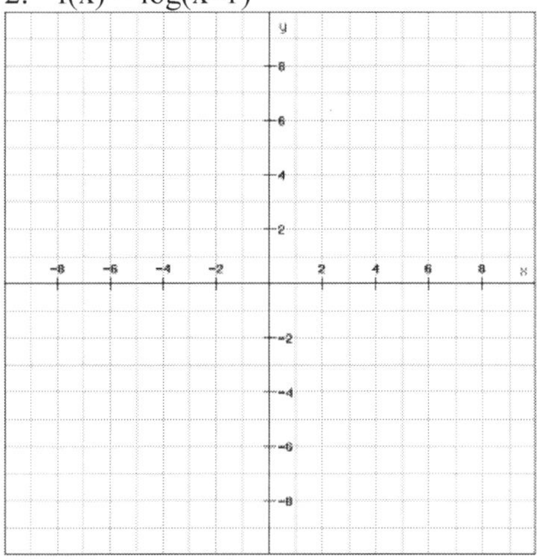

Horizontal asymptote:______ Domain: __________

Lim

Range: ___________

Lim

Increases: ________

Vertical asymptote: _______ Decreases: _______

Lim

y intercept:(___, ___)

Lim

x intercept:(___, ___)

3. f(x) = log(x^2)

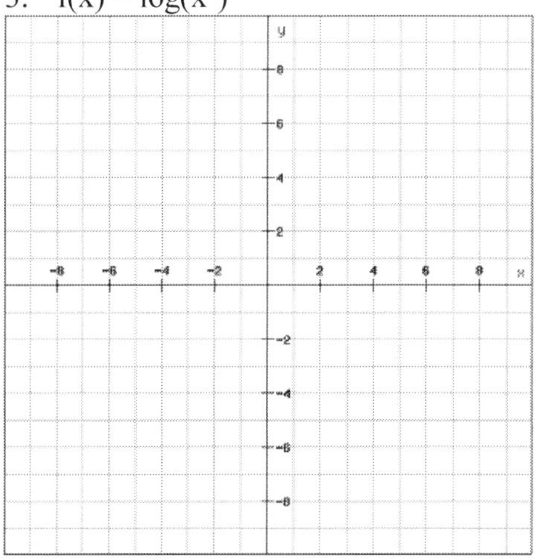

Horizontal asymptote:______ Domain: __________

Lim

Range: ___________

Lim

Increases: ________

Vertical asymptote: _______ Decreases: _______

Lim

y intercept:(___, ___)

Lim

x intercept:(___, ___)

4. $f(x) = -\log(5 - x)$

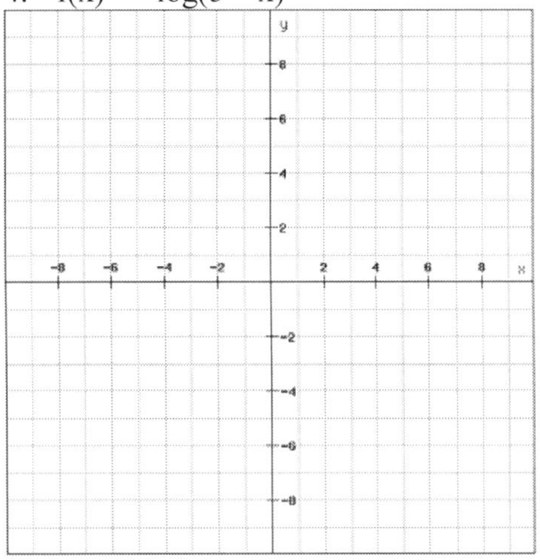

Horizontal asymptote:______ Domain: __________

Lim

Range: ___________

Lim

Increases: _________

Vertical asymptote: ________ Decreases: ________

Lim

y intercept:(___, ___)

Lim

x intercept:(___, ___)

5. $f(x) = \log(x - 3) + 5$

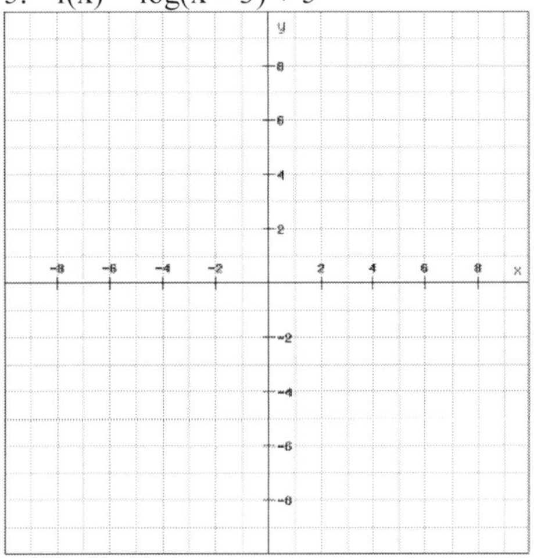

Horizontal asymptote:______ Domain: __________

Lim

Range: ___________

Lim

Increases: _________

Vertical asymptote: ________ Decreases: ________

Lim

y intercept:(___, ___)

Lim

x intercept:(___, ___)

6. $f(x) = \log(-x + 3) - 2$

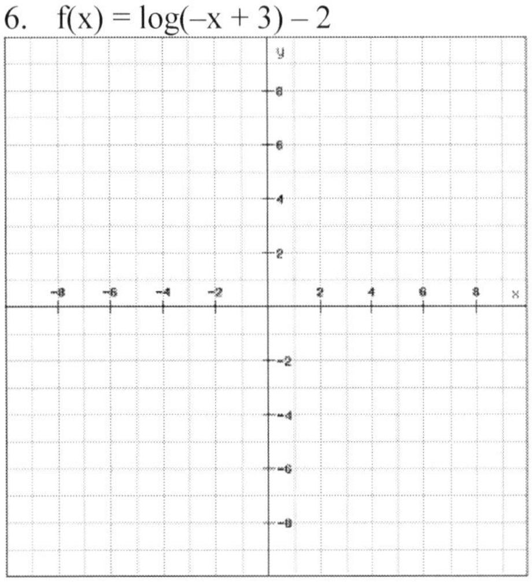

Horizontal asymptote:______ Domain: __________

Lim

Range: ___________

Lim

Increases: _________

Vertical asymptote: ________ Decreases: ________

Lim

y intercept:(___, ___)

Lim

x intercept:(___, ___)

7. $f(x) = -\log(x) - 5$

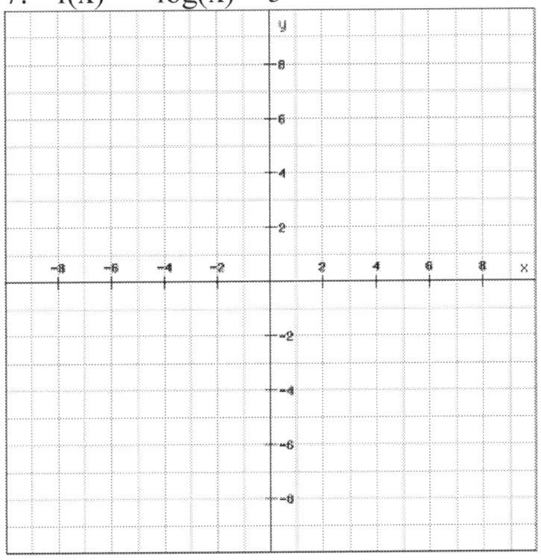

Horizontal asymptote:______ Domain: __________

Lim

Range: ___________

Lim

Increases: _________

Vertical asymptote: ________ Decreases: ________

Lim

y intercept:(___, ___)

Lim

x intercept:(___, ___)

8. $f(x) = \log(2x)$

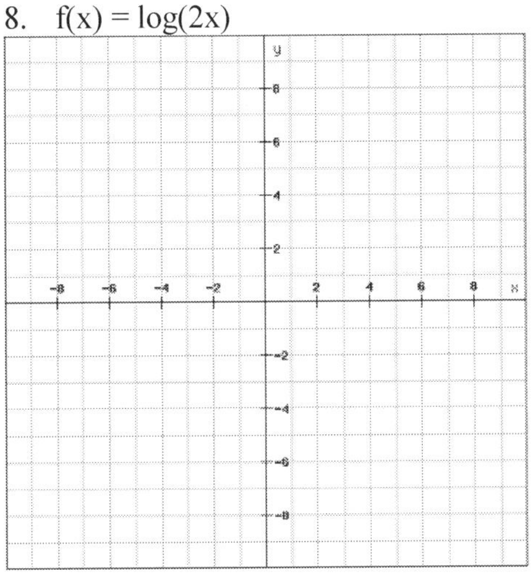

Horizontal asymptote:______ Domain: __________

Lim

Range: ___________

Lim

Increases: _________

Vertical asymptote: ________ Decreases: ________

Lim

y intercept:(___, ___)

Lim

x intercept:(___, ___)

9. $f(x) = -\log(-2x + 3)$

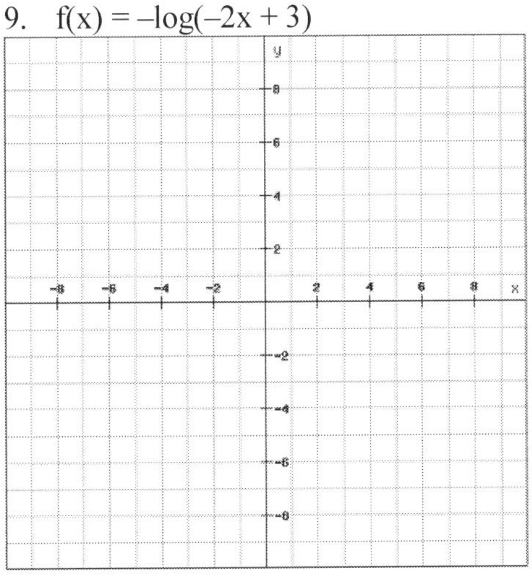

Horizontal asymptote:______ Domain: __________

Lim

Range: ___________

Lim

Increases: _________

Vertical asymptote: ________ Decreases: ________

Lim

y intercept:(___, ___)

Lim

x intercept:(___, ___)

10. $f(x) = \log(2x - 3) - 1$.

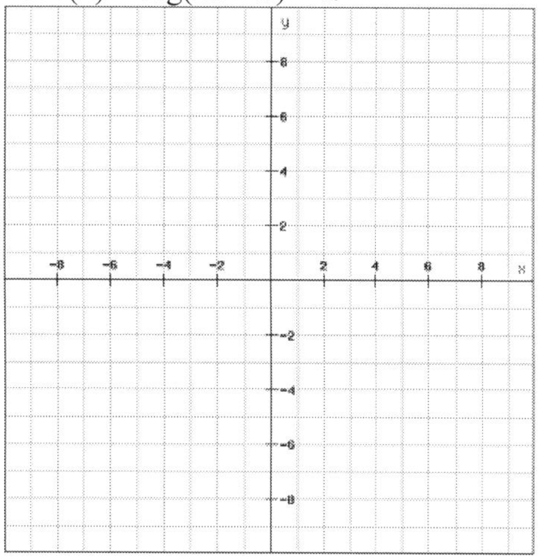

Horizontal asymptote:______ Domain: __________

Lim

Range: ___________

Lim

Increases: _________

Vertical asymptote: ________ Decreases: ________

Lim

y intercept:(___, ___)

Lim

x intercept:(___, ___)

11. $f(x) = \log(3x - 5) - 6$

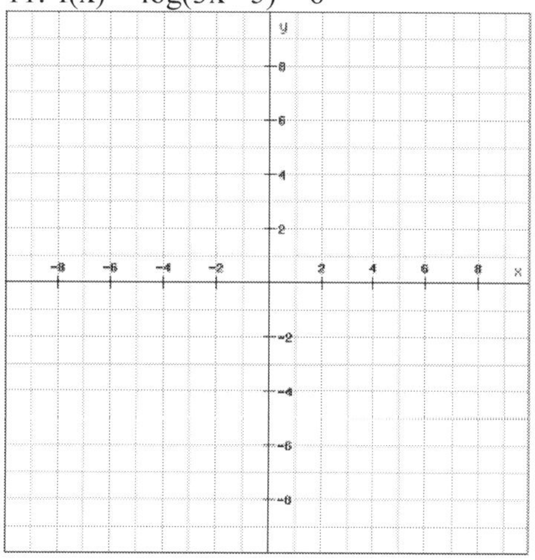

Horizontal asymptote:______ Domain: __________

Lim

Range: ___________

Lim

Increases: _________

Vertical asymptote: ________ Decreases: ________

Lim

y intercept:(___, ___)

Lim

x intercept:(___, ___)

12. $f(x) = -\log(x^2) + 5$

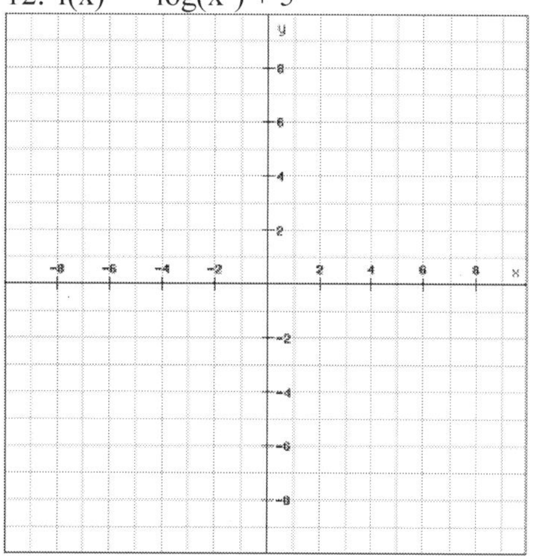

Horizontal asymptote:______ Domain: __________

Lim

Range: ___________

Lim

Increases: _________

Vertical asymptote: ________ Decreases: ________

Lim

y intercept:(___, ___)

Lim

x intercept:(___, ___)

13. $f(x) = \log(x^2) - 3$

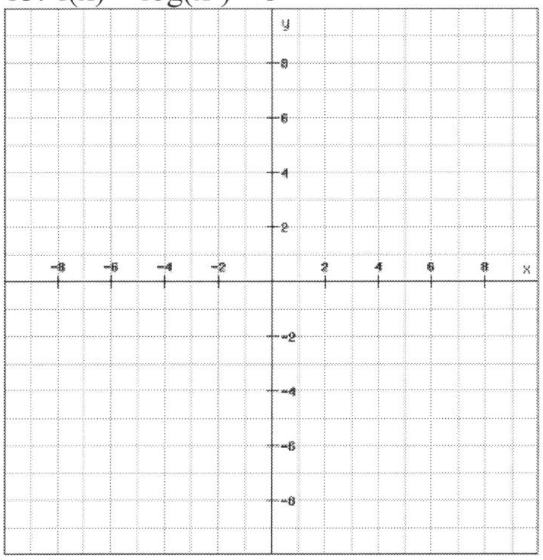

Horizontal asymptote:______ Domain: __________

Lim

Range: ___________

Lim

Increases: _________

Vertical asymptote: ________ Decreases: ________

Lim

y intercept:(___, ___)

Lim

x intercept:(___, ___)

14. $f(x) = -\log(|x|) - 3$

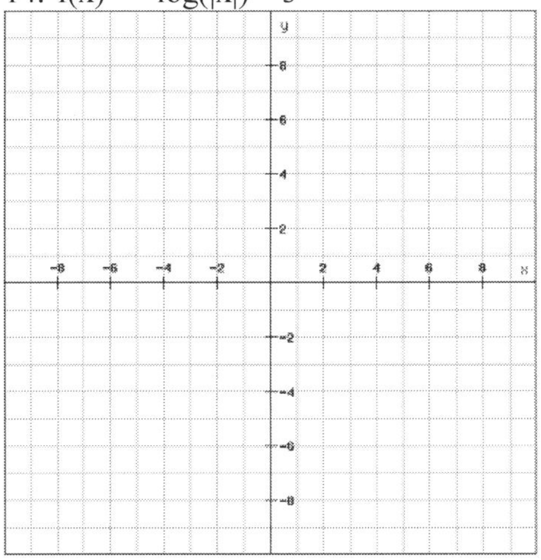

Horizontal asymptote:______ Domain: __________

Lim

Range: ___________

Lim

Increases: _________

Vertical asymptote: ________ Decreases: ________

Lim

y intercept:(___, ___)

Lim

x intercept:(___, ___)

15. $f(x) = \log(|x - 2|)$

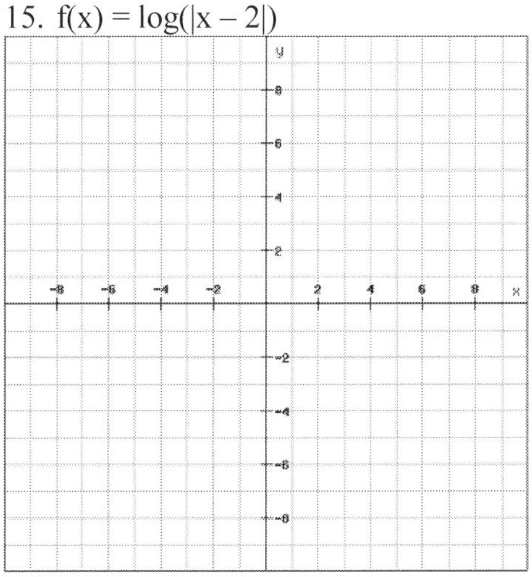

Horizontal asymptote:______ Domain: __________

Lim

Range: ___________

Lim

Increases: _________

Vertical asymptote: ________ Decreases: ________

Lim

y intercept:(___, ___)

Lim

x intercept:(___, ___)

16. $f(x) = \log(|x + 2|) - 5$

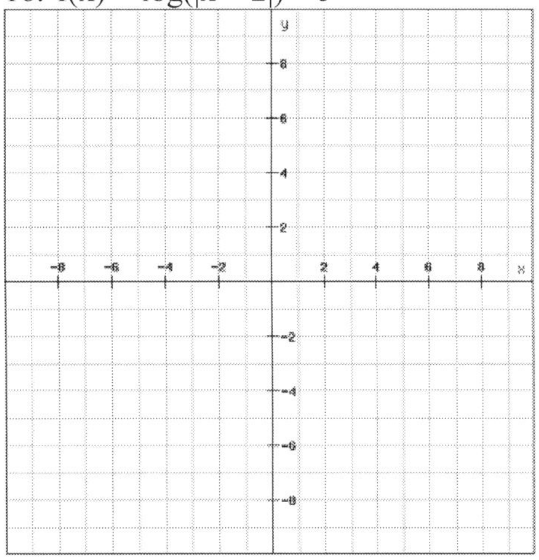

Horizontal asymptote:______ Domain: __________

Lim

Range: ___________

Lim

Increases: _________

Vertical asymptote: ________ Decreases: ________

Lim

y intercept:(___, ___)

Lim

x intercept:(___, ___)

17. $f(x) = -\log(|x + 6|) - 3$

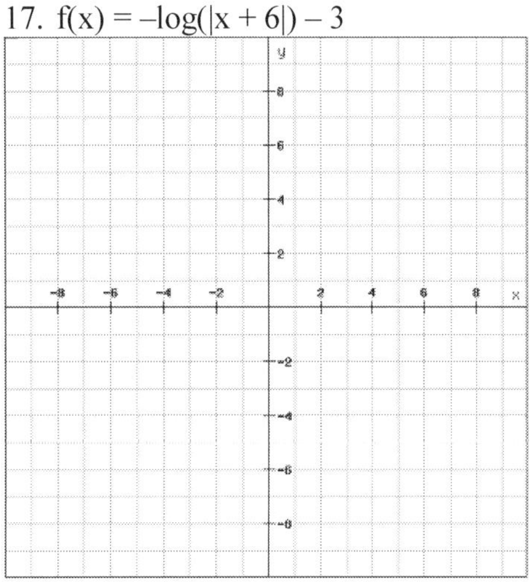

Horizontal asymptote:______ Domain: __________

Lim

Range: ___________

Lim

Increases: _________

Vertical asymptote: ________ Decreases: ________

Lim

y intercept:(___, ___)

Lim

x intercept:(___, ___)

18. $f(x) = \ln(x) - 3$

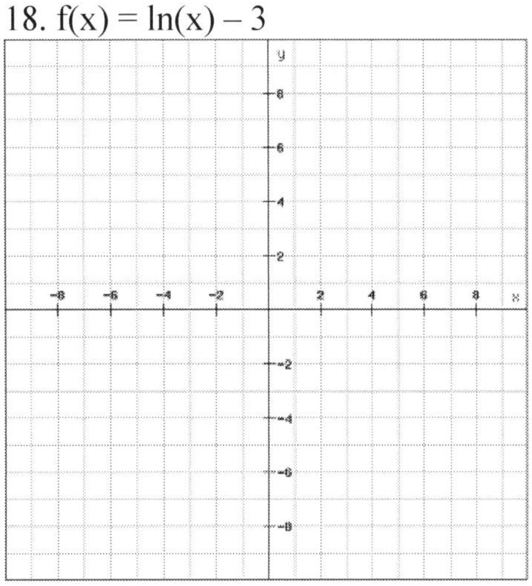

Horizontal asymptote:______ Domain: __________

Lim

Range: ___________

Lim

Increases: _________

Vertical asymptote: ________ Decreases: ________

Lim

y intercept:(___, ___)

Lim

x intercept:(___, ___)

19. $f(x) = \log(x) - 3$

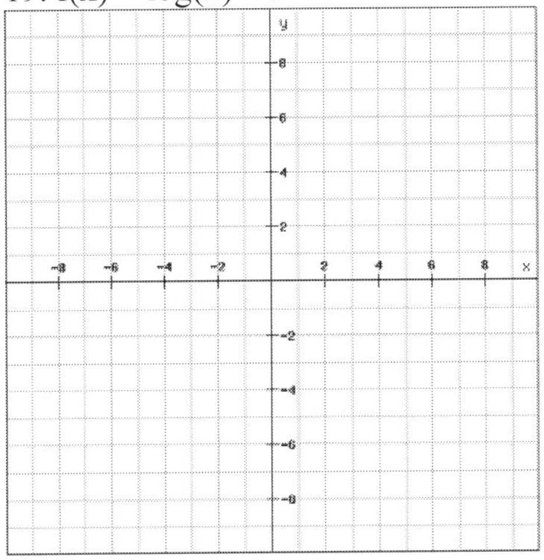

Horizontal asymptote:______ Domain: __________

Lim

Range: ___________

Lim

Increases: ________

Vertical asymptote: ________ Decreases: ________

Lim

y intercept:(___, ___)

Lim

x intercept:(___, ___)

20. $f(x) = \ln(x) - 2$

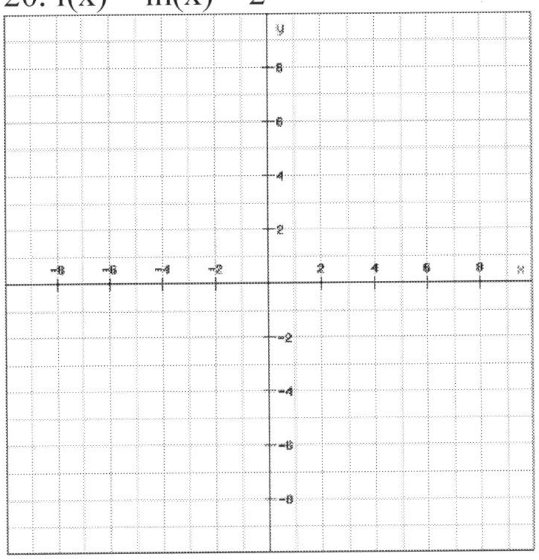

Horizontal asymptote:______ Domain: __________

Lim

Range: ___________

Lim

Increases: ________

Vertical asymptote: ________ Decreases: ________

Lim

y intercept:(___, ___)

Lim

x intercept:(___, ___)

21. $f(x) = \ln(-x-1)$

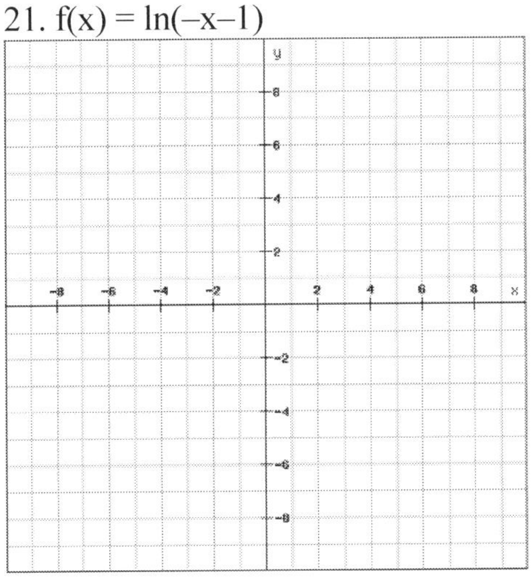

Horizontal asymptote:______ Domain: __________

Lim

Range: ___________

Lim

Increases: ________

Vertical asymptote: ________ Decreases: ________

Lim

y intercept:(___, ___)

Lim

x intercept:(___, ___)

22. $f(x) = \log_2(2 - x)$

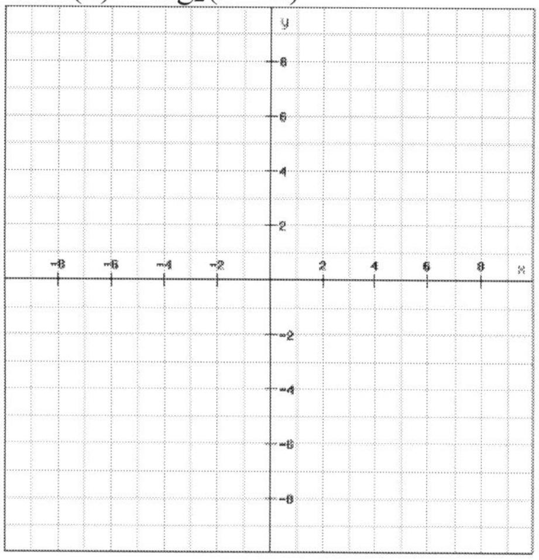

Horizontal asymptote:______ Domain: __________

Lim

Range: ___________

Lim

Increases: _________

Vertical asymptote: ________ Decreases: ________

Lim

y intercept:(___, ___)

Lim

x intercept:(___, ___)

23. $f(x) = -\ln(x+5)$

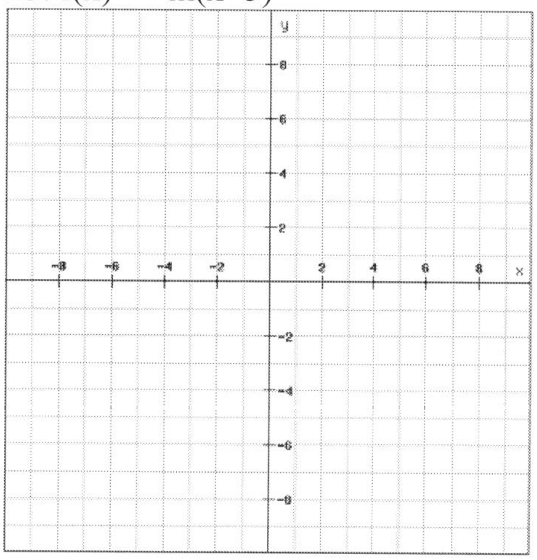

Horizontal asymptote:______ Domain: __________

Lim

Range: ___________

Lim

Increases: _________

Vertical asymptote: ________ Decreases: ________

Lim

y intercept:(___, ___)

Lim

x intercept:(___, ___)

24. $f(x) = \log_3(4 - 2x) + 1$

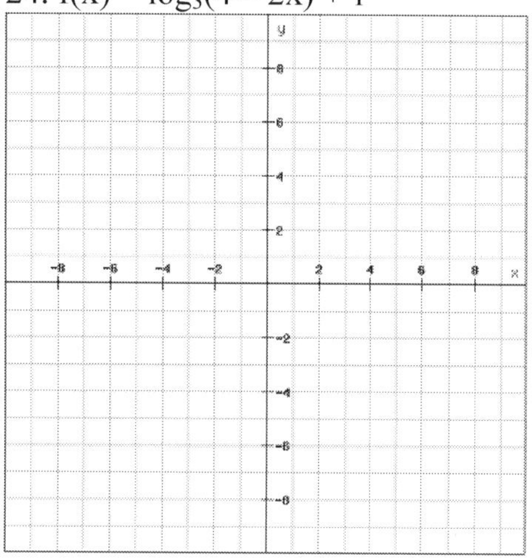

Horizontal asymptote:______ Domain: __________

Lim

Range: ___________

Lim

Increases: _________

Vertical asymptote: ________ Decreases: ________

Lim

y intercept:(___, ___)

Lim

x intercept:(___, ___)

25. $f(x) = \ln(2 - 2x) - 3$

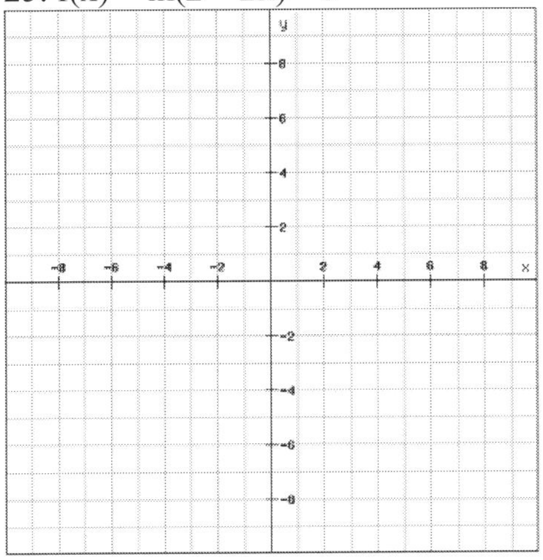

Horizontal asymptote:______ Domain: __________

Lim

Range: ___________

Lim

Increases: ________

Vertical asymptote: _______ Decreases: ________

Lim

y intercept:(___, ___)

Lim

x intercept:(___, ___)

26. $f(x) = -\ln(x) - 5$

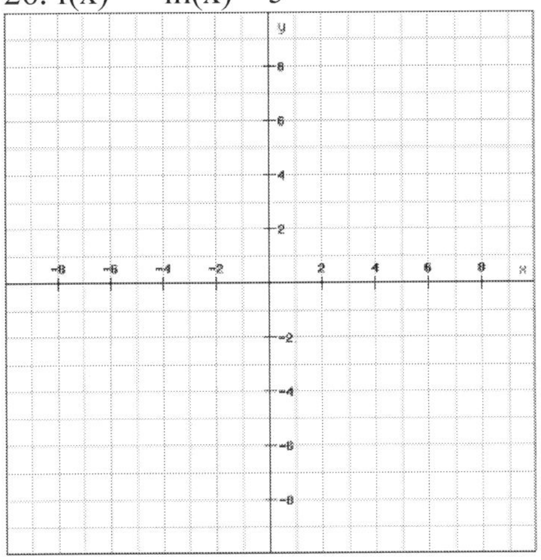

Horizontal asymptote:______ Domain: __________

Lim

Range: ___________

Lim

Increases: ________

Vertical asymptote: _______ Decreases: ________

Lim

y intercept:(___, ___)

Lim

x intercept:(___, ___)

27. $f(x) = \log_4(2x)$

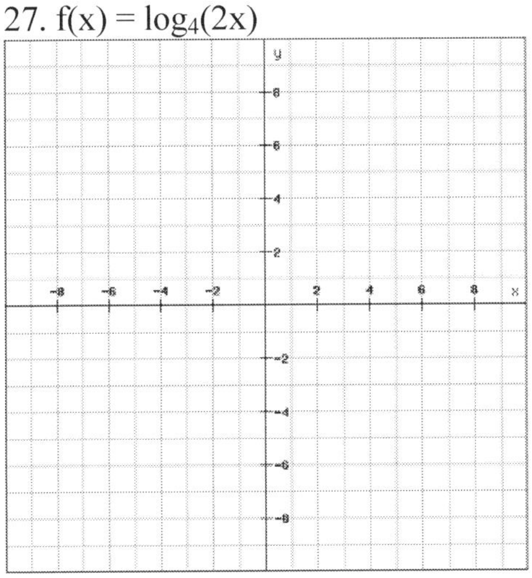

Horizontal asymptote:______ Domain: __________

Lim

Range: ___________

Lim

Increases: ________

Vertical asymptote: _______ Decreases: ________

Lim

y intercept:(___, ___)

Lim

x intercept:(___, ___)

28. $f(x) = -\log_6(-2x) + 1$

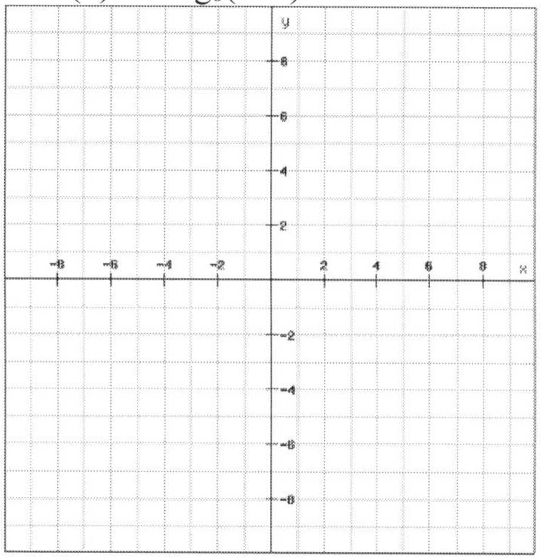

Horizontal asymptote:______ Domain: __________

Lim

Range: ___________

Lim

Increases: _________

Vertical asymptote: ________ Decreases: ________

Lim

y intercept:(___, ___)

Lim

x intercept:(___, ___)

29. $f(x) = \ln(-2x - 3) - 1$

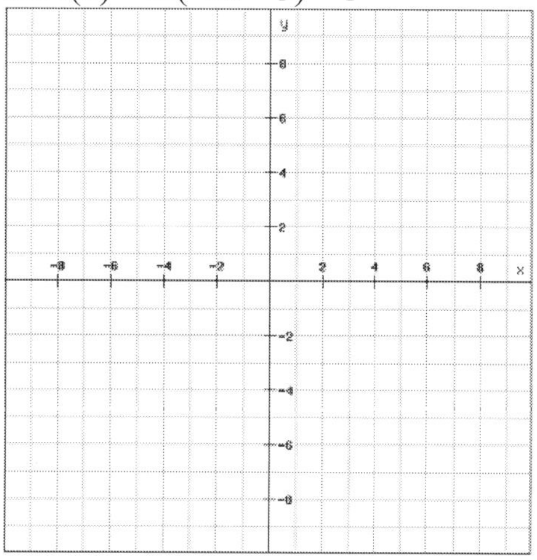

Horizontal asymptote:______ Domain: __________

Lim

Range: ___________

Lim

Increases: _________

Vertical asymptote: ________ Decreases: ________

Lim

y intercept:(___, ___)

Lim

x intercept:(___, ___)

30. $f(x) = -\log(10x - 5) - 1$

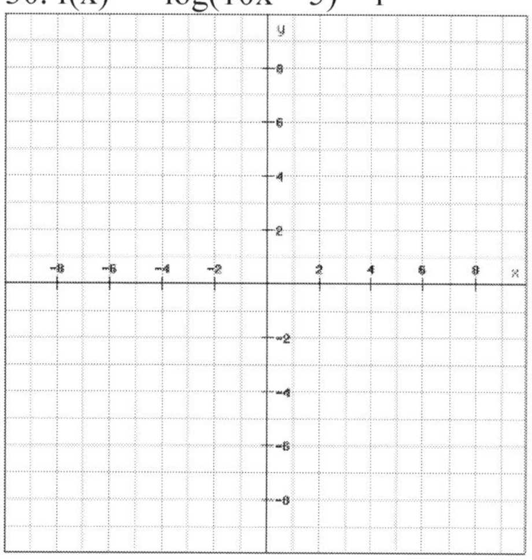

Horizontal asymptote:______ Domain: __________

Lim

Range: ___________

Lim

Increases: _________

Vertical asymptote: ________ Decreases: ________

Lim

y intercept:(___, ___)

Lim

x intercept:(___, ___)

31. The population of a city increases by 5% every year. Find the number of years it will take it to double.

32. The population of a town increases by k% every year; find the time it will take it to triple in terms of k.

33. The population of a city increases by k% every month; find k in case the population grew by 50% after 3 years.

34. The PH level in a substance is given by: $PH = -\log(H^+)$, where H^+ is the concentration of hydrogen ions (only proton) in moles/litter.

a. Given that the PH level of different substances complete the following table:

Substance	PH Level	Concentration of Hydrogen ions
Battery Acid	0	
Lemon Juice	2	
Milk	6	
Pure Water	7	
Human Blood	7.4	
Great salt lake	10	
Liquid drain cleaner	14	

b. People who have cancer have about a 100 times more acid blood than normal blood, find their level of PH.

35. Richter scale for measuring earthquake strength as felt in a particular place (M) can be approximated by $M = \log(x)$, where x depends on the strength of the earthquake and the distance from its centre.

a. Given that in a certain location A the Richter scale measure M was 5 and in location B the Richter scale measure M was 6. Find how much stronger was the earthquake in location B?

b. Given that in a certain location A the Richter scale measure was 5 and in location B the earthquake was 3 times as strong, what was the Richter scale measure in location B?

36. The Weber – Fechner law can be approximated by: $S = k\log_{10} I$, where I is the intensity of light and S is the sensation of brightness.

a. This law means that:

Big changes in the Intensity will cause _______ changes in the sensation.

b. Find the change needed in the intensity that will double the sensation of brightness.

37. Decibels (DB) are used for measuring the volume of sound. They are given by: $I = 10\log(P/P_0)$ where P_0 is the minimum intensity of sound detected by the human ear.

a. What is the threshold in DB of the human ear?

b. In normal conversation 60 DB will be measured. Express P in terms of P_0. How many times louder is this than the threshold?

c. In a rock concert 120 DB will be measured. Express P in terms of P_0. How many times louder is this than a normal conversation?

d. Find the number of DB of a sound twice is strong as the threshold.

2.8. – RADICAL FUCNTIONS

1. Given the functions: $f(x) = \sqrt{x}$, $g(x) = -\sqrt{x}$, Complete the following table:

x	–2	–1	0	1	2	3	4	5	6	7	8	9
f(x)												
g(x)												

- Sketch the points of the table on a graph.
- State the domain of the function: ________________
- State the *y* intercept (sketched on the graph: (____, ____)
- State the *x* intercept(s): (____, ____), (____, ____)
- Write the corresponding limits and the equation of the vertical asymptote: _____
- Write the corresponding limits and the equation of the horizontal asymptote: ___
- Function is increasing on the interval: _____, decreasing on the interval:______
- Find the max/min point(s): (____, ____)
- State the range of the function: ________

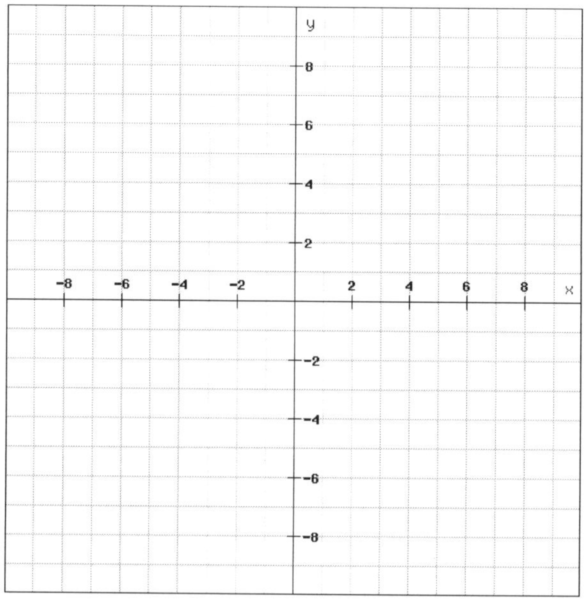

2. Given the functions: $f(x) = \sqrt{-x+1}$, $g(x) = -\sqrt{x-3}$, Complete the table:

x	−2	−1	0	1	2	3	4	5	6	7	8	9
f(x)												
g(x)												

- Sketch the points of the table on a graph.
- State the domain of the function: ________________
- State the *y* intercept (sketched on the graph: (____, ____)
- State the *x* intercept(s): (____, ____), (____, ____)
- Write the corresponding limits and the equation of the vertical asymptote: _____
- Write the corresponding limits and the equation of the horizontal asymptote: ___
- Function is increasing on the interval: _____, decreasing on the interval:______
- Find the max/min point(s): (____, ____)
- State the range of the function: ________

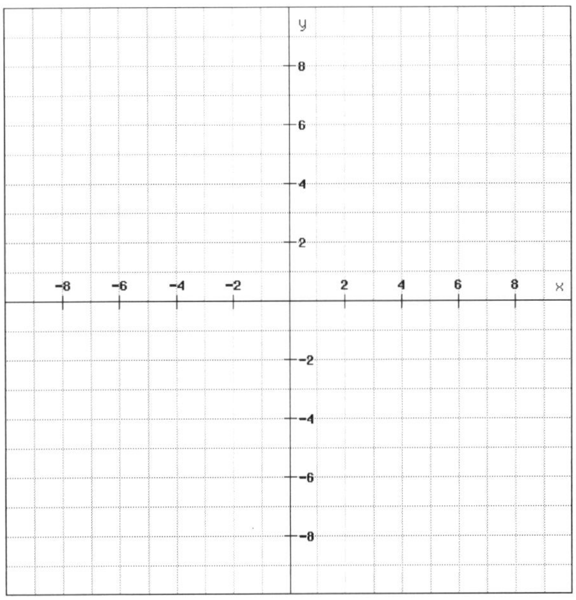

3. Given the functions: f(x) = $\sqrt{x+1}+3$, g(x) = $-\sqrt{x-3}-6$. Complete the table:

x	–2	–1	0	1	2	3	4	5	6	7	8	9
f(x)												
g(x)												

- Sketch the points of the table on a graph.
- State the domain of the function: ________________
- State the *y* intercept (sketched on the graph: (____, ____)
- State the *x* intercept(s): (____, ____), (____, ____)
- Write the corresponding limits and the equation of the vertical asymptote: _____
- Write the corresponding limits and the equation of the horizontal asymptote: ___
- Function is increasing on the interval: _____, decreasing on the interval:______
- Find the max/min point(s): (____, ____)
- State the range of the function: ________

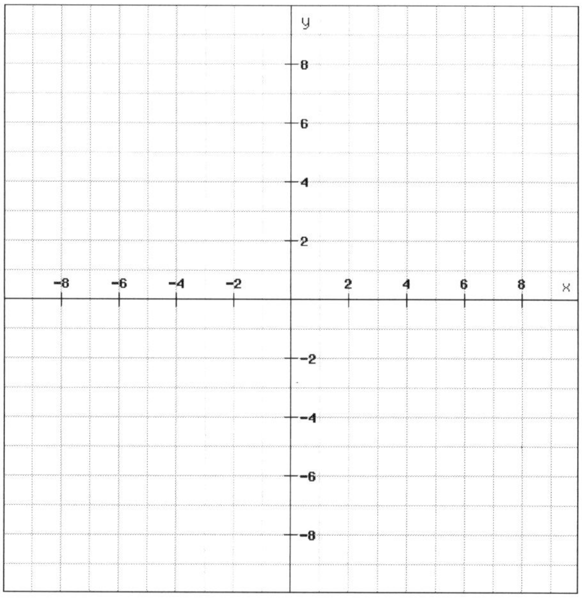

4. Given the graph, complete the table below:

Function	On the graph
$f(x)=3\sqrt{x-2}-3$	
$f(x)=\sqrt{3x+2}$	
$f(x)=\sqrt{-2x+1}$	
$f(x)=\sqrt{x+1}$	
$f(x)=\sqrt{-x-2}$	
$f(x)=2-\sqrt{x-2}$	
$f(x)=-2\sqrt{x-1}$	
$f(x)=-1-\sqrt{-x+4}$	
$f(x)=-\sqrt{2x-5}-1$	

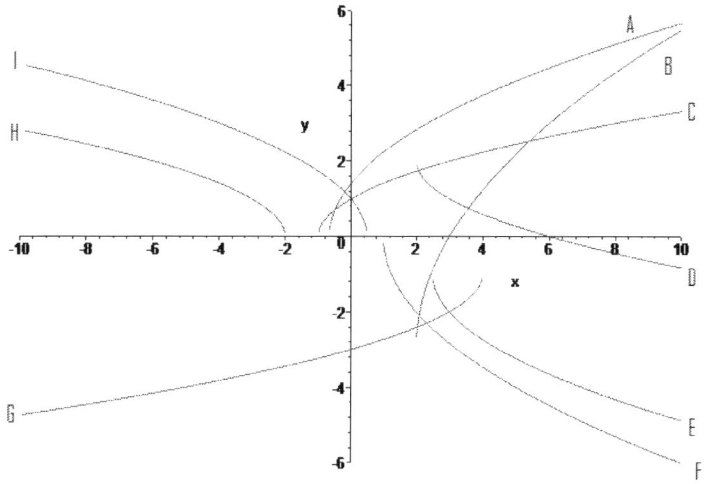

5. Given the function $f(x)=\sqrt{x}$

a. Write the same function translated 2 positions up.

b. Write the same function translated 2 positions left.

c. Write the same function translated 4 positions up and 3 right.

d. Sketch the 3 functions:

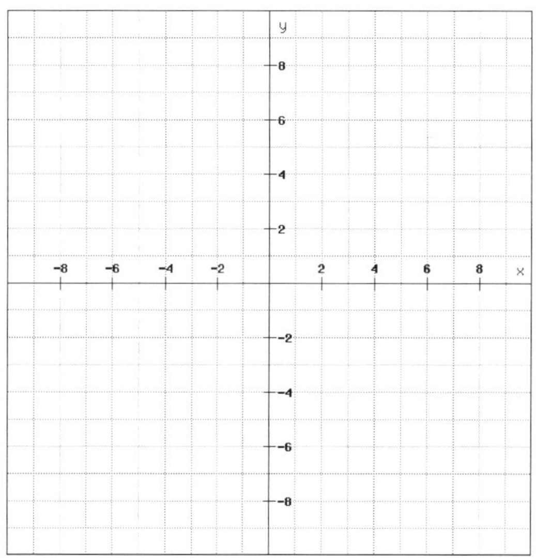

6. Given the function $f(x) = 4\sqrt{-2x+1}$

a. Write the same function translated 2 positions up.

b. Write the same function translated 2 positions left.

c. Write the same function translated 4 positions up and 3 right.

e. Sketch the 3 functions:

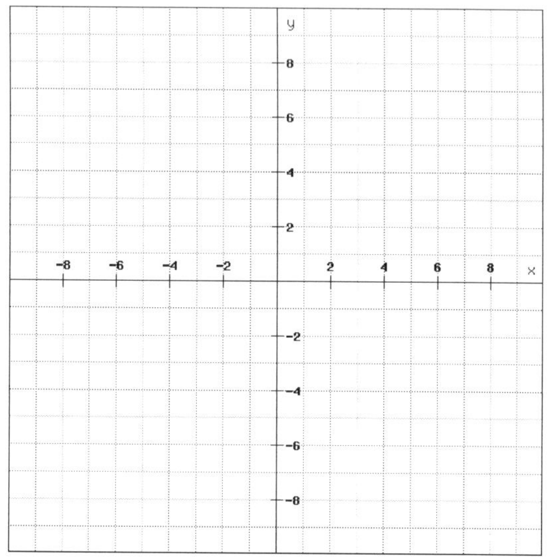

Analyze the following functions:

1. f(x) = $\sqrt{x+3}$

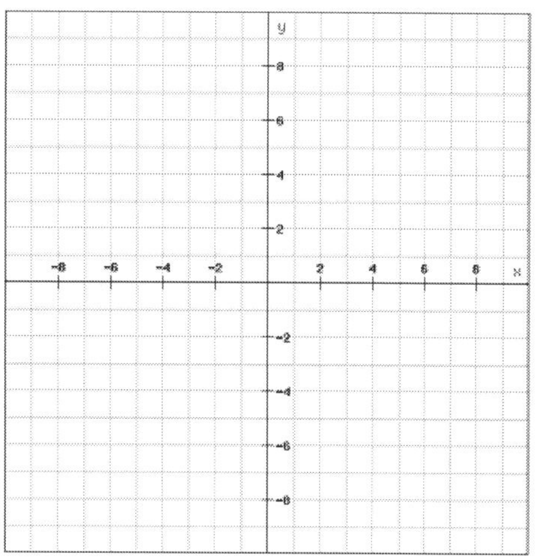

Domain: ___________ x intercept:(___, ___)

Range: ___________

Increases: ___________

Decreases: ___________ y intercept:(___, ___)

Max/Min:(___, ___)

2. $f(x) = 3\sqrt{x-2}$

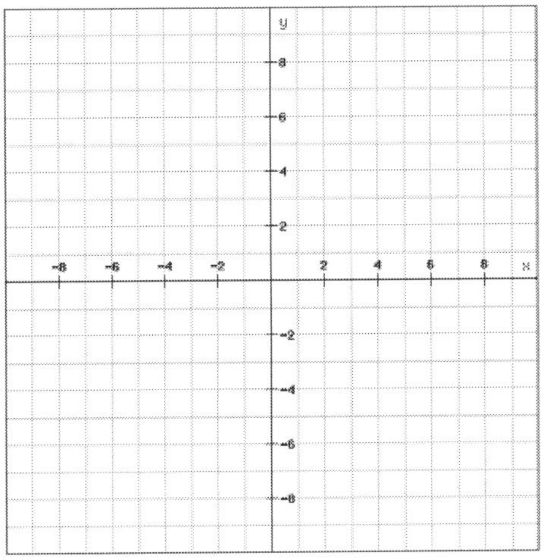

Domain: __________

Range: ___________

Increases: _________

Decreases: ________

Max/Min:(___, ___)

x intercept:(___, ___)

y intercept:(___, ___)

3. $f(x) = \sqrt{5x+6}$

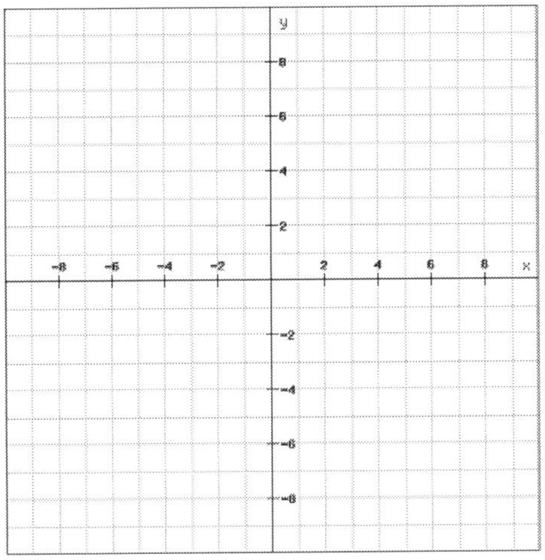

Domain: __________

Range: ___________

Increases: _________

Decreases: ________

Max/Min:(___, ___)

x intercept:(___, ___)

y intercept:(___, ___)

4. $f(x) = 2\sqrt{-4x-2}$

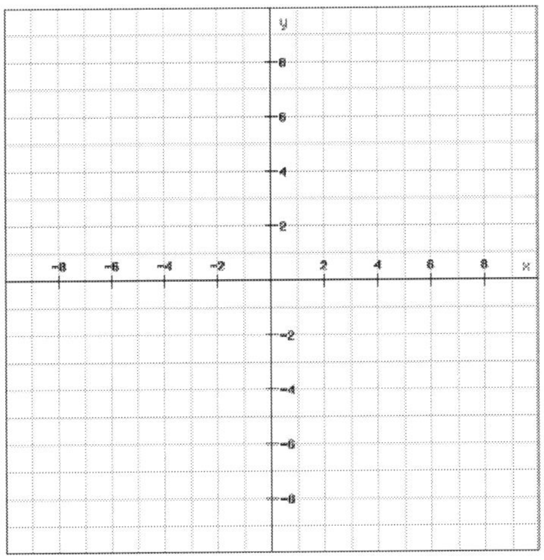

Domain: __________

Range: ___________

Increases: _________

Decreases: ________

Max/Min:(___, ___)

x intercept:(___, ___)

y intercept:(___, ___)

5. $f(x) = -\sqrt{x-3}$

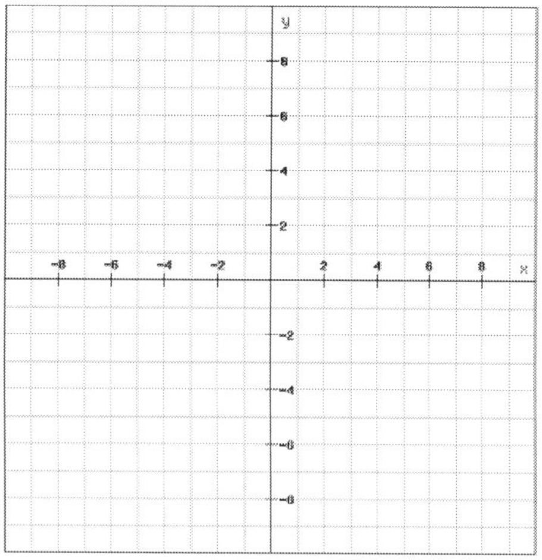

Domain: __________ x intercept:(___, ___)

Range: ___________

Increases: _________

Decreases: ________ y intercept:(___, ___)

Max/Min:(___, ___)

6. $f(x) = \sqrt{2x-5}$

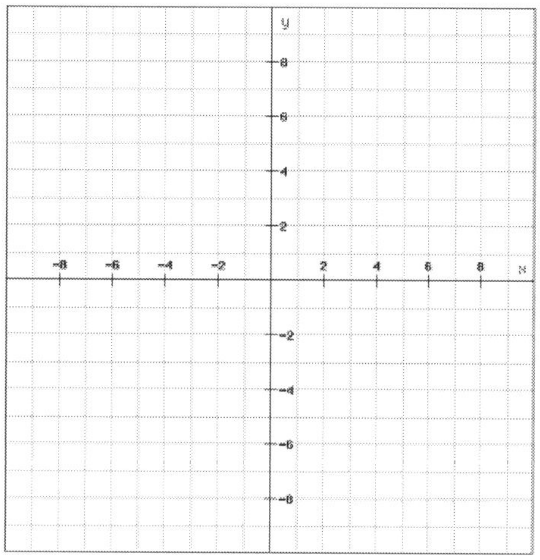

Domain: __________ x intercept:(___, ___)

Range: ___________

Increases: _________

Decreases: ________ y intercept:(___, ___)

Max/Min:(___, ___)

7. $f(x) = 2\sqrt{-3x-2}$

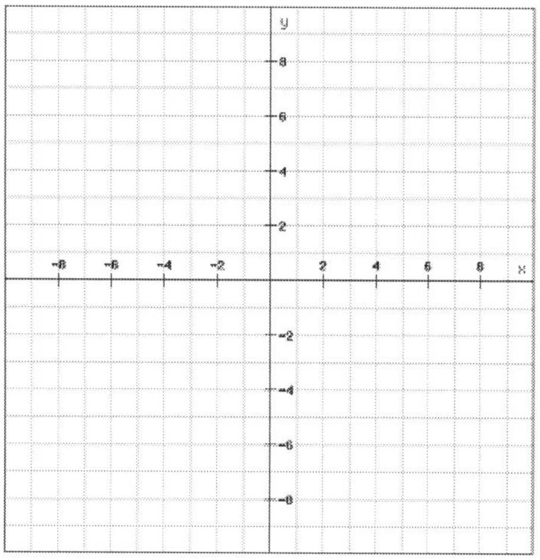

Domain: __________ x intercept:(___, ___)

Range: ___________

Increases: _________

Decreases: ________ y intercept:(___, ___)

Max/Min:(___, ___)

8. $f(x) = \sqrt{x-5}+6$

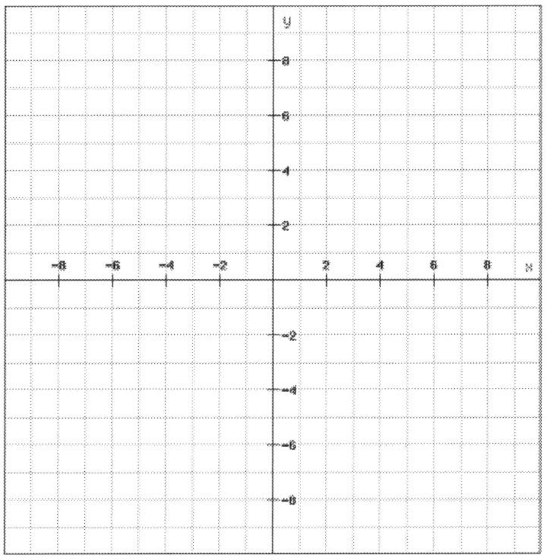

Domain: __________ x intercept:(___, ___)

Range: ___________

Increases: ________

Decreases: ________ y intercept:(___, ___)

Max/Min:(___, ___)

9. $f(x) = \sqrt{-x+3}-8$

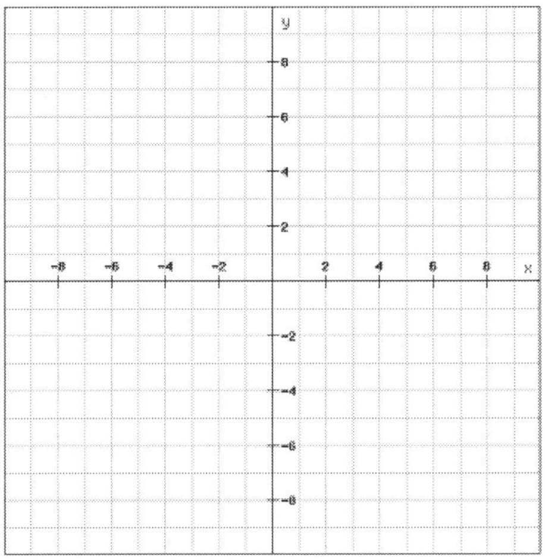

Domain: __________ x intercept:(___, ___)

Range: ___________

Increases: ________

Decreases: ________ y intercept:(___, ___)

Max/Min:(___, ___)

10. $f(x) = \sqrt{4x+3}+4$

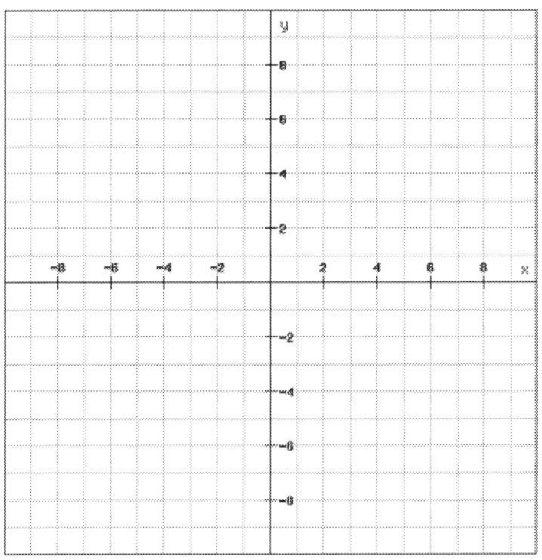

Domain: __________ x intercept:(___, ___)

Range: ___________

Increases: ________

Decreases: ________ y intercept:(___, ___)

Max/Min:(___, ___)

11. f(x) = $\sqrt{x-6}-2$

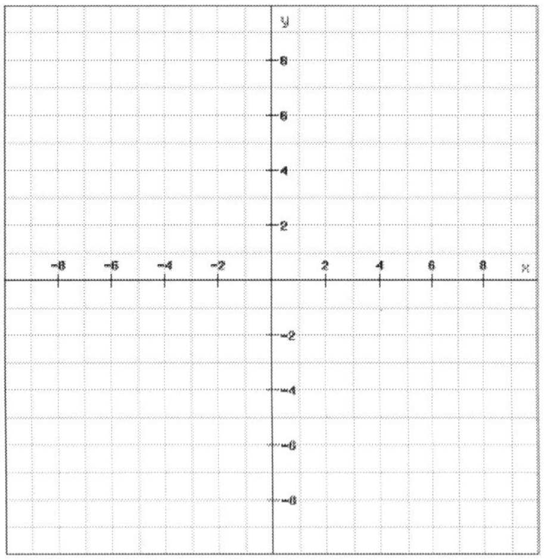

Domain: __________ x intercept:(___, ___)

Range: ___________

Increases: _________

Decreases: ________ y intercept:(___, ___)

Max/Min:(___, ___)

12. f(x) = $5\sqrt{x}-5$

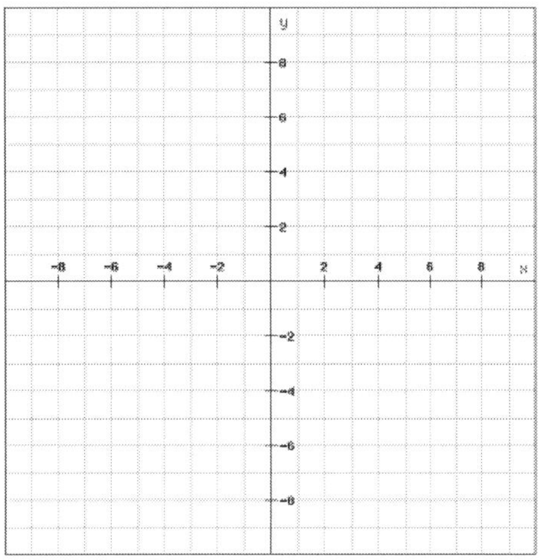

Domain: __________ x intercept:(___, ___)

Range: ___________

Increases: _________

Decreases: ________ y intercept:(___, ___)

Max/Min:(___, ___)

13. f(x) = $\sqrt{x+3}-1$

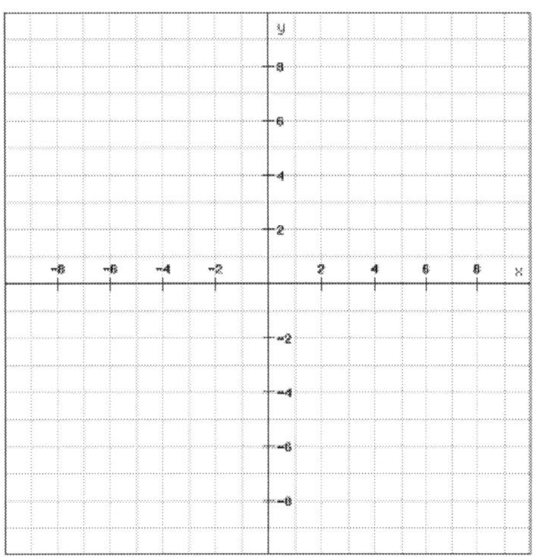

Domain: __________ x intercept:(___, ___)

Range: ___________

Increases: _________

Decreases: ________ y intercept:(___, ___)

Max/Min:(___, ___)

14. f(x) = $-2\sqrt{x}+9$

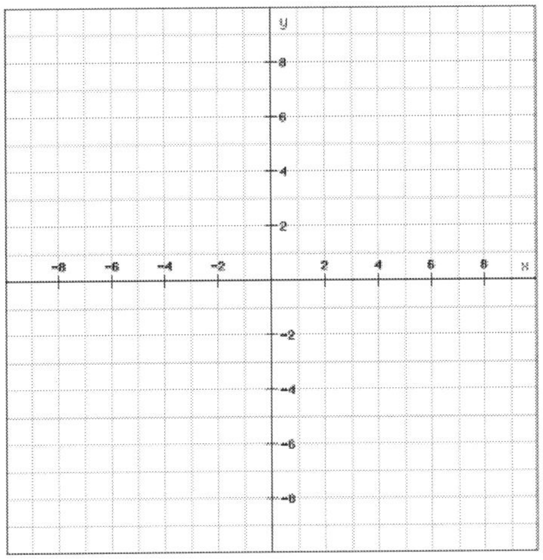

Domain: ___________ x intercept:(___, ___)

Range: ____________

Increases: _________

Decreases: ________ y intercept:(___, ___)

Max/Min:(___, ___)

15. f(x) = $-\sqrt{-x+3}$

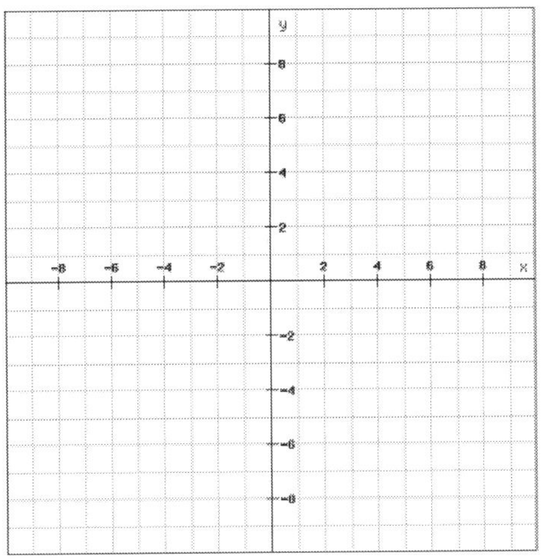

Domain: ___________ x intercept:(___, ___)

Range: ____________

Increases: _________

Decreases: ________ y intercept:(___, ___)

Max/Min:(___, ___)

16. f(x) = $\sqrt{x-2}$

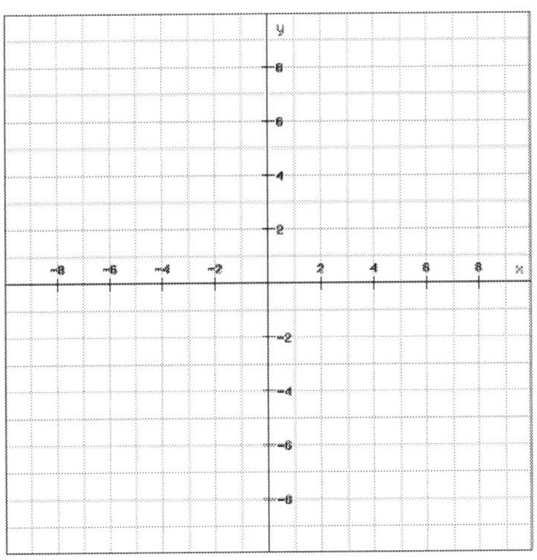

Domain: ___________ x intercept:(___, ___)

Range: ____________

Increases: _________

Decreases: ________ y intercept:(___, ___)

Max/Min:(___, ___)

17. f(x) = $\sqrt{x-5}+6$

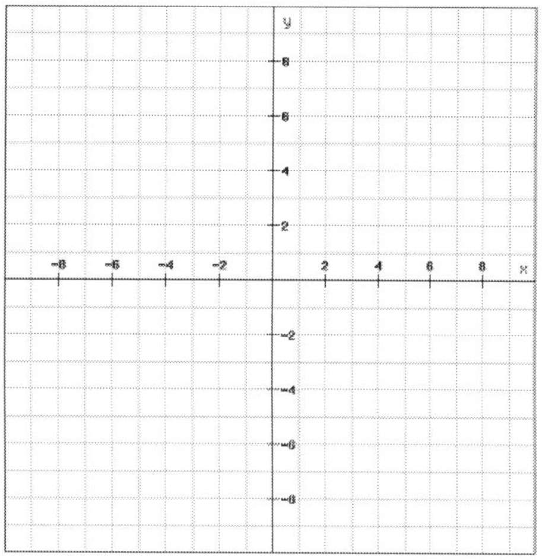

Domain: __________ x intercept:(___, ___)

Range: ___________

Increases: _________

Decreases: ________ y intercept:(___, ___)

Max/Min:(___, ___)

18. f(x) = $-\sqrt{-x+2}-8$

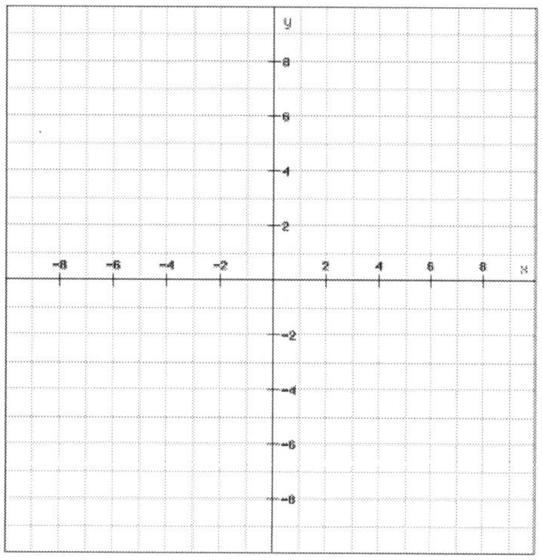

Domain: __________ x intercept:(___, ___)

Range: ___________

Increases: _________

Decreases: ________ y intercept:(___, ___)

Max/Min:(___, ___)

19. f(x) = $\sqrt{x}-5$

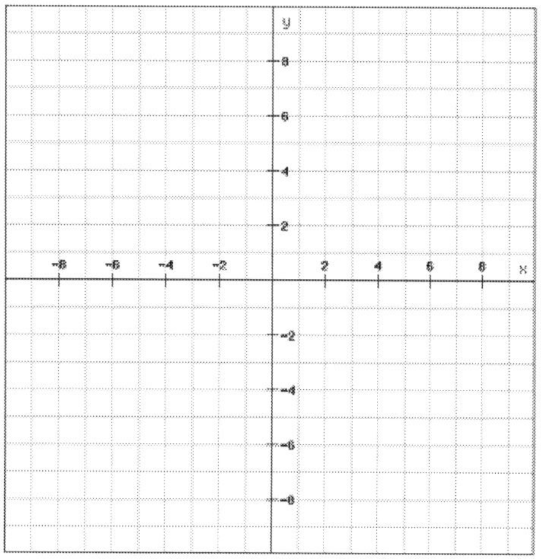

Domain: __________ x intercept:(___, ___)

Range: ___________

Increases: _________

Decreases: ________ y intercept:(___, ___)

Max/Min:(___, ___)

2.9. – HYBRID (OR PIECEWISE) FUNCTIONS

1. Analyze a function means that we should discuss the following:

    a. Domain
    b. Range
    c. Interceptions (x and y)
    d. Asymptotes
    e. Critical Points (max, min)
    f. Write in all forms
    g. Decrease and increase intervals
    h. Sketch
    i. Continuity

Analyze the following functions:

2. $f(x) = \begin{cases} -x & x < 0 \\ x & 0 \le x \end{cases}$

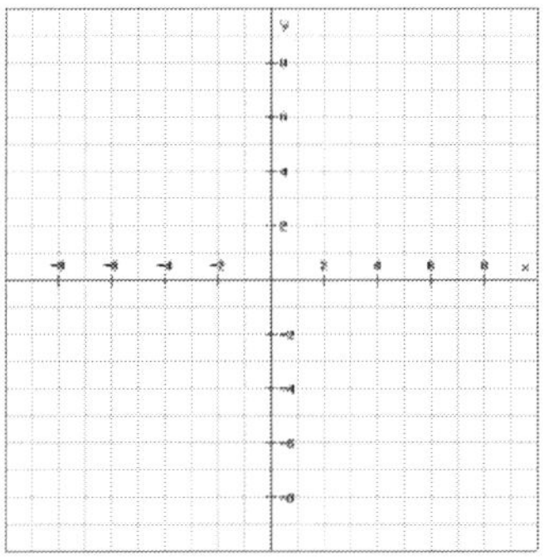

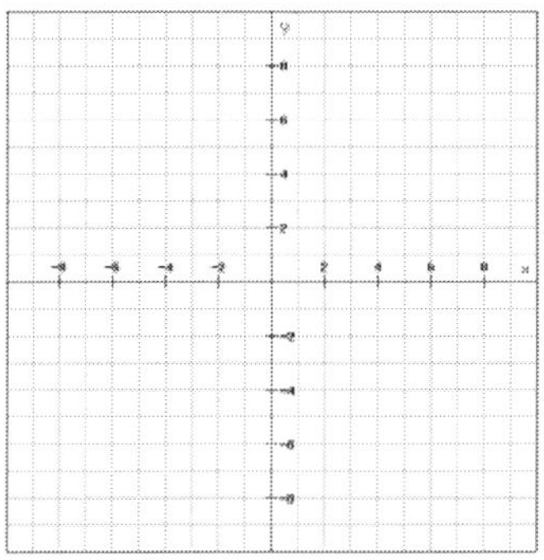

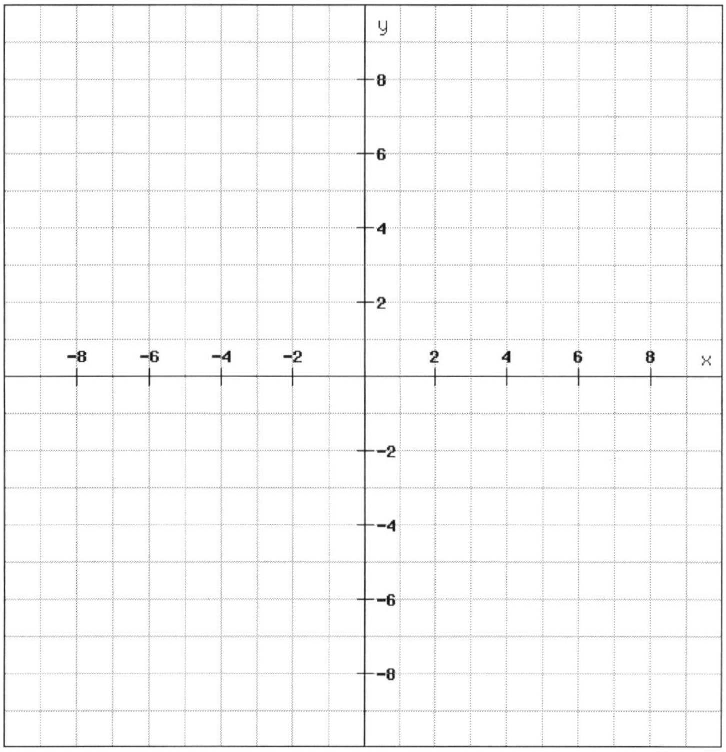

3. $f(x) = \begin{cases} -x & x < 2 \\ x & 2 \leq x \end{cases}$

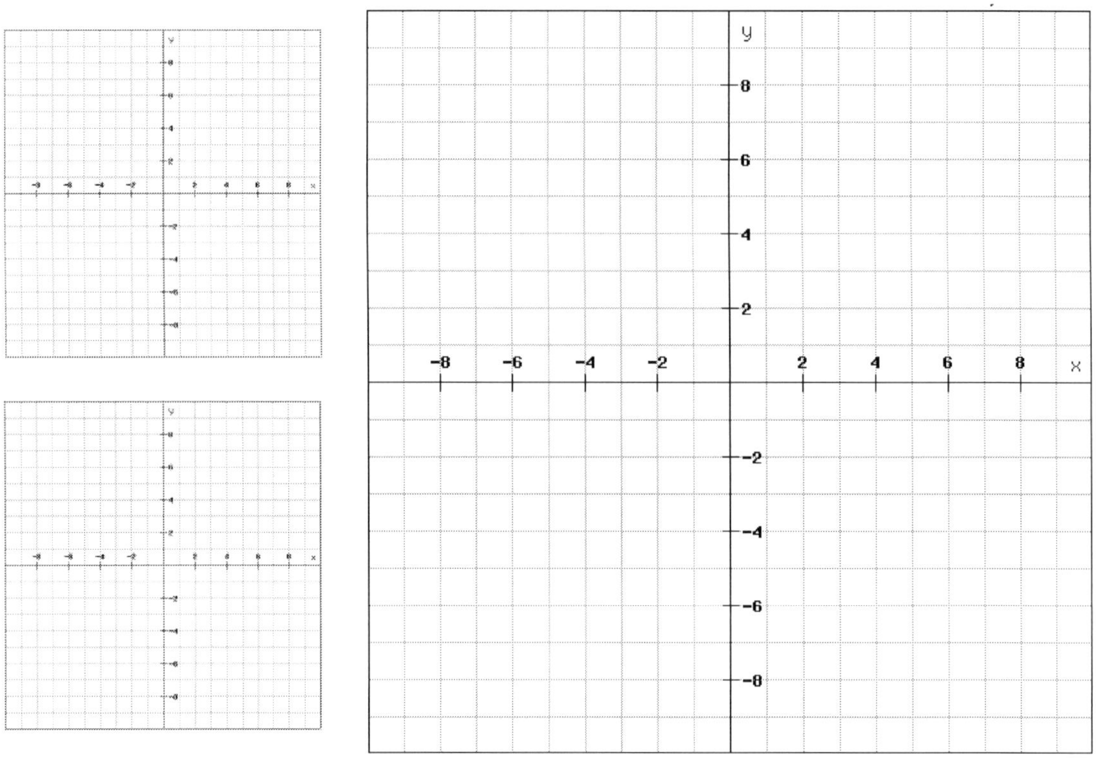

4. $f(x) = \begin{cases} 3 & x < -3 \\ x^2 & -3 \leq x \end{cases}$

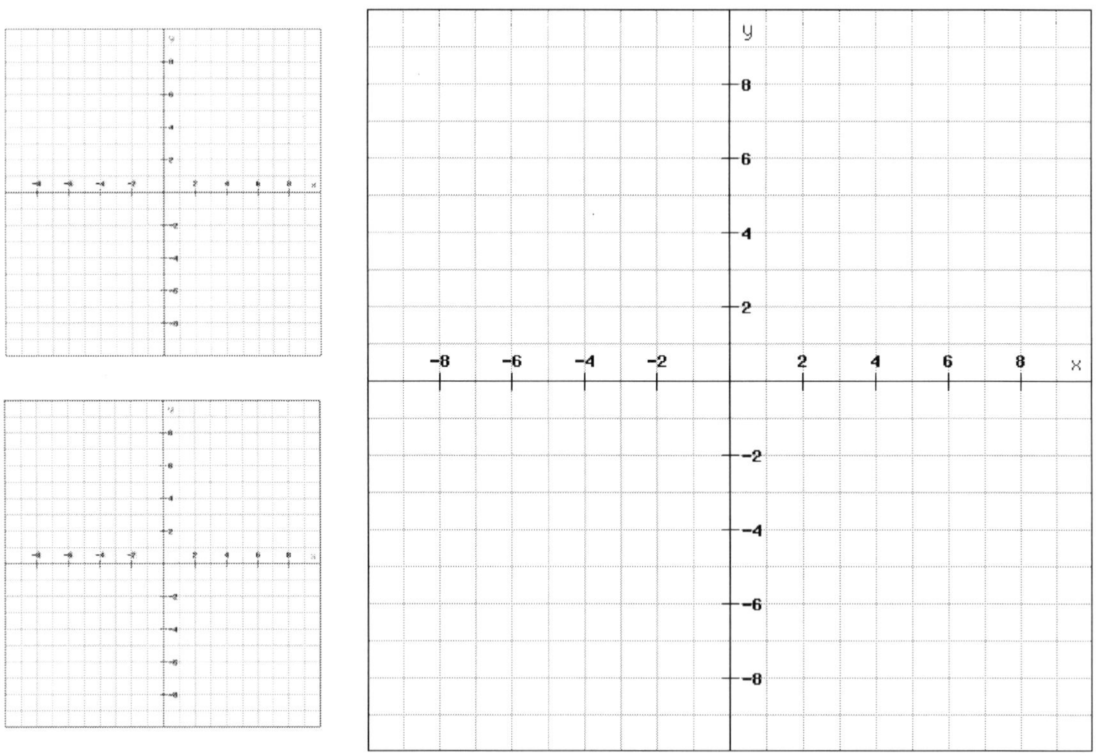

5. $f(x) = \begin{cases} 3x & x \le 2 \\ -x^2 - 2 & 2 < x \end{cases}$

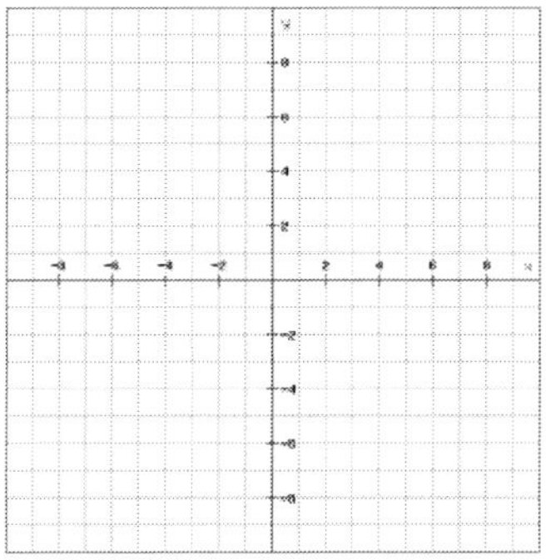

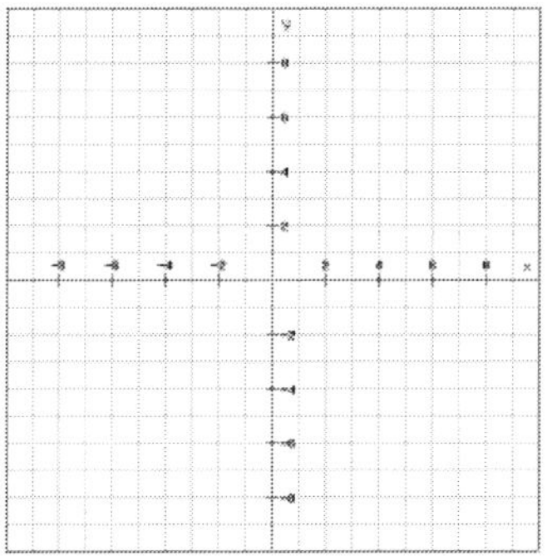

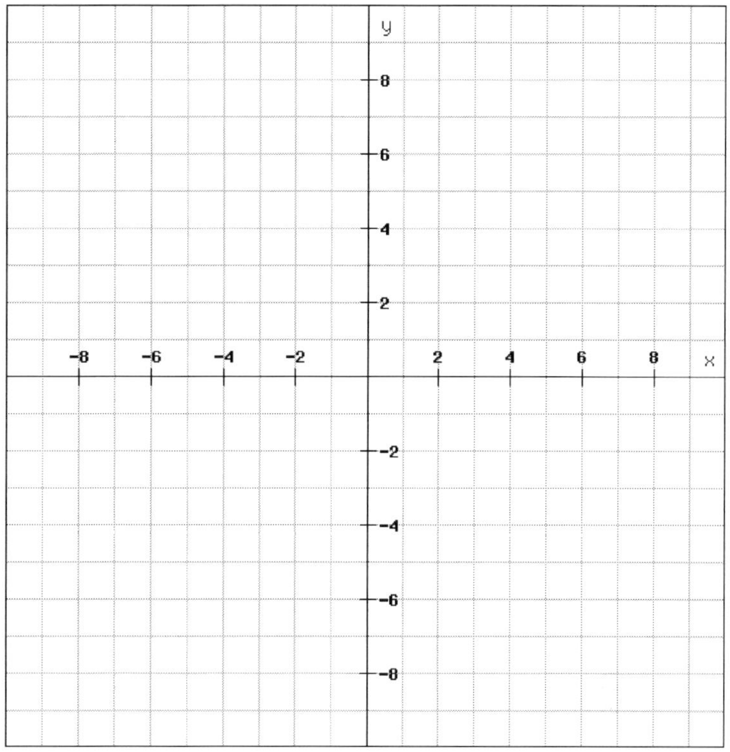

6. $f(x) = \begin{cases} e^x & x \le 2 \\ -(x-2)^2 & 2 < x \end{cases}$

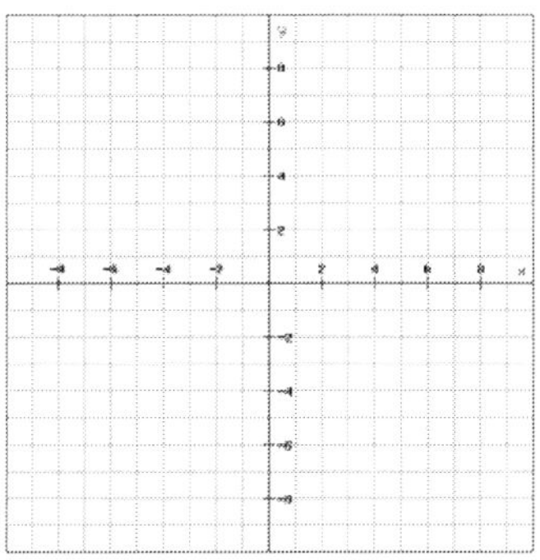

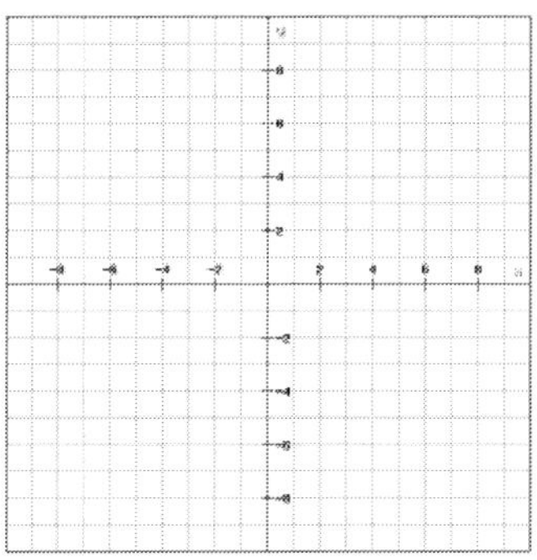

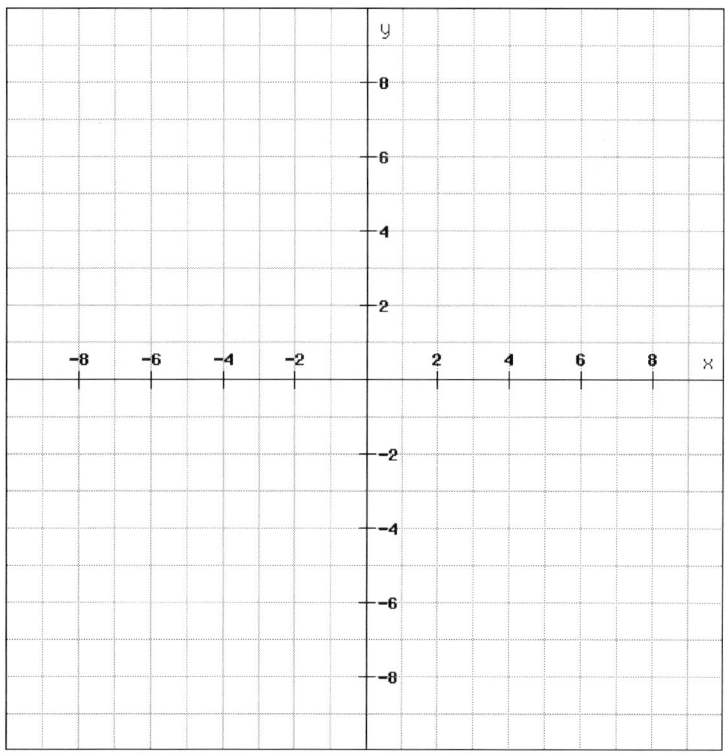

7. $f(x) = \begin{cases} -2^{x} & x \leq -3 \\ (x+1)^2 - 2 & -3 < x \end{cases}$

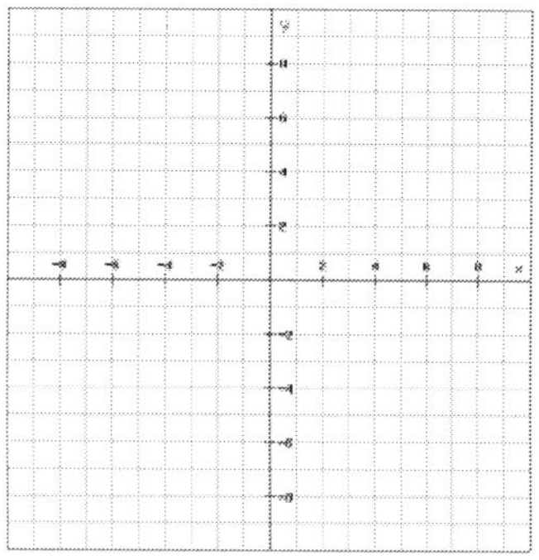

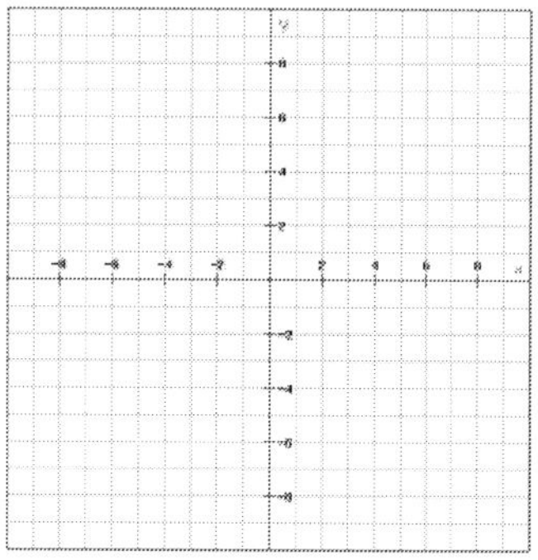

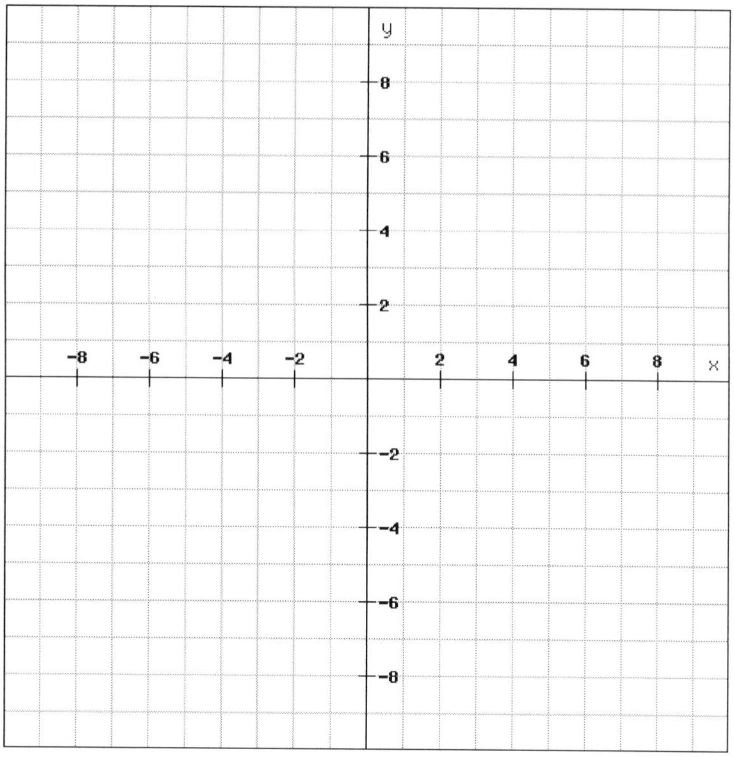

8. $f(x) = \begin{cases} x & x < 2 \\ x^2 - 1 & 2 \leq x \end{cases}$

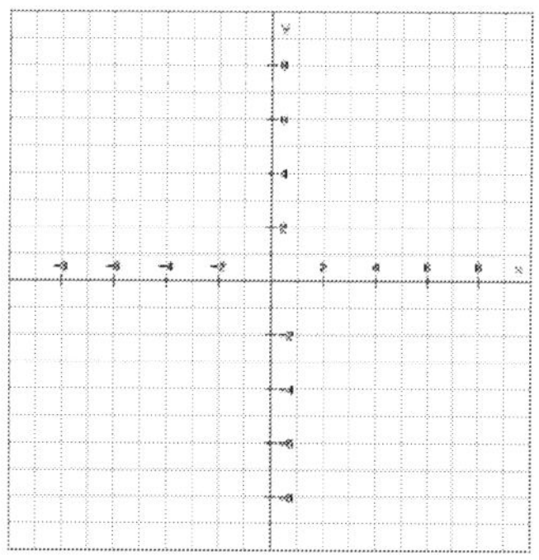

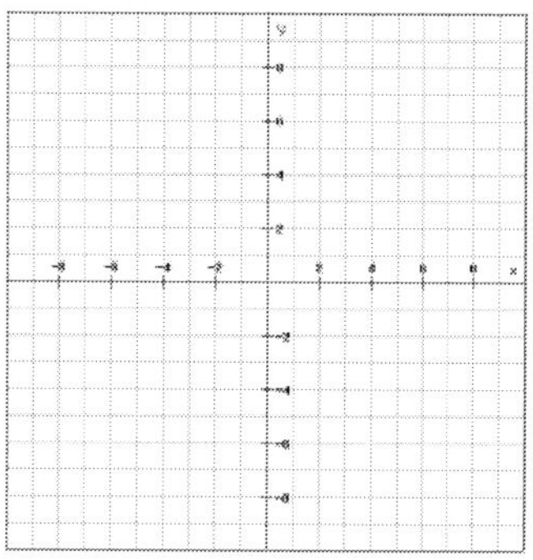

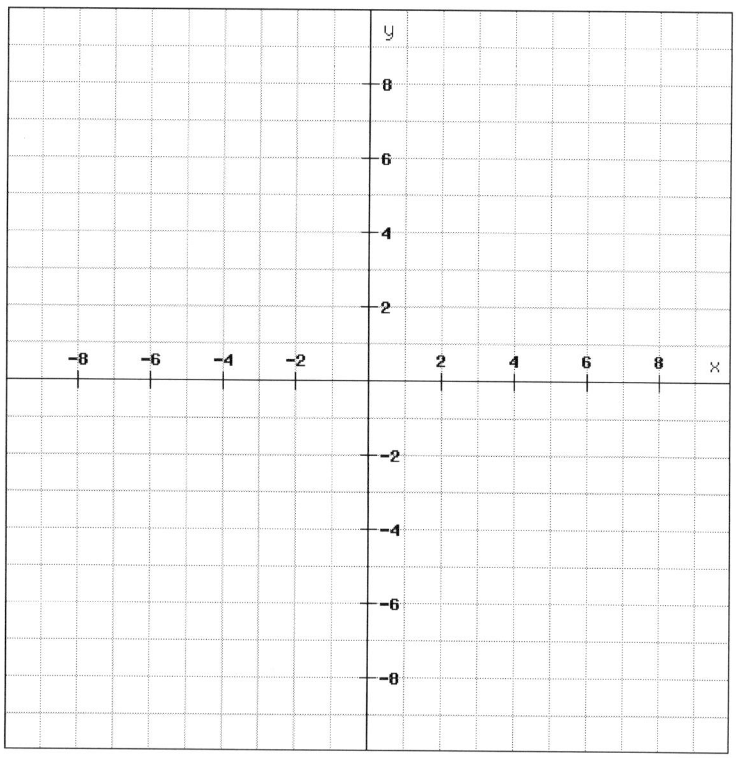

9. $f(x) = \begin{cases} -x^2 + 3 & x < -2 \\ x^2 - 1 & -2 \le x \end{cases}$

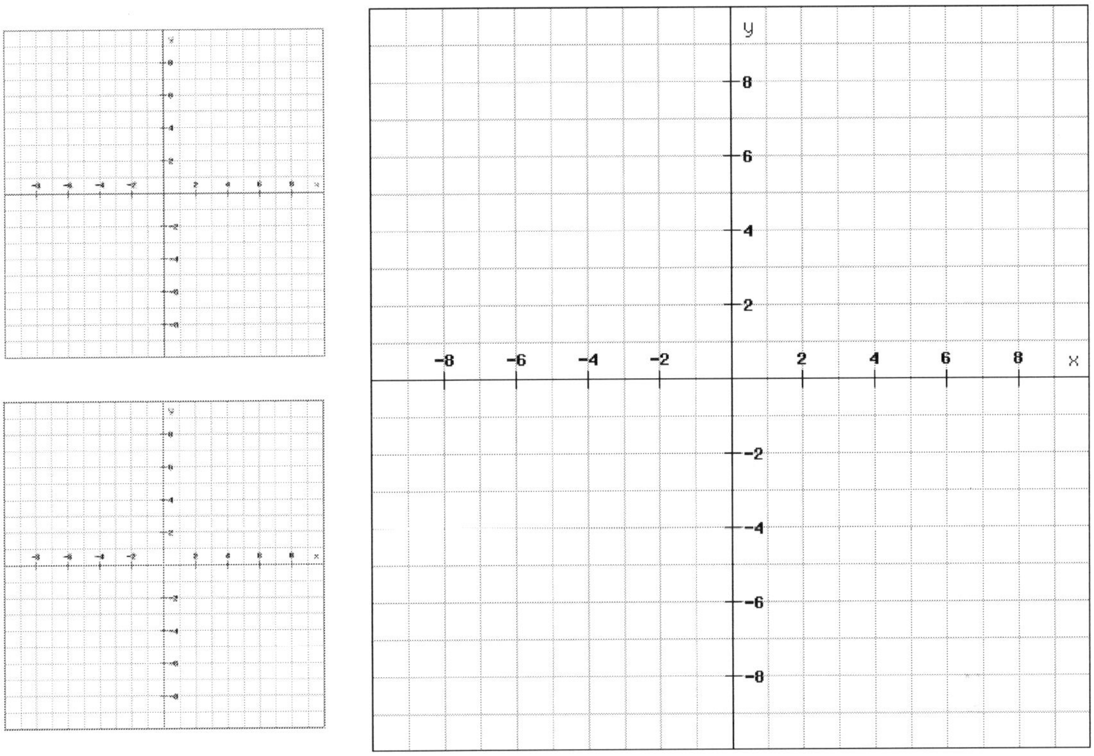

10. $f(x) = \begin{cases} -2x^2 + 47 & x < -5 \\ x + 2 & -5 \le x \end{cases}$

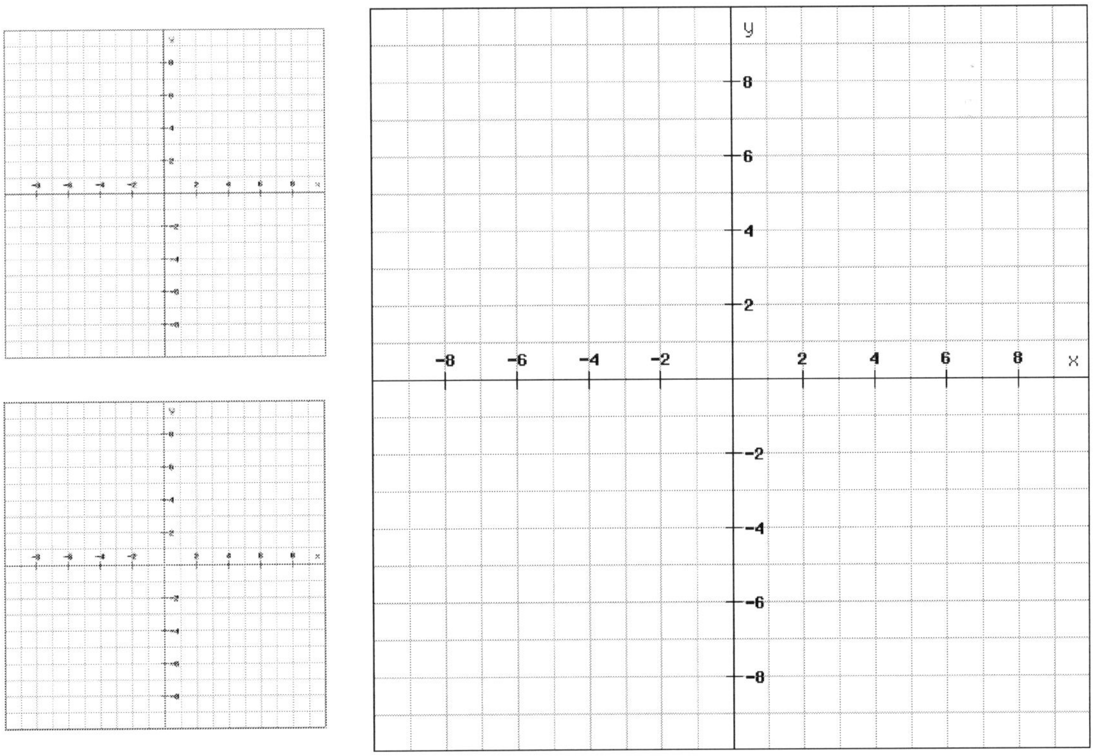

11. $f(x) = \begin{cases} x & x < 3 \\ \ln(x) & 3 < x \end{cases}$

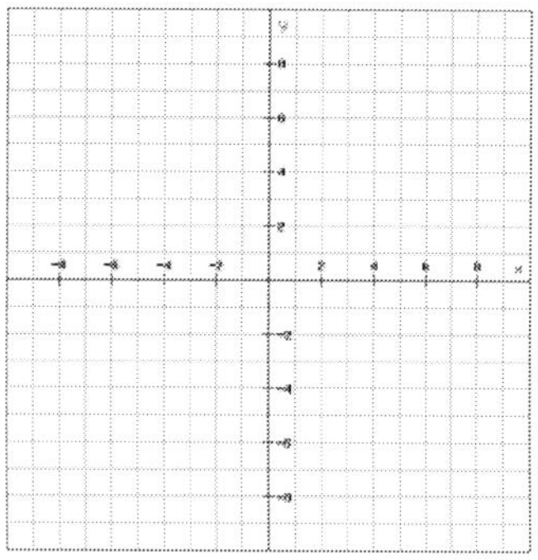

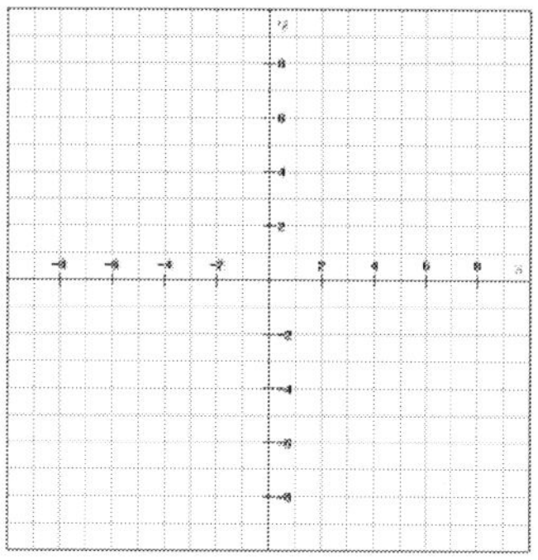

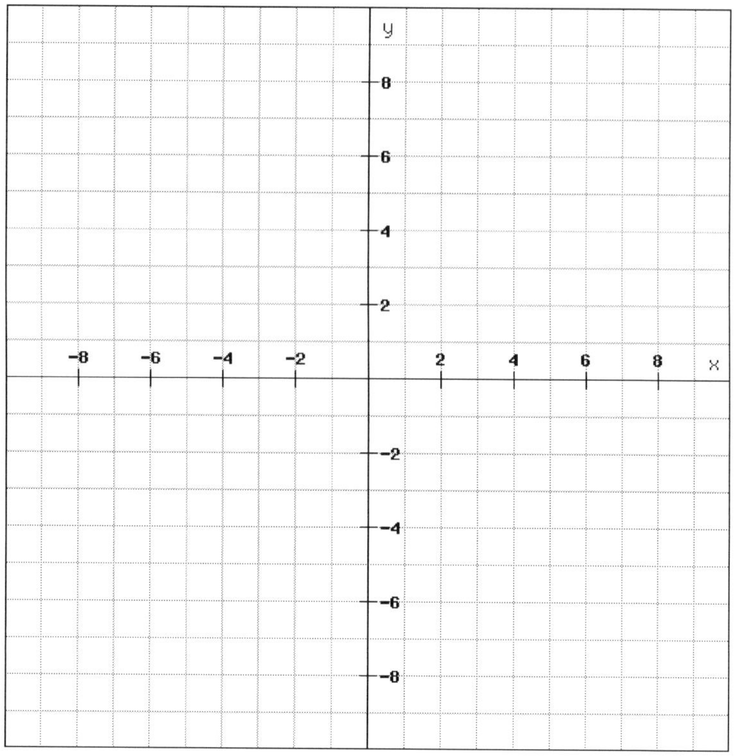

12. $f(x) = \begin{cases} x - \dfrac{8}{3} & x < 3 \\ \dfrac{1}{x} & 3 \le x \end{cases}$

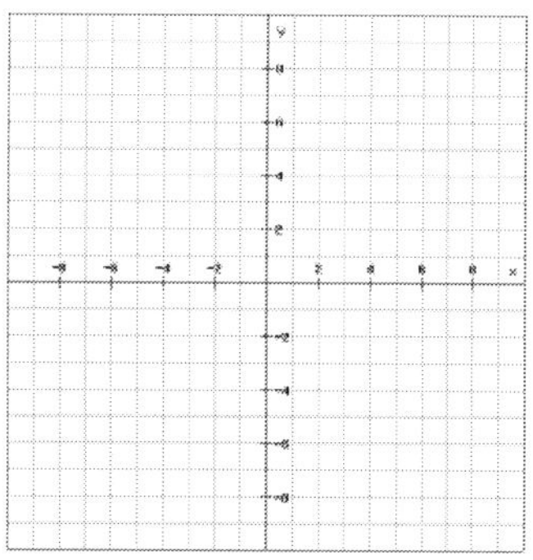

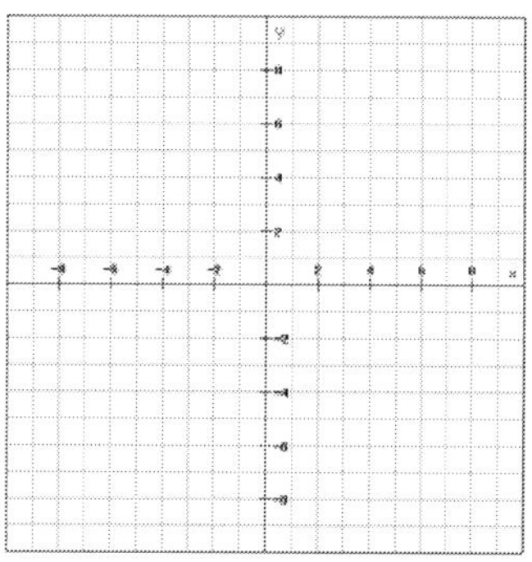

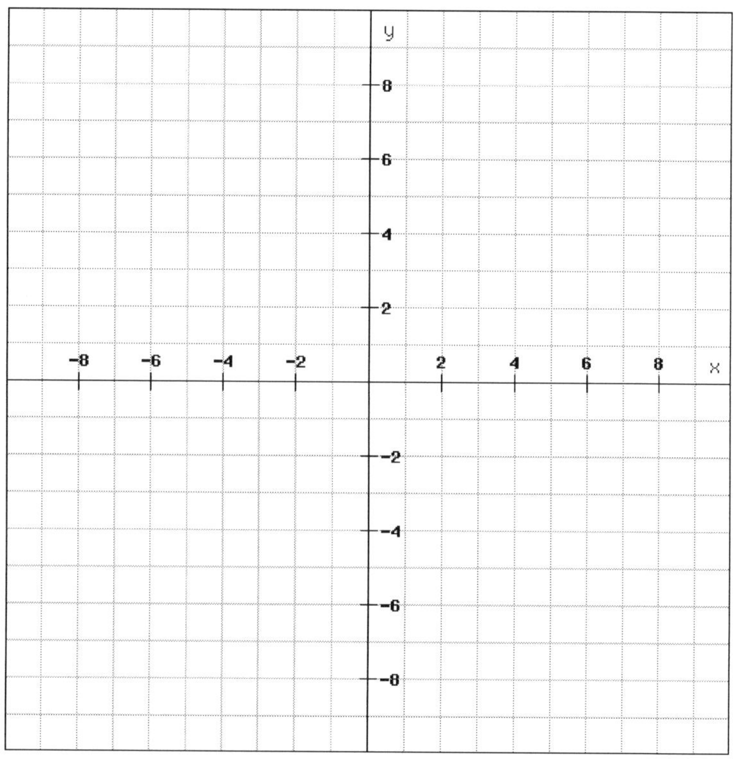

13. $$f(x) = \begin{cases} \dfrac{1}{x+1} & x \le 2 \\ \dfrac{1}{x} & 2 < x \end{cases}$$

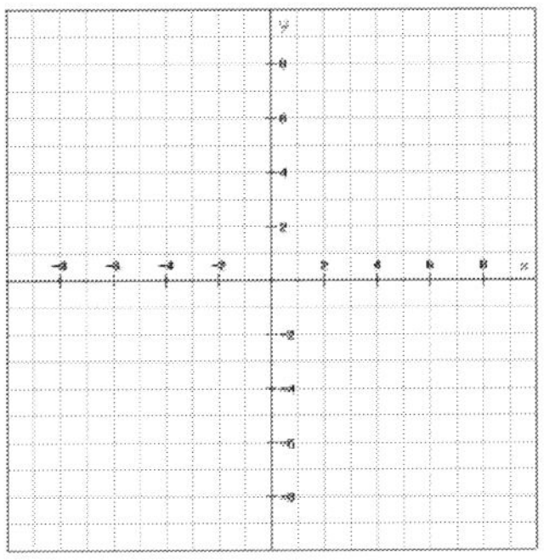

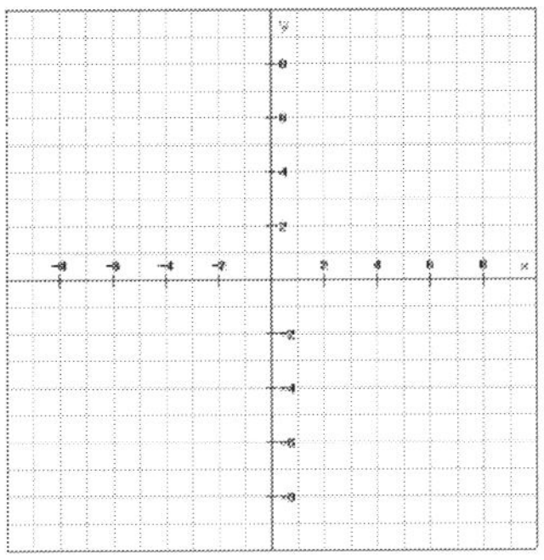

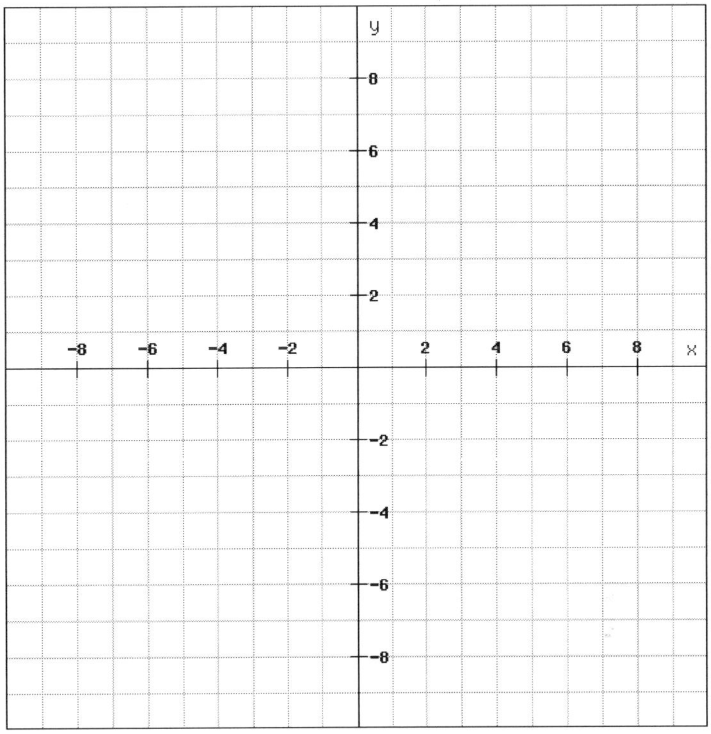

14. $$f(x) = \begin{cases} \dfrac{1}{x+1} & x < \dfrac{-1}{2} \\ \dfrac{1}{x} & \dfrac{-1}{2} < x \end{cases}$$

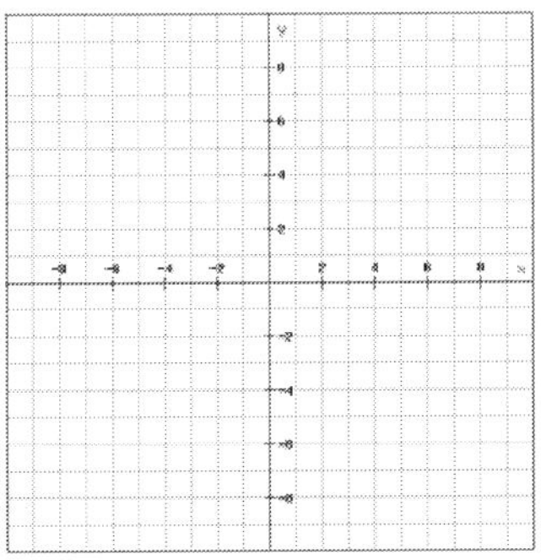

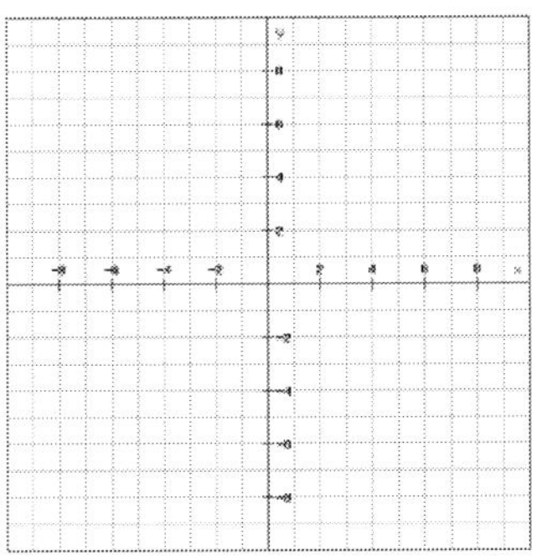

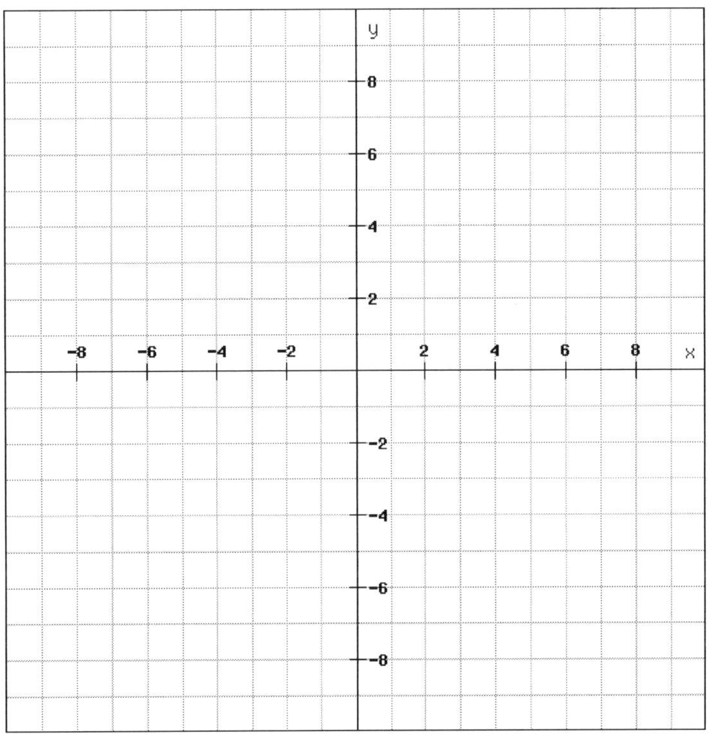

15. $f(x) = \begin{cases} \dfrac{1}{x-2} + 2 & x < 3 \\ \ln(x) & 3 \le x \end{cases}$

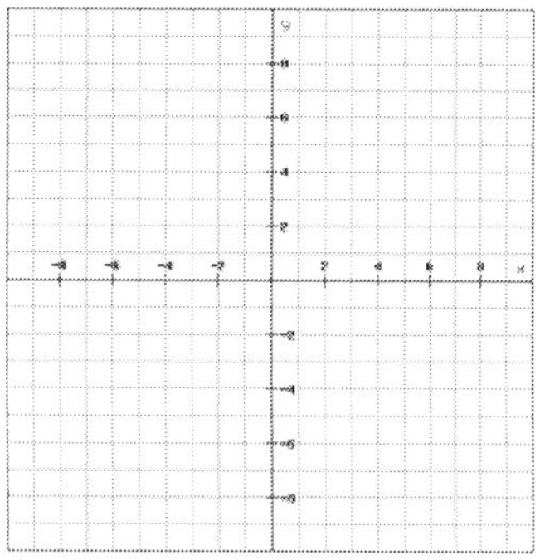

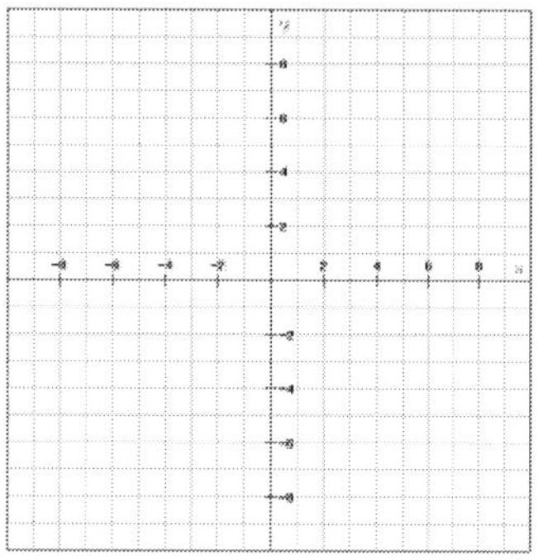

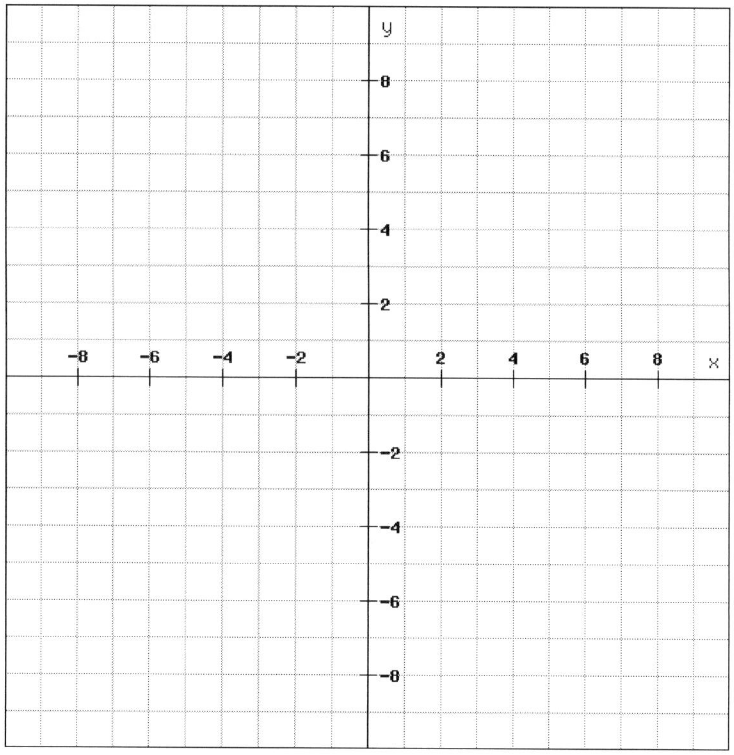

16. $f(x) = \begin{cases} e^{x} + 2 & x < -2 \\ \dfrac{1}{x} - 2 & -2 \le x \end{cases}$

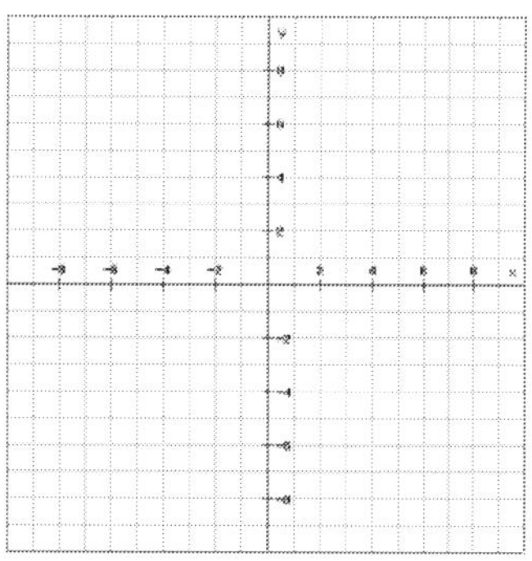

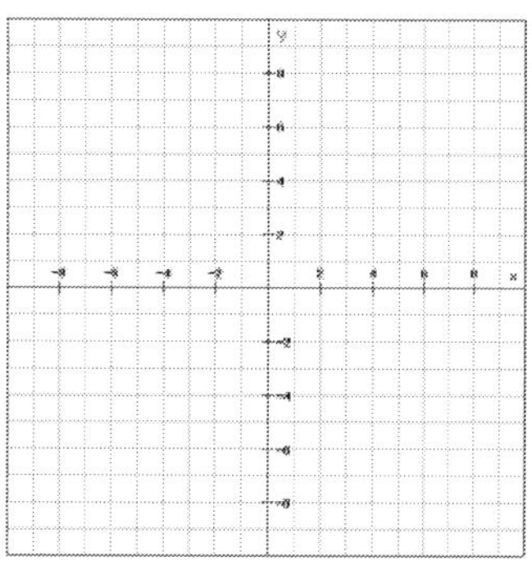

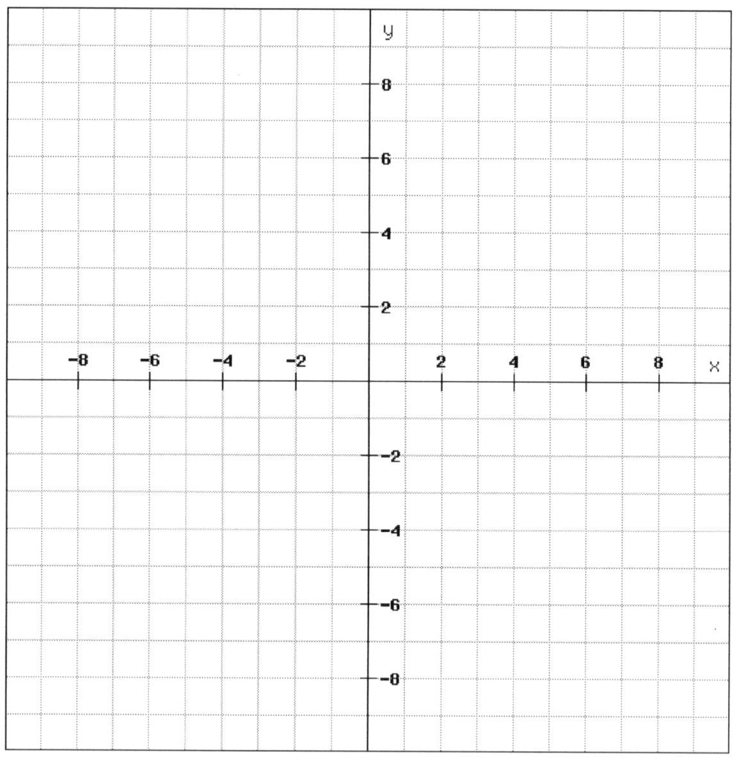

17. $f(x) = \begin{cases} e^{(-x)} - 2 & x < 1 \\ \dfrac{1}{x-2} + 1 & 1 \le x \end{cases}$

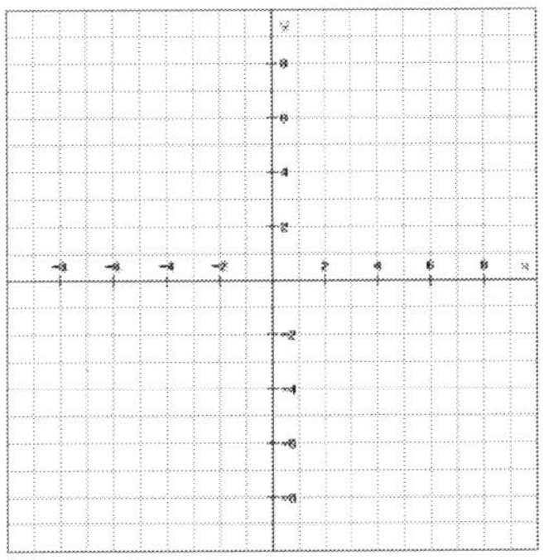

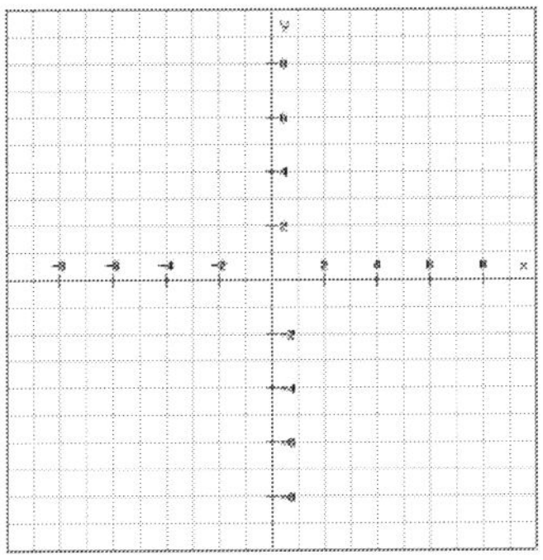

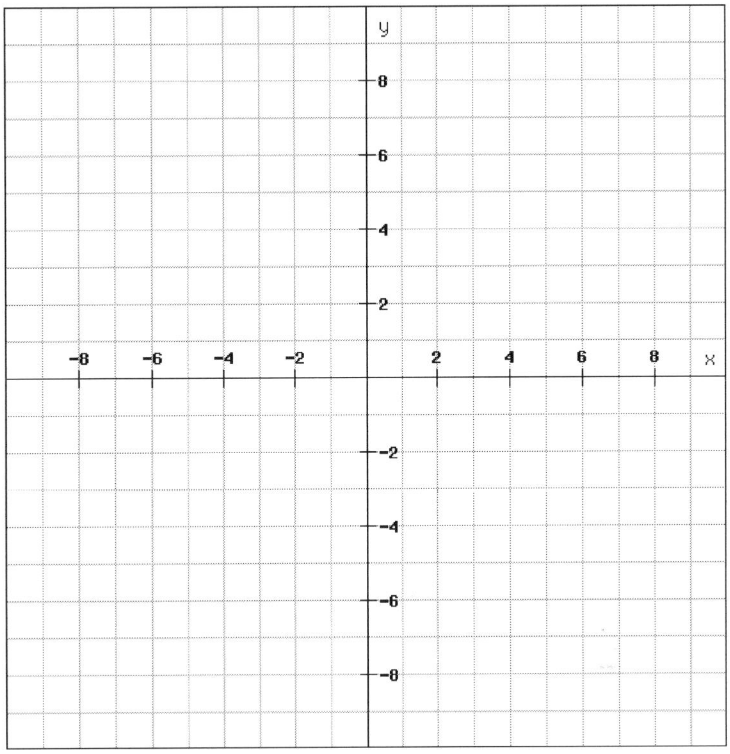

18. $f(x) = \begin{cases} -x^2 - 2 & x < 1 \\ \dfrac{1}{-3+x} & 1 \le x \end{cases}$

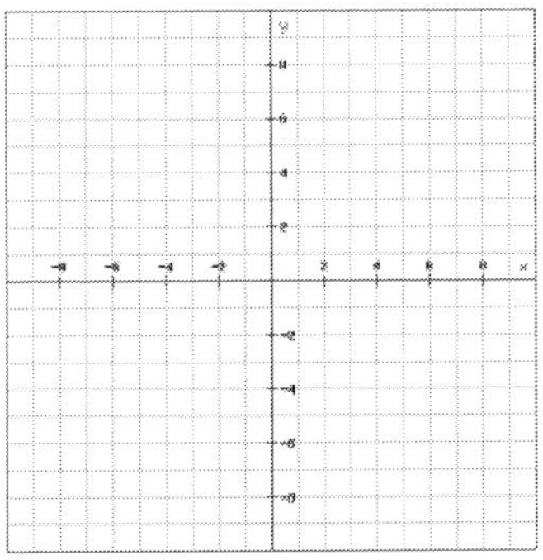

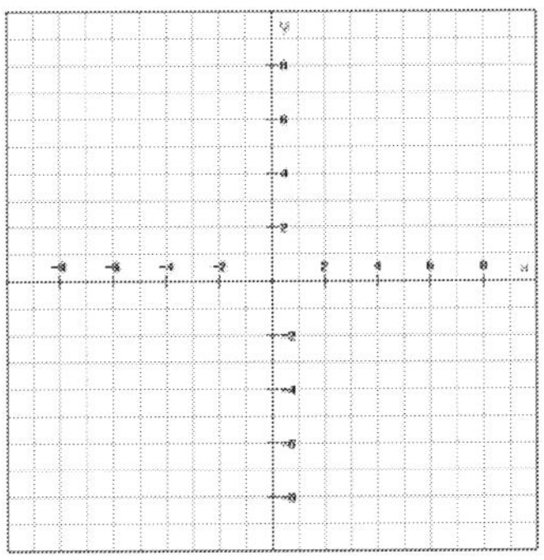

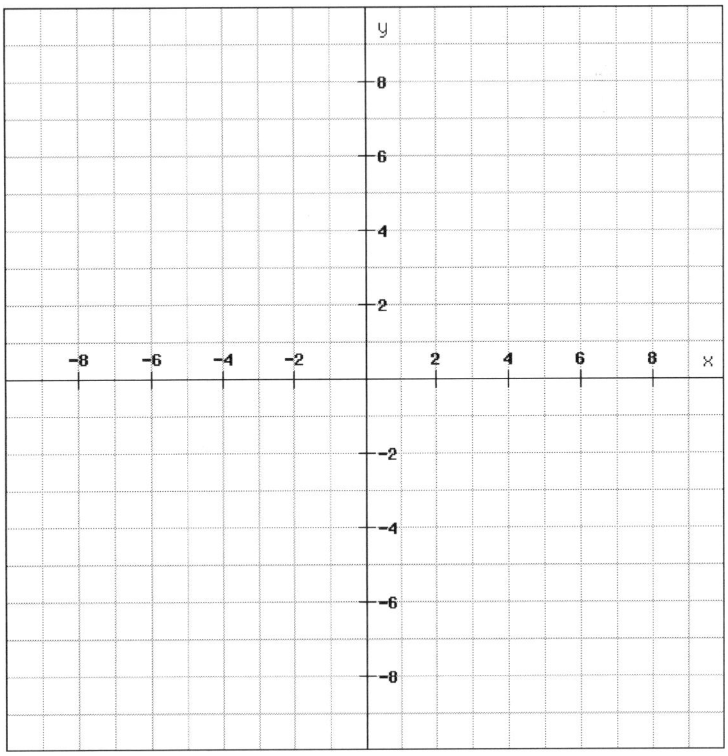

19. $f(x) = \begin{cases} x^2 + 3 & x < 2 \\ \ln(3 + x) & 2 \le x \end{cases}$

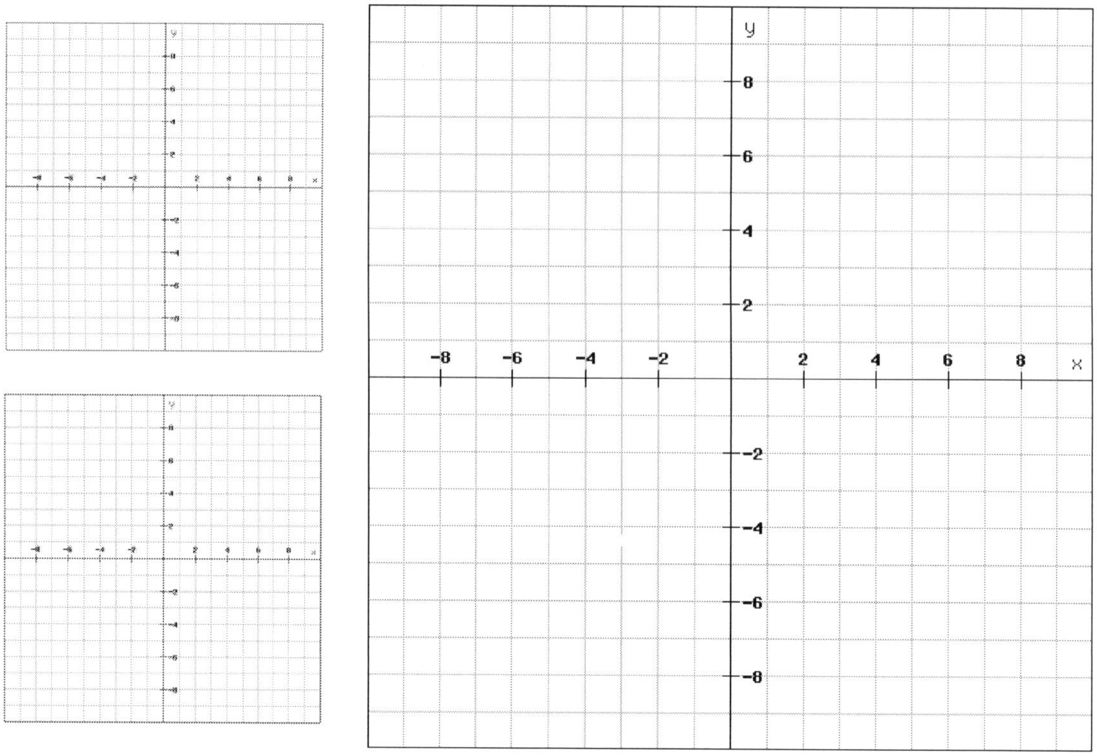

20. $f(x) = \begin{cases} x^2 + 3 & x < 2 \\ \ln(-3 + x) & 2 \le x \end{cases}$

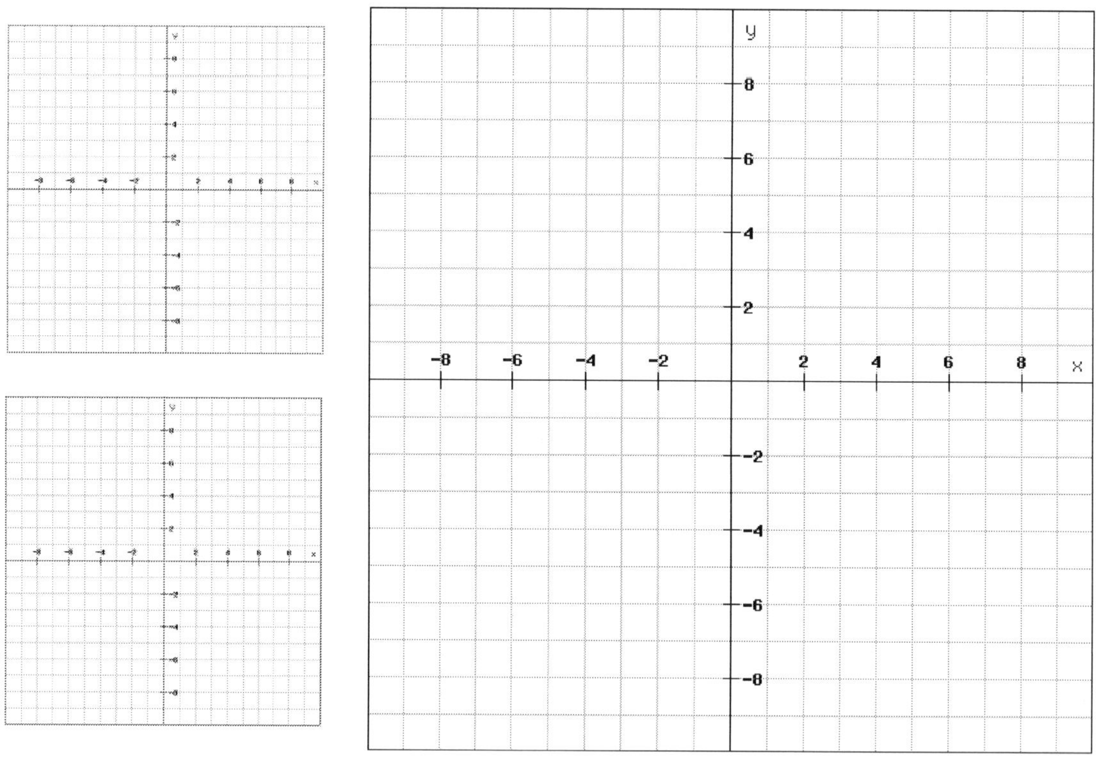

21. $$f(x) = \begin{cases} 3x - 2 & x < 0 \\ \ln(3 + x) - 1 & 0 \le x \end{cases}$$

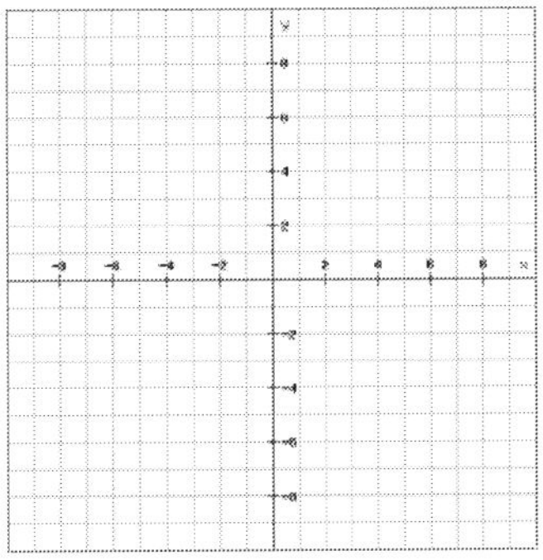

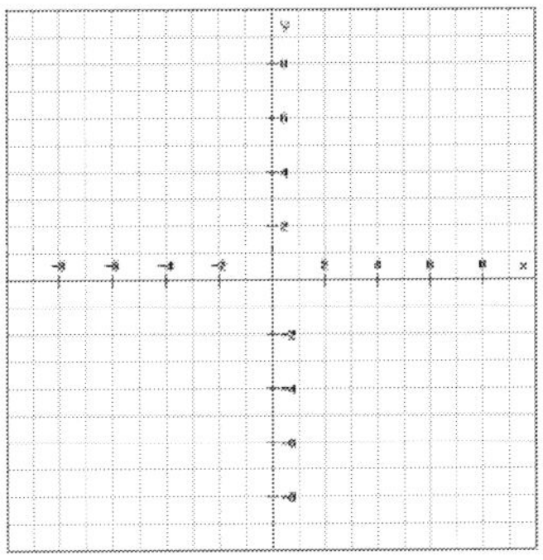

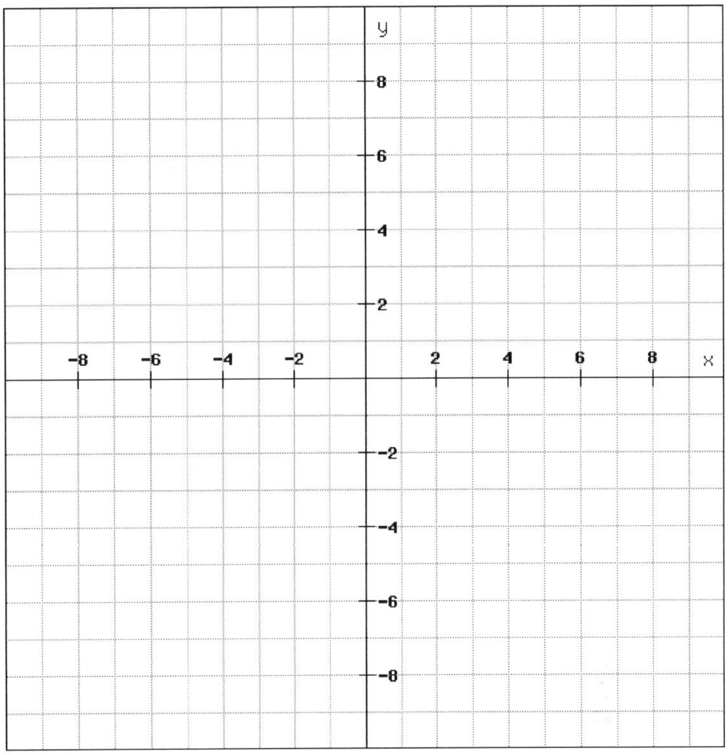

Find the value(s) of a for which the following functions will be continuous and then analyze the function:

22. $f(x) = \begin{cases} ax + 7 & x < -3 \\ x + 1 & -3 \le x \end{cases}$

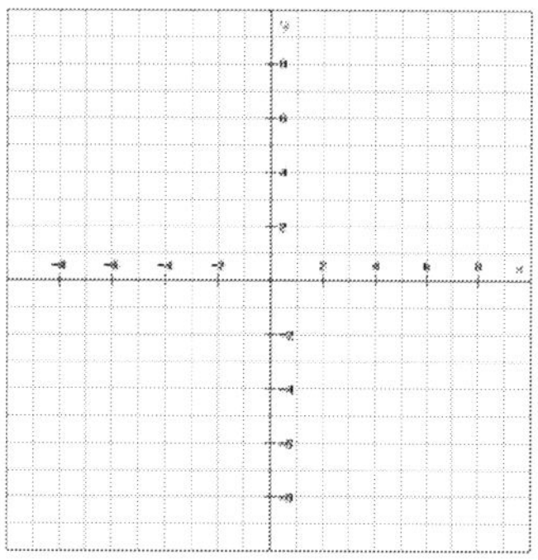

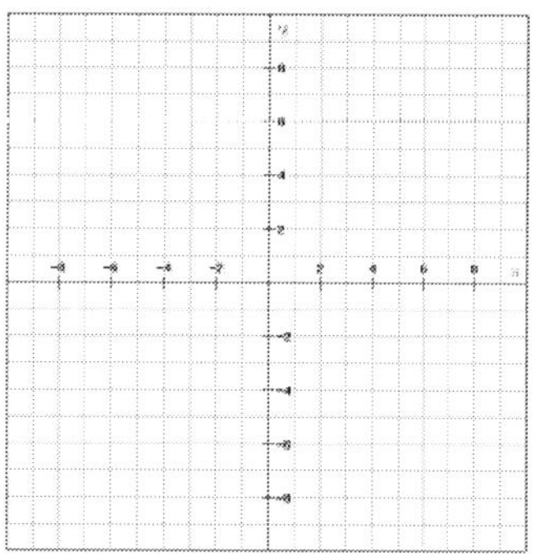

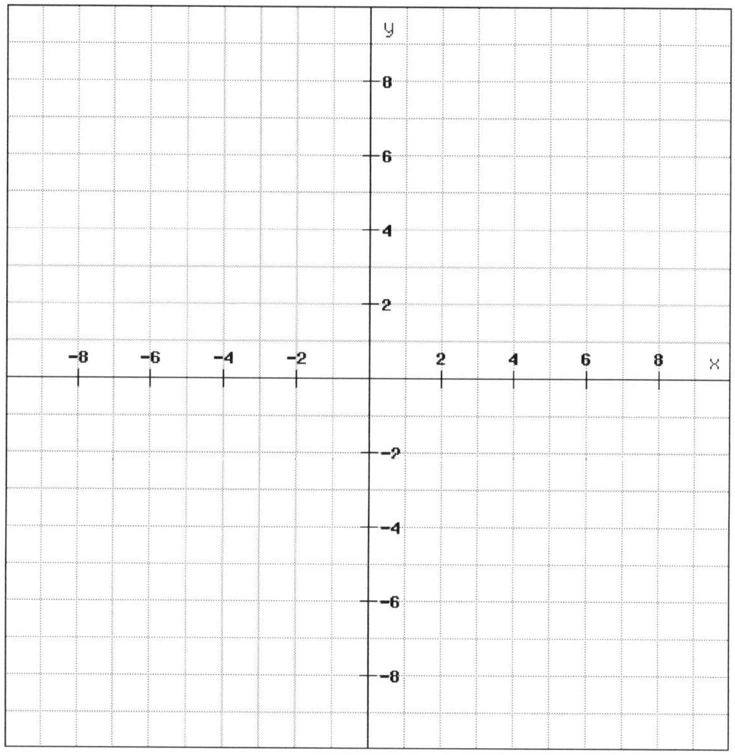

23. $f(x) = \begin{cases} a x^2 + 7 & x < -1 \\ 2x - 6 & -1 \le x \end{cases}$

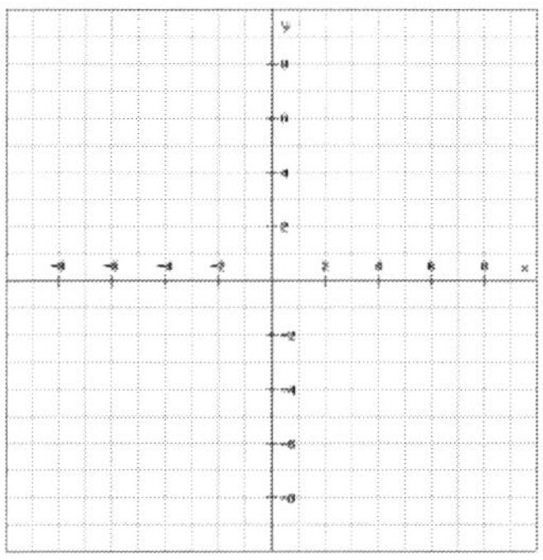

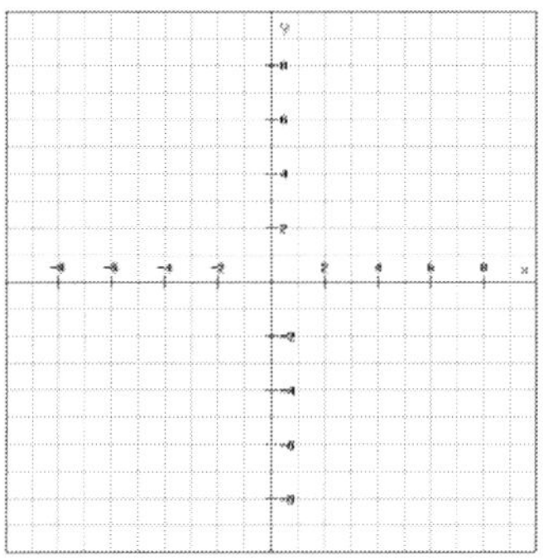

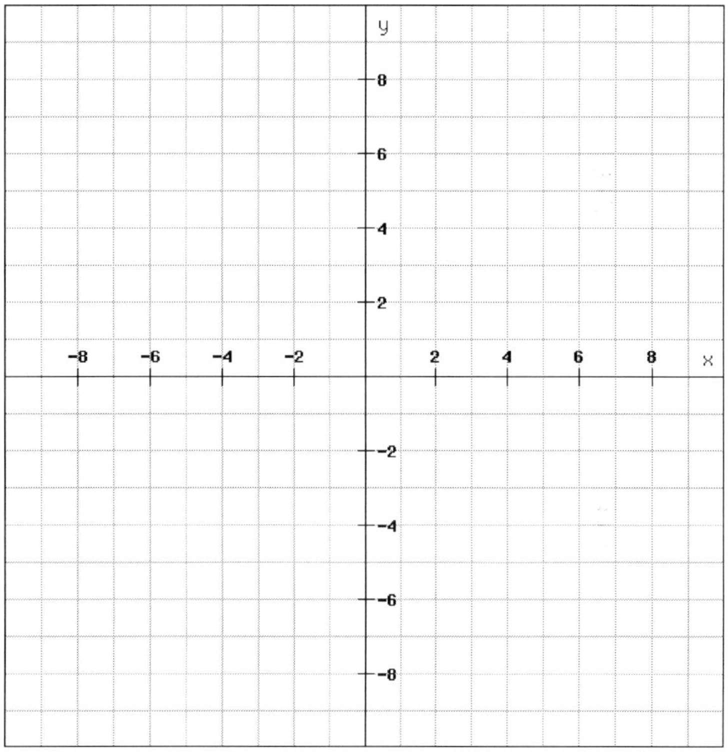

24. $$f(x) = \begin{cases} x^2 + a & x < -1 \\ 2x - 6 & -1 \le x \end{cases}$$

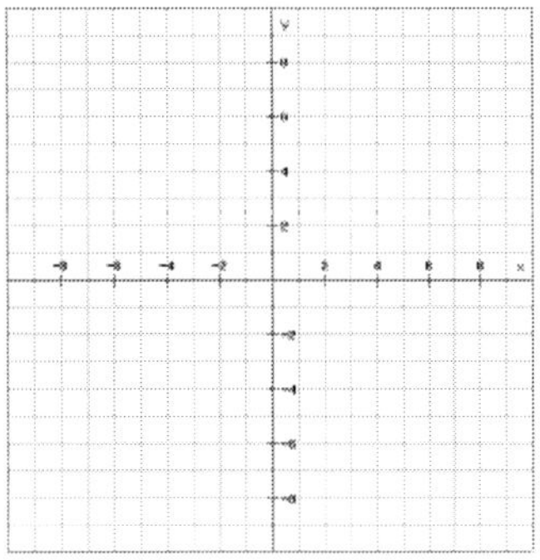

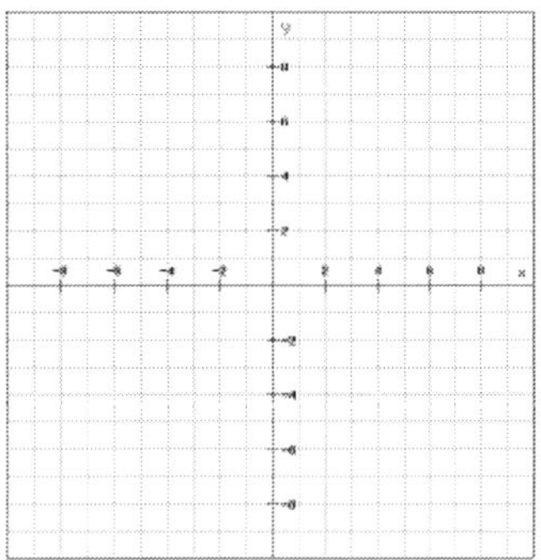

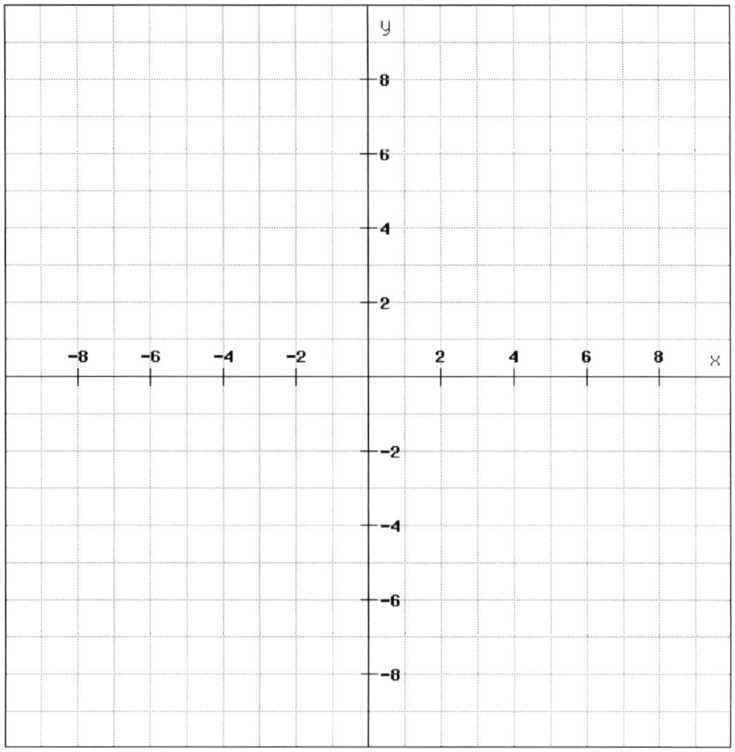

25. $$f(x) = \begin{cases} -x^2 + 2 & x < 3 \\ 2x^2 - a & 3 \le x \end{cases}$$

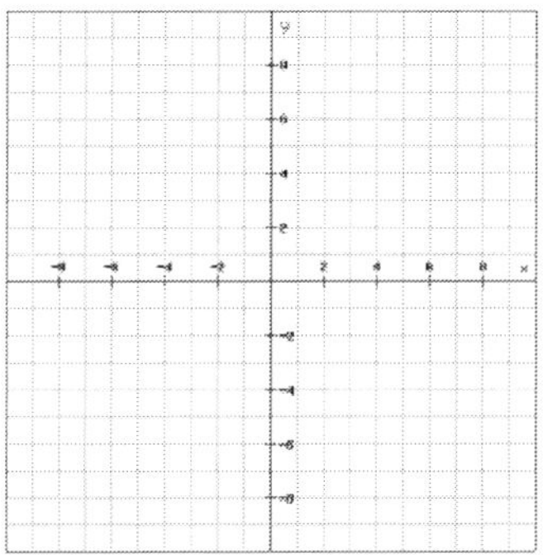

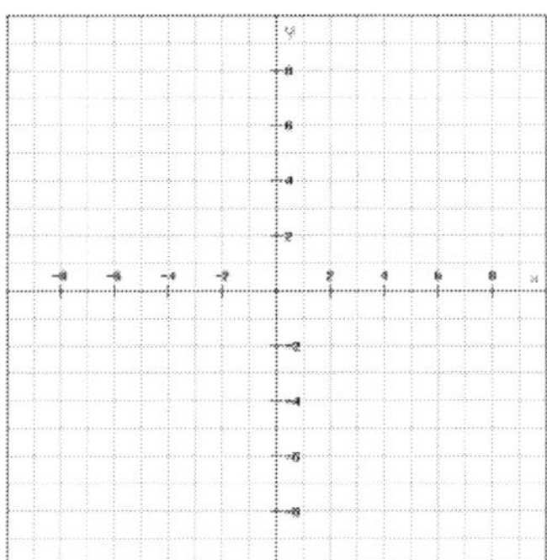

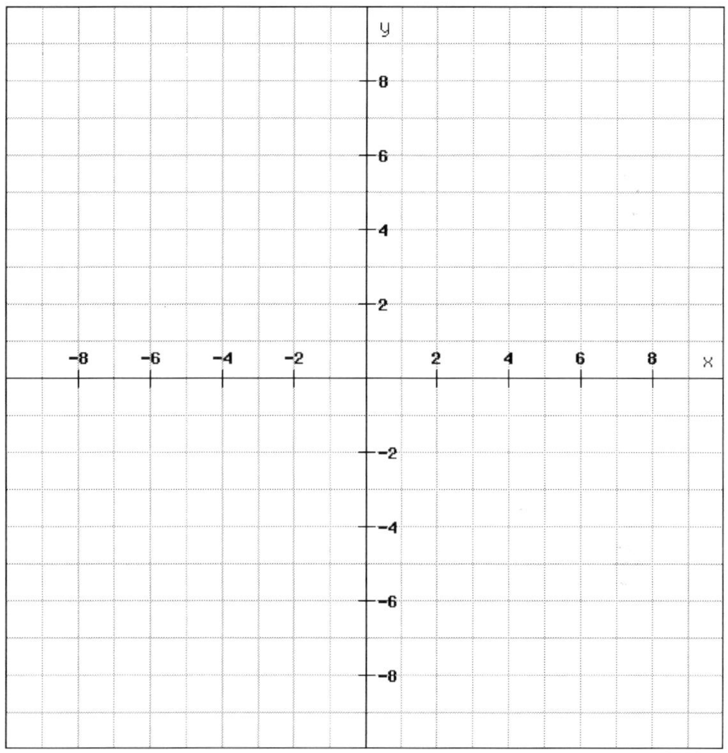

Analyze the following functions:

26. $f(x)=\begin{cases}\sqrt{x}-1 & x<2\\ \dfrac{2}{x}+1 & 2\le x\end{cases}$

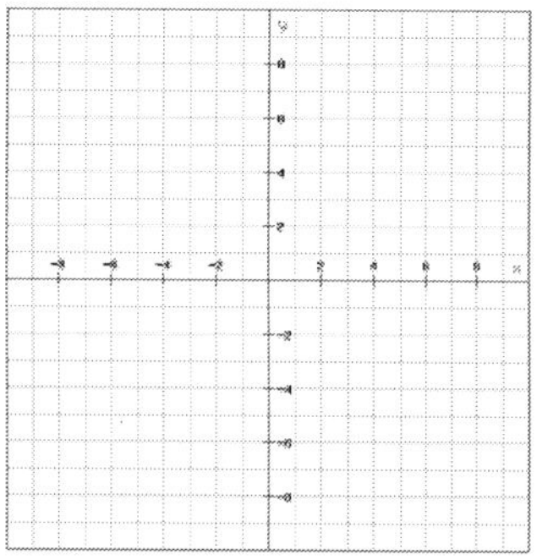

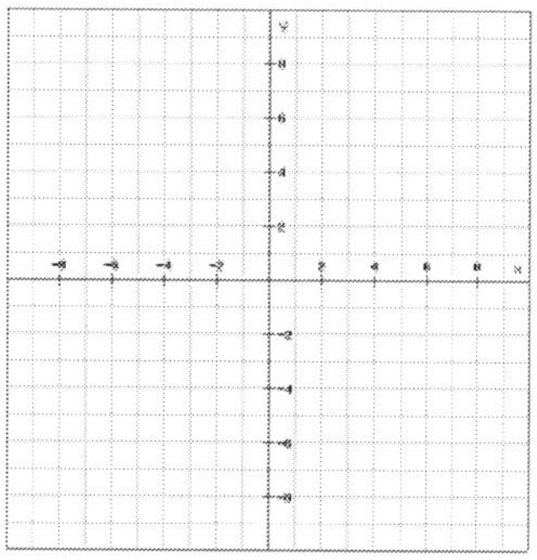

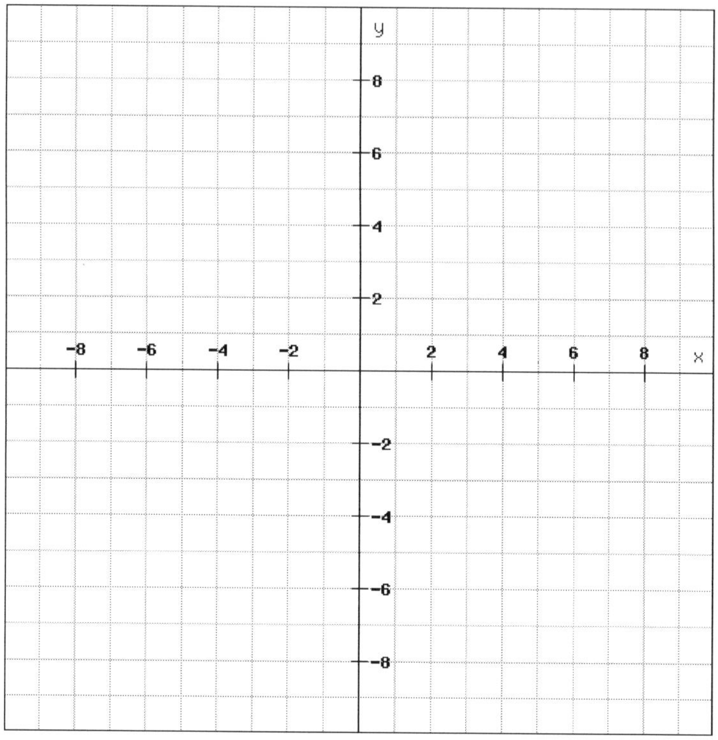

27. $f(x)=\begin{cases}\sqrt{x+2}-2 & x<7\\ \dfrac{16}{x+1}-1 & 7\le x\end{cases}$

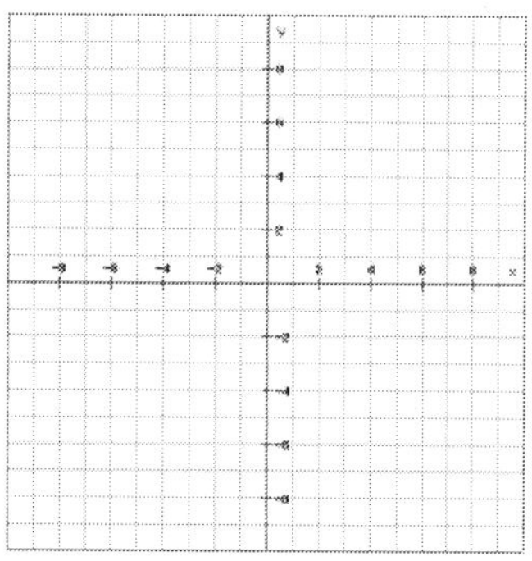

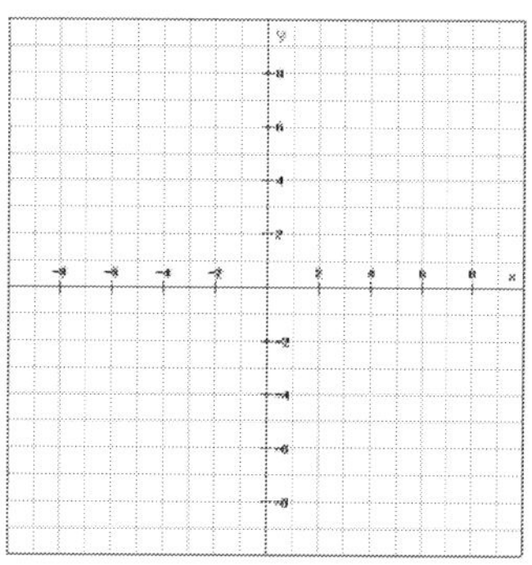

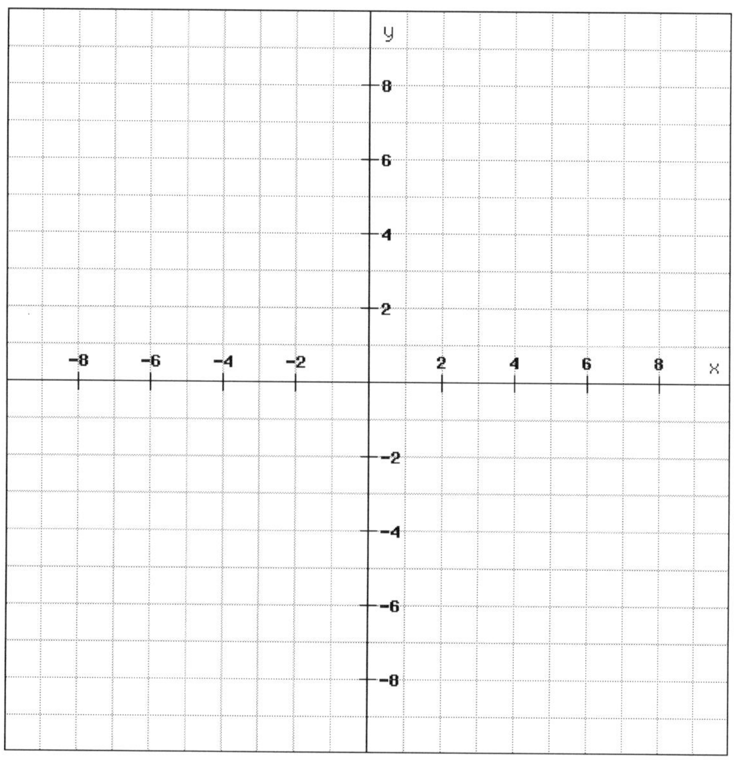

28. The sketch below shows the graph of a function y = f(x) between x = 0 and x = 6. The function f(x) is defined as follows

$$f(x) = \begin{cases} x & 0 < x \text{ and } x < 2 \\ a & 2 < x \text{ and } x < 3 \\ m\,x + b & 3 < x \text{ and } x < 6 \end{cases}$$

Where a, m and b are constants.

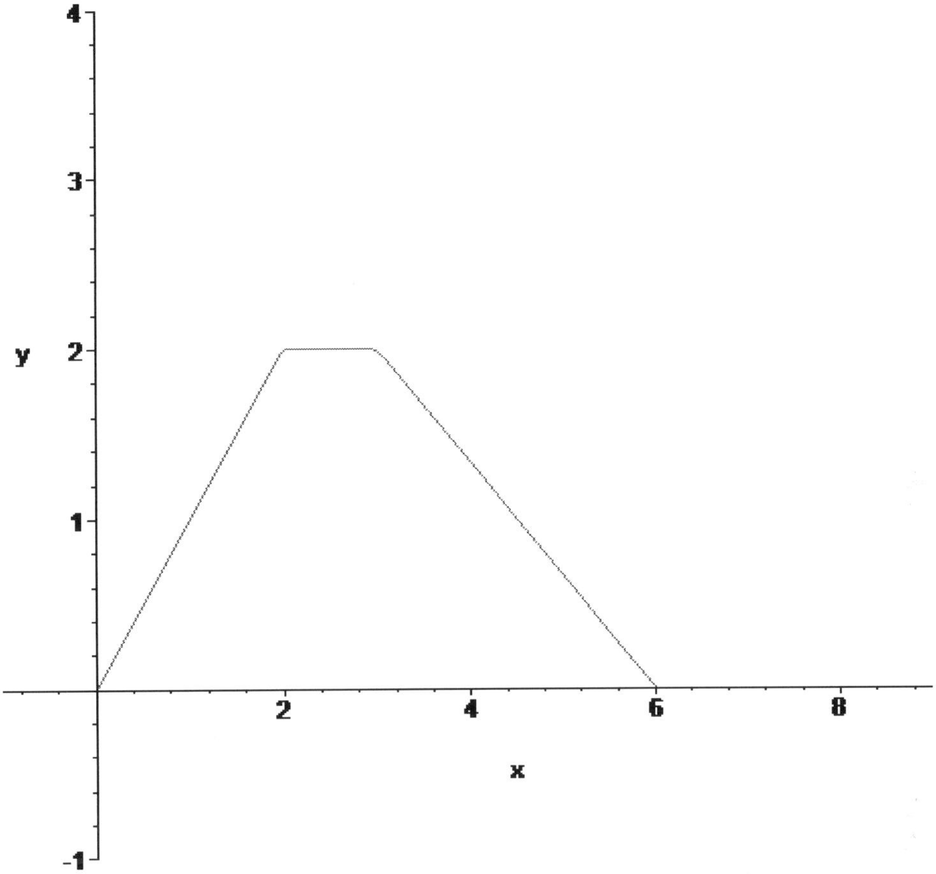

a. State the value of a.

b. Find the values of m and b

29. $$f(x) = \begin{cases} -1 & x \le 5 \\ 1 & 5 < x \text{ and } x < 6 \\ 2 & 6 \le x \end{cases}$$

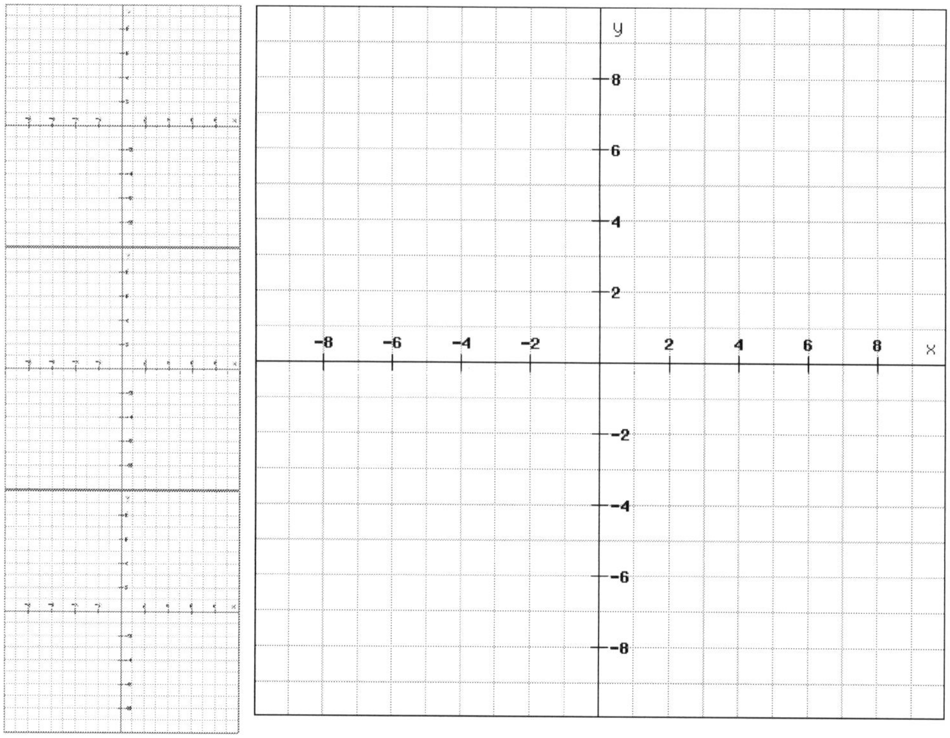

30. $$f(x) = \begin{cases} 2x + 7 & x < -6 \\ x + 1 & -6 \le x \text{ and } x < 2 \\ x^2 & 2 \le x \end{cases}$$

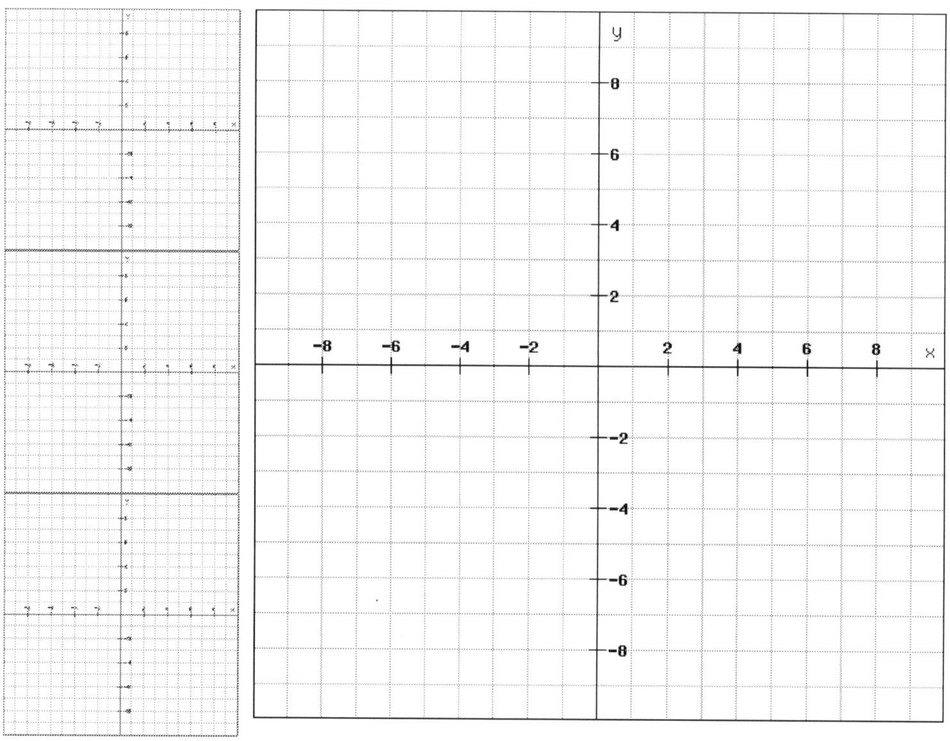

31. $f(x) = \begin{cases} -(3+x)^2 & x \le -2 \\ x^2 - 5 & -1 < x \text{ and } x < 1 \\ -2x - 5 & 1 \le x \end{cases}$

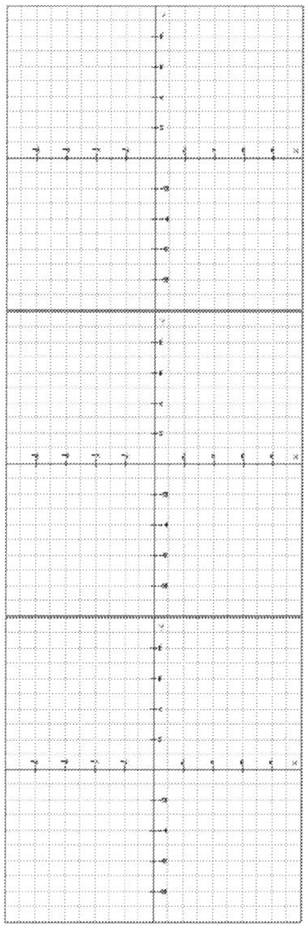

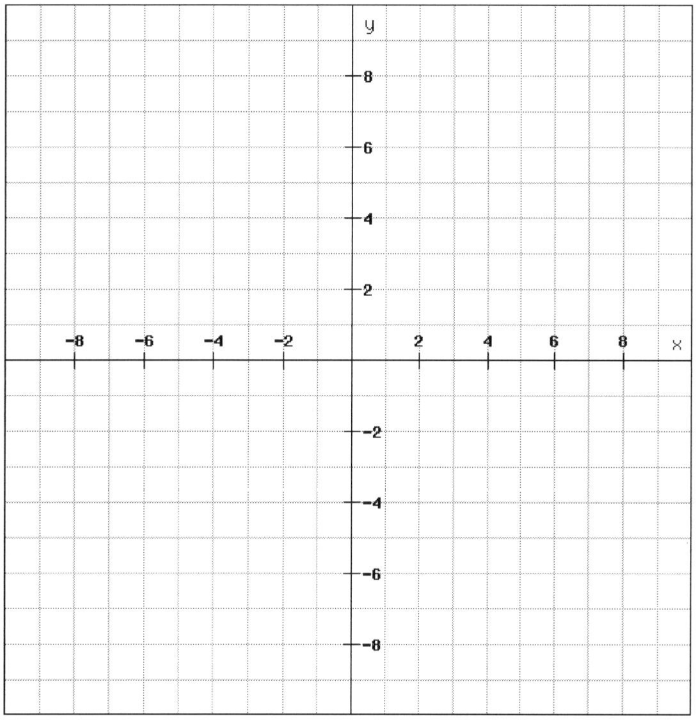

32. $f(x) = \begin{cases} 2x & x \le -3 \\ (x+2)^2 & -3 < x \text{ and } x \le 0 \\ \ln(x) & 0 < x \end{cases}$

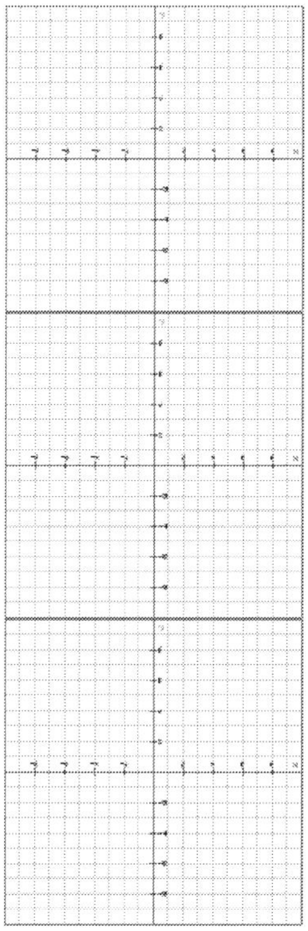

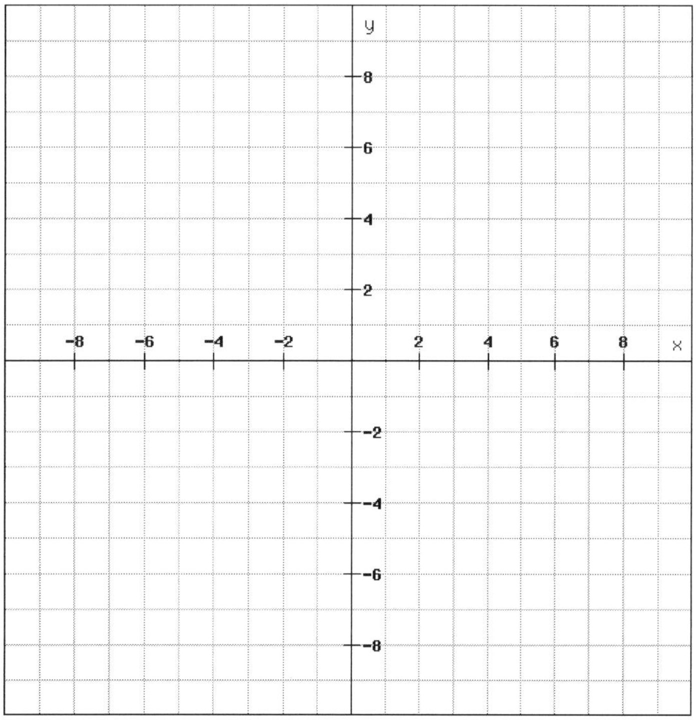

33. $f(x) = \begin{cases} -2x+1 & x \le 2 \\ e^{x} & 2 < x \text{ and } x < 4 \\ \dfrac{1}{x} & 4 < x \end{cases}$

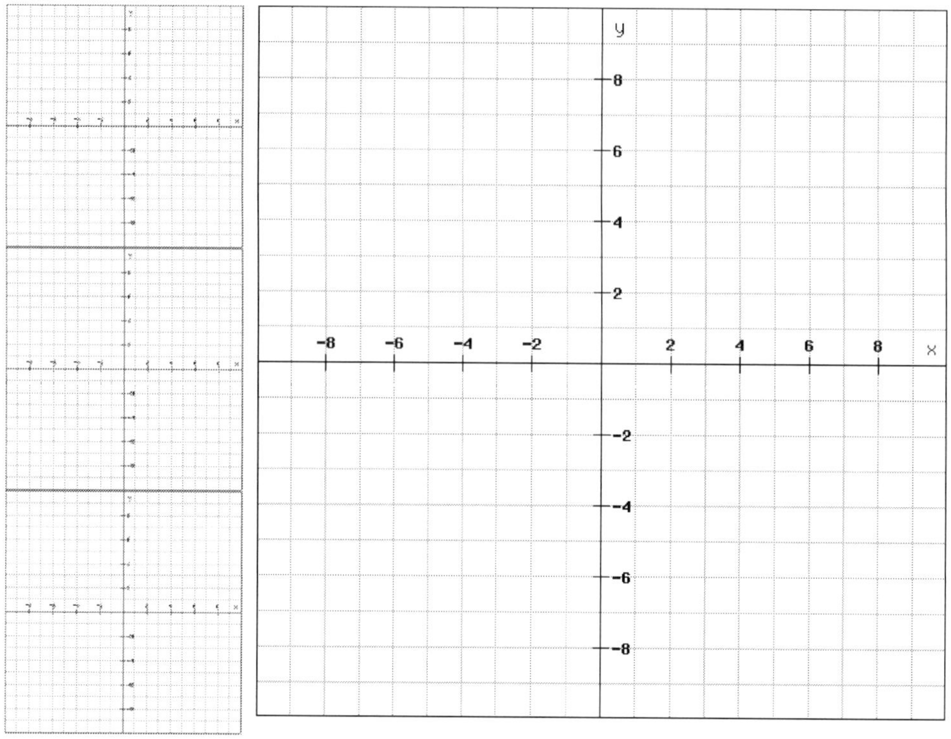

34. $f(x) = \begin{cases} x & x \le -2 \\ -3x-2 & -2 < x \text{ and } x < 0 \\ \ln(2x+1)-1 & 0 \le x \end{cases}$

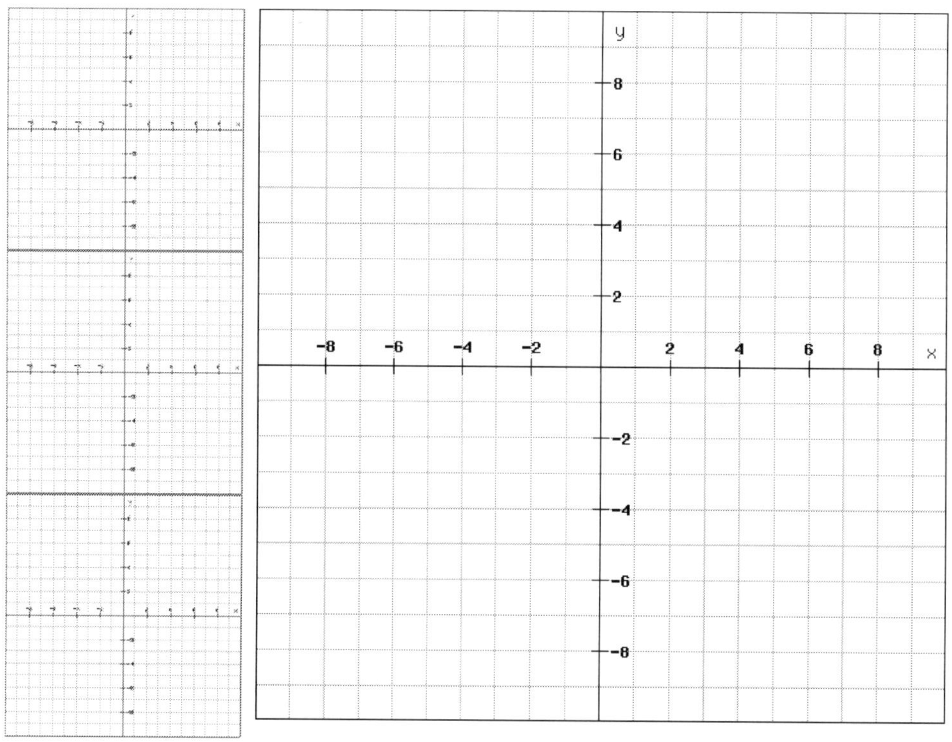

Find the value(s) of *a* for which the following functions will be continuous and then analyze the function:

35. $$f(x) = \begin{cases} \sqrt{x+1} & x < 2 \\ \dfrac{a}{x+1} - 1 & 2 \le x \end{cases}$$

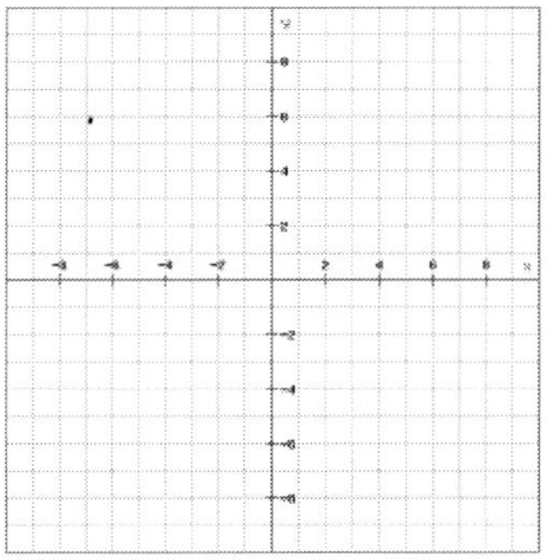

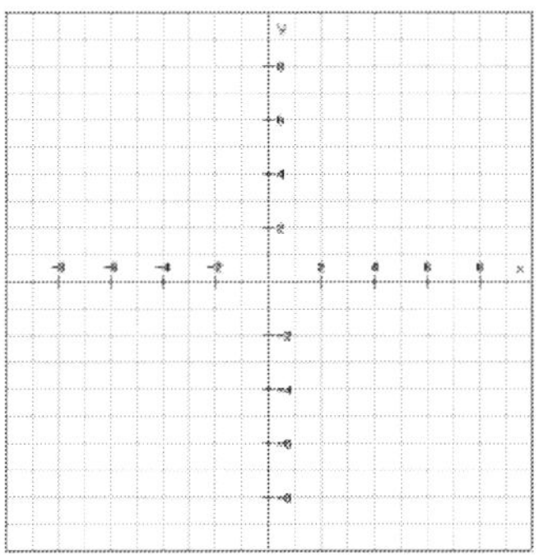

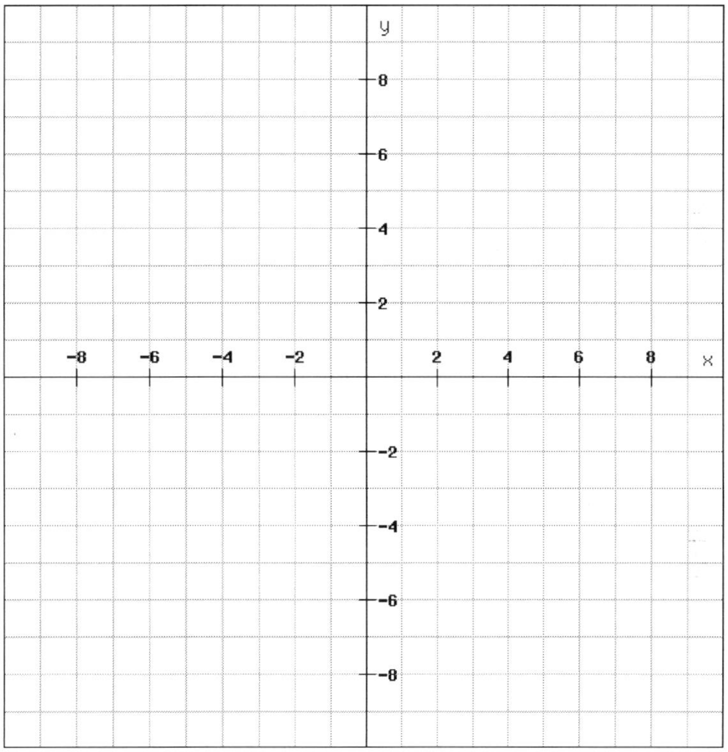

36. $$f(x) = \begin{cases} \ln(x) + 1 & x < 1 \\ \dfrac{a}{2x+1} - 3 & 1 \leq x \end{cases}$$

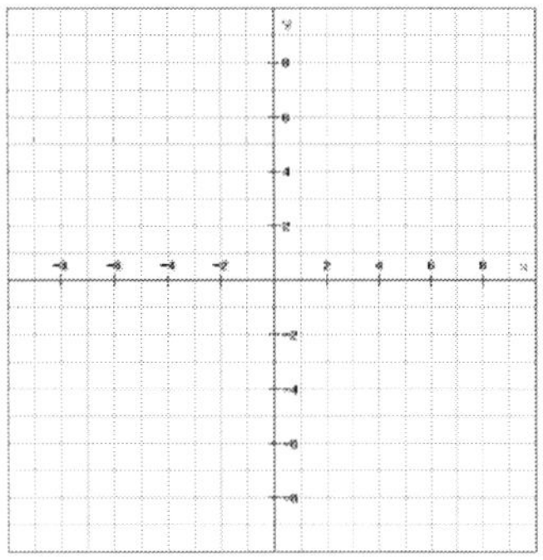

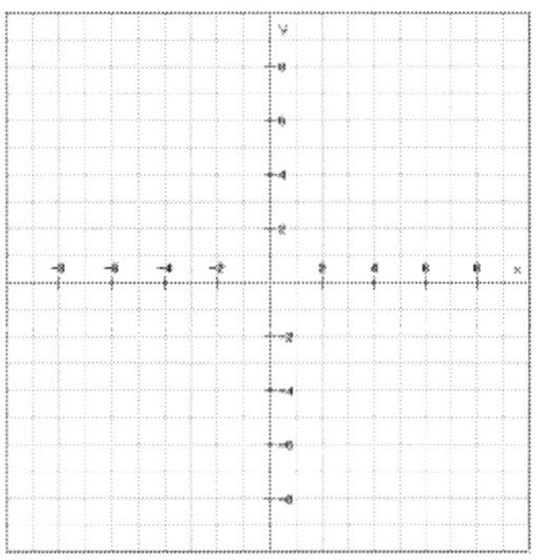

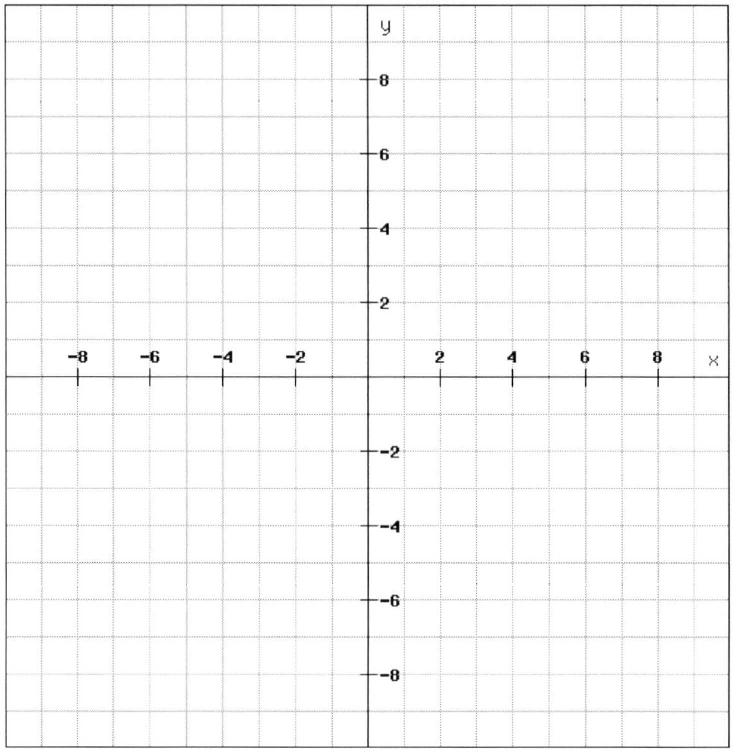

37. $$f(x) = \begin{cases} x^2 & x < -2 \\ \dfrac{a}{x+3} - 3 & -2 \le x \end{cases}$$

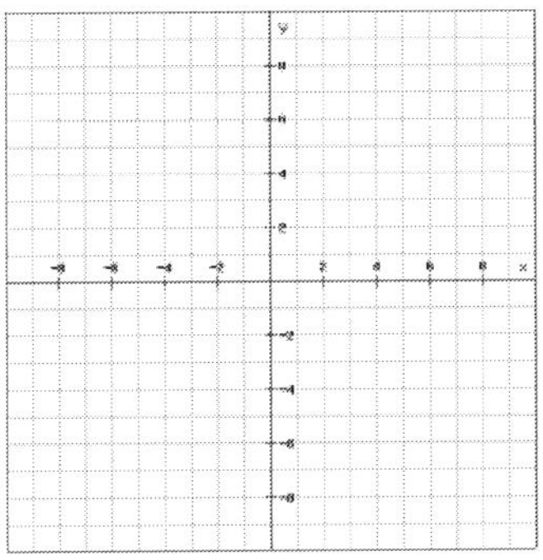

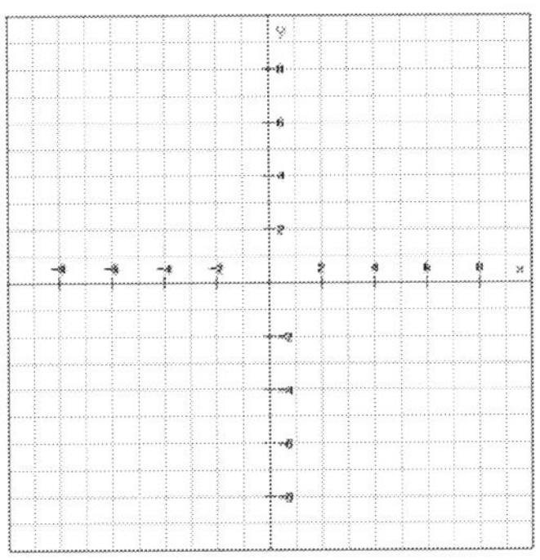

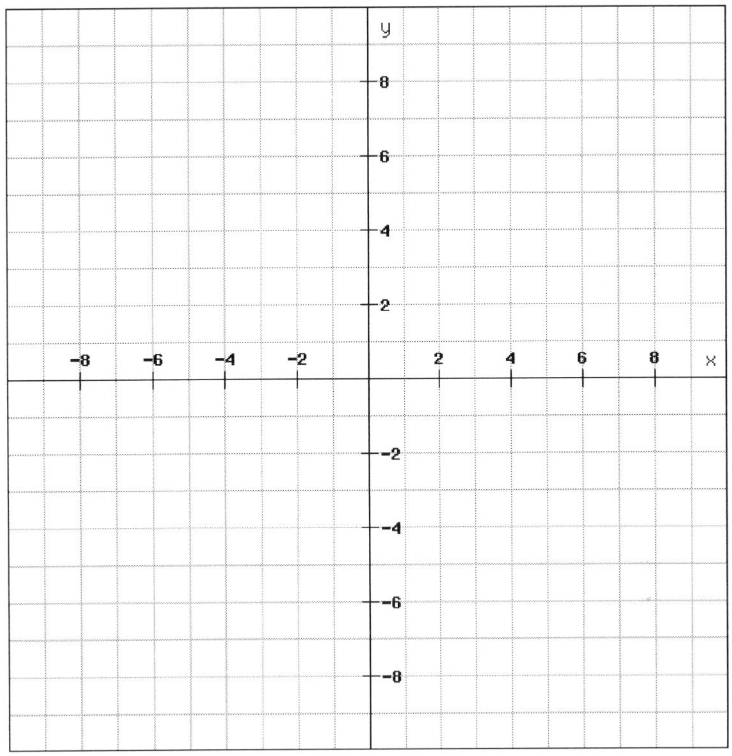

38. $$f(x) = \{ \begin{array}{ll} x^2 & x < -2 \\ \sqrt{x+3} - a & -2 \le x \end{array}$$

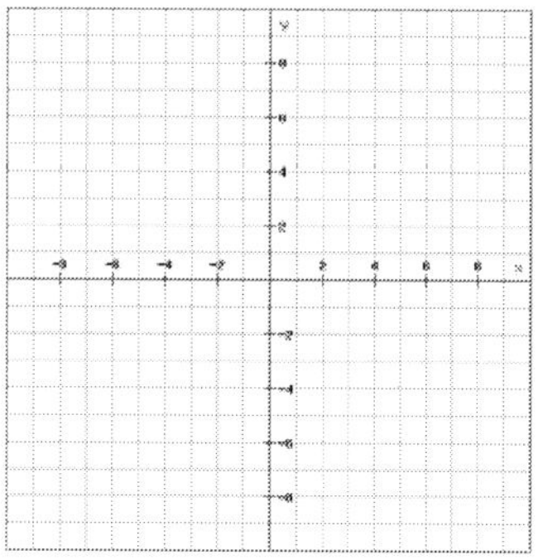

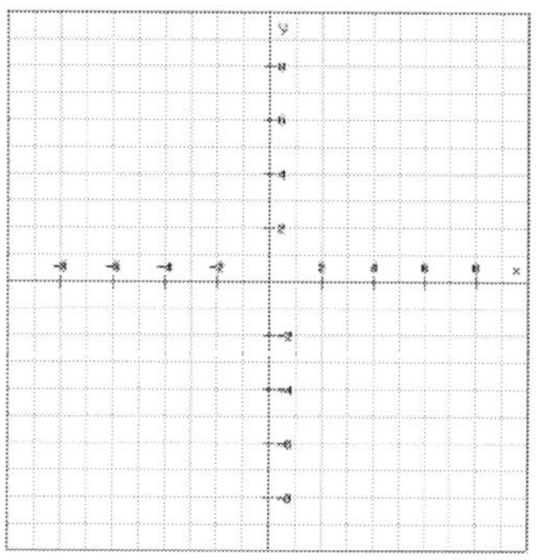

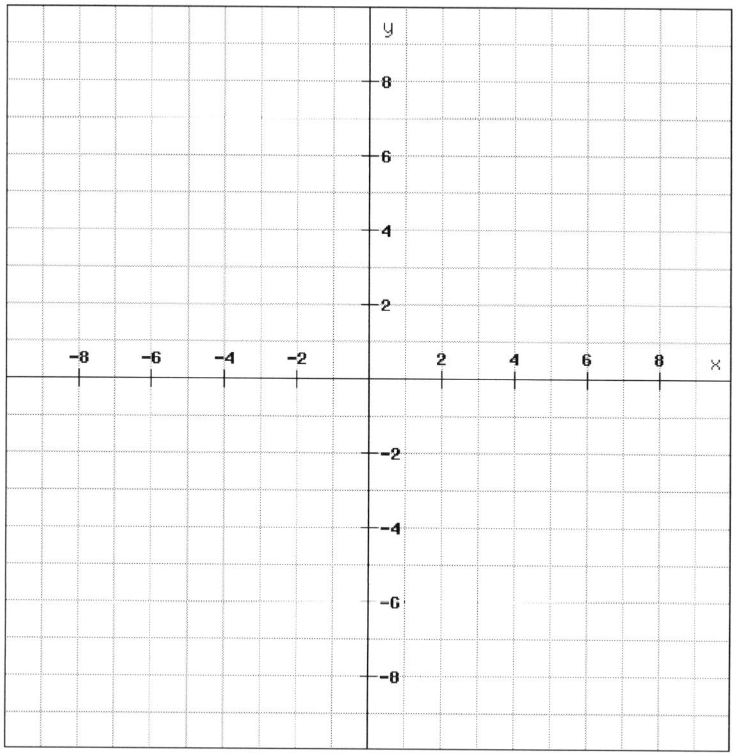

Analyze the following functions:

39. $f(x) = \begin{cases} -x + 1 & x < 0 \\ x & 0 \le x \end{cases}$

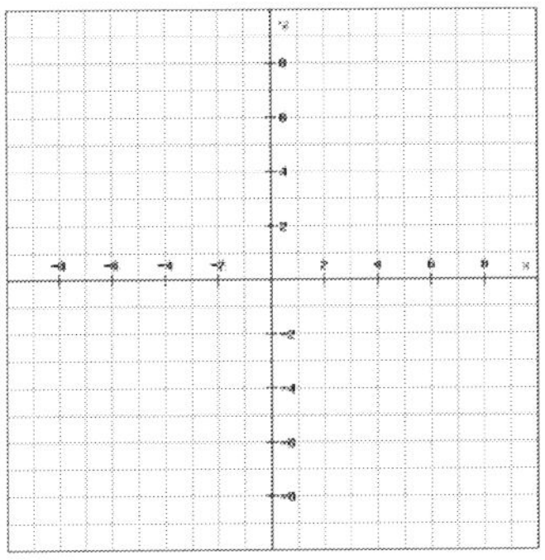

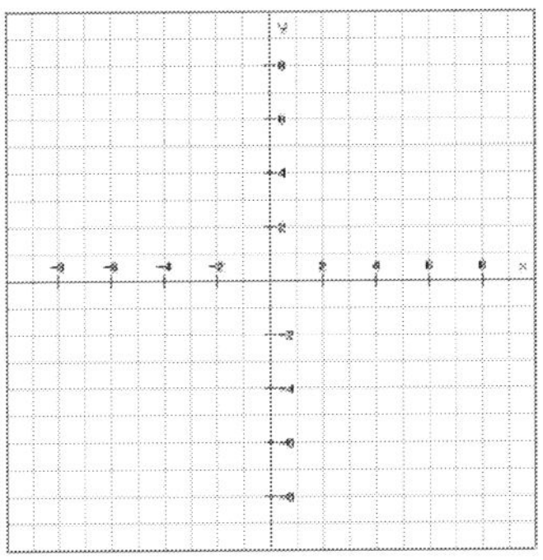

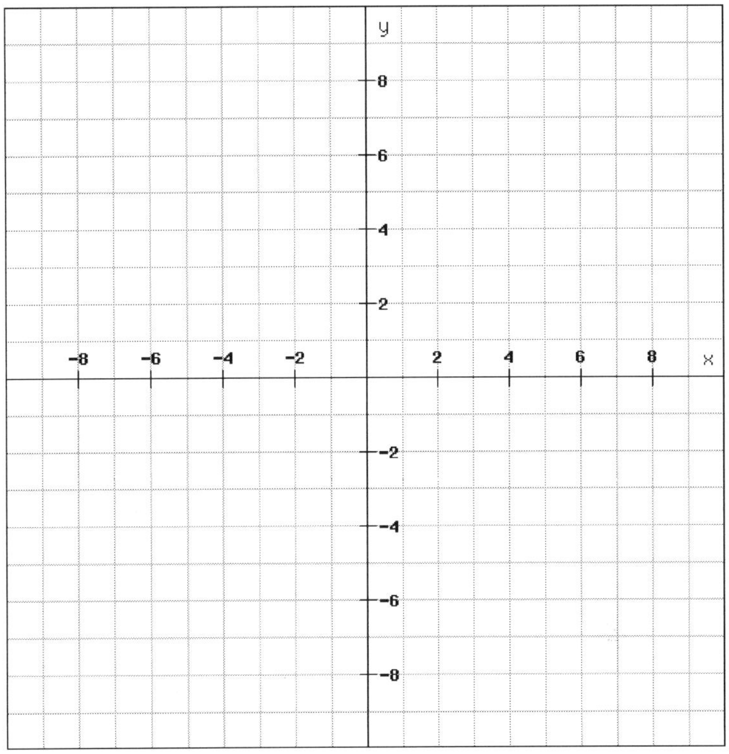

40. $f(x) = \begin{cases} -2x + 2 & x < 1 \\ \dfrac{1}{x} & 1 \le x \end{cases}$

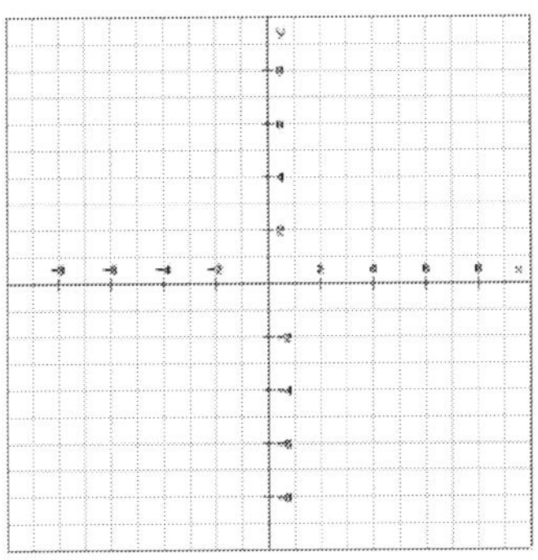

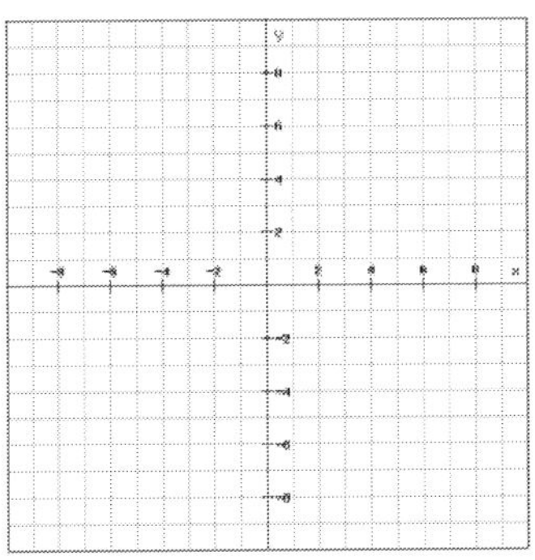

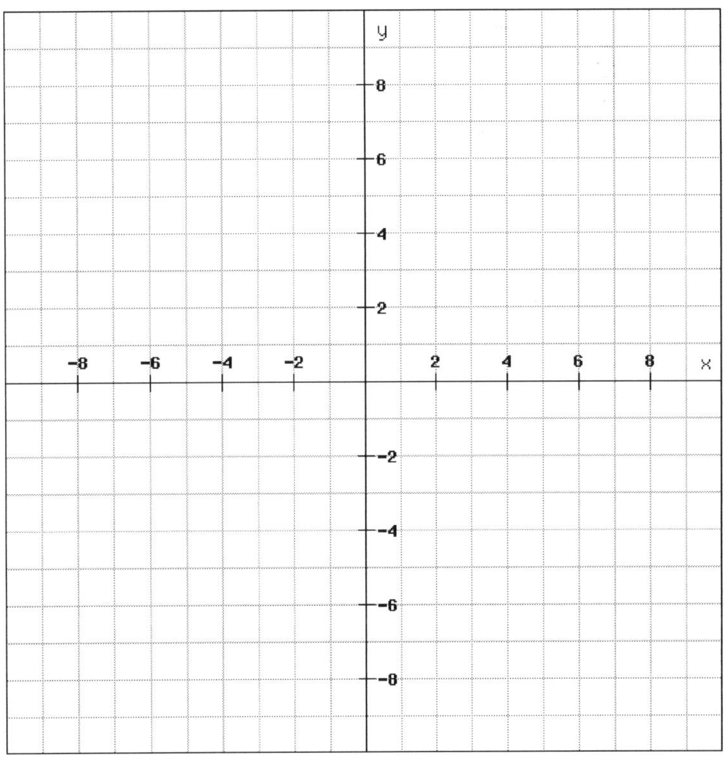

41. $f(x) = \begin{cases} x^2 - 2 & x < -3 \\ \dfrac{1}{x+1} & -3 \le x \end{cases}$

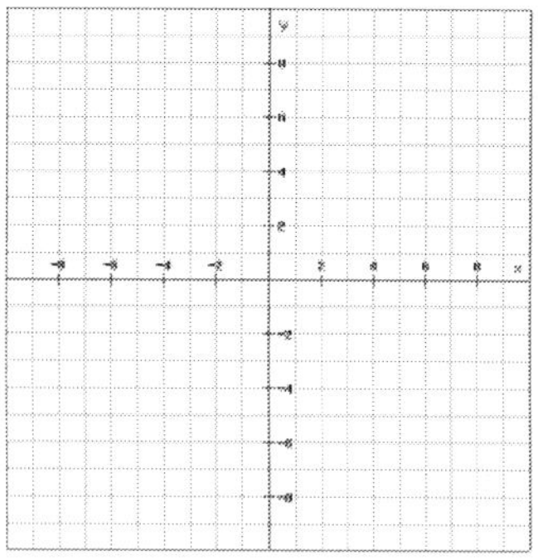

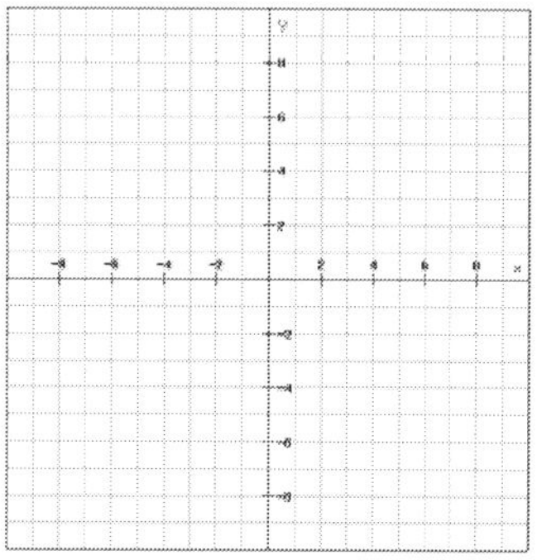

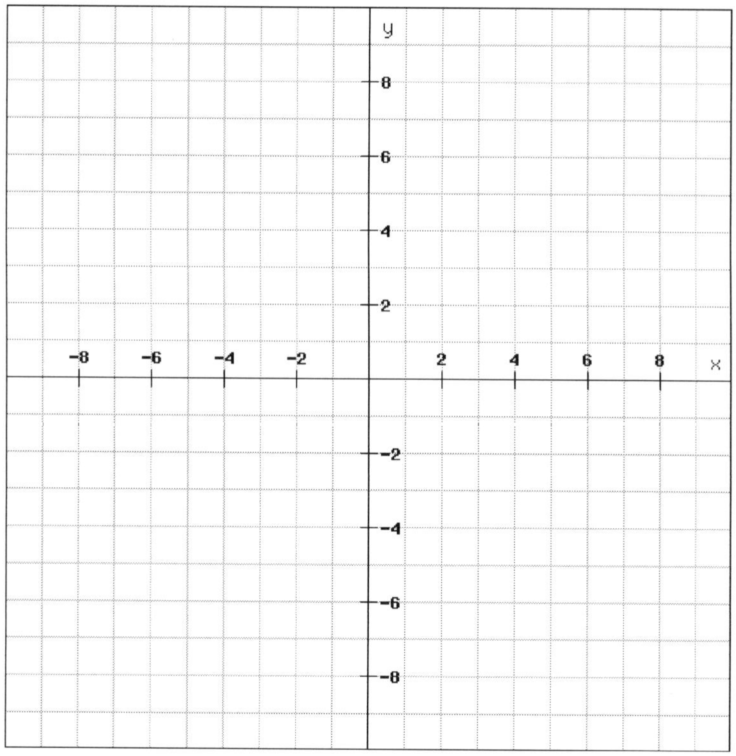

42. $f(x) = \{ \begin{matrix} x^2 - 2 & x < 2 \\ \ln(x) & 2 \le x \end{matrix}$

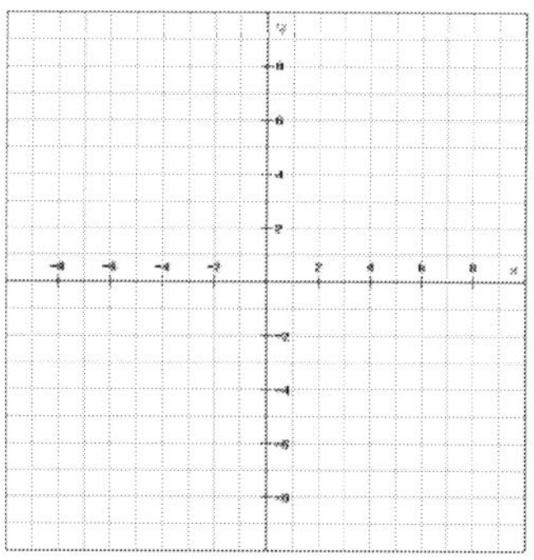

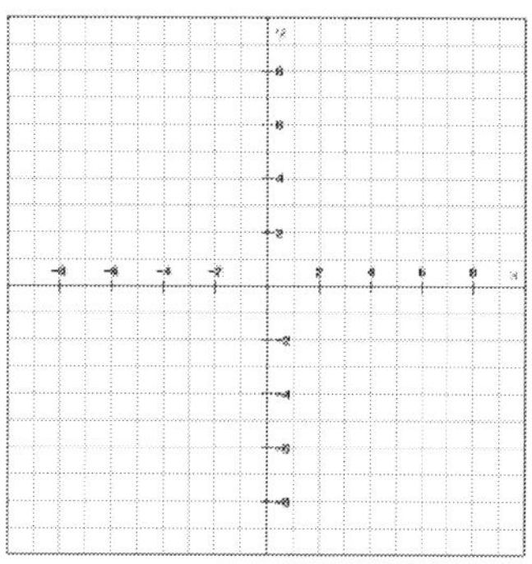

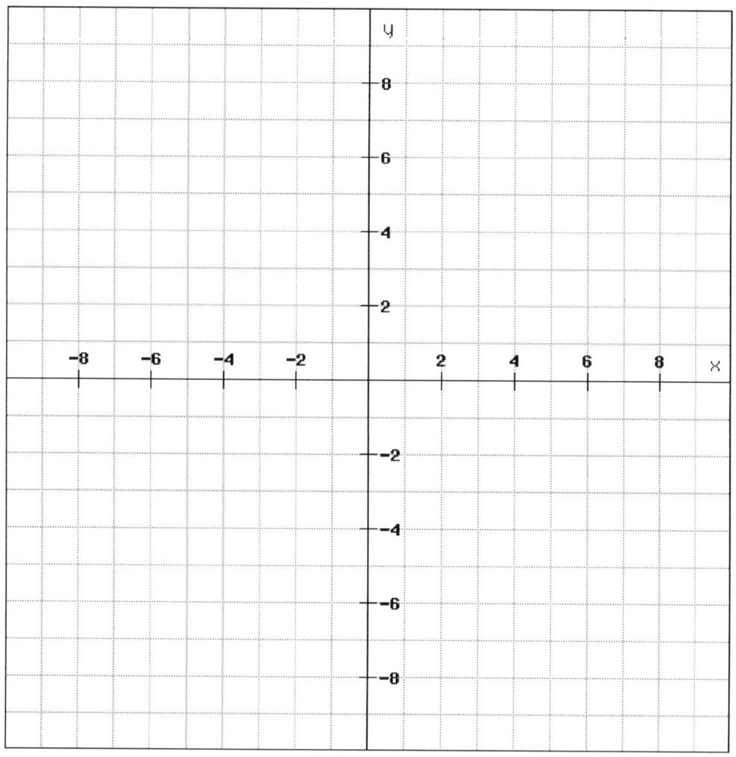

43. Find the value of *a* that will make f(x) continuous:

$$f(x) = \begin{cases} 2x^2 - 5 & x < 2 \\ a & 2 \le x \end{cases}$$

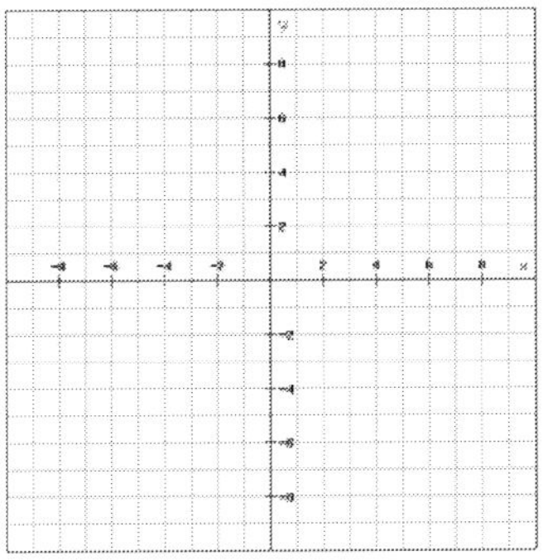

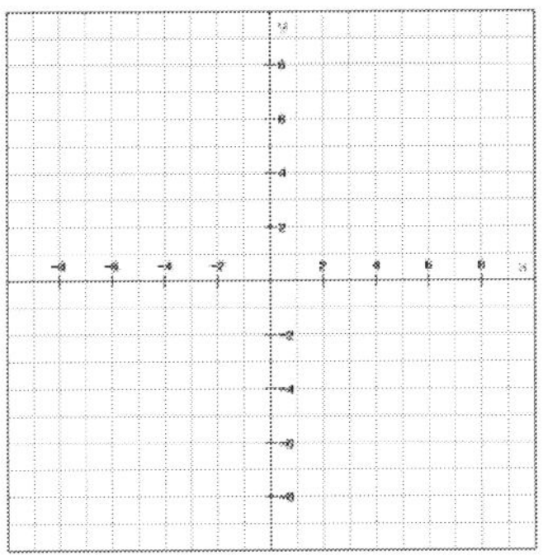

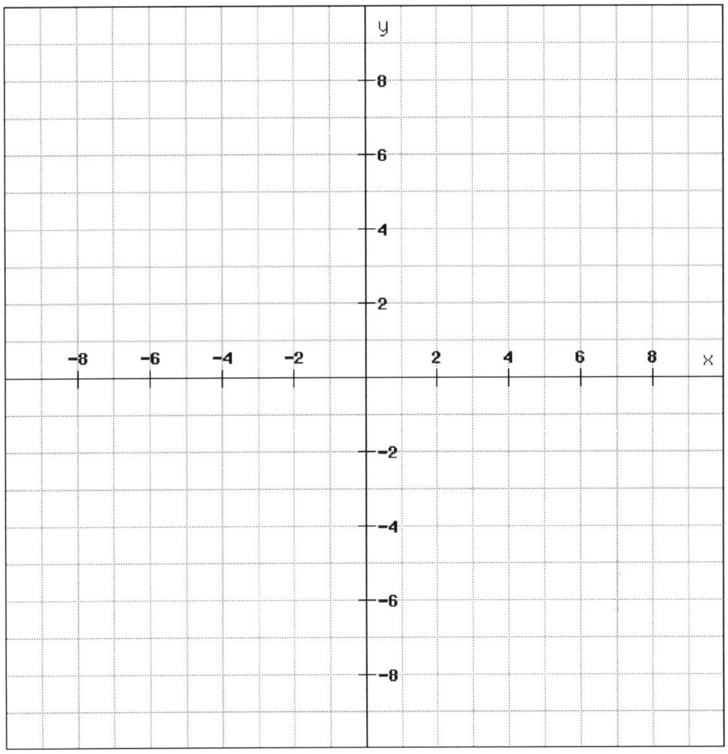

44. $$f(x) = \begin{cases} \ln(x + 1) & x < 2 \\ -x^2 & 2 \le x \end{cases}$$

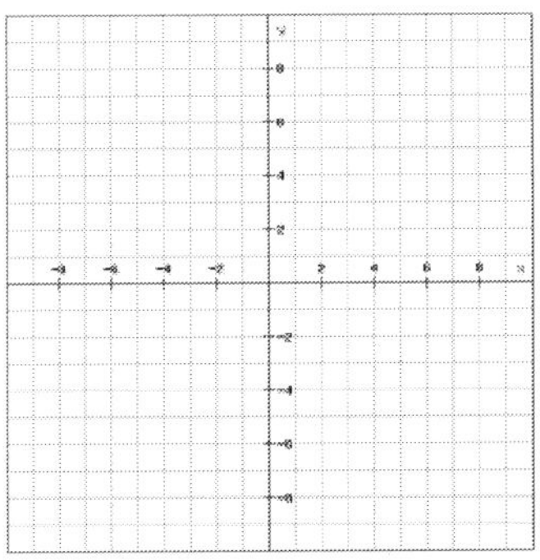

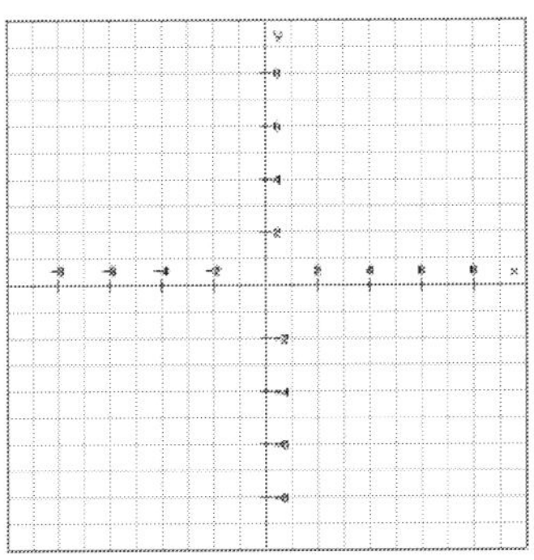

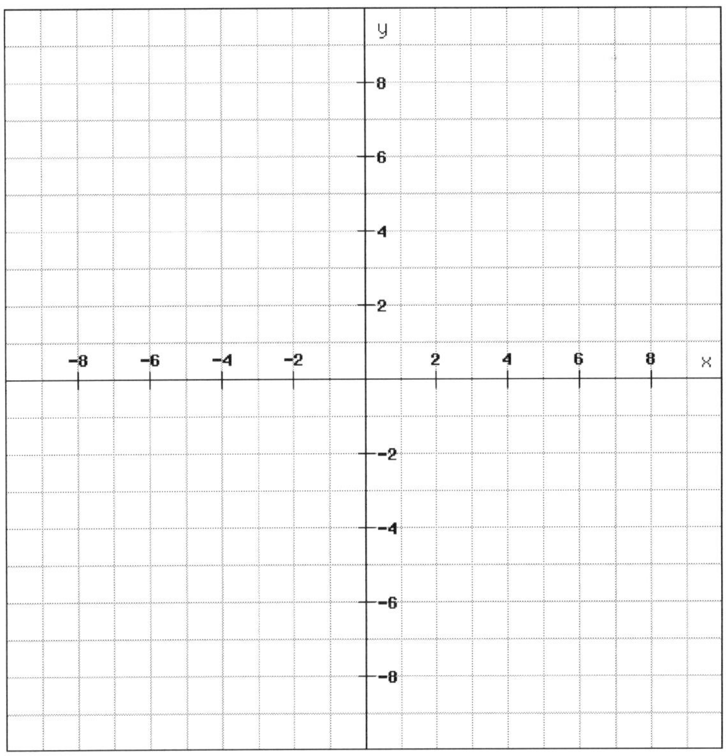

45. $f(x) = \begin{cases} \ln(x-1) & 2 < x \\ (x-2)^2 & x \le 2 \end{cases}$

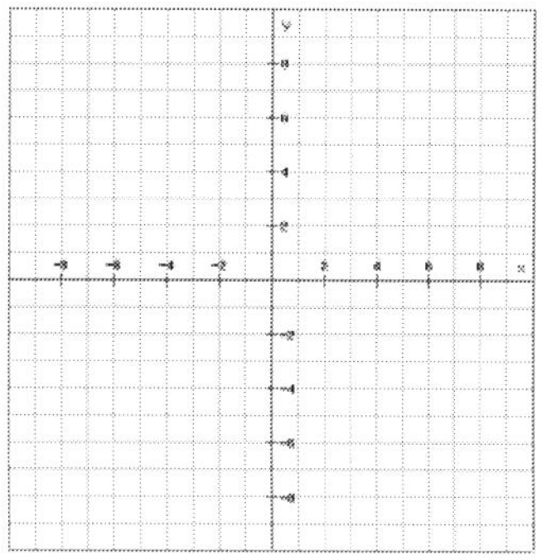

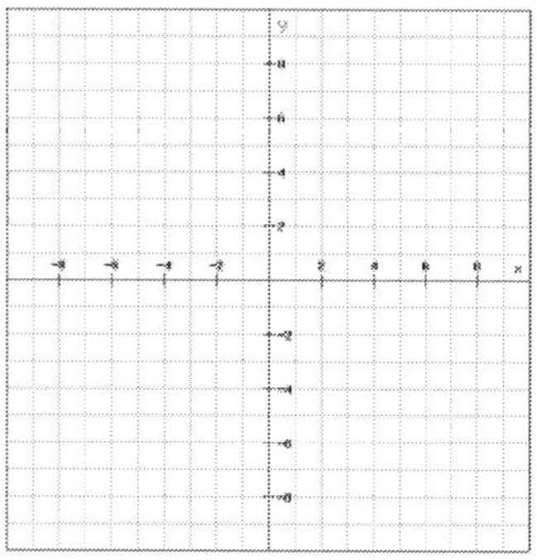

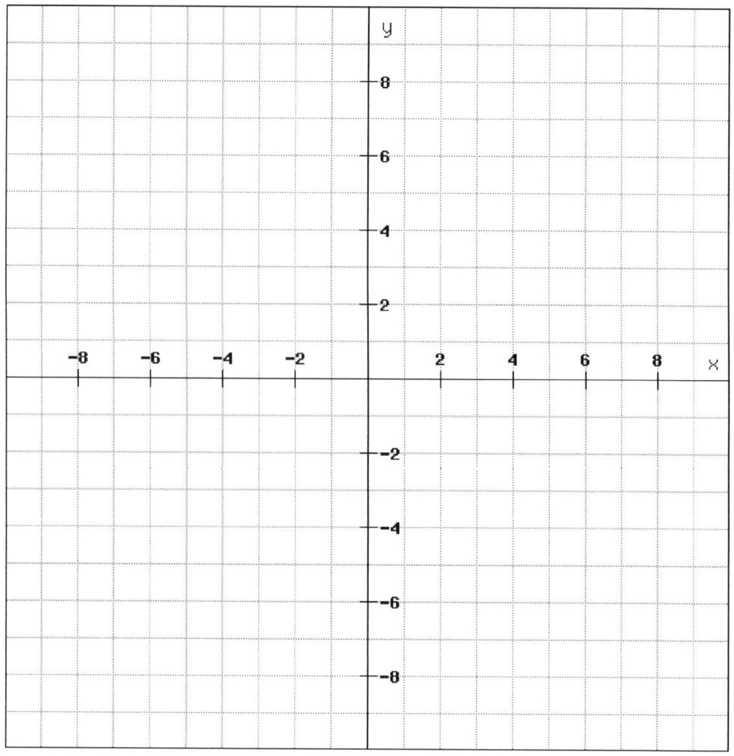

46. Find the value of a that will make f(x) continuous:

$$f(x) = \begin{cases} x^2 + a & x \le 1 \\ (x-3)^2 & 1 < x \end{cases}$$

47. $f(x) = \begin{cases} 1 & x < 0 \\ x & 0 \le x \text{ and } x < 2 \\ -(x-3)^2 & 2 \le x \end{cases}$

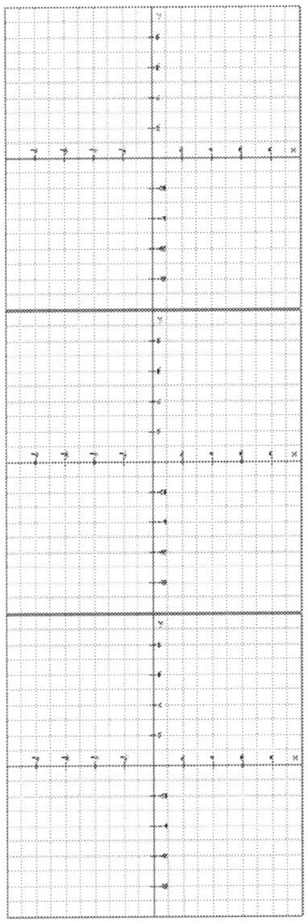

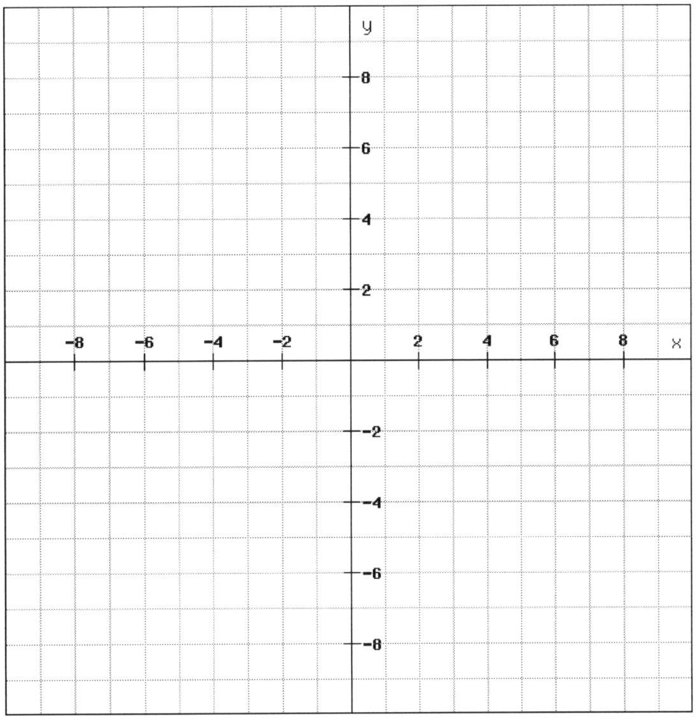

48. $f(x) = \begin{cases} -2x & x < -1 \\ x^2 & -1 \le x \text{ and } x < 3 \\ (x+1)^2 & 3 \le x \end{cases}$

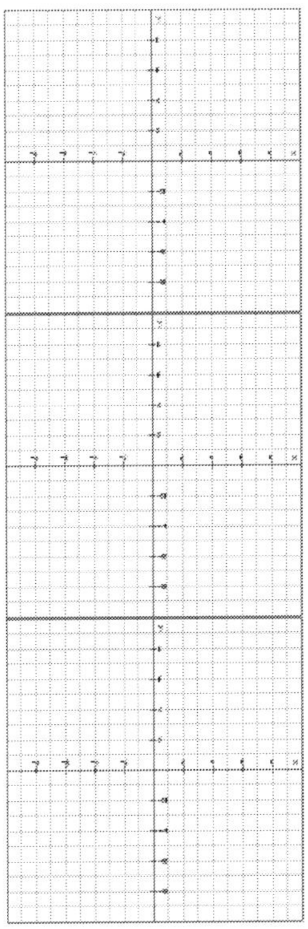

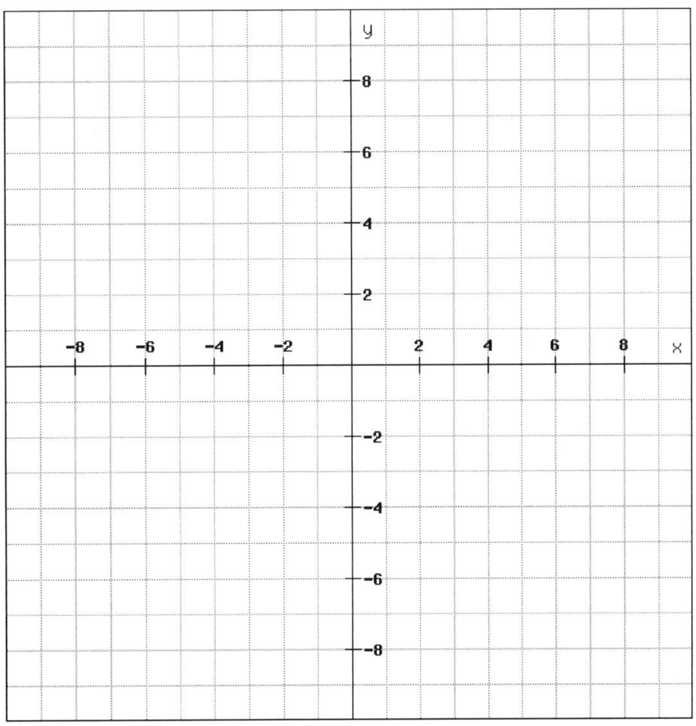

49. $$f(x) = \begin{cases} x+3 & x < -2 \\ \sqrt{x+4} & -2 \le x \text{ and } x < 0 \\ -x^2 & 0 \le x \end{cases}$$

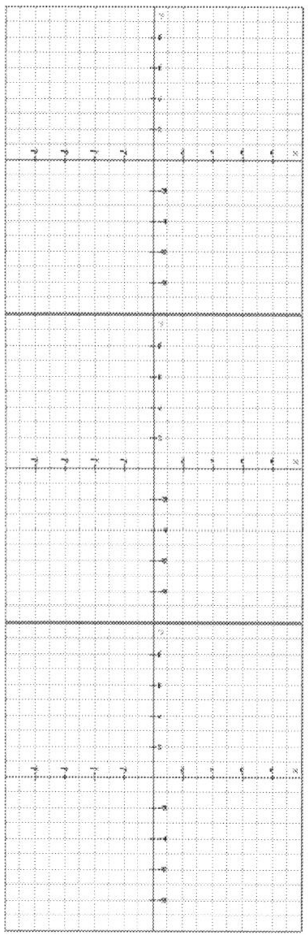

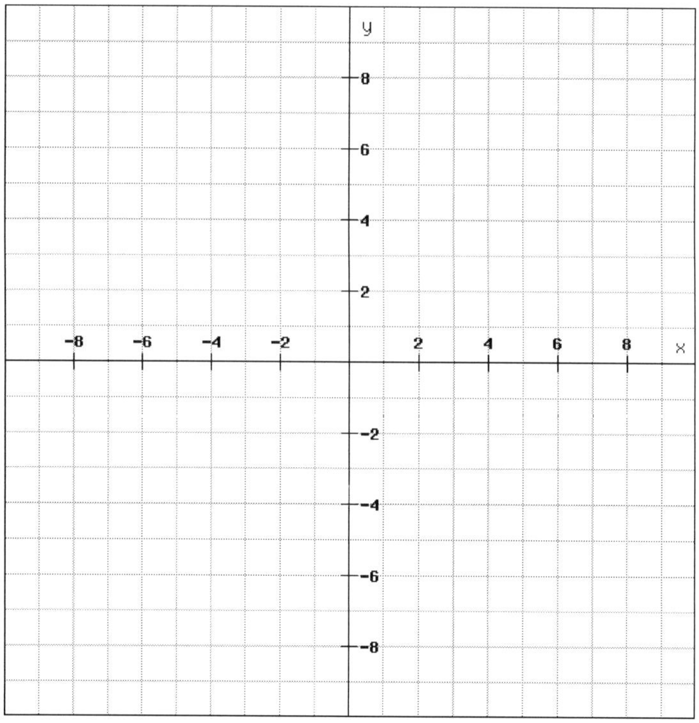

50. $$f(x) = \begin{cases} -3x-1 & x < 0 \\ \ln(x-1) & 0 \le x \text{ and } x < 4 \\ \sqrt{x} & 4 \le x \end{cases}$$

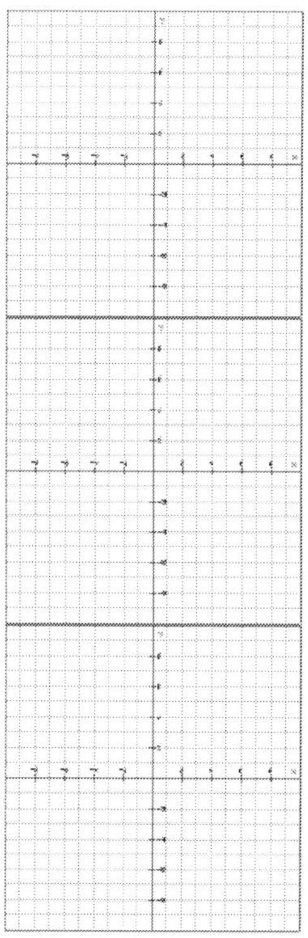

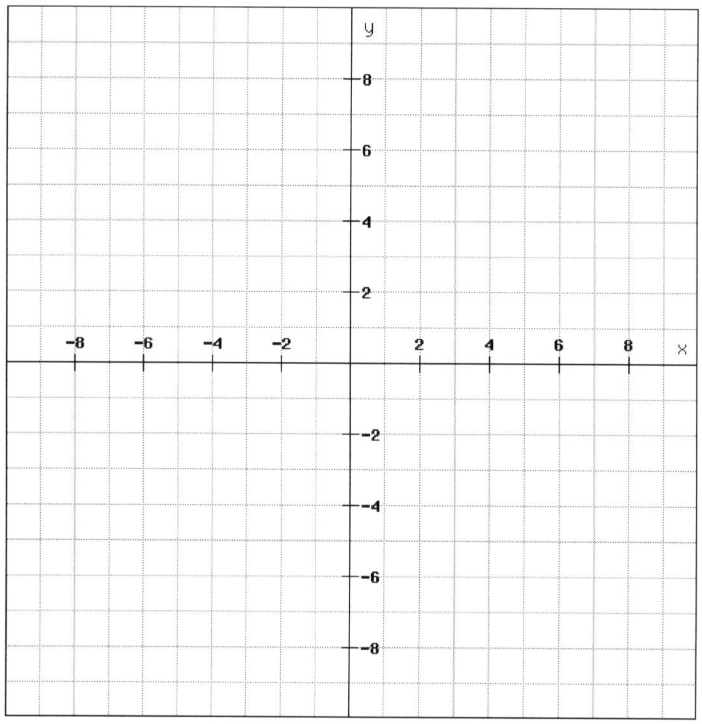

51. $$f(x) = \begin{cases} e^{x} & x < -1 \\ -x^2 & -1 \le x \text{ and } x < 2 \\ e^{(-x)} & 2 \le x \end{cases}$$

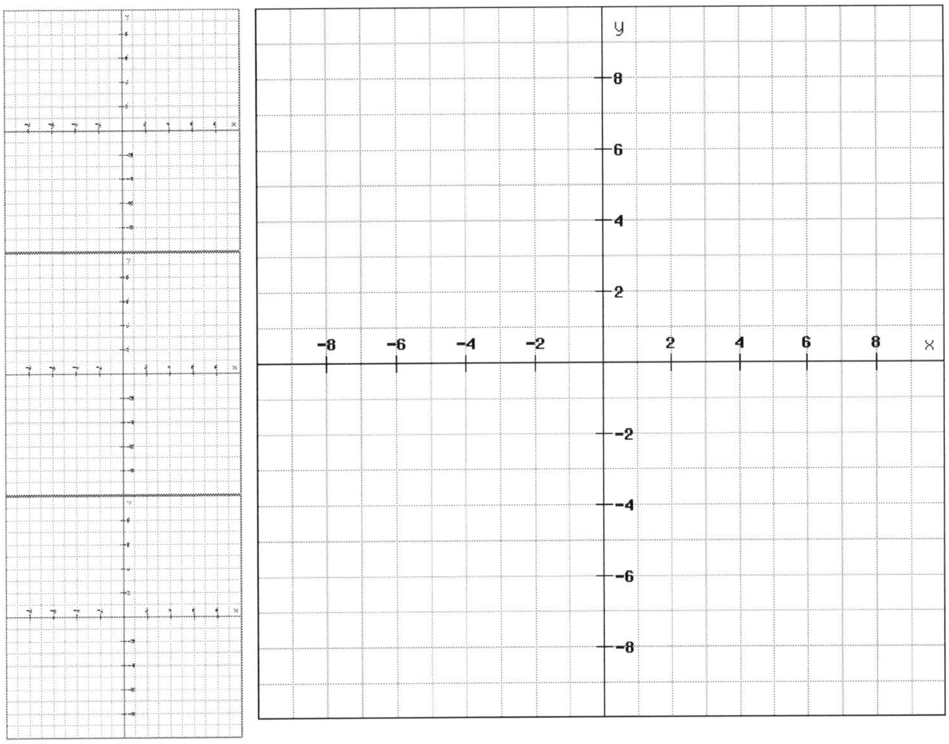

52. $$f(x) = \begin{cases} -(x+2)^2 & x < 0 \\ 3^{(-x)} & 0 \le x \text{ and } x < 3 \\ x - 6 & 3 \le x \end{cases}$$

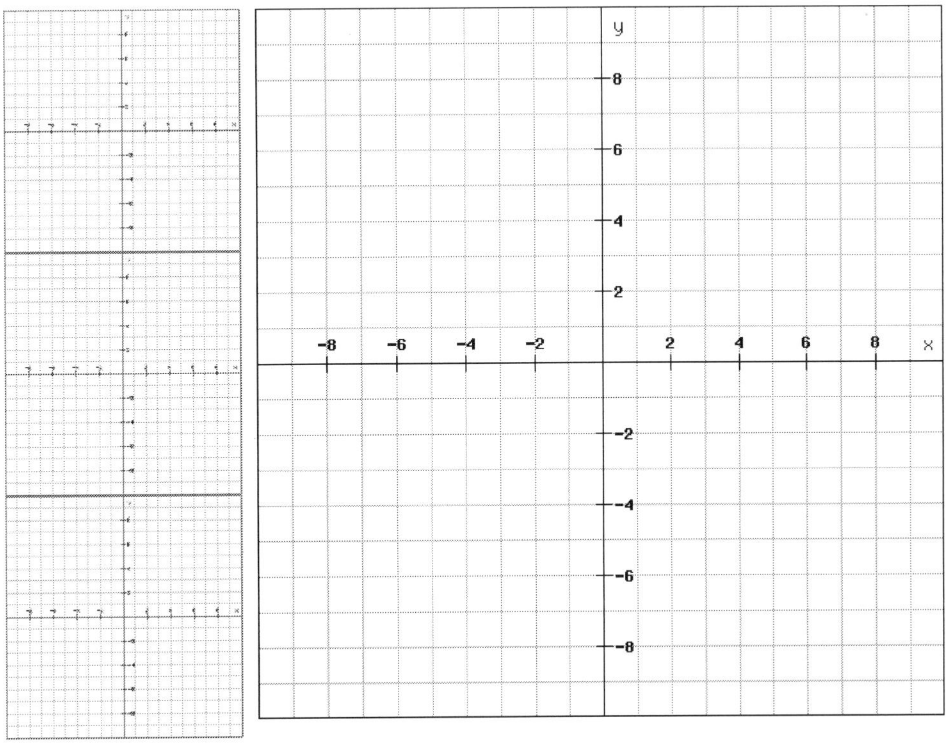

53. $$f(x) = \begin{cases} x^2 - 1 & x < 0 \\ 2^x & 0 \le x \text{ and } x < 3 \\ \dfrac{1}{x-6} & 4 \le x \end{cases}$$

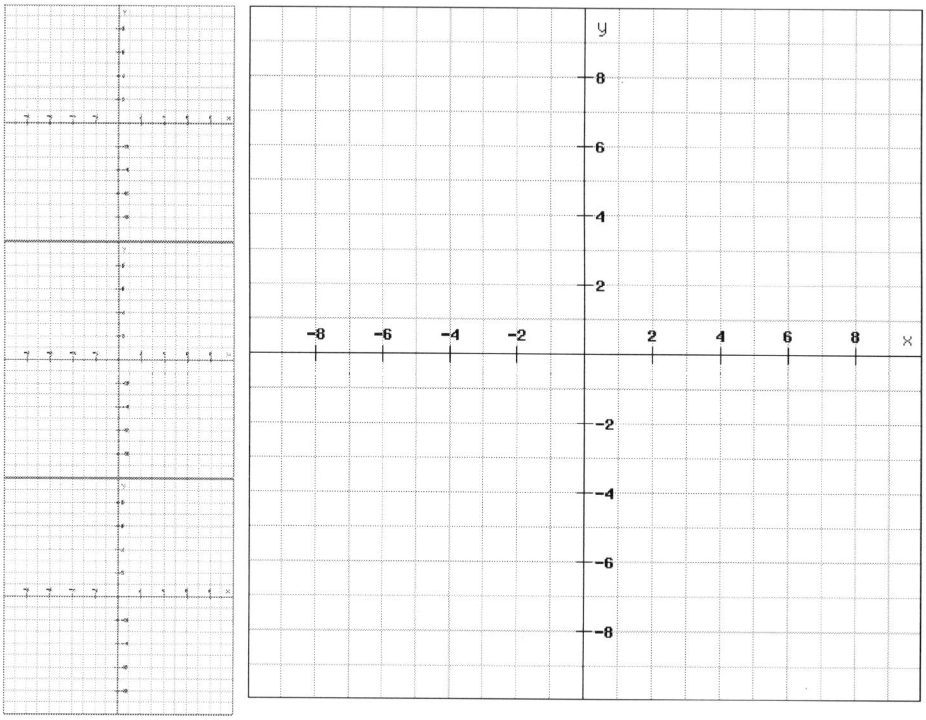

54. $$f(x) = \begin{cases} \dfrac{1}{x} & x < -1 \\ e^x & -1 \le x \text{ and } x < 2 \\ \ln(x) & 2 \le x \end{cases}$$

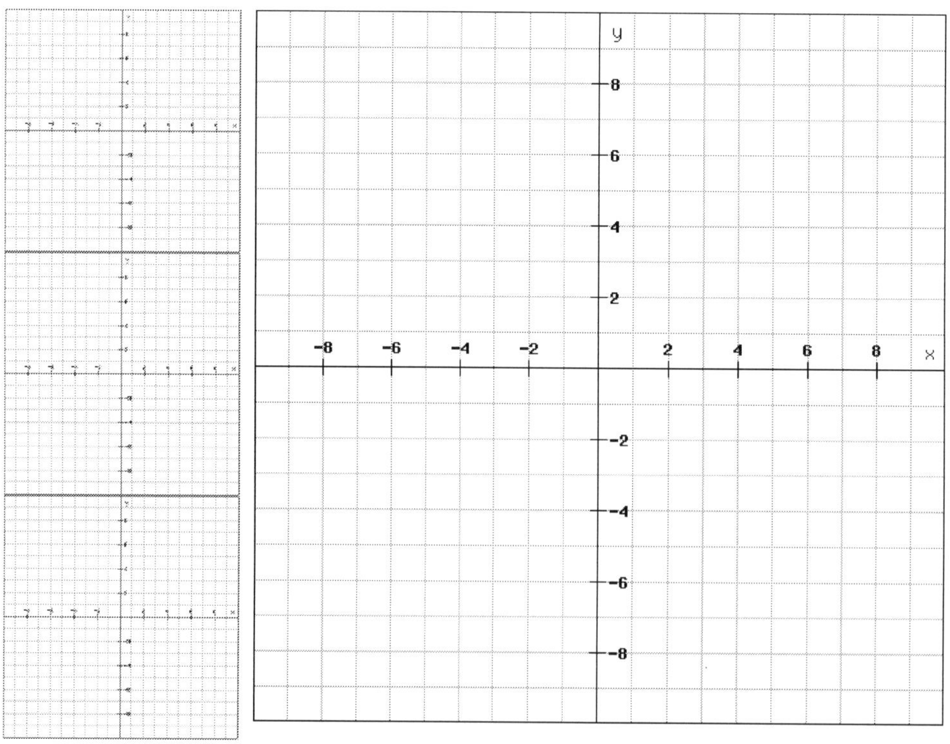

55. $$f(x) = \begin{cases} \dfrac{1}{x+3} & x < -2 \\ \sqrt{x+2} & -2 \le x \text{ and } x < 0 \\ \ln(x) & 0 \le x \end{cases}$$

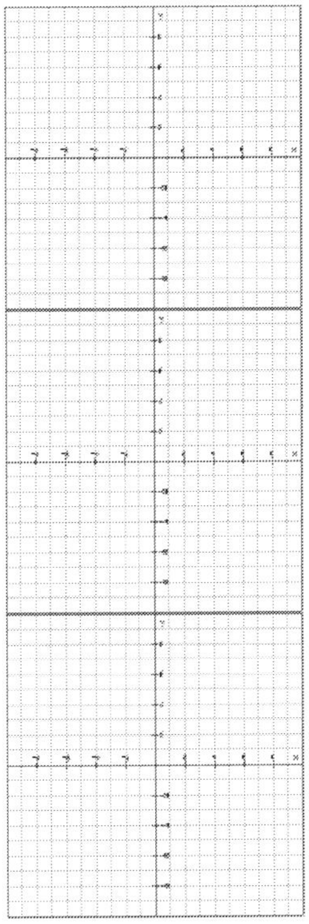

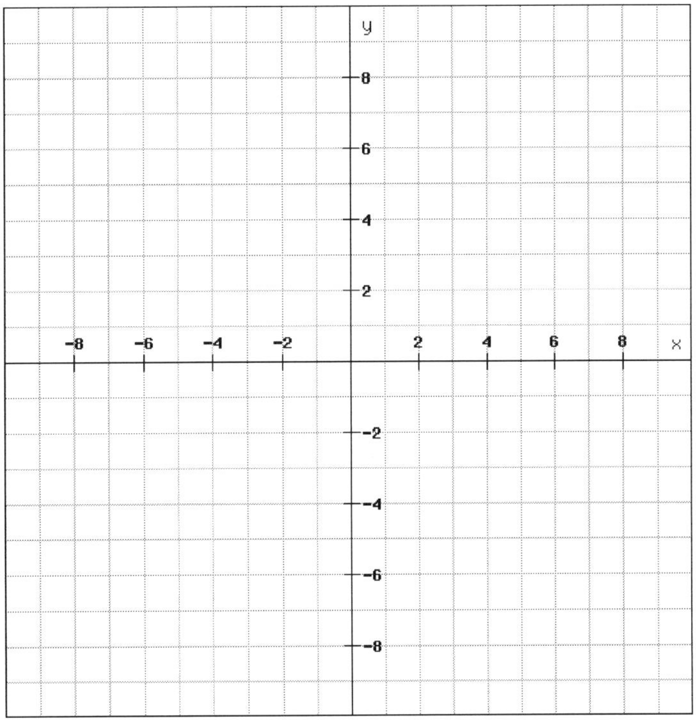

2.10. – COMPOSITE FUCNTIONS

1. Given The functions $f(x) = x + 4$ and $g(x) = 2x^2$, find

   a. f(g(x)) =   g(f(x)) =

   b. f(f(x)) =   g(g(x)) =

   c. f(g(f(x)x)) =   g(f(g(x))) =

2. Given The functions $f(x) = 2x^3 + x$ and $g(x) = Ln(x + 1)$, find

   a. f(g(x)) =   g(f(x)) =

   b. f(f(x)) –   g(g(x)) =

   c. f(g(f(x)x)) =   g(f(g(x))) =

3. Given The functions $f(x) = \sqrt{x+1}$ and $g(x) = 3^x - 2$, find

   a. f(g(x)) =   g(f(x)) =

   b. f(f(x)) =   g(g(x)) =

   c. f(g(f(x)x)) =   g(f(g(x))) =

4. Given The functions $f(x) = \dfrac{2}{x^2+1}$ and $g(x) = Sin(x + 1)$, find

   a. f(g(x)) =   g(f(x)) =

   b. f(f(x)) =   g(g(x)) =

   c. f(g(f(x)x)) =   g(f(g(x))) =

5. Given The functions $f(x) = \dfrac{1}{x}$ and $g(x) = x^2$, find

   a. f(g(x)) =   g(f(x)) =

   b. f(f(x)) =   g(g(x)) =

   c. f(g(f(x)x)) =   g(f(g(x))) =

6. In general, is $f(g(x)) = g(f(x))$?

7. Given The functions $f(x) = x$ and $g(x) = x^2$, $s(x) = \sin(x^2 + 3)$, $a(x) = \mathrm{Ln}(\frac{1}{x})$ find

   a. $f(g(x)) =$ $g(f(x)) =$

   b. $f(s(x)) =$ $s(f(x)) =$

   c. $f(a(x)) =$ $a(f(x)) =$

   d. What is your conclusion?

2.11. – INVERSE FUCNTIONS

1. Given The functions $f(x) = x + 4$ and $g(x) = x - 4$, find

   a. $f(g(x)) =$ $g(f(x)) =$

2. Given The functions $f(x) = 2x^3$ and $g(x) = \sqrt[3]{\frac{x}{2}}$, find

   a. $f(g(x)) =$ $g(f(x)) =$

3. What is your conclusion?

4. Given The functions $f(x) = \sqrt{x+1}$, find $f^{-1}(x)$

5. Given The functions $f(x) = \frac{2x-3}{x+5}$, find $f^{-1}(x)$

6. Given The functions f(x) = $2^{3x-5}+3$, find $f^{-1}(x)$

7. Given The functions f(x) = $e^{\sqrt{x-2}}+5$, find $f^{-1}(x)$

8. Given The functions f(x) = $Ln(x^2+2)+3$, find $f^{-1}(x)$

9. Given The functions f(x) = $Log_2(2x-3)$, find $f^{-1}(1)$

10. Given The functions f(x) = $(2x-4)^2$, find $f^{-1}(0)$

11. Given The functions $f(x) = x^2 + 2x$, find $f^{-1}(x)$

12. Given the function, sketch the inverse function:

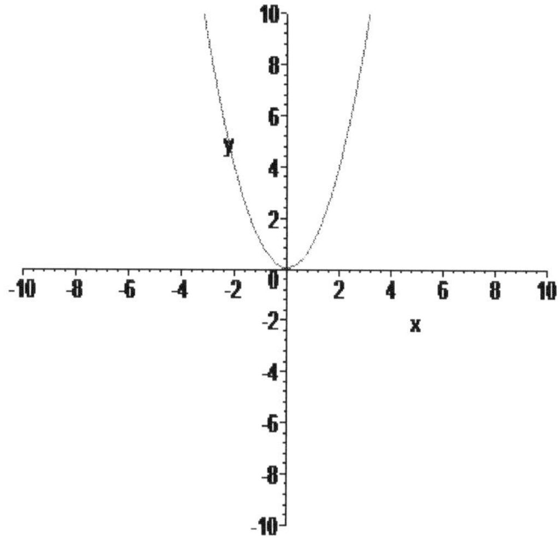

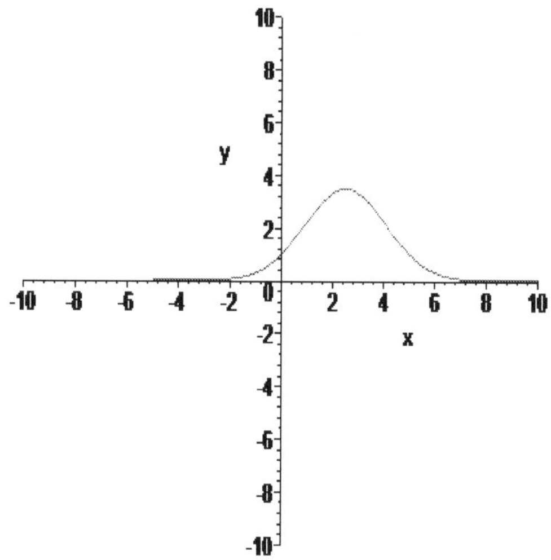

13. Given the function, sketch the inverse function:

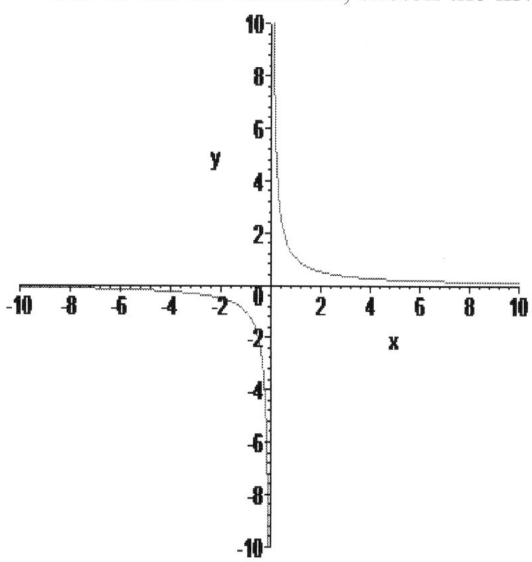

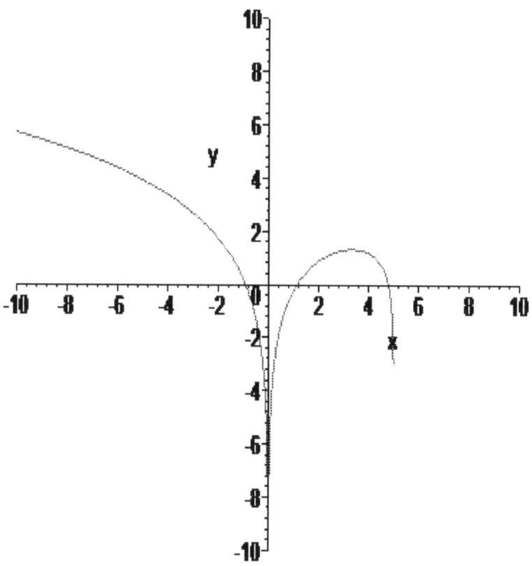

14. Graphically, the inverse function is a ______________________________.

15. (T/F) In case the inverse curve is not a function, the inverse function is not well defined.

CHAPTER 3 – TRIGONOMETRIC FUNCTIONS

3.1. – DEGREES AND RADIANS

Since we were "young" angles were measured in degrees, we were told that the size of a circular angle is 360º. In reality the number 360º is meaningless; it is merely used because of historical reasons. If we go back to the definition of an angle in a circle it is the following:

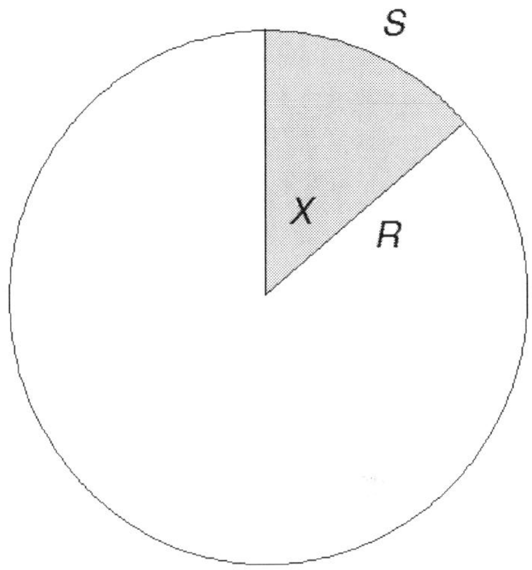

$$X = -$$

In case that S is the entire circle we obtain:

$$X = \frac{S}{R} = \frac{Length\_\_\_\_\_\_\_\_\_\_}{\_\_\_\_\_\_\_\_ of - Circle} = 6.2831... = 2\pi$$

So what we see is that the angle of the entire circle is approximately 6.28 or exactly 2π. That means:

$$2\pi_{rad} = \_\_\_\_\_\_\_^{o}$$

$$1^{o} = \frac{2\pi}{360} rad \approx 0.017_{rad}$$

$$1_{rad} = \left(\frac{\_\_\_\_\_\_}{\_\_\_\_\_\_}\right)^{0} \approx 57.3^{o}$$

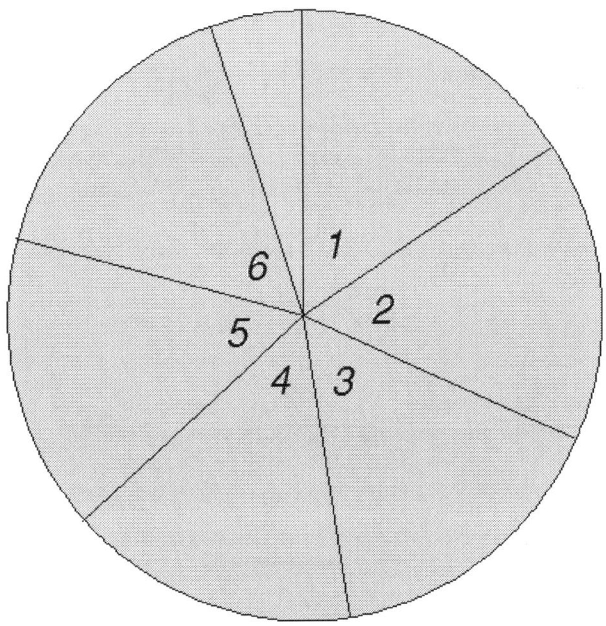

In the image we can observe that in a circle 6 radians are equivalent to a bit less than 360º, the exact number is 2π, approximately 6.28 radians

Exercises:

1. Complete the table:

Degrees	360°	-180°	90°	45°	22.5°
Radians					

2. Complete the table:

Degrees	0°	30°	60°	-120°	150°
Radians					

3. Complete the table:

Degrees	315°	-225°	135°	330°	420°
Radians					

4. Complete the table:

Degrees	54°	18°	-36°	15°	75°
Radians					

5. Complete the table:

Degrees	54°	-18°	36°	15°	75°
Radians					

6. Complete the table:

Degrees	5°	1°	-10°	660°	540°
Radians					

7. Complete the table:

Degrees					
Radians	π	$\frac{\pi}{10}$	$-\frac{5\pi}{3}$	$\frac{12\pi}{7}$	$\frac{22\pi}{5}$

8. Complete the table:

Degrees					
Radians	1	2.4	3.5	-2	-3.1

9. Given the following circles, find θ or L in each one of the cases (in degrees and radians):

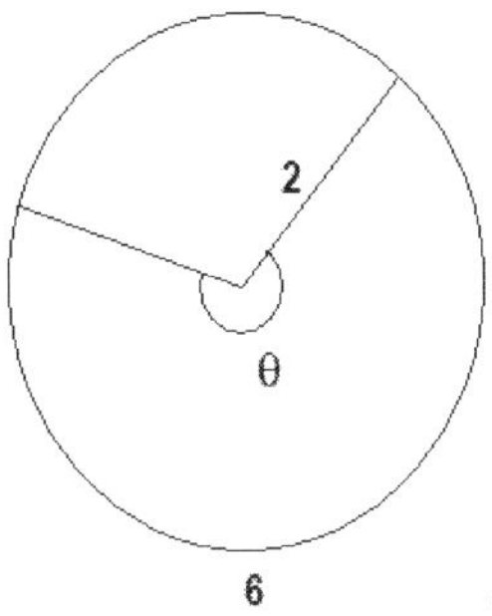

θ = _____ rad = _____°

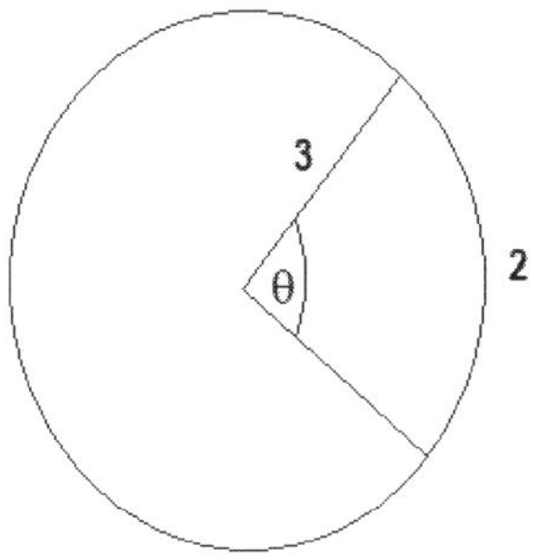

θ = _____ rad = _____°

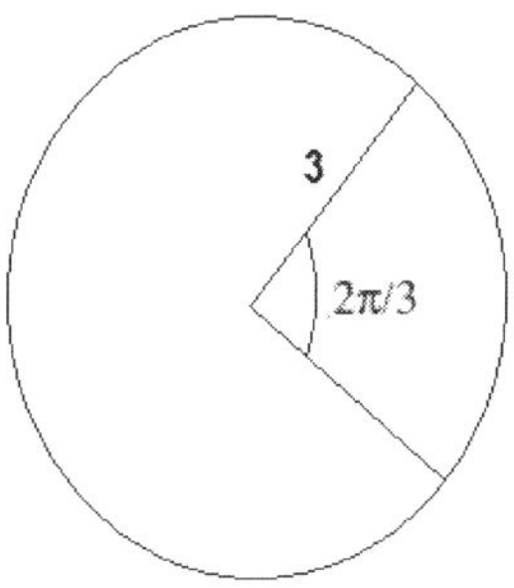

L = _____________

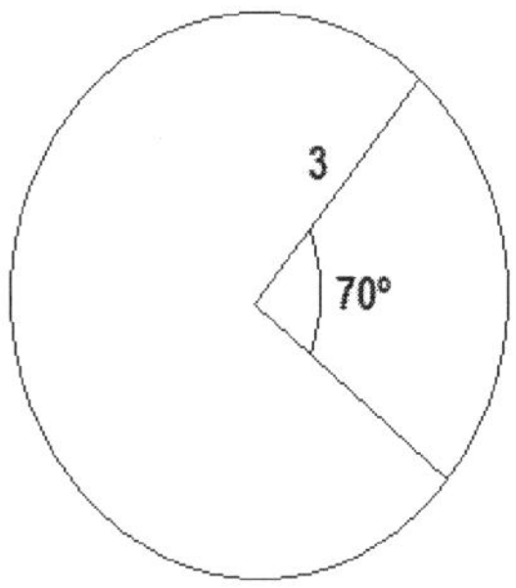

L = _____________

10. The length of the perimeter of a circle with radius r is _______________. The length of the arc that corresponds an angle x° is _______________. In case the angle x is measured in radians it would be _______________.

11. The area of a circle with radius r is _______________. The area of the sector that corresponds an angle x° is _______________. In case the angle x is measured in radians it would be _______________.

12. Given the circle with r = 2cm :

a. Show the arc corresponding an angle of 45°.
b. Calculate its length.
c. Shade Show the corresponding sector area.
d. Calculate it.

13. Given the circle with r = 3.2m:

a. Show Shade the arc corresponding an angle of 20°.
b. Calculate its length.
c. Shade the corresponding sector area.
d. Calculate it.

14. Given the circle with r = 3.2m:

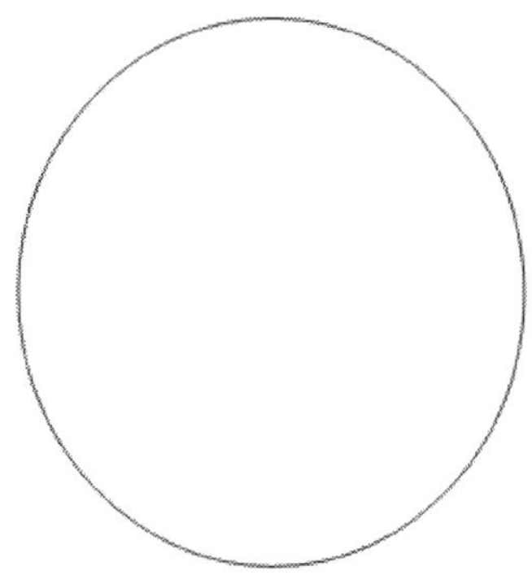

a. Show Shade the arc corresponding an angle of $\frac{\pi}{10} rad$.
b. Calculate its length.
c. Shade the corresponding sector area.
d. Calculate it.

15. Given the circle with r = 3.2m:

    a. Show Shade the arc corresponding an angle of 1 radian.
    b. Calculate its length.
    c. Shade the corresponding sector area.
    d. Calculate it.

16. Given the following concentric circles with radii 3 cm and 5 cm correspondingly. Calculate the shaded area.

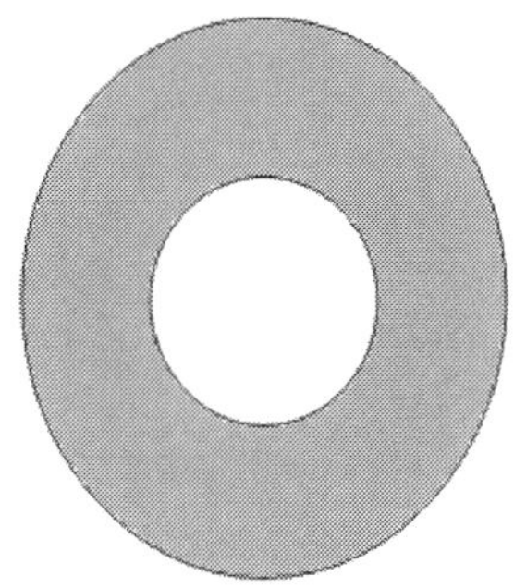

17. Given the following concentric circles with radii 10m and 14m correspondingly. Calculate the shaded area.

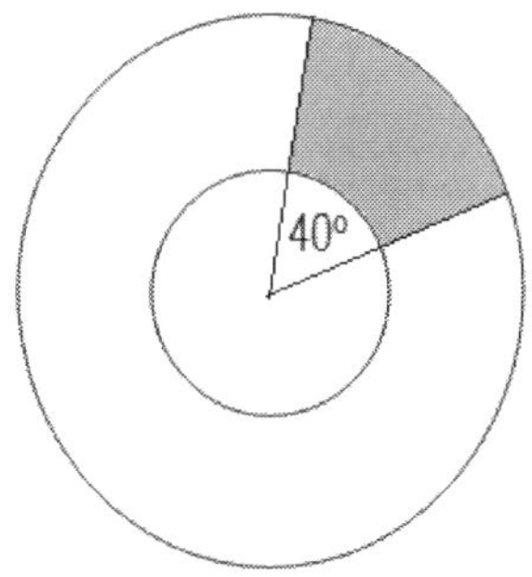

3.2. – TRIGONOMETRIC FUNCTIONS

Definition: The trigonometric functions are defined using the so called "unit circle" which is simply a circle with radius 1:

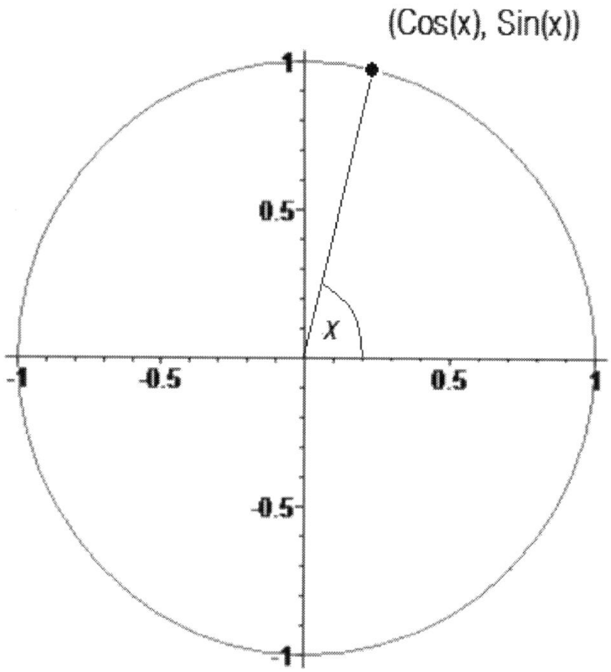

Definition of Sin(x):

1st Quadrant:

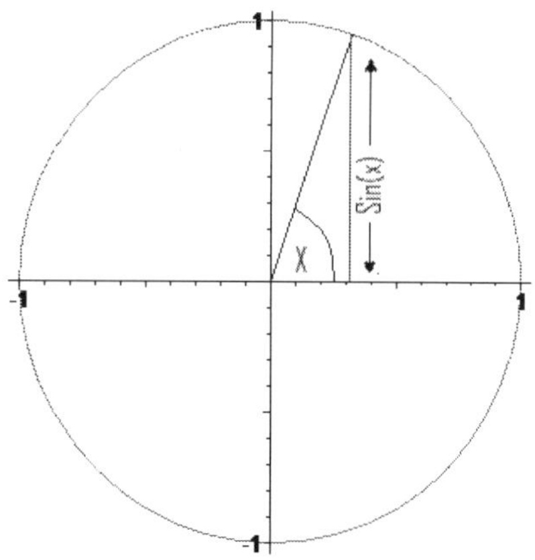

3rd Quadrant:

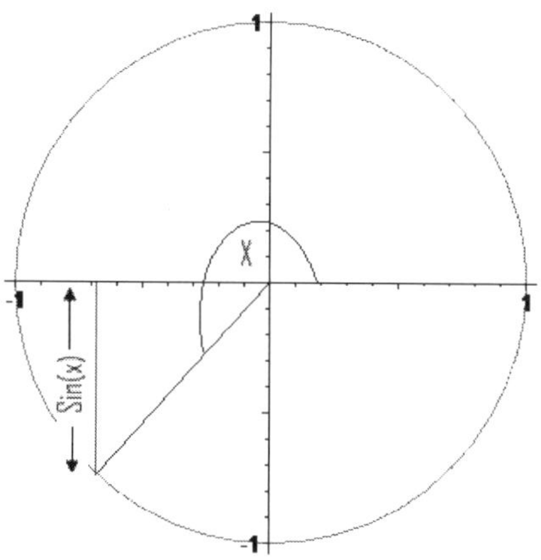

As can be deduced from the unit circle in the ____________ and ____________ quadrants the Sin(x) function is ___________, while in the ____________ and ____________ quadrants it is ___________.

Definition of Cos(x):

2nd Quadrant:

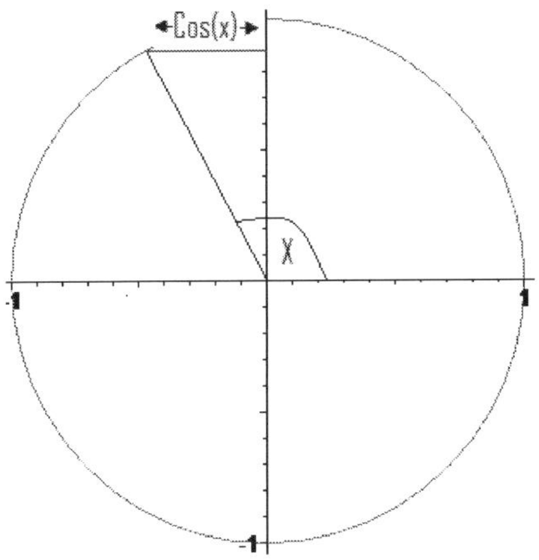

4th Quadrant:

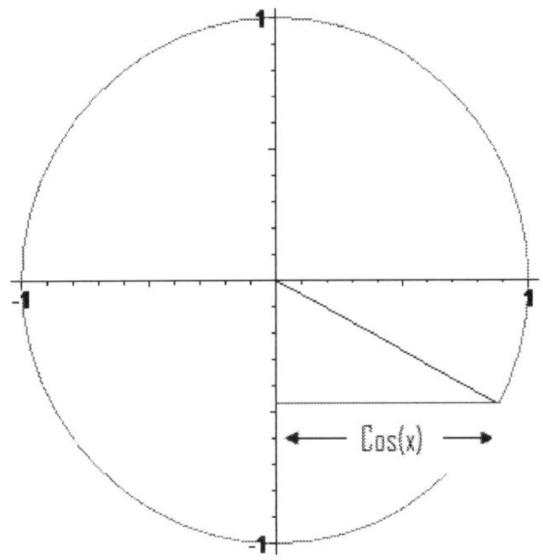

As can be deduced from the unit circle in the ____________ and ____________ quadrants the Sin(x) function is ___________, while in the ____________ and _____________ quadrants it is ___________.

Exercises:

In each one of the cases sketch the unit circle and the corresponding angle and then find the corresponding value:

1. Sin(0º) =

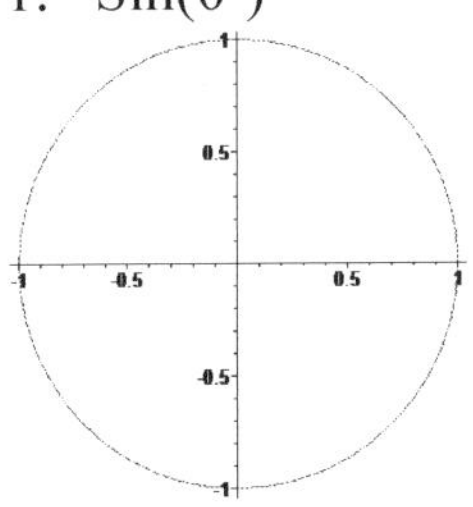

2. $\text{Cos}(0_{\text{rad}})$ =

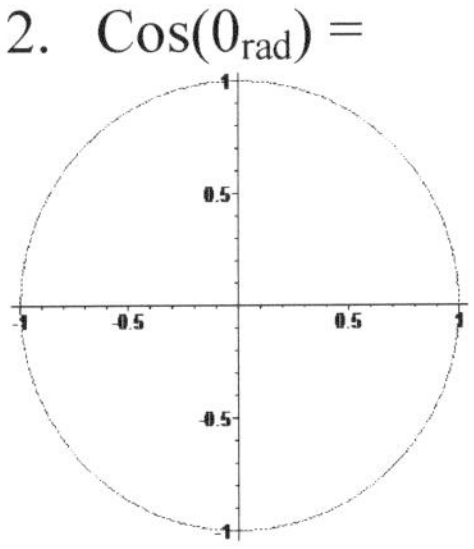

3. $\text{Sin}(0_{\text{rad}})$ =

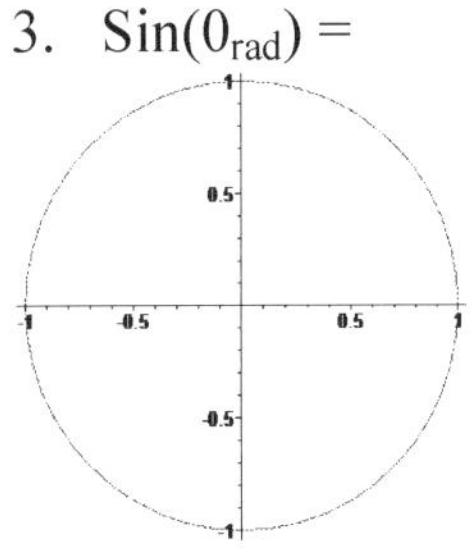

4. Cos(0º) =

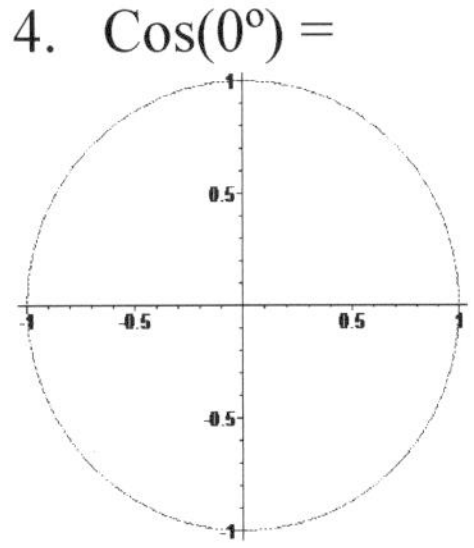

5. $\mathrm{Sin}(90^{\circ}) =$

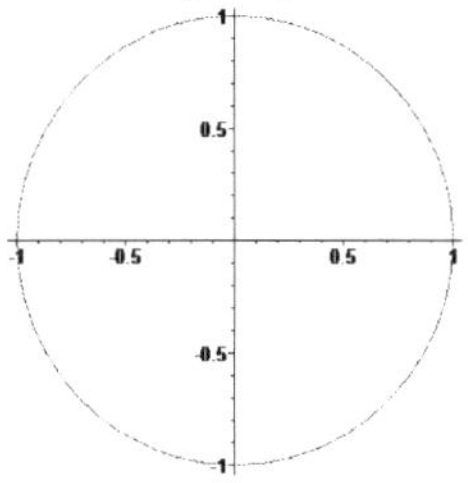

6. $\mathrm{Cos}(\pi_{rad}) =$

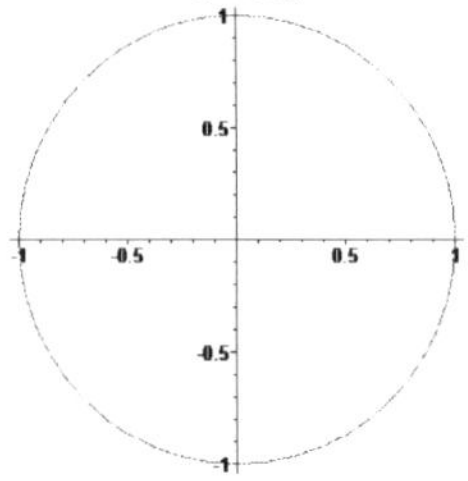

7. $\mathrm{Sin}(3\pi/4_{\ rad}) =$

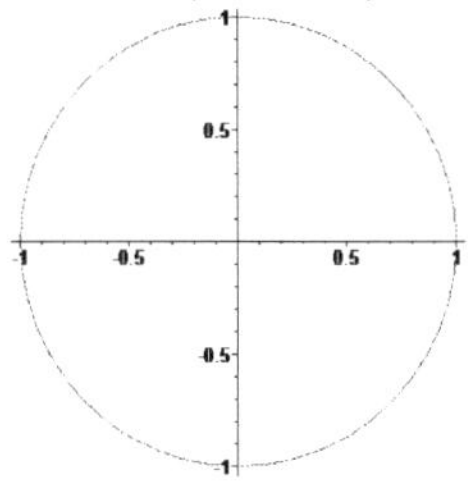

8. $\mathrm{Cos}(225^{\circ}) =$

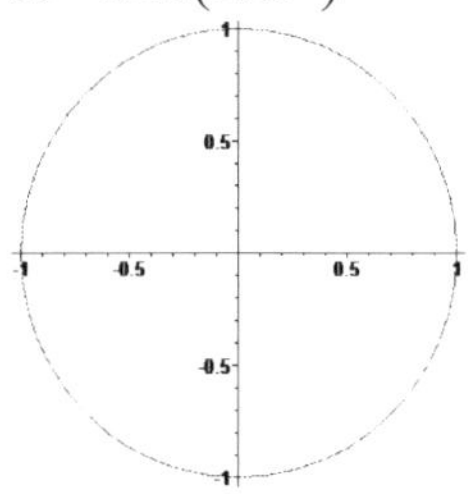

9. $\mathrm{Sin}(225^{\circ}) =$

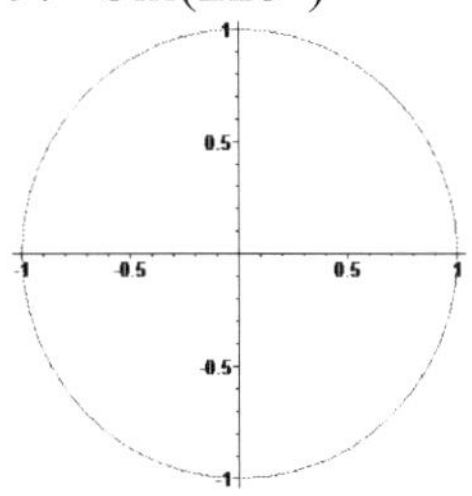

10. $\mathrm{Cos}(4\pi/3_{\ rad}) =$

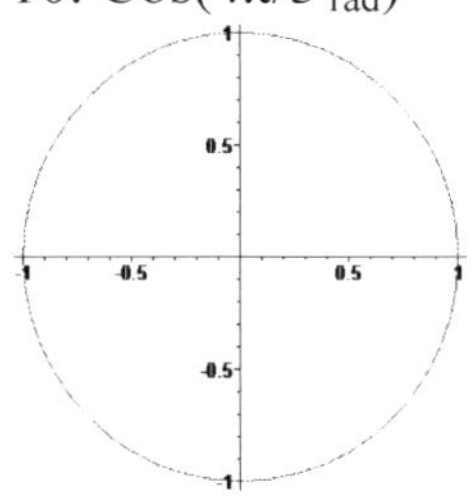

11. $\mathrm{Sin}(4\pi/3_{\ rad}) =$

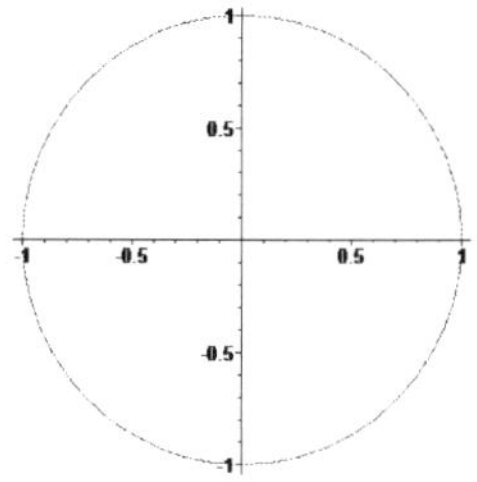

12. $\mathrm{Cos}(210^{\circ}) =$

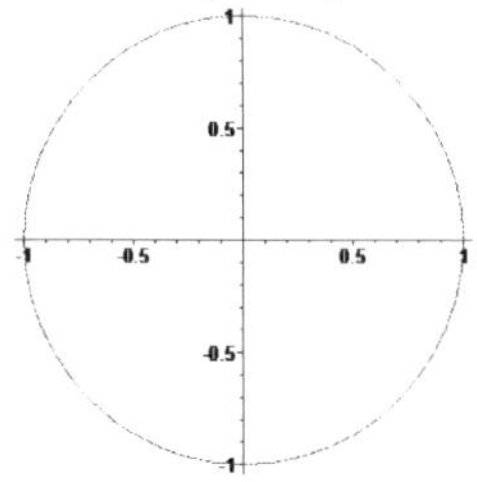

13. $\mathrm{Sin}(210^{\circ}) =$

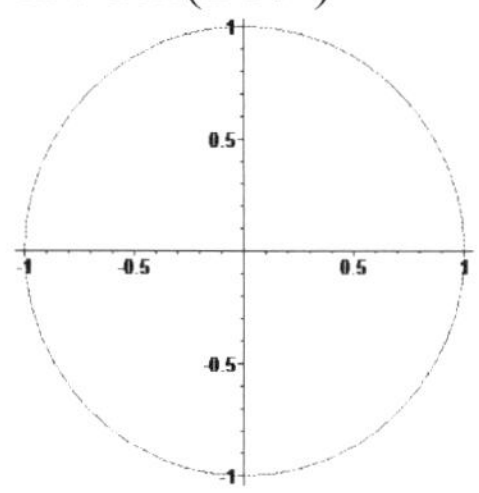

14. $\mathrm{Sin}(3\pi/4_{\ rad}) =$

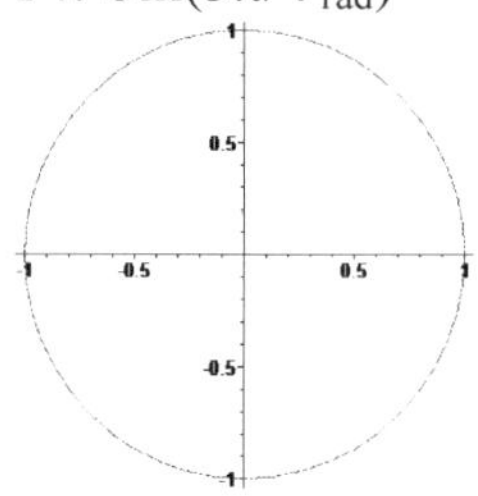

15. $\mathrm{Cos}(225^{\circ}) =$

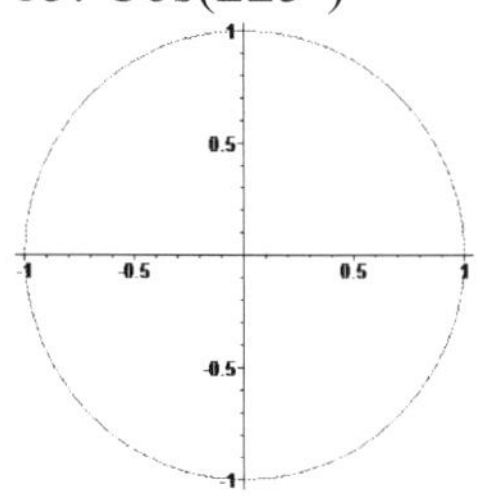

16. $\mathrm{Sin}(-225^{\circ}) =$

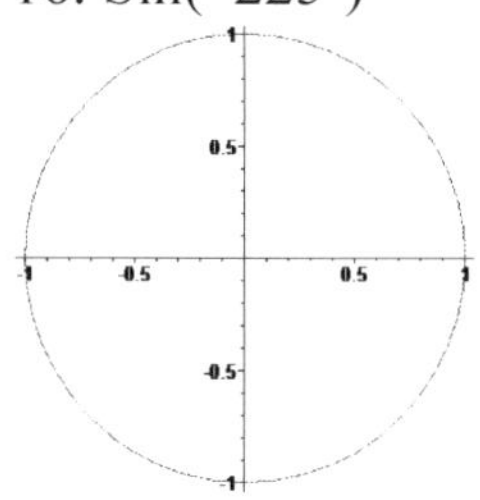

17. $\text{Cos}(4\pi/3_{\text{ rad}}) =$

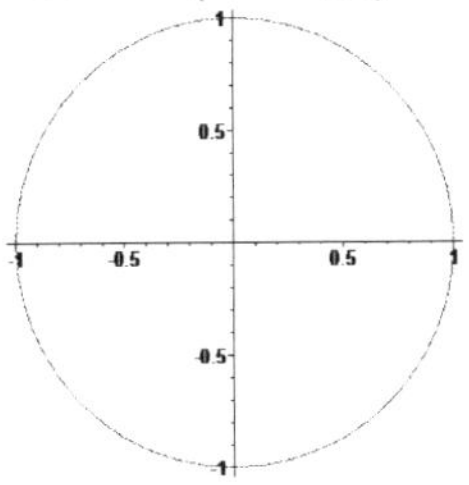

18. $\text{Sin}(4\pi/3_{\text{ rad}}) =$

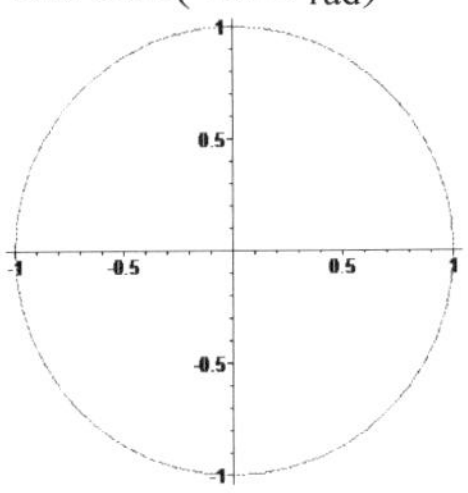

19. $\text{Cos}(210^{\circ}) =$

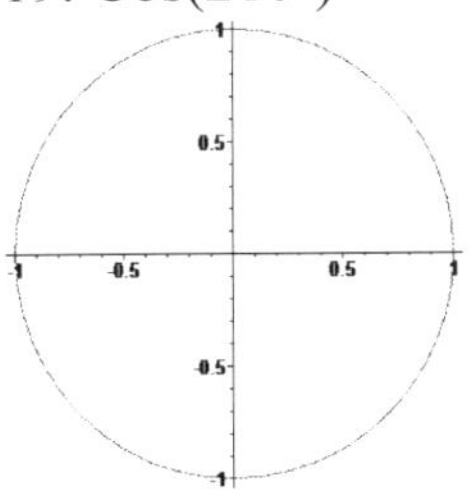

20. $\text{Sin}(-210^{\circ}) =$

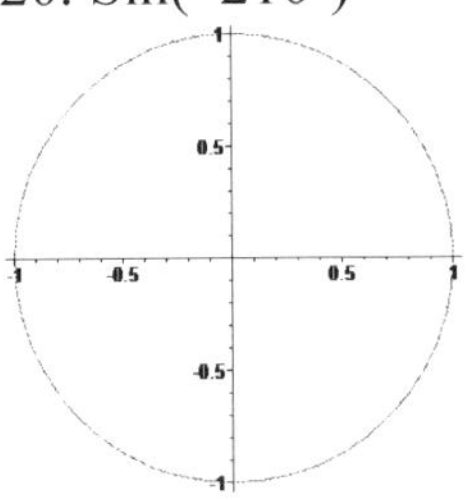

21. $\text{Sin}(-\pi_{\text{rad}}) =$

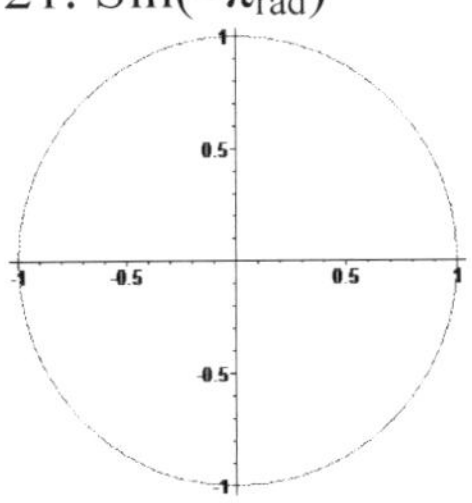

22. $\text{Cos}(90^{\circ}) =$

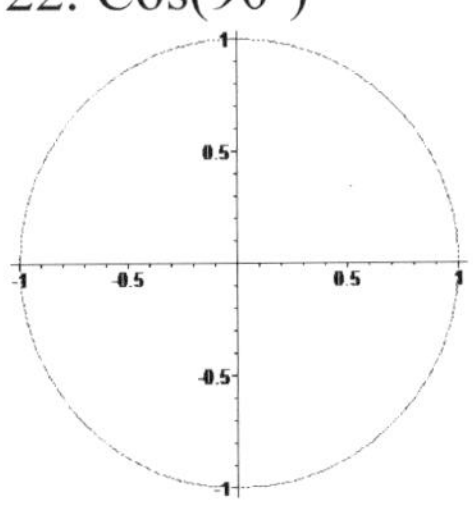

23. $\text{Sin}(270^{\circ}) =$

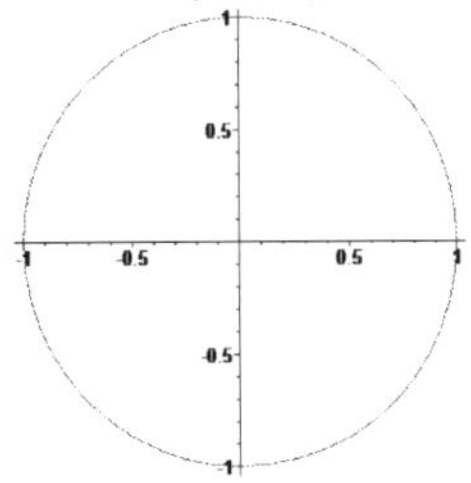

24. $\text{Cos}(\pi/2_{\text{rad}}) =$

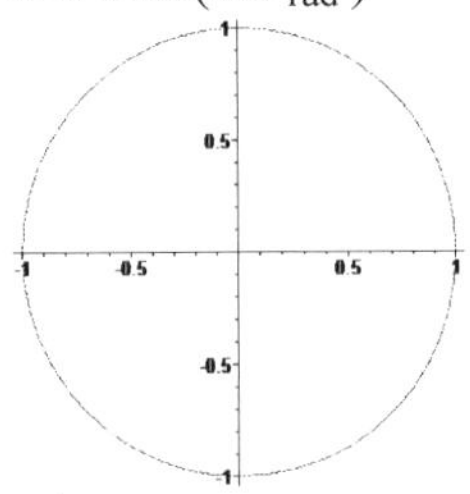

25. $\text{Sin}(3\pi/2_{\text{rad}}) =$

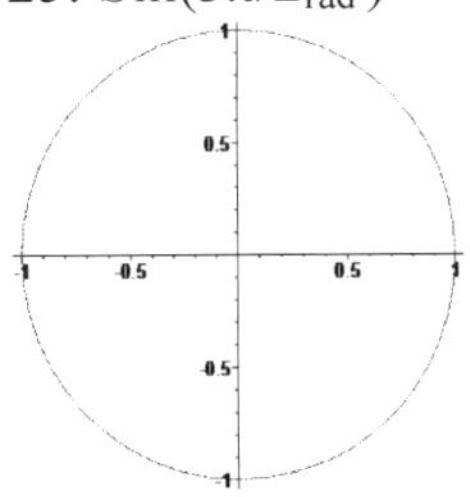

26. $\text{Cos}(270^{\circ}) =$

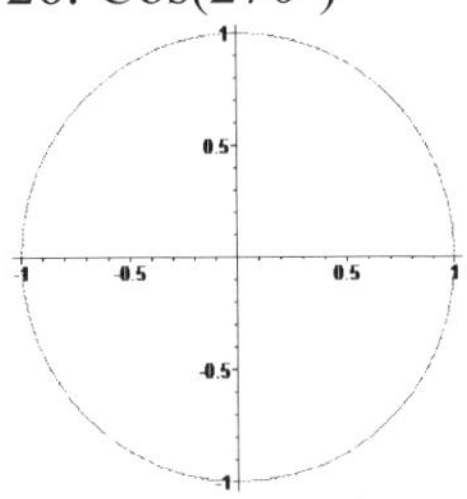

27. $\text{Sin}(360^{\circ}) =$

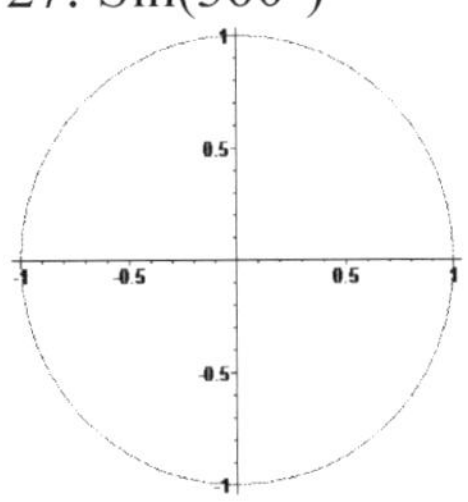

28. $\text{Cos}(-\pi/2_{\text{rad}}) =$

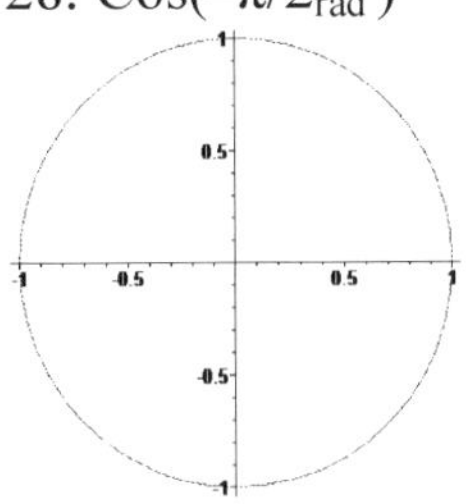

29. $\text{Sin}(2\pi_{\text{rad}}) =$

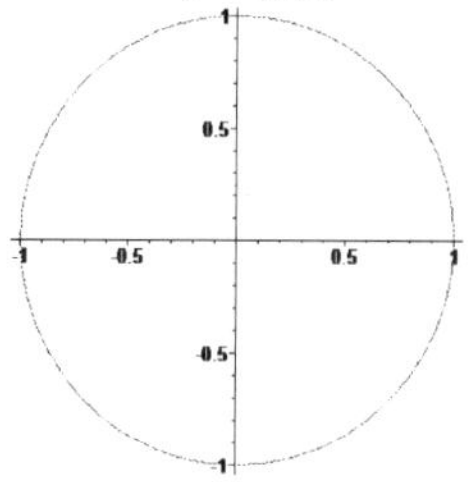

30. Cos(180°) =

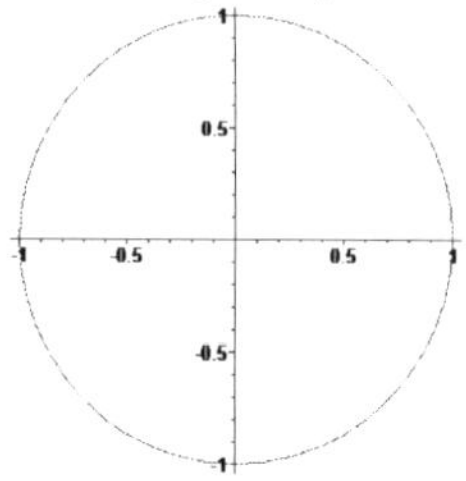

31. Sin(180°) =

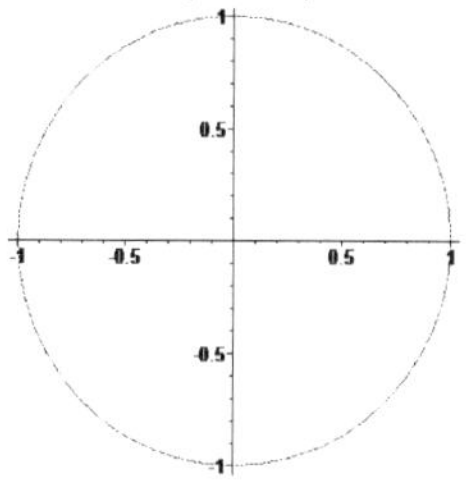

32. $\text{Cos}(\pi/3_{\text{rad}}) =$

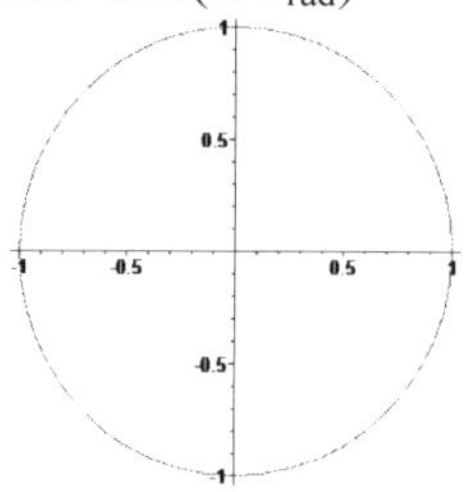

33. $\text{Sin}(\pi/4_{\text{rad}}) =$

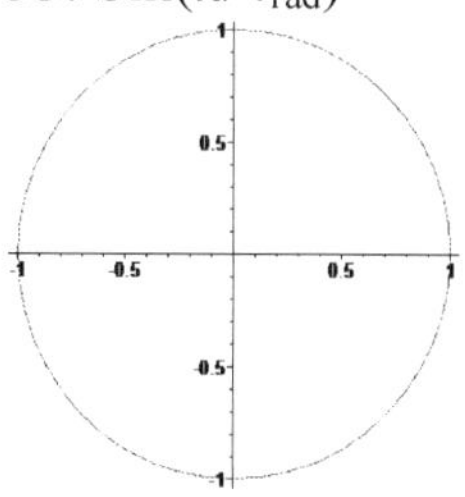

34. Cos(–45°) =

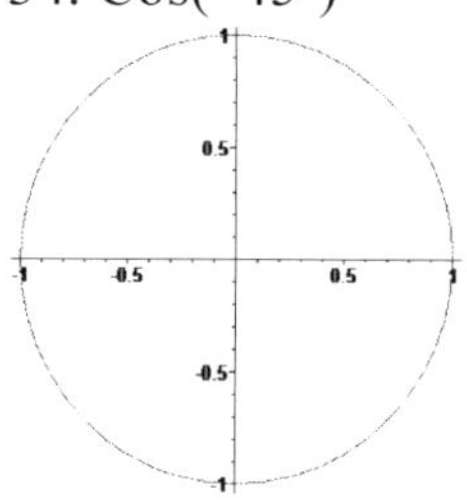

35. $\text{Sin}(3\pi/2_{\text{ rad}}) =$

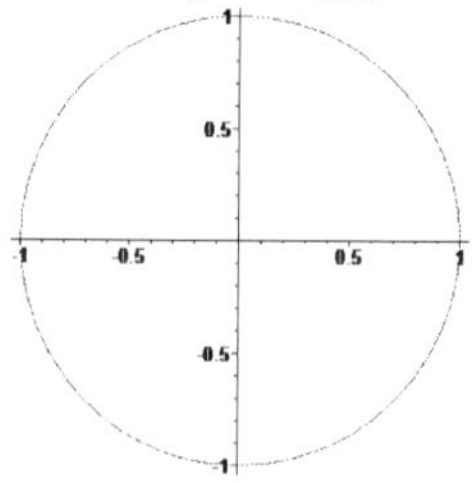

36. $\text{Cos}(-2\pi/3_{\text{ rad}}) =$

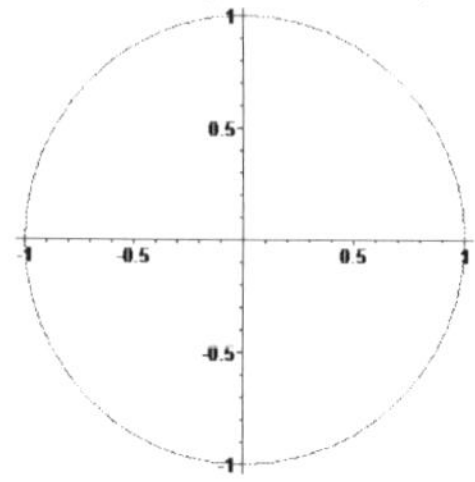

37. $\text{Sin}(2\pi/3_{\text{ rad}}) =$

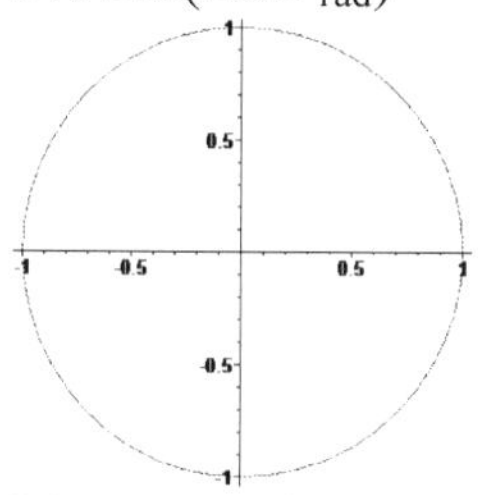

38. $\text{Cos}(3\pi/4_{\text{ rad}}) =$

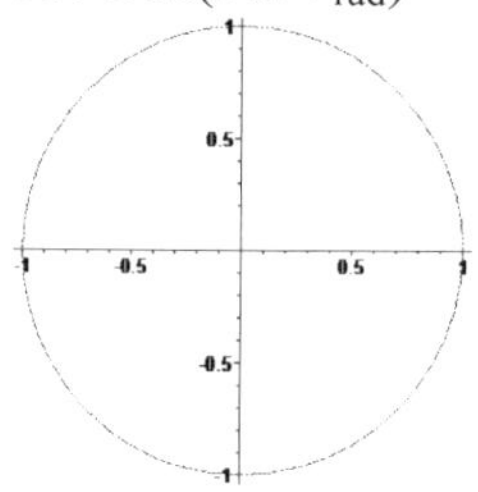

39. Cos(300°) =

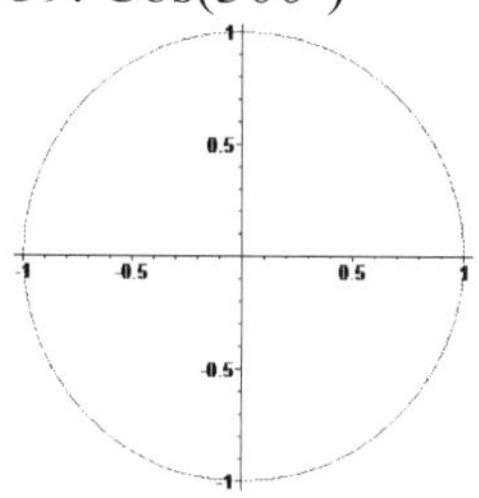

40. Sin(300°) =

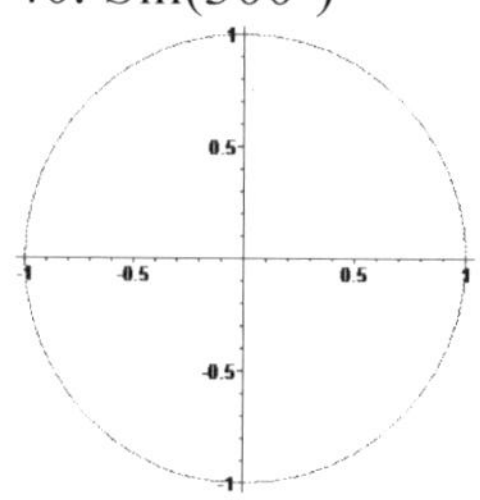

41. $\text{Cos}(2\pi_{\text{rad}}) =$

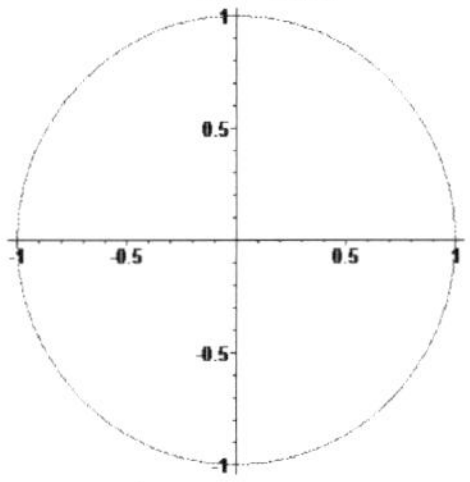

42. $\text{Sin}(2\pi_{\text{rad}}) =$

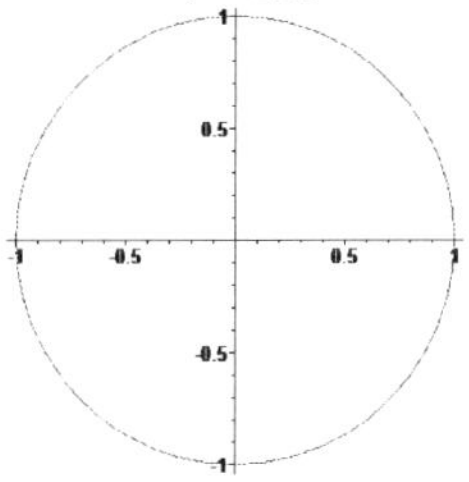

43. $\text{Sin}(330^{\circ}) =$

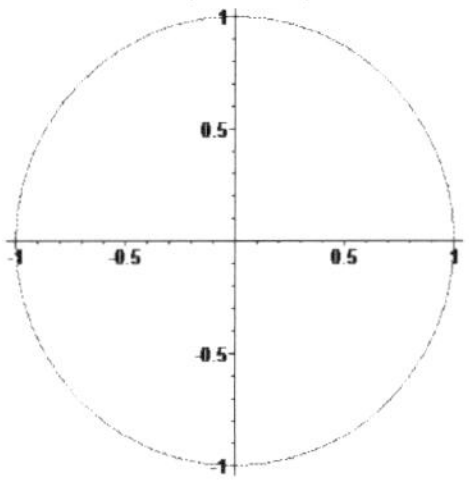

44. $\text{Cos}(390^{\circ}) =$

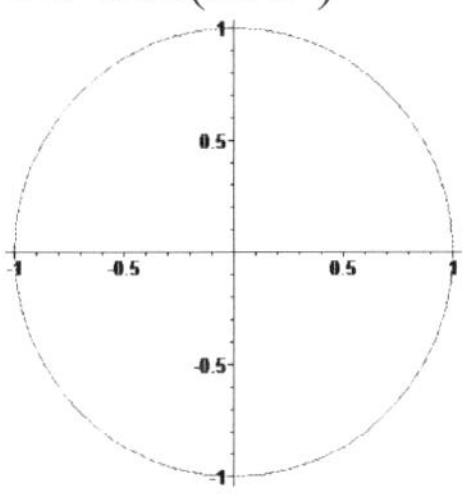

45. $\text{Cos}(135^{\circ}) =$

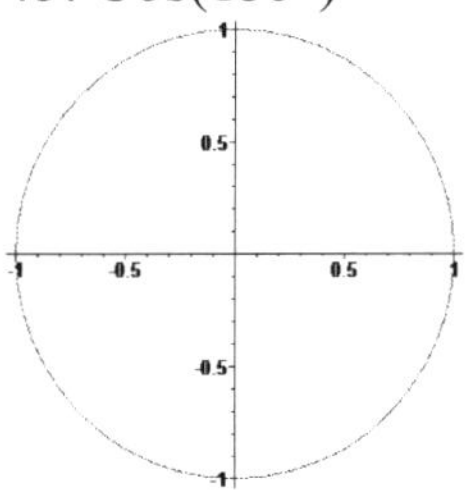

46. $\text{Sin}(135^{\circ}) =$

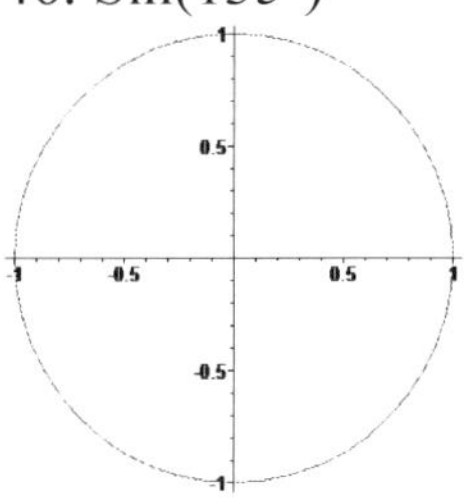

47. $\text{Sin}(45^{\circ}) =$

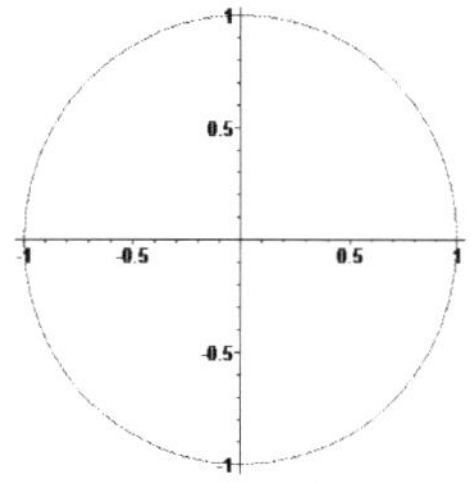

48. $\text{Cos}(-3\pi/2_{\text{ rad}}) =$

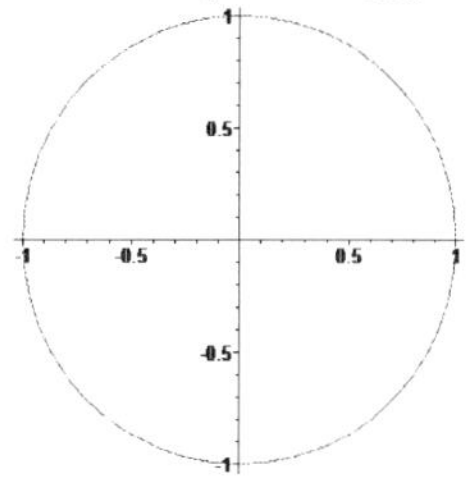

49. $\text{Cos}(70^{\circ}) =$

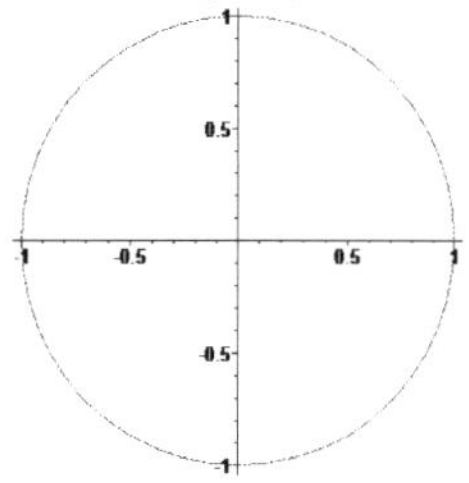

50. $\text{Cos}(130^{\circ}) =$

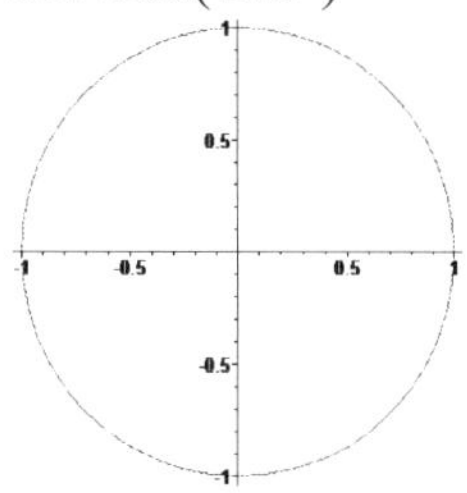

51. $\text{Cos}(1^{\circ}) =$

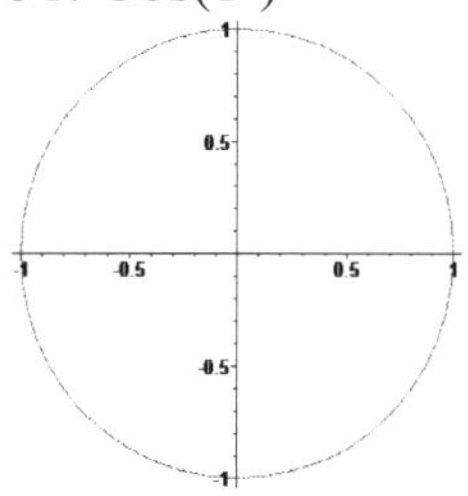

52. $\text{Cos}(3_{\text{rad}}) =$

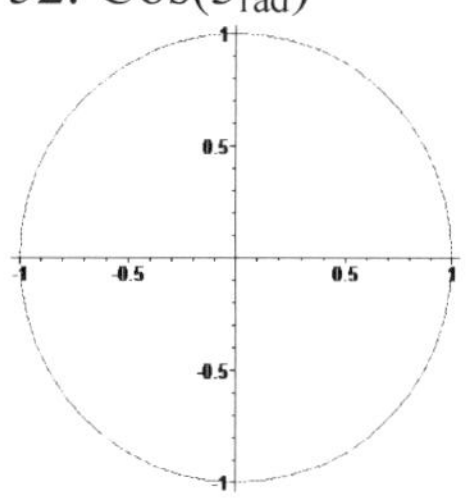

53. Sin(1 $_{rad}$) =

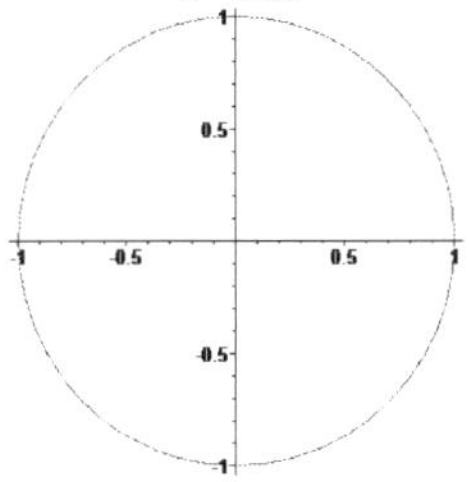

54. Cos(Π/5 $_{rad}$) =

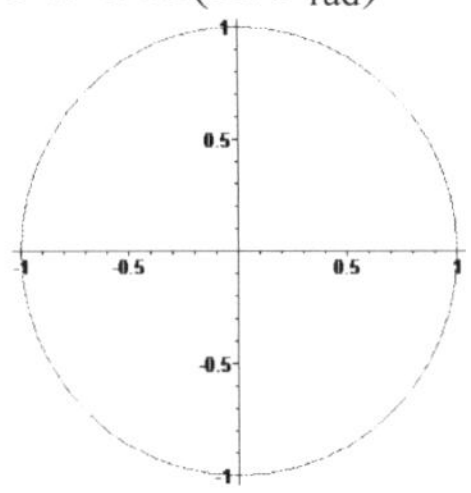

55. Sin(2Π/7 $_{rad}$) =

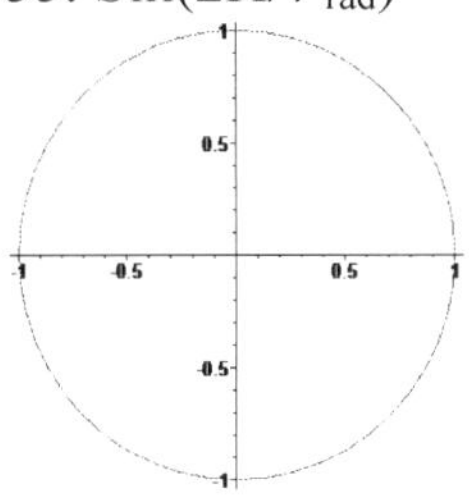

For each one of the following, fill in the blank with an angle between 0º and 360º different than the first one.

56. Sin(25º) = Sin (____)

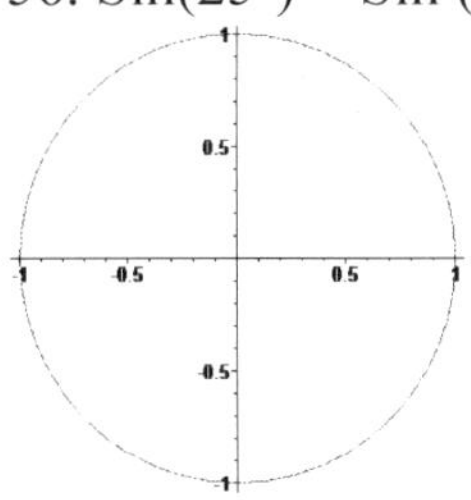

57. Sin(145º) = Sin (____)

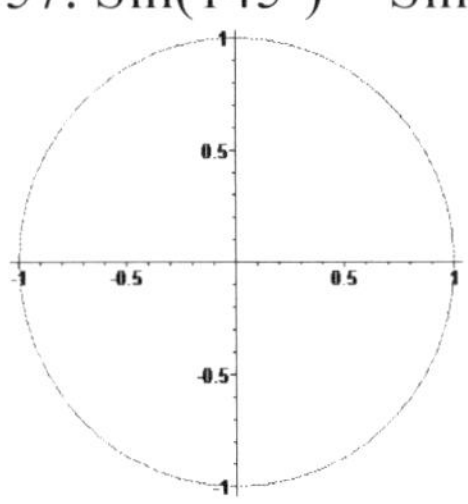

58. Sin(70º) = Sin (____)

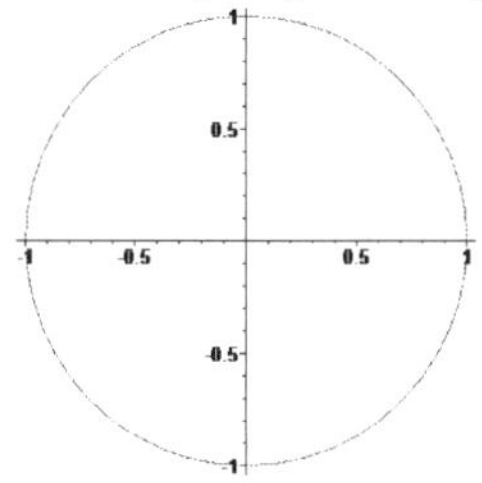

59. Sin(–20º) = Sin (____)

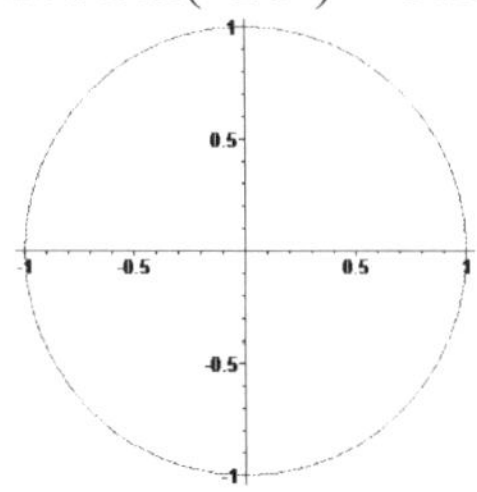

60. Sin(–30º) = Sin (____)

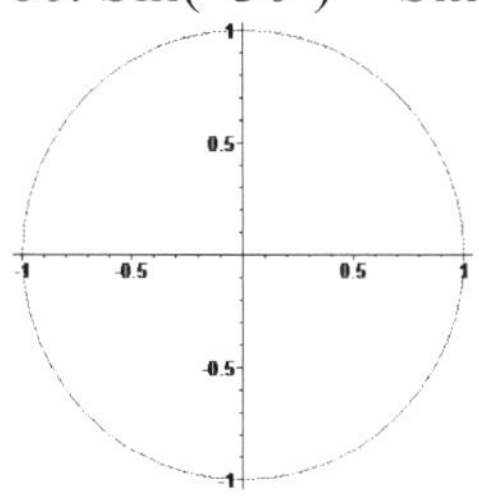

61. Sin(225º) = Sin (____)

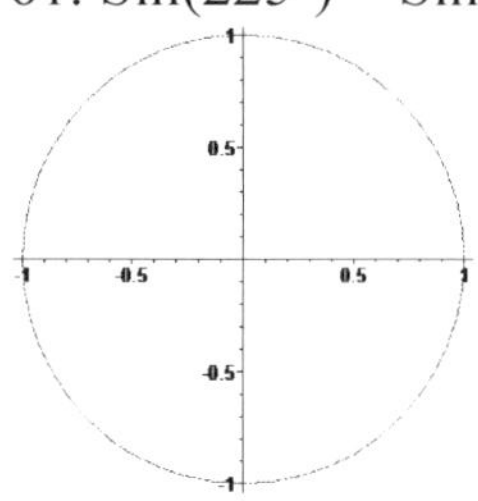

62. Sin(250º) = Sin (____)

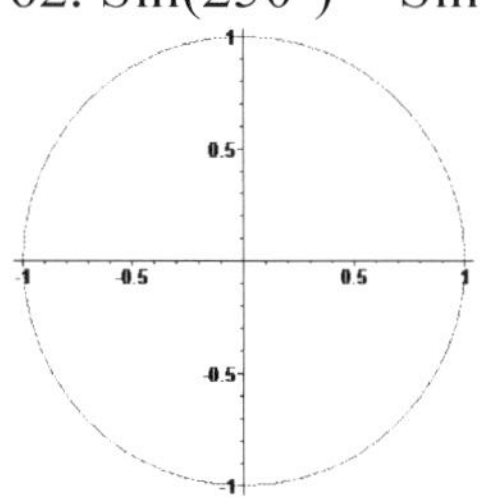

63. Cos(250º) = Cos (____)

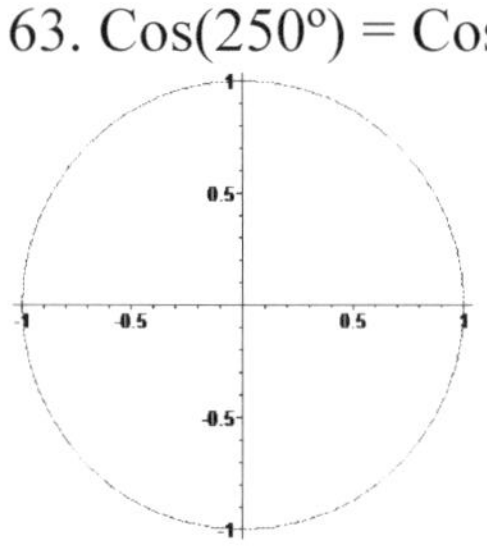

64. Cos(350°) = Cos (____)

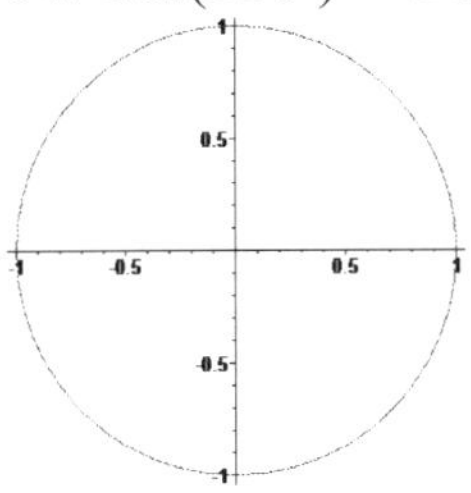

65. Cos(450°) = Cos (____)

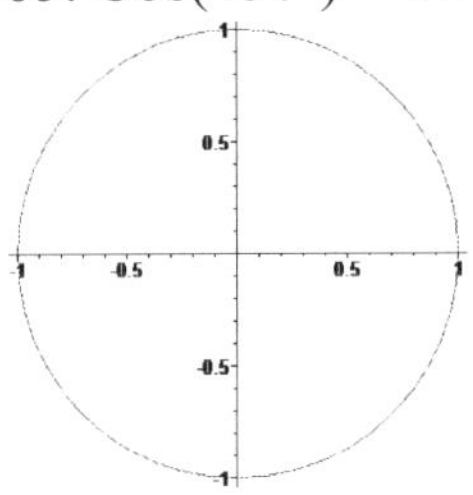

66. Cos(–250°) = Cos (____)

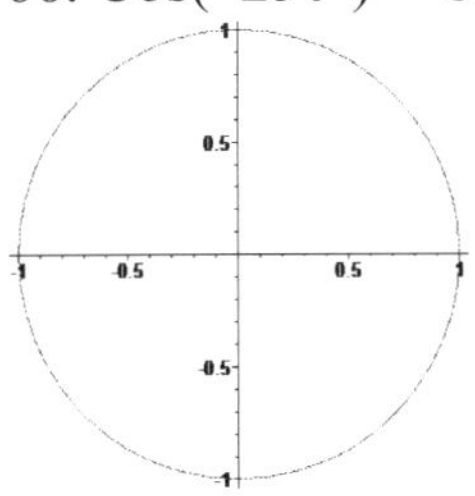

67. Cos(–50°) = Cos (____)

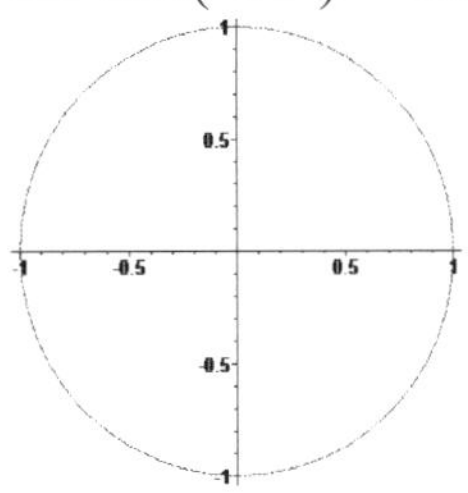

68. Cos(–73°) = Cos (____)

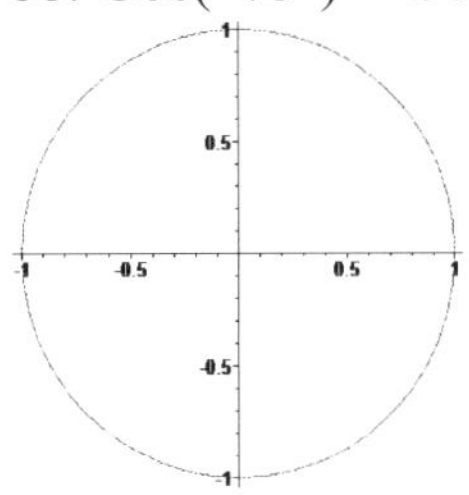

<u>Definitions of Tan (x), Cot(x), Sec(x) Cosec(x)</u>

$$Tan(x)=\left(\frac{\_\_\_\_\_\_}{\_\_\_\_\_\_}\right), Cos(x)\neq 0 \qquad Cot(x)=\left(\frac{\_\_\_\_\_\_}{\_\_\_\_\_\_}\right), Sin(x)\neq 0$$

$$Sec(x)=\left(\frac{1}{\_\_\_\_\_\_}\right), Cos(x)\neq 0 \qquad Csc(x)=\left(\frac{1}{\_\_\_\_\_\_}\right), Sin(x)\neq 0$$

In Consequence:

Tan(x) = tg(x) is positive in the __________and __________ quadrants and negative in the __________and __________ quadrants. Cotg(x) = Cot(x) =Cotan(x) is positive in the _________and __________ quadrants and negative in the __________and __________ quadrants.

69. Calculate the following trigonometric functions in terms of a and b:

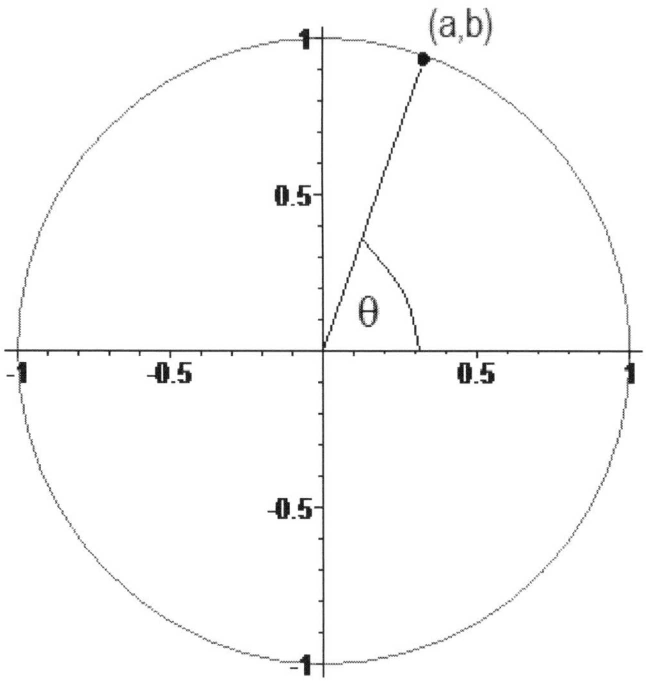

a. $\text{Sin}(\theta) =$ $\text{Cos}(\theta) =$

b. $\text{Sin}(\theta + 360^\circ) =$

c. $\text{Sin}(\theta + 180^\circ) =$

d. $\text{Sin}(180^\circ - \theta) =$

e. $\text{Cos}(180^\circ - \theta) =$

f. $\text{Sin}(360^\circ - \theta) =$

g. $\text{Cos}(360^\circ - \theta) =$

h. $\text{Sin}(90^\circ - \theta) =$

i. $\text{Cos}(90^\circ - \theta) =$

j. $\text{Tan}(\theta) =$

k. $\text{Cotan}(\theta) =$

l. $\text{Sec}(\theta) =$

m. $\text{Csc}(\theta) =$

n. $\text{Tan}(\theta + 180^\circ) =$

o. $\text{Tan}(\theta + 90^\circ) =$

p. $\text{Cos}(270^\circ - \theta)$

q. $\text{Sin}(270^\circ + \theta)$

Complete the following table:

Angle in degrees	Angle in Radians	Sin(x)	Cos(x)	Tan(x)	Cot(x)	Sec(x)	Csc(x)
0	0						
30°							
45°							
60°							
90°							
120°							
135°							
150°							
180°							
360°							
390°							

Exercises:

1. Given that $\sin(x) = \dfrac{2}{7}$ and $0 < x < \dfrac{\pi}{2}$, find:

a. $\text{Cos}(x) =$

b. $\text{Tan}(x) =$

c. $\text{Cot}(x) =$

d. $\text{Csc}(x) =$

e. $\text{Sin}(2x) =$

f. $\text{Cos}(2x) =$

g. $\text{Sin}(3x) =$

h. $\text{Cos}(3x) =$

i. $\text{Sin}(\pi - x) =$

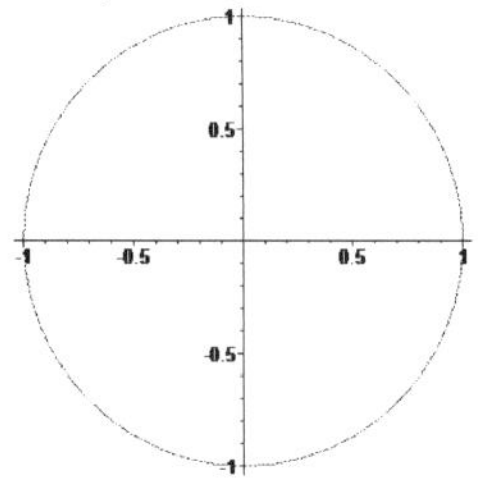

j. $\text{Cos}(\pi - x) =$

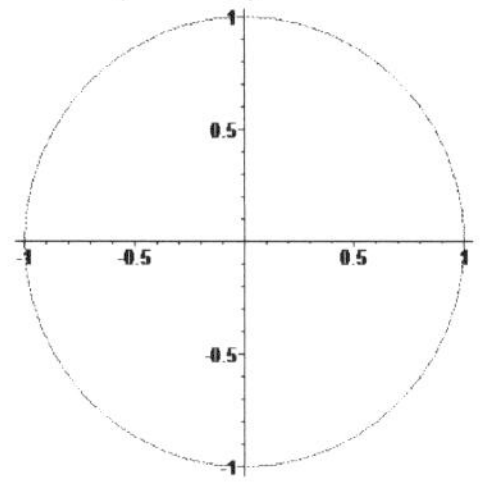

k. $\text{Sin}(2\pi - x) =$

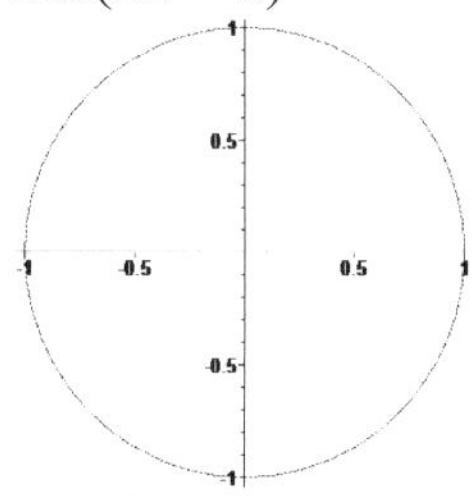

l. $\text{Cos}(2\pi - x) =$

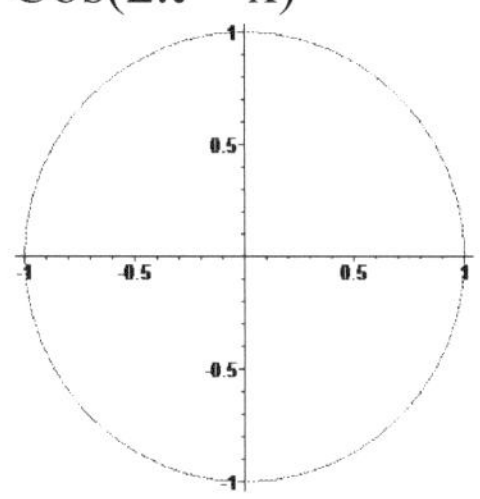

m. $\text{Sin}(x + \dfrac{\pi}{2}) =$

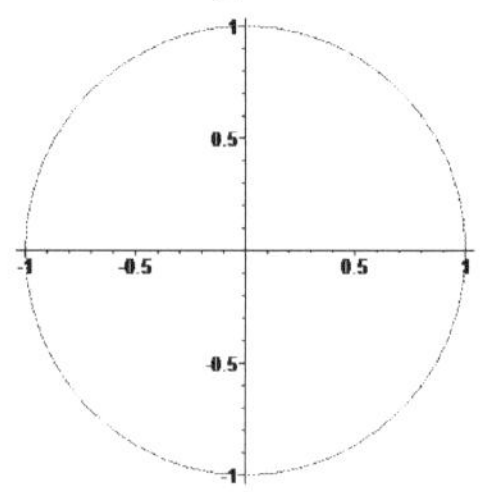

2. Given that $\text{Cos}(x) = -\frac{1}{6}$ and $\pi < x < \frac{3\pi}{2}$, find:

a. Sin(x) =

b. Tan(x) =

c. Cot(x) =

d. Csc(x) =

e. Sin(2x) =

f. Cos(2x) =

g. Sin(4x) =

h. Cos(4x) =

i. Sin(π – x) =

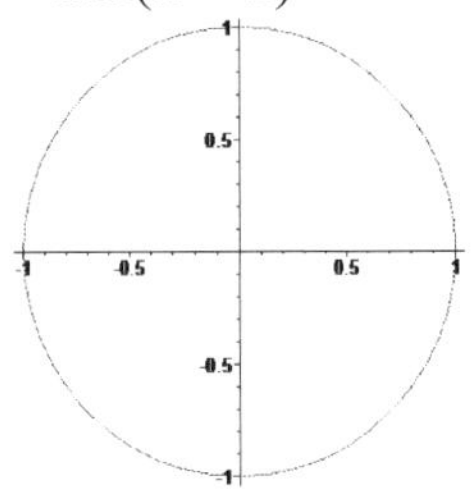

j. Cos(π – x) =

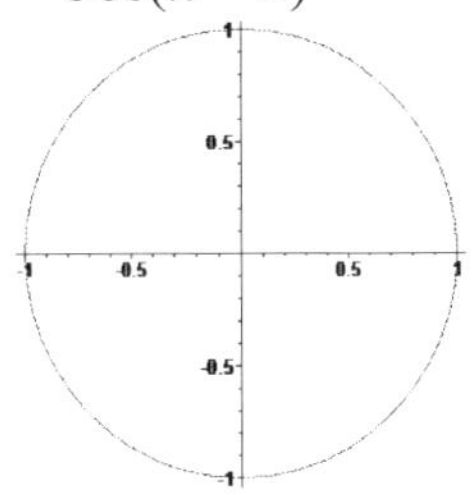

k. Sin(2π – x) =

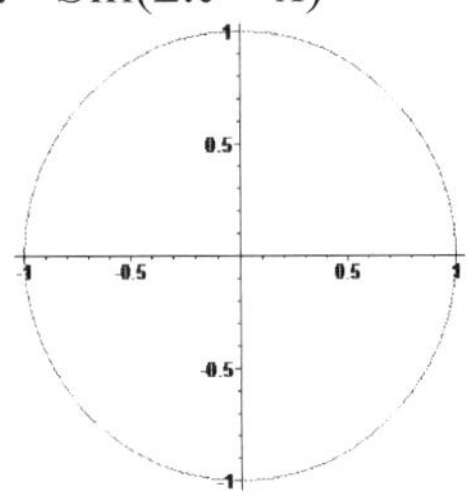

l. Cos(2π – x) =

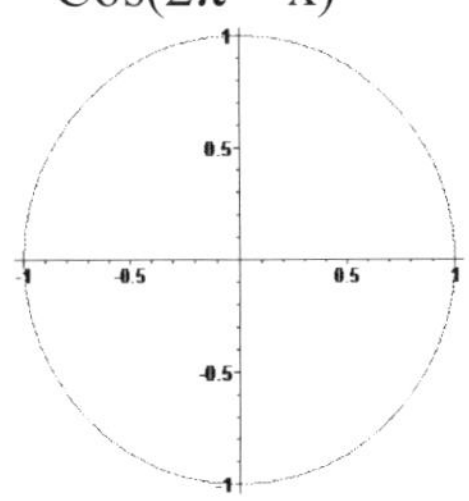

m. $\text{Cos}(x + \frac{\pi}{2}) =$

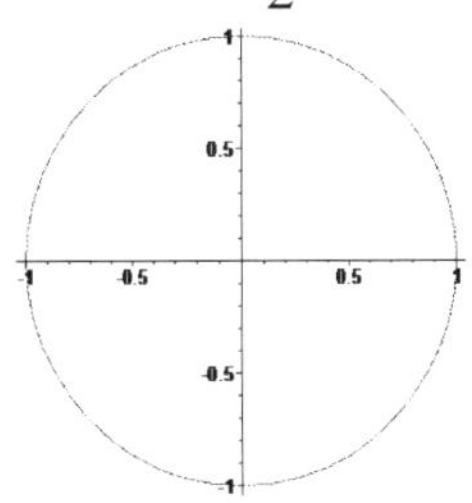

3. Given that Tan(x) = 3 and π < x < 2π, so x is in the ________ quadrant. find:

a. Cos(x) =

b. Tan(x) =

c. Cot(x) =

d. Csc(x) =

e. Tan(2x) =

f. Sin(3x) =

g. Cos(3x) =

h. Sin(π – x) =

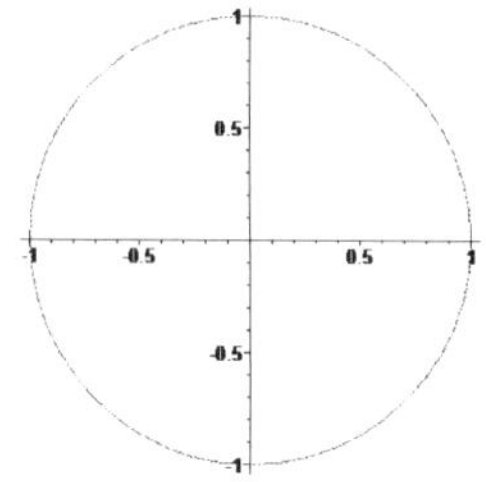

i. Cos(π – x) =

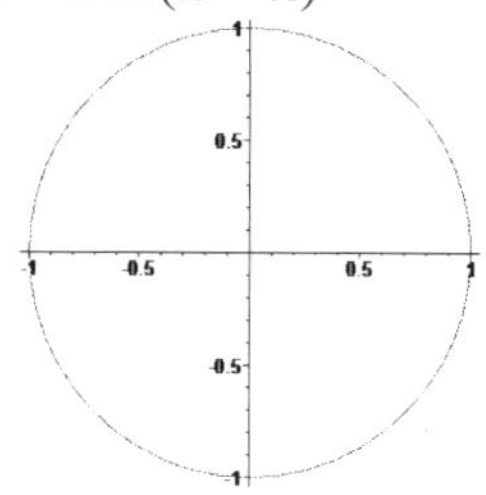

j. Sin(2π – x) =

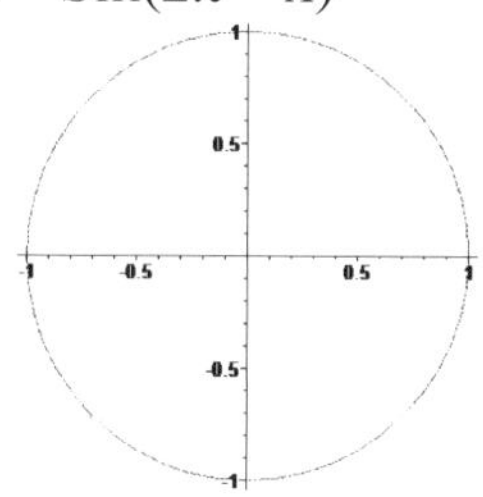

k. Cos(2π – x) =

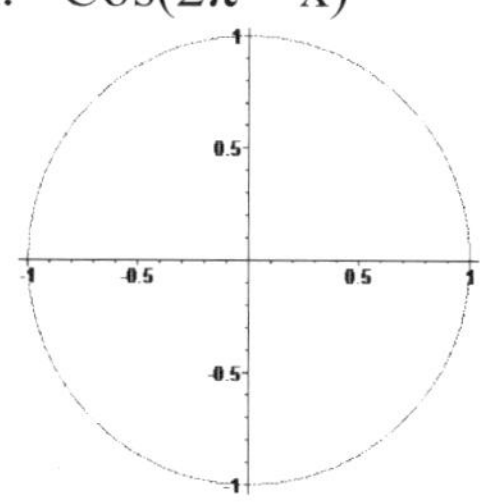

l. $\text{Sin}(x + \frac{\pi}{2}) =$

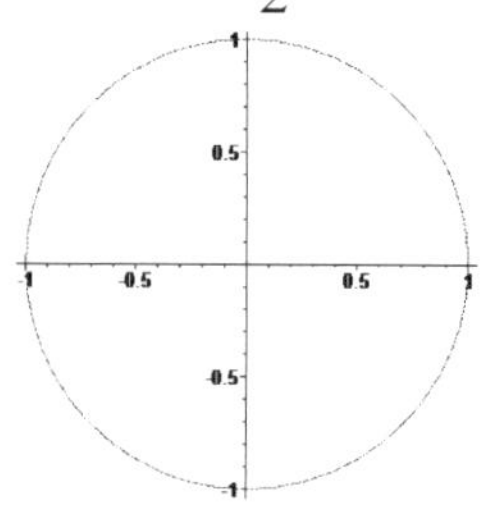

3.3. – TRIGONOMETRIC FUNCTIONS

1. Write next to each one of the functions if it's periodic or not. Determine the period of the periodic ones.

a.

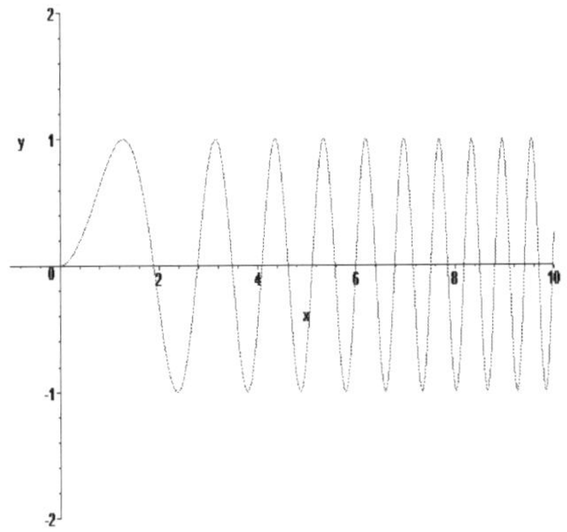

b.

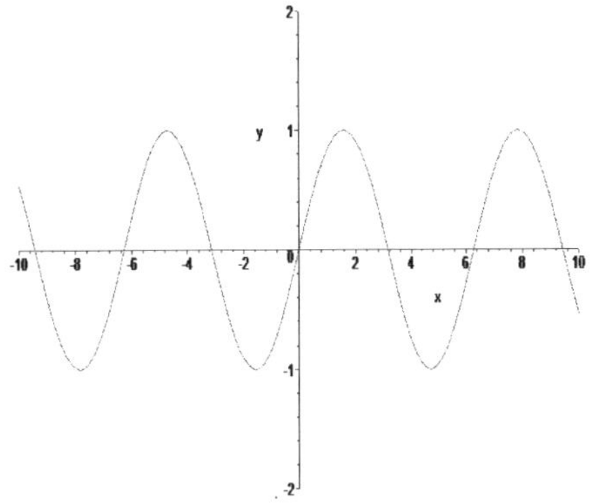

c.

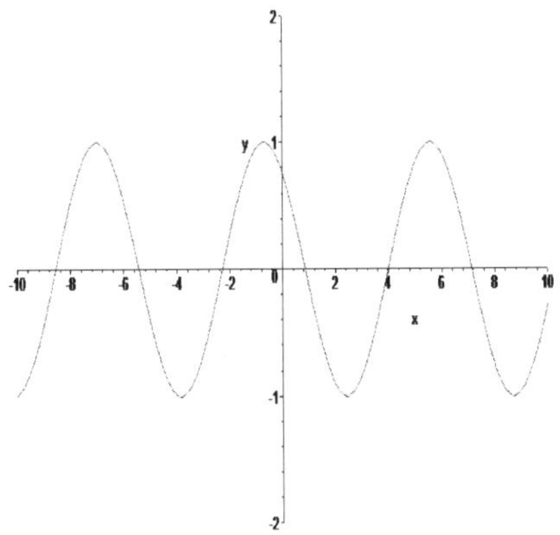

d.

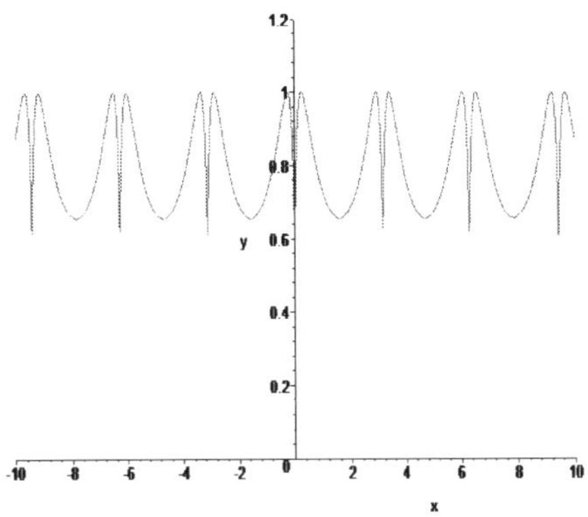

2. Given the function f(x) = Sin(x), g(x) = cos(x), Complete the following table:

x°	0	15	30	45	60	75	90	105	120	135	150	165	180	195	210	225	240	255
Rad																		
f(x)																		
g(x)																		

- Sketch the points of the table on a graph.
- State the domain of the function: ________________
- State the y intercept (sketched on the graph: (____, ____)
- State the x intercept(s): (____, ____), (____,)
- Write the corresponding limits and the equation of the vertical asymptote: _____
- Write the corresponding limits and the equation of the horizontal asymptote: ___
- Function is increasing on the interval: _____, decreasing on the interval:______
- Find the max/min point(s): (____, ____)
- State the range of the function: ________

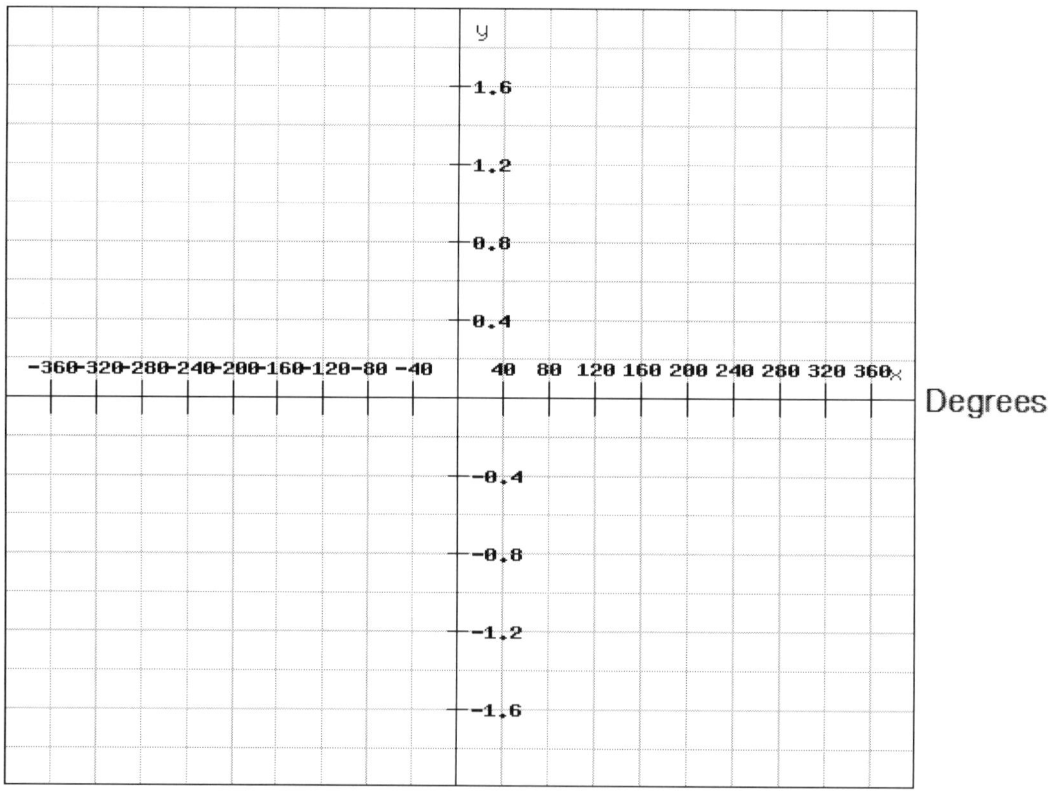

3. Given the function f(x) = Sin(x)

   a. Write in all forms the same function translated 2 positions up.

   b. Write in all forms the same function translated 3 positions left.

   c. Write in all forms the same function translated 3 positions left and 1 up.

   d. Write in all forms the same function translated 4 positions right and 1 up.

   e. Change the function so that the period would be 2.

   f. Change the function so that the period would be 3 and the amplitude 2.

   g. Change the function so that the period would be π and the amplitude 4.

   h. Change the function so that the period would be $\frac{\pi}{3}$ and the amplitude k.

   i. Change the function so that the period would be 6, the amplitude 3, then shift the function 2 positions right and 1 down.

   j. Change the function so that the period would be $\frac{\pi}{3}$, the amplitude 1.3, then shift the function 4 positions left and 2 down.

   k. Change the function so that the period would be $\frac{\pi}{5}$, the amplitude 4, then shift the function π positions left and 5 down.

4. Given the function $f(x) = 3Sin(5(x - 2)) + 3$

   a. Amplitude = ___________

   b. Period = ___________

   c. Horizontal Translation = ___________

   d. Vertical Translation (midline) = ___________

5. Given the function $f(x) = -5Cos(3x - 2) - 3.4$

   a. Amplitude = ___________

   b. Period = ___________

   c. Horizontal Translation = ___________

   d. Vertical Translation (midline) = ___________

6. Given the function $f(x) = 2.4Sin(\pi x - \frac{\pi}{2}) - 3$

   a. Amplitude = ___________

   b. Period = ___________

   c. Horizontal Translation = ___________

   d. Vertical Translation (midline) = ___________

7. Given the function $f(x) = 4 - (2.4)Cos(2\pi x - \frac{\pi}{3})$

   a. Amplitude = ___________

   b. Period = ___________

   c. Horizontal Translation = ___________

   d. Vertical Translation (midline) = ___________

8. Given the function $f(x) = 1 + 4\text{Sin}(\frac{\pi}{3}x - 3)$

   a. Amplitude = ___________

   b. Period = ___________

   c. Horizontal Translation = ___________

   d. Vertical Translation (midline) = ___________

9. Given the function $f(x) = -\text{Sin}(\frac{\pi}{5}x - 1) + 1$

   a. Amplitude = ___________

   b. Period = ___________

   c. Horizontal Translation = ___________

   d. Vertical Translation (midline) = ___________

10. Given the function $f(x) = 4 - 3\text{Cos}(3x^{\circ})$

   a. Amplitude = ___________

   b. Period = ___________

   c. Horizontal Translation = ___________

   d. Vertical Translation

   e. Midline: ___________

11. Given the function $f(x) = -\text{Sin}(\frac{x^{\circ}}{10}) + 1$

   a. Amplitude = ___________

   b. Period = ___________

   c. Horizontal Translation = ___________

   d. Vertical Translation

   e. Midline: ___________

12. Given the graph, complete:

a. Amplitude = ____________

b. Period = ____________

c. Horizontal Translation: ____________

d. Midline: ____________

e. f(x) =

f. Range: ________________________

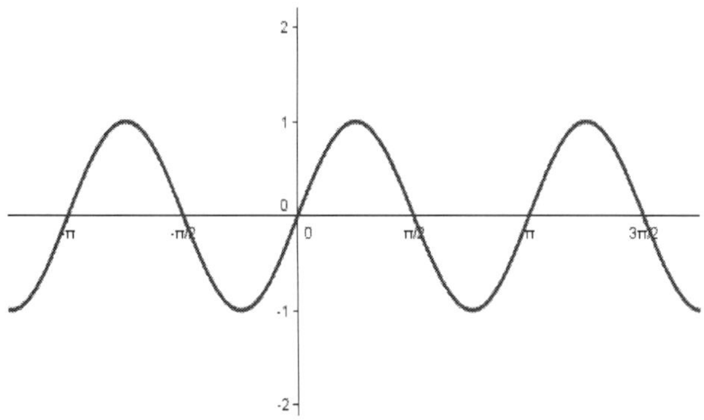

13. Given the graph, complete:

a. Amplitude = ____________

b. Period = ____________

c. Horizontal Translation: ____________

d. Midline: ____________

e. f(x) =

f. Range: ________________________

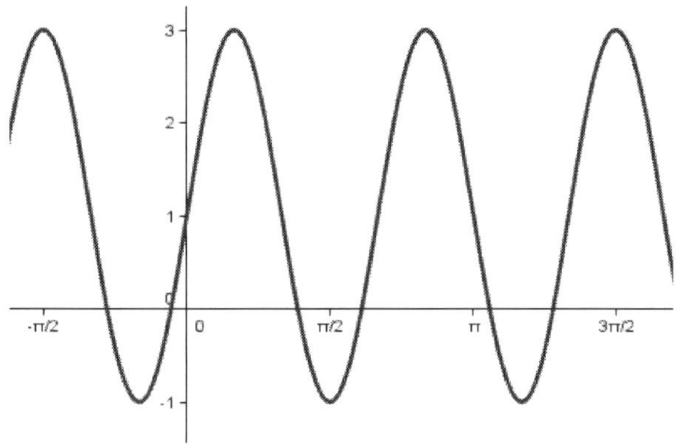

14. Given the graph, complete:

a. Amplitude = ____________

b. Period = ____________

c. Horizontal Translation:____________

d. Midline: ____________

e. f(x) =

f. Range: ________________________

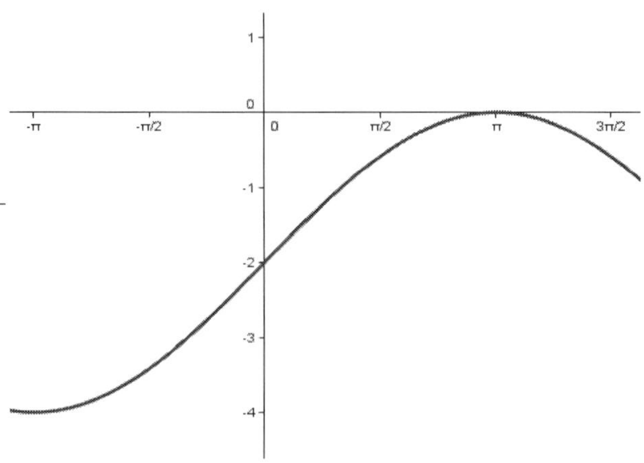

15. Given the graph, complete:

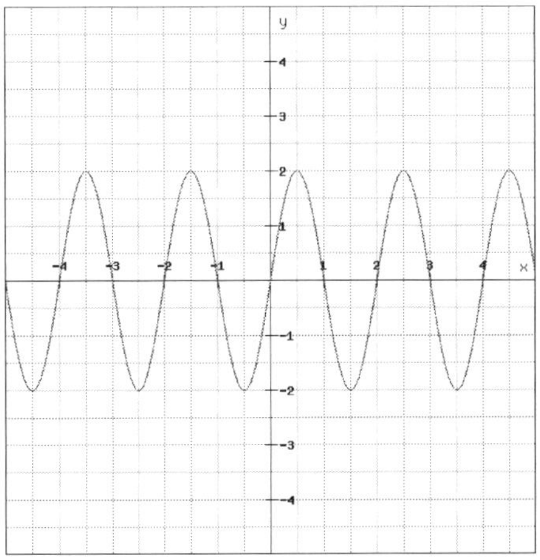

a. Amplitude = ____________

b. Period = ____________

c. Horizontal Translation:___________

d. Midline: ____________

e. f(x) =

f. Range: _______________________

16. Given the graph, complete:

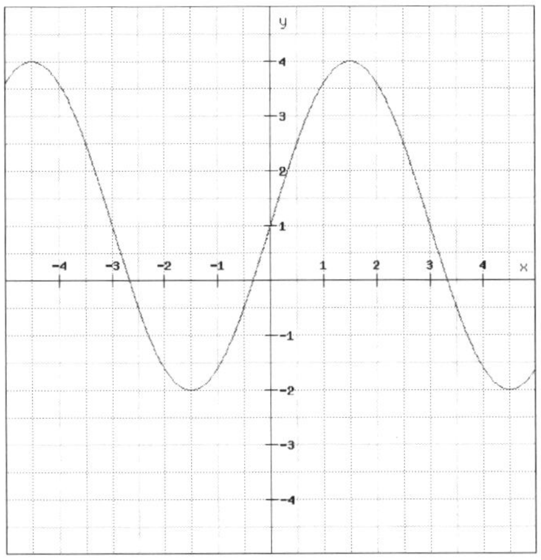

a. Amplitude = ____________

b. Period = ____________

c. Horizontal Translation: ___________

d. Midline: ____________

e. f(x) =

f. Range: ___________________________

17. Given the graph, complete:

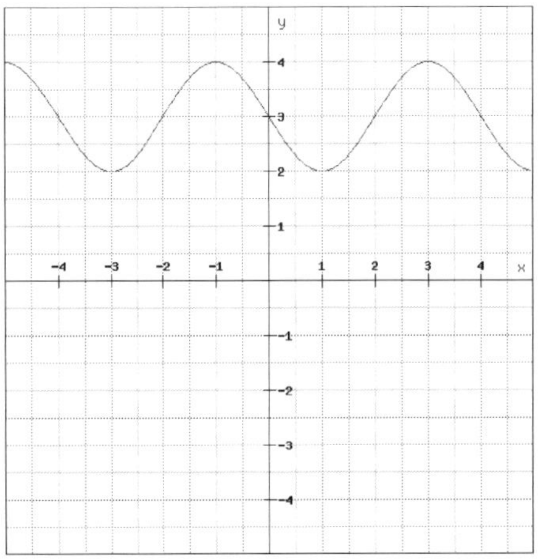

a. Amplitude = ____________

b. Period = ____________

c. Horizontal Translation:___________

d. Midline: ____________

e. f(x) =

f. Range: ___________________________

18. Given the graph, complete:

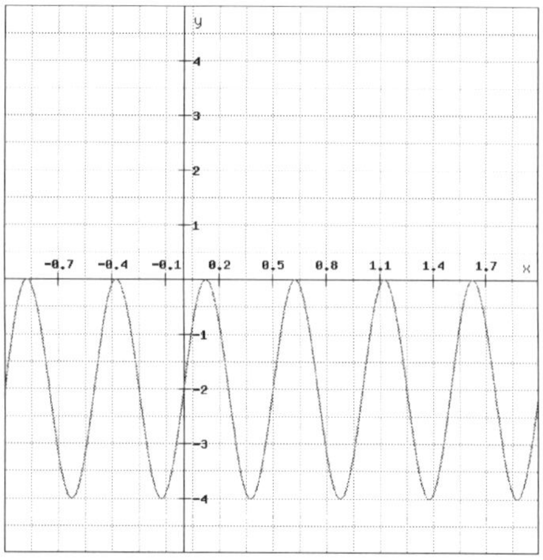

a. Amplitude = ___________

b. Period = ___________

c. Horizontal Translation: ___________

d. Midline: ___________

e. f(x) =

f. Range: _________________________

19. Given the graph, complete:

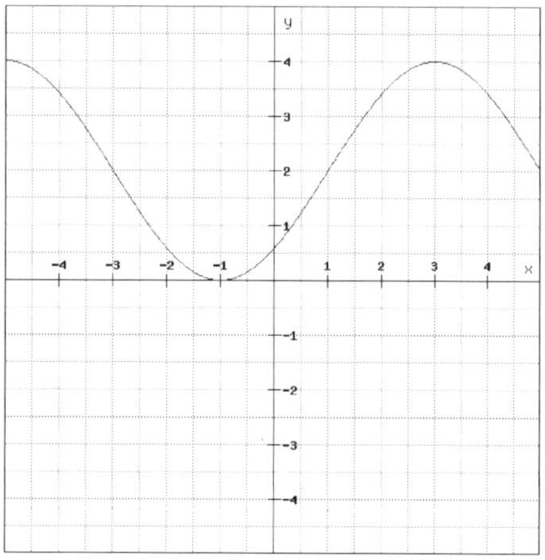

a. Amplitude = ___________

b. Period = ___________

c. Horizontal Translation = ___________

d. Midline: ___________

e. f(x) =

f. Range: _________________________

20. Given the graph, complete:

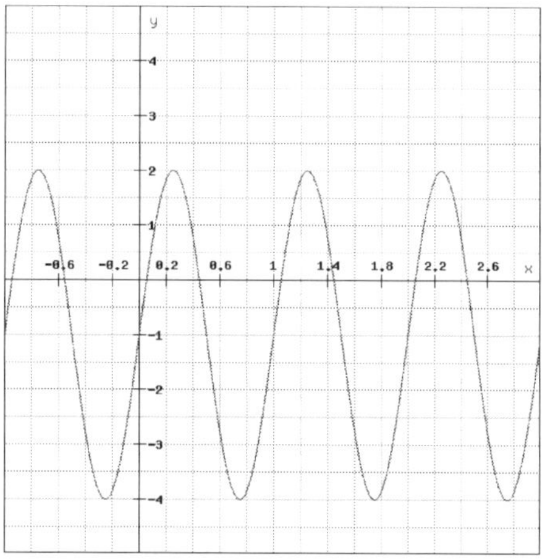

a. Amplitude = ___________

b. Period = ___________

c. Horizontal Translation = ___________

d. Midline: ___________

e. f(x) =

f. Range: _________________________

21. Given the graph, complete:

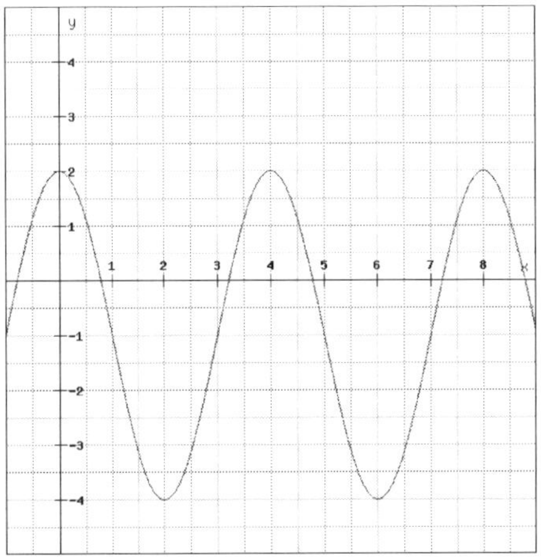

a. Amplitude = ____________

b. Period = ____________

c. Horizontal Translation:___________

d. Midline____________

e. f(x) =

f. Range: ___________________________

22. Given the graph, complete:

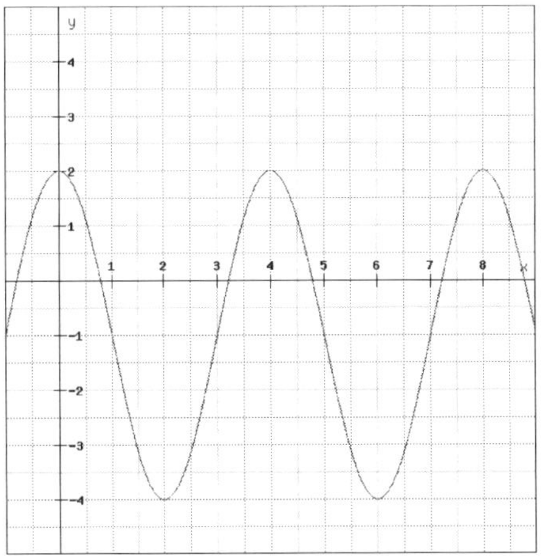

a. Amplitude = ____________

b. Period = ____________

c. Horizontal Translation: ___________

d. Midline____________

e. f(x) =

f. Range: ___________________________

23. Given the graph, complete:

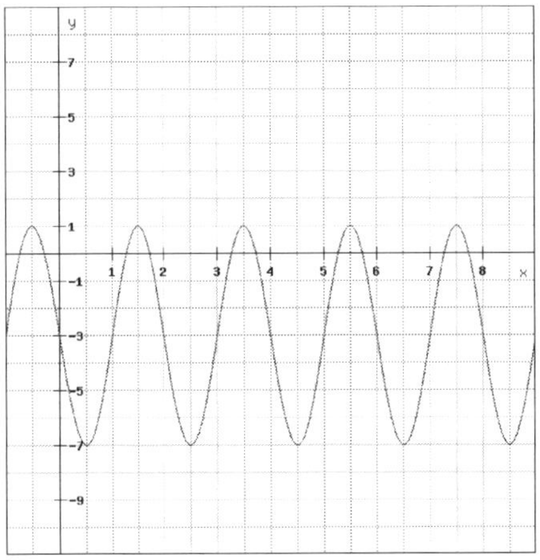

a. Amplitude = ____________

b. Period = ____________

c. Horizontal Translation: ___________

d. Midline: ____________

e. f(x) =

f. Range: _________________________

24. Given the function f(x) = Tan(x), Complete the following table:

x°	0	15	30	45	60	75	90	105	120	135	150	165	180	195	210	225	240	255
Rad																		
f(x)																		

- Sketch the points of the table on a graph.
- State the domain of the function: ________________
- State the *y* intercept (sketched on the graph: (____, ____)
- State the *x* intercept(s): (____, ____), (____, ____)
- Write the corresponding limits and the equation of the vertical asymptote: _____
- Write the corresponding limits and the equation of the horizontal asymptote: ___
- Function is increasing on the interval: _____, decreasing on the interval:______
- Find the max/min point(s): (____, ____)
- State the range of the function: ________

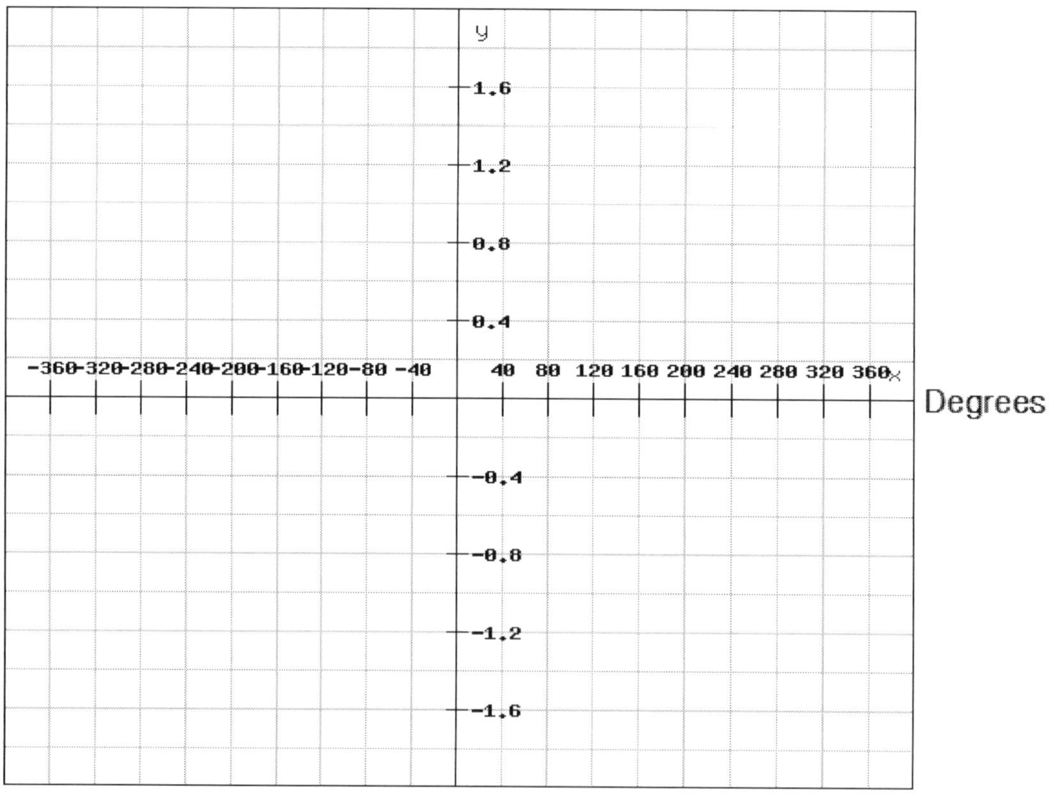

25. Given the function f(x) = Tan(x)

a. Write in all forms the same function translated 2 positions up.

b. Write in all forms the same function translated 3 positions left.

c. Write in all forms the same function translated 3 positions left and 1 up.

d. Write in all forms the same function translated 4 positions right and 1 up.

e. Change the function so that the period would be 2.

f. Change the function so that the period would be 3 and the amplitude 2.

g. Change the function so that the period would be π.

h. Change the function so that the period would be $\frac{\pi}{3}$.

i. Change the function so that the period would be 6, then shift the function 2 positions right and 1 down.

j. Change the function so that the period would be $\frac{\pi}{3}$, then shift the function 4 positions left and 2 down.

k. Change the function so that the period would be $\frac{\pi}{5}$, then shift the function π positions left and 5 down.

26. Given the graph, complete:

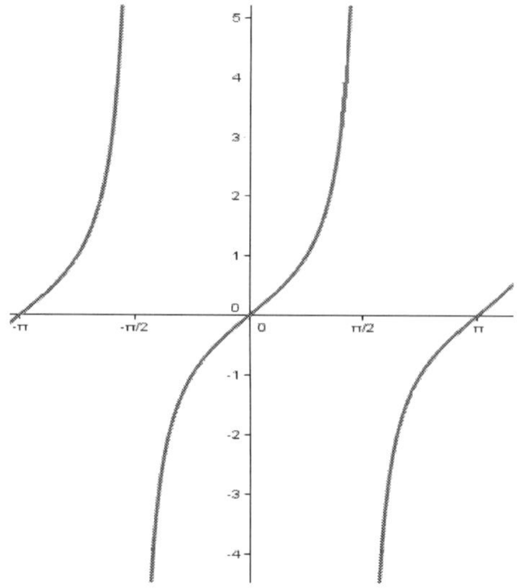

a. Amplitude = ____________

b. Period = ____________

c. Horizontal Translation: ___________

d. Midline: ________

e. f(x) =

f. Range: ____________________________

27. Given the graph, complete:

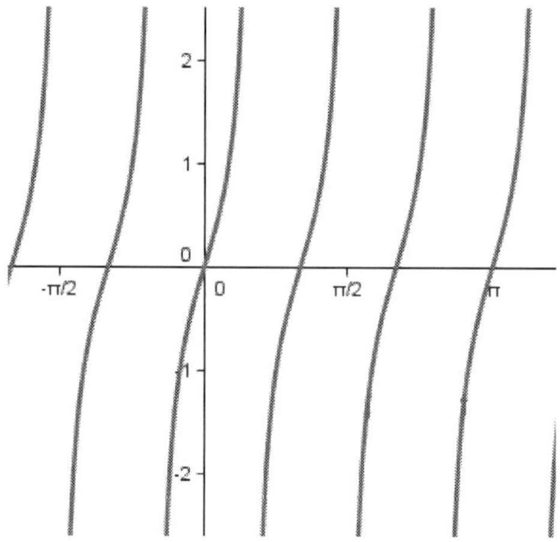

a. Amplitude = ____________

b. Period = ____________

c. Horizontal Translation: ___________

d. Midline: ________

e. f(x) =

f. Range: ____________________________

28. Given the graph, complete:

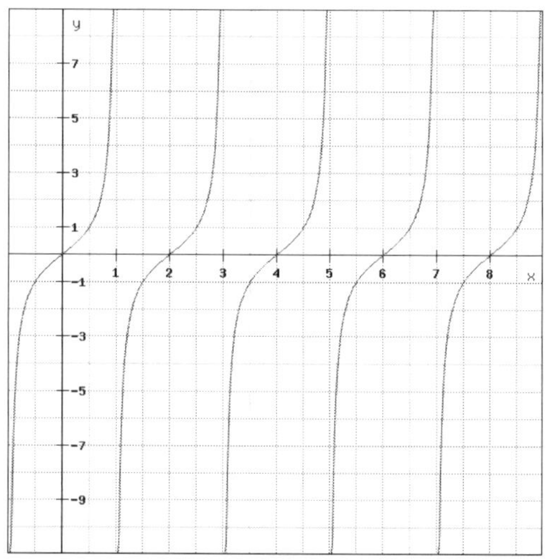

a. Amplitude = ____________

b. Period = ____________

c. Horizontal Translation: ___________

d. Midline: ________

e. f(x) =

f. Range: ____________________________

Analyze the following functions:

1. $f(x) = Sin(x)$
2. $f(x) = Sin(2x)$
3. $f(x) = 2Sin(3x)$
4. $f(x) = \frac{1}{2}Sin(x) + 1$
5. $f(x) = 2Sin(x) + 5$
6. $f(x) = 3Sin(x) - 1$
7. $f(x) = -3Sin(x) - 3$
8. $f(x) = Sin(2x) - 2$
9. $f(x) = -Sin(3x) + 4$
10. $f(x) = -2Sin(\pi x)$
11. $f(x) = \frac{1}{2}Sin(\pi x)$
12. $f(x) = 2Sin(2\pi x)$
13. $f(x) = -Sin(k\pi x)$
14. $f(x) = Sin(\pi x + \pi)$
15. $f(x) = Sin(\frac{\pi}{2}x)$
16. $f(x) = Sin(\frac{\pi}{2}x - \frac{\pi}{2}) - 3$
17. $f(x) = 2Sin(\frac{\pi}{4}x - \frac{\pi}{2})$
18. $f(x) = -2Sin(\frac{\pi}{4}x + \frac{\pi}{2})$
19. $f(x) = \frac{1}{2}Sin(\frac{\pi}{4}x - \pi) + 1$
20. $f(x) = Sin(\pi x - 1)$

22. $f(x) = Cos(x)$
23. $f(x) = Cos(2x)$
24. $f(x) = 2Cos(3x)$
25. $f(x) = \frac{1}{2}Cos(x) + 1$
26. $f(x) = 2Cos(x) + 5$
27. $f(x) = 3Cos(x) - 1$
28. $f(x) = -3Cos(x) - 3$
29. $f(x) = Cos(2x) - 2$
30. $f(x) = -Cos(3x) + 4$
31. $f(x) = -2Cos(\pi x)$
32. $f(x) = \frac{1}{2}Cos(\pi x)$
33. $f(x) = 2Cos(2\pi x)$

<u>Analyze a function:</u>

I. Domain
II. Amplitude
III. Period
IV. Range
V. Interceptions
VI. Critical Points (max, min)
VII. Write in all forms
VIII. Decrease and increase intervals
IX. Sketch

34. $f(x) = -\text{Cos}(k\pi x)$
35. $f(x) = \text{Cos}(\pi x + \pi)$
36. $f(x) = \text{Cos}(\frac{\pi}{2}x)$
37. $f(x) = \text{Cos}(\frac{\pi}{2}x - \frac{\pi}{2})$
38. $f(x) = 2\text{Cos}(\frac{\pi}{4}x - \frac{\pi}{2})$
39. $f(x) = -2\text{Cos}(\frac{\pi}{4}x + \frac{\pi}{2})$
40. $f(x) = \frac{1}{2}\text{Cos}(\frac{\pi}{4}x - \pi) - 2$
41. $f(x) = \text{Cos}(\pi x + 2)$

43. $f(x) = \tan(x)$
44. $f(x) = \tan(2x)$
45. $f(x) = 2\tan(3x)$
46. $f(x) = \frac{1}{2}\tan(x) + 1$
47. $f(x) = 2\tan(x) + 5$
48. $f(x) = 3\tan(x) - 1$
49. $f(x) = -3\tan(x) - 3$
50. $f(x) = \tan(2x) - 2$
51. $f(x) = -\tan(3x) + 4$
52. $f(x) = -2\tan(\pi x)$
53. $f(x) = \frac{1}{2}\tan(\pi x)$
54. $f(x) = 2\tan(2\pi x)$
55. $f(x) = -\tan(k\pi x)$
56. $f(x) = \tan(\pi x+\pi)$
57. $f(x) = \tan(\frac{\pi}{2}x)$
58. $f(x) = \tan(\frac{\pi}{2}x - \frac{\pi}{2})$
59. $f(x) = 2\tan(\frac{\pi}{4}x - \frac{\pi}{2}) + 2$
60. $f(x) = -2\tan(\frac{\pi}{4}x + \frac{\pi}{2})$
61. $f(x) = \frac{1}{2}\tan(\frac{\pi}{4}x - \pi)$
62. $f(x) = \tan(\pi x + 1)$

3.4. – SINE AND COSINE RULE

The sine rule: For any triangle, given the sides a, b and c and their corresponding opposite angles, A, B and C:

$$\frac{Sin(A)}{a} = \frac{Sin(B)}{b} = \frac{Sin(C)}{c}$$

How many equations are written above? ___

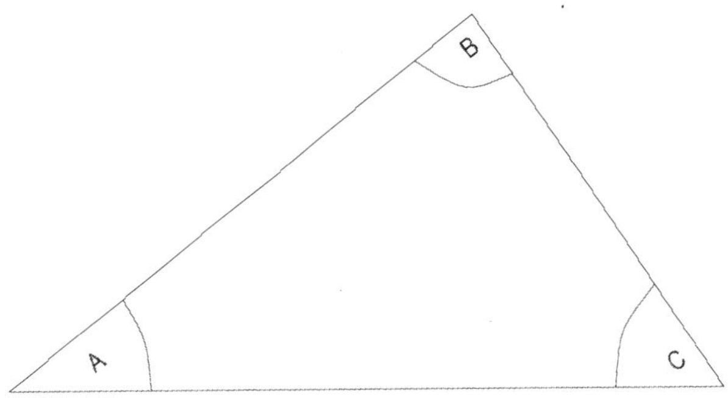

I. ________________

II. ________________

III. ________________

The cosine rule: For any triangle, given the sides a, b and c and their corresponding opposite angles, A, B and C:

$$a^2 = b^2 + c^2 - 2bc\cos(A)$$

$b^2 =$ ____________________

$c^2 =$ ____________________

Given the following triangle:

a. Find AD in terms of AC and angle C.

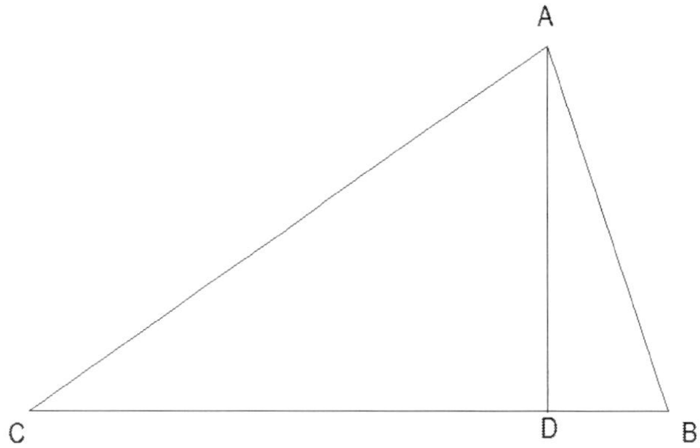

b. Find the Area of the triangle in terms of AC, CB and the angle C.

c. Conclusion:

Exercises

1. Sketch a triangle with angles: 20º, 80º, C and sides 10, b, c .Write the Sine and Cosine rule for this triangle.

2. Find all the missing sides, angles and area of the triangles below. If there is more than one set of solutions, try to find them all.

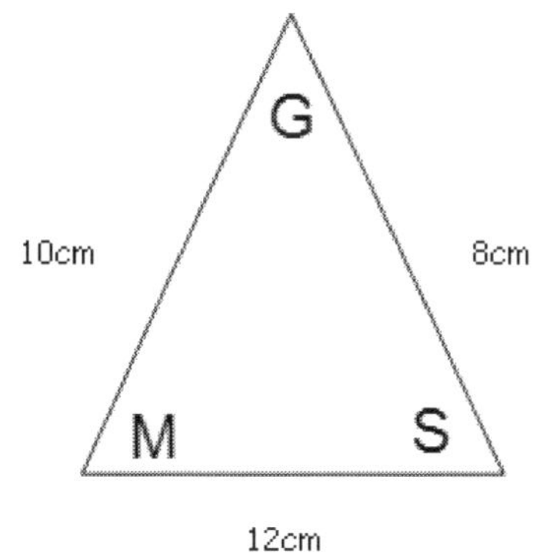

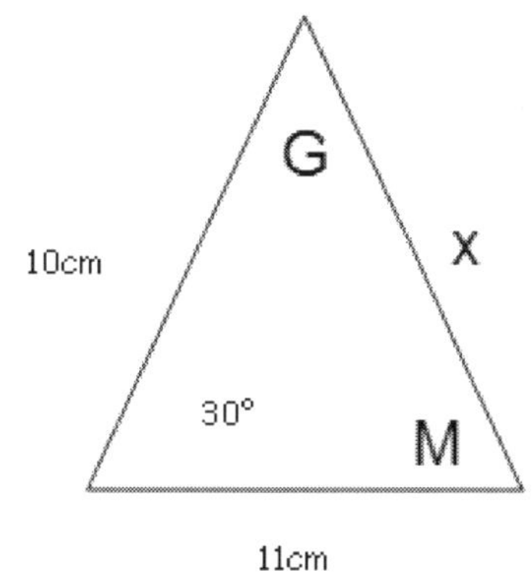

Conclusion: The cosine rule must be used in the following cases:

I. ____

II. ____

3. Find all the sides, angles and the area of the following triangles:
<u>Ambiguous Case (2 possible solutions)</u>

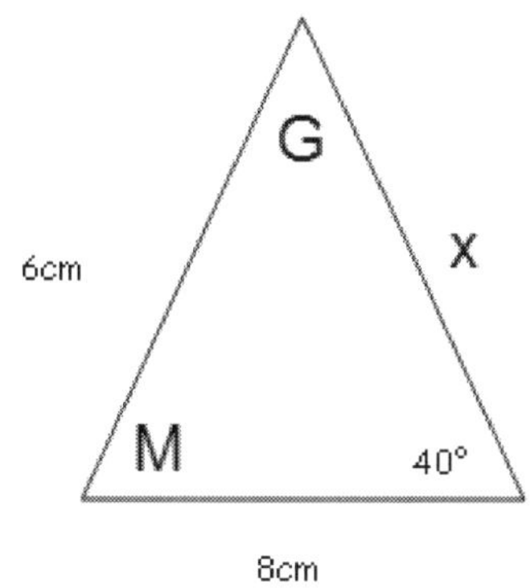

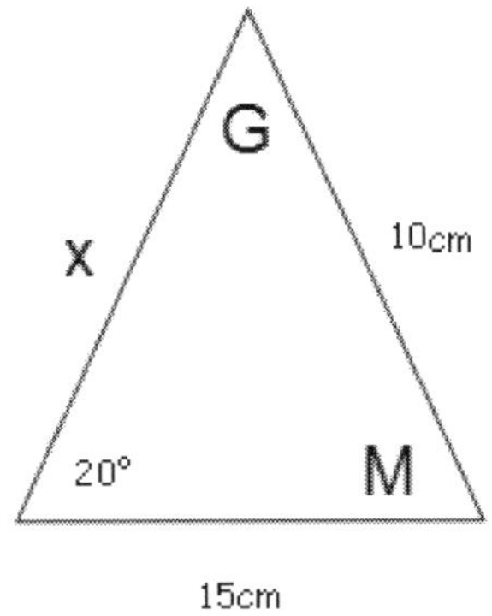

Conclusion: ____

4. Find all the sides, angles and the area of the following triangles:

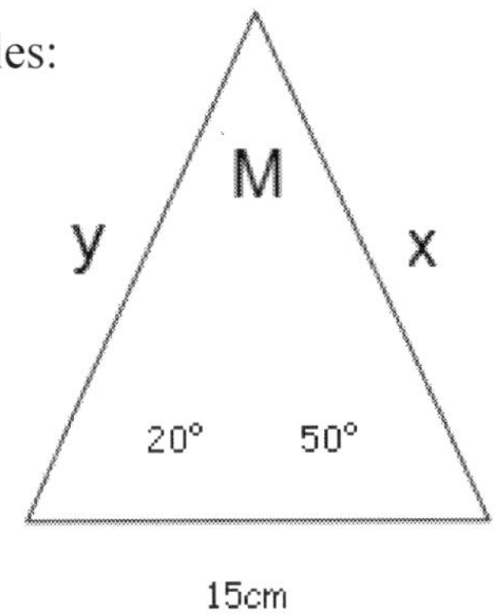

5. Find all the sides, angles and the area of the triangle:

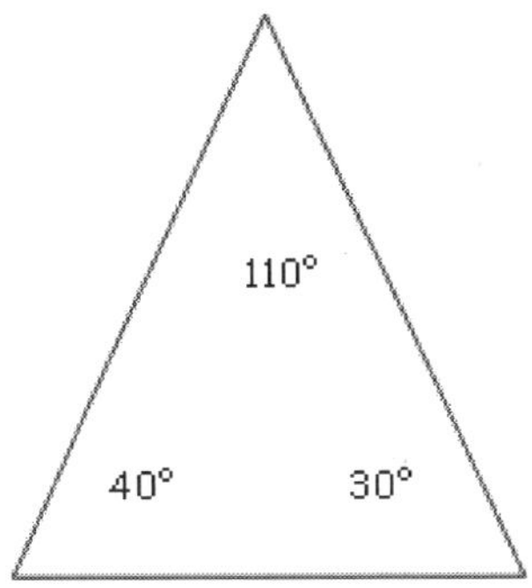

6. Find all the sides, angles and the area of the triangle:

.

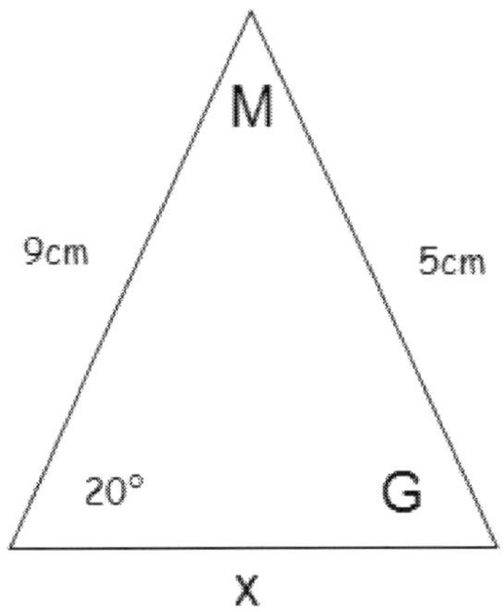

7. Find all the sides, angles and the area of the triangle:

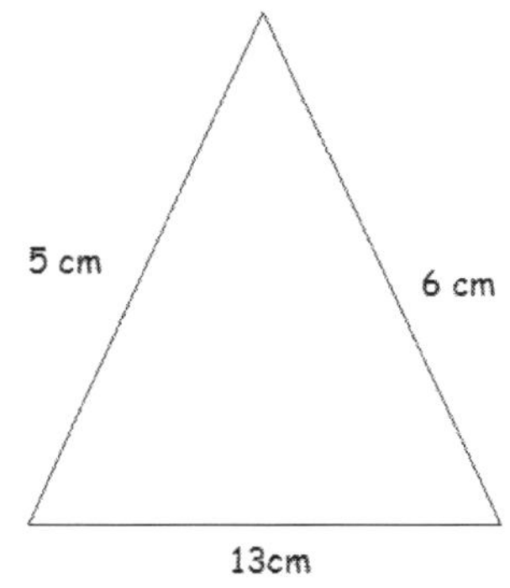

8. Find all the sides, angles and the area of the triangle:

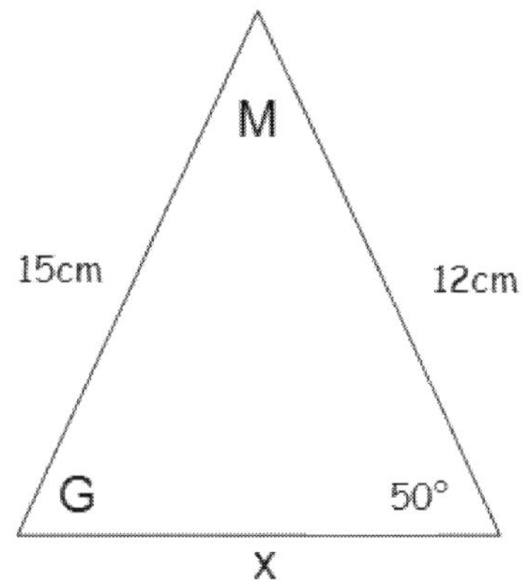

9. Find all the sides, angles and the area of the triangle:

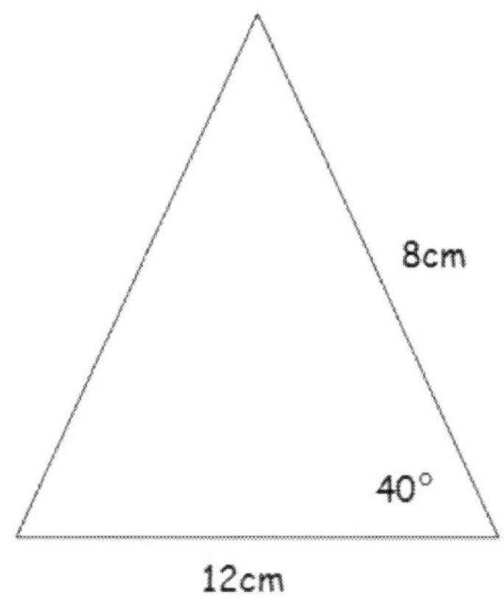

10. Find all the sides, angles and the area of the triangle:

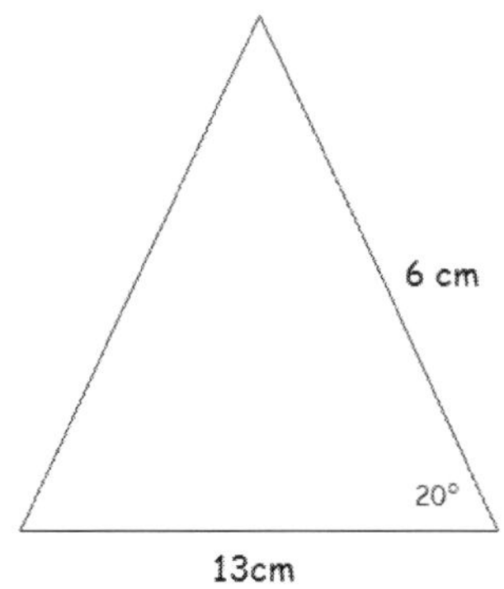

11. Can you identify how many triangles (not to scale) you could draw using the given information? In which example could you find the ambiguous case? Sketch (to scale as possible) both triangles in that case.

a.

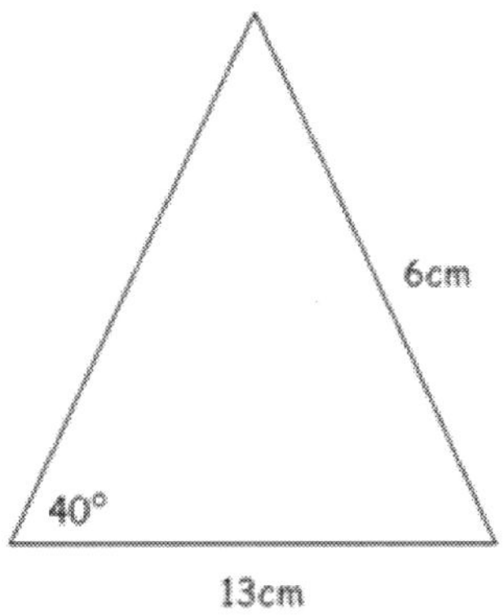

b.

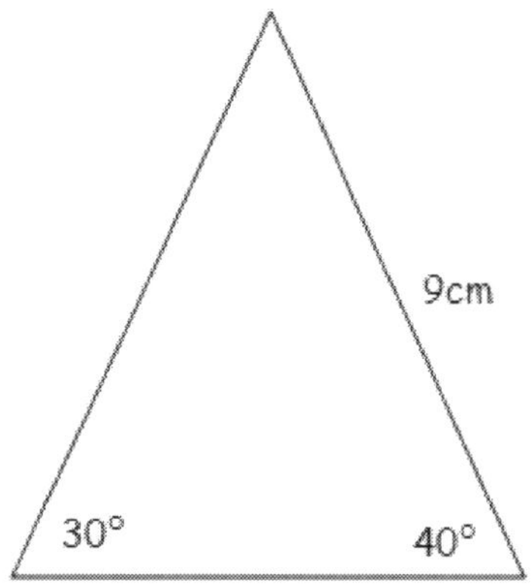

c.

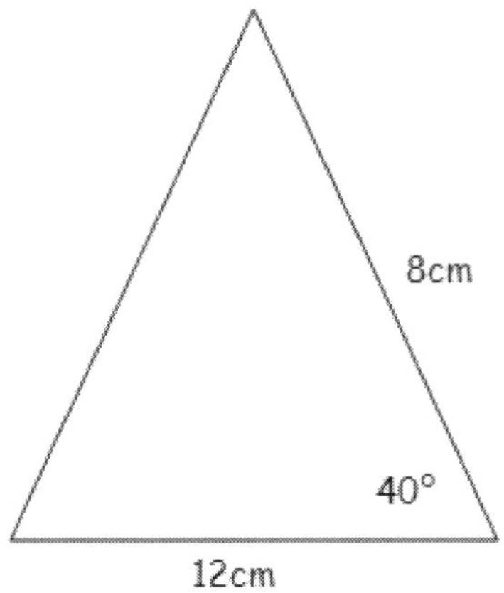

d.

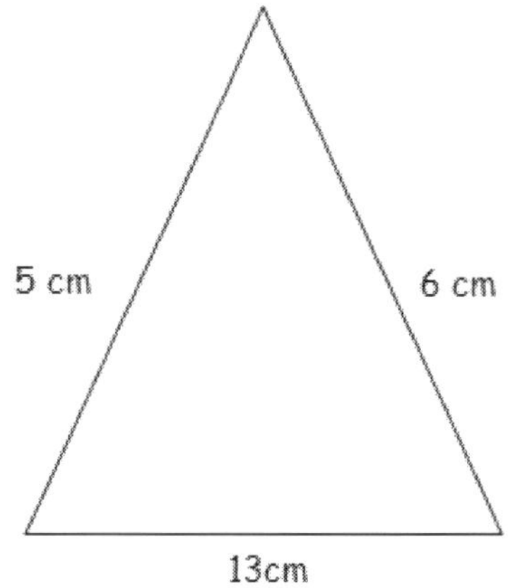

e.

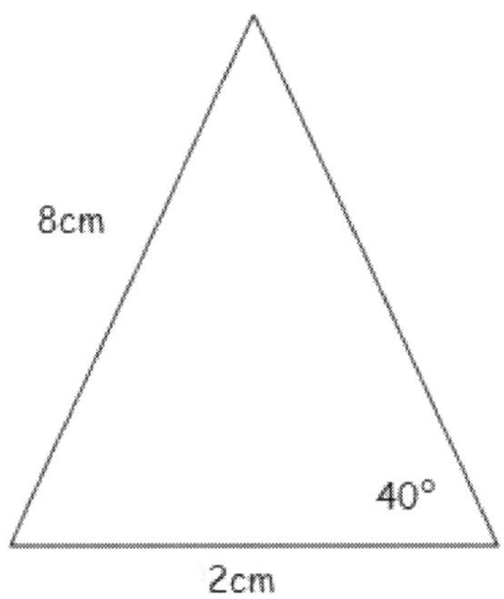

f.

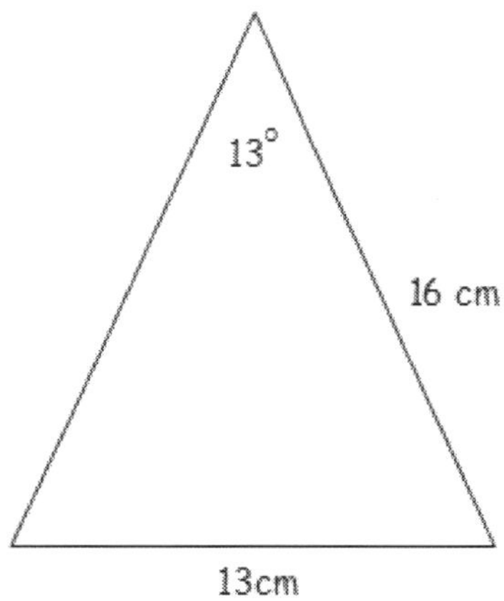

3.5. – TRIGONOMETRIC RATIOS

Following directly from the unit circle are the trigonometric ratios:

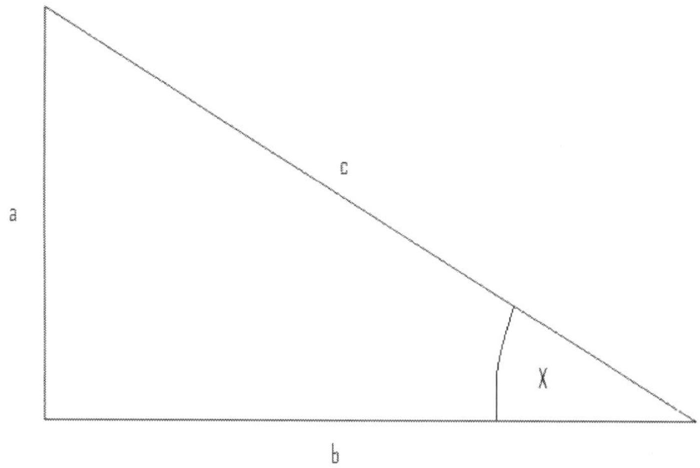

$$Sin(x) = -$$

$$Cos(x) = -$$

$$Tan(x) = \frac{Sin(x)}{Cos(x)} = -$$

Exercises:

1. Find x and y in the following cases:

    a.

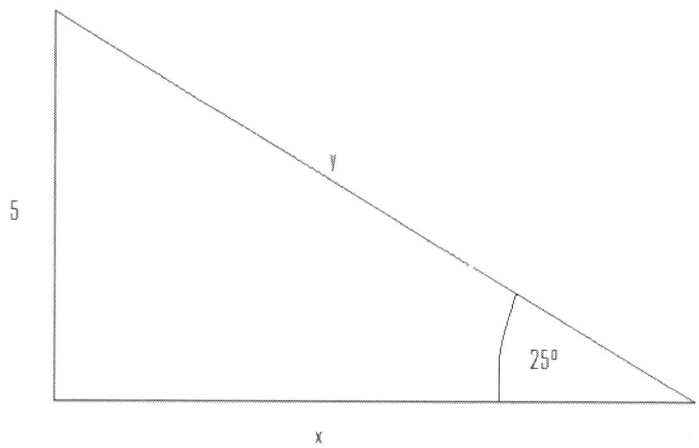

    b.

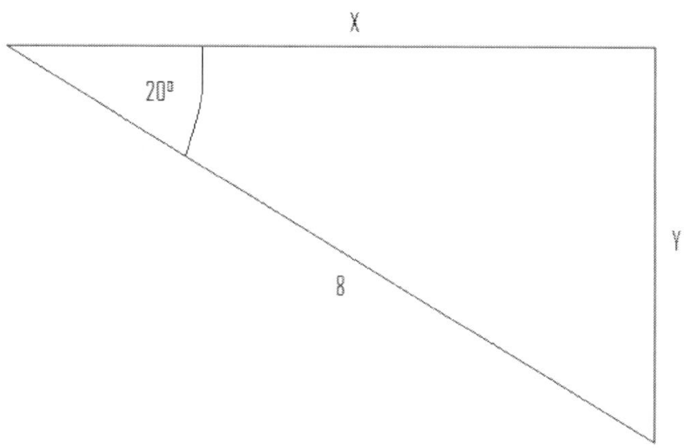

2. The Triangle in the diagram (not to scale) is <u>not</u> right angled, find X and Y.

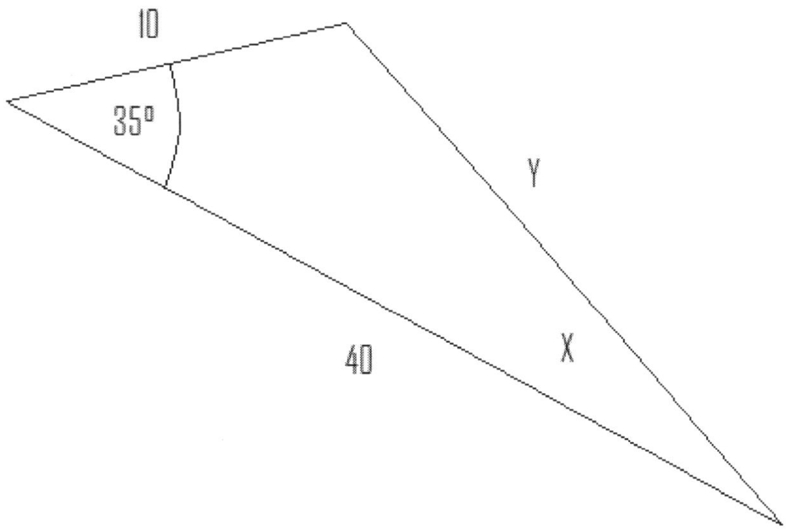

3. The shade formed by building is 100m long. The depression angle of the light as it approaches the ground is 40º.

    a. Sketch a diagram that describes the situation.
    b. Find the height of the building.

4. The height of building is 120m. The depression angle of the light as it approaches the ground is 30°.

    a. Sketch a diagram that describes the situation.
    b. Find the length of the shade on the ground.

5. In its search for food the lion is observing a certain prey located 2 m above the ground. The lion's head forms an angle of 12° as he looks at his prey.

    a. Sketch a diagram that describes the situation.
    b. Find the distance from the lion's mouth to its prey.

6. Measuring the height and distance of objects:

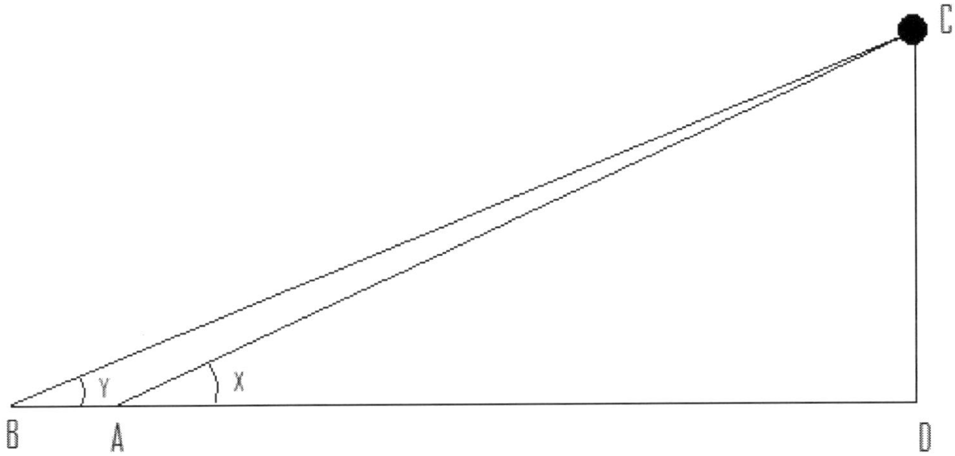

Assuming we start at point A and the object that we want to measure its distance (ground distance AD or Air distance AC) is located at point C. We need to use a device (in real life a **theodolite** is used) the measure the angle x (elevation angle), let's assume that we measured it and got 20º. Later we move a certain distance (backwards or forward) and measure the angle y. Let assume that we moved backwards 4 meters (that is AB = 4m) and the angle y is 18º. Find AD, AC, CD.

3.6. – INVERSE TRIGONOMETRIC FUNCTIONS

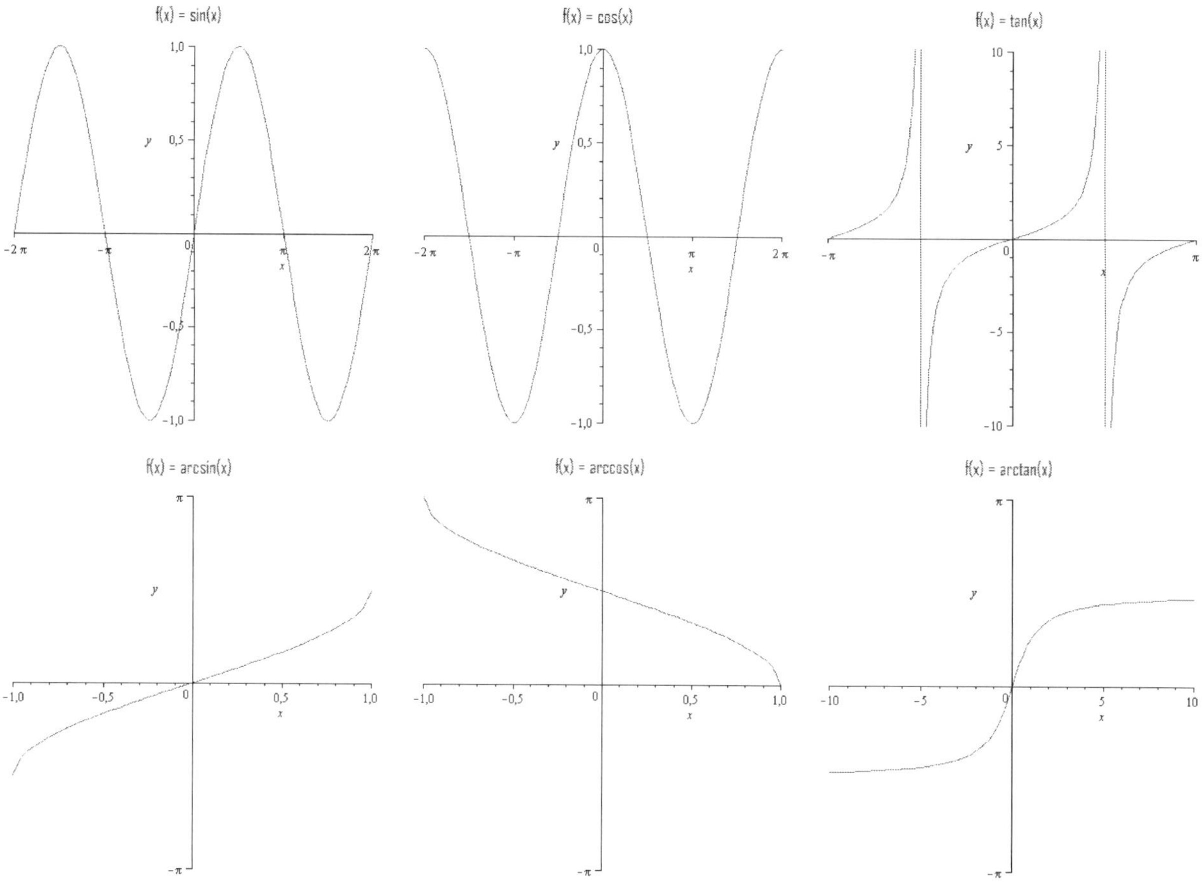

Inverse Trigonometric Function	Domain	Range	In words
f(x) = arcsin(x)	[-1, 1]	$[-\frac{\pi}{2}, \frac{\pi}{2}]$	f(x) is the angle (whose sine is x)
f(x) = arcos(x)	[-1, 1]	$[0, \pi]$	f(x) is the angle (whose cosine is x)
f(x) = arctan(x)	$[-\infty, \infty]$	$[-\frac{\pi}{2}, \frac{\pi}{2}]$	f(x) is the angle (whose tangent is x)

Give your answer(s) in radians and degrees, use a calculator if necessary:

1. Arcsin(0) =

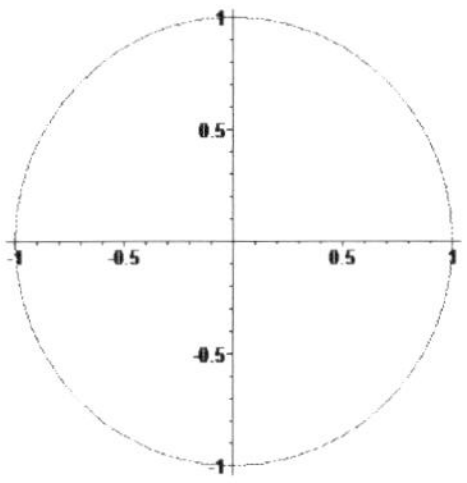

2. Arcos(0) =

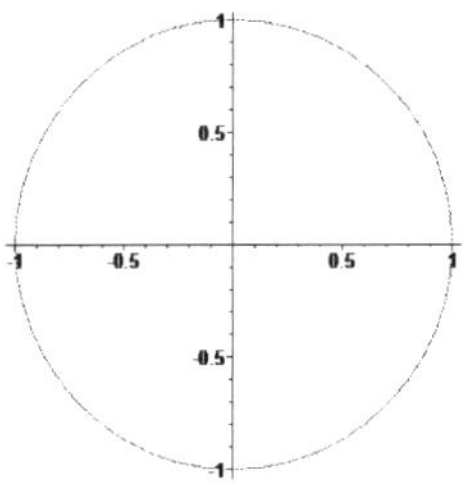

3. Arcsin(1) =

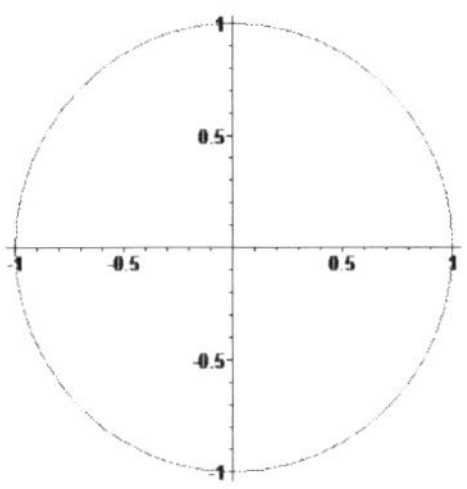

4. Arcos(2) =

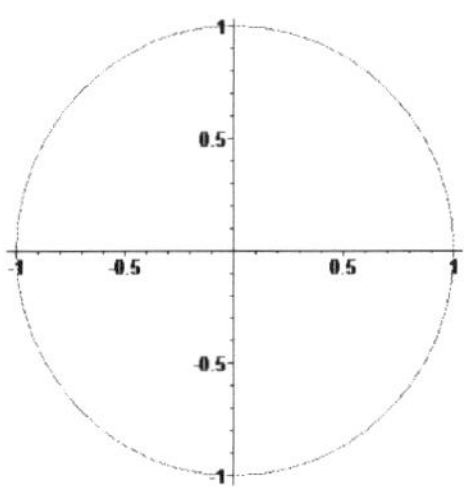

5. Arcsin(0.5) =

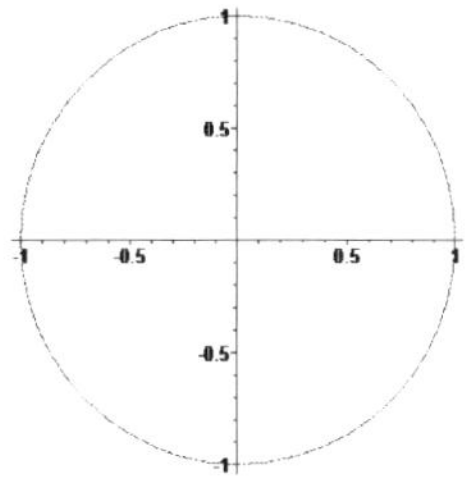

6. Arcos(-0.5) =

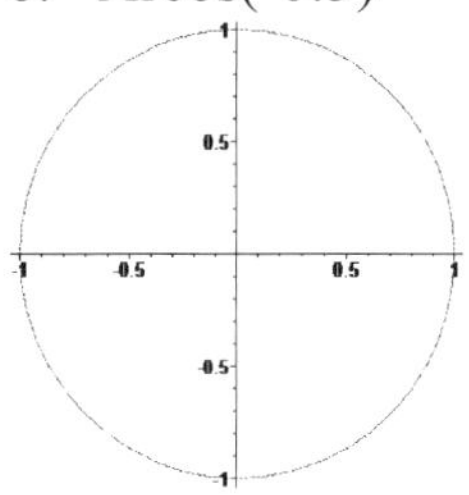

7. Arcsin($\frac{\sqrt{3}}{2}$) =

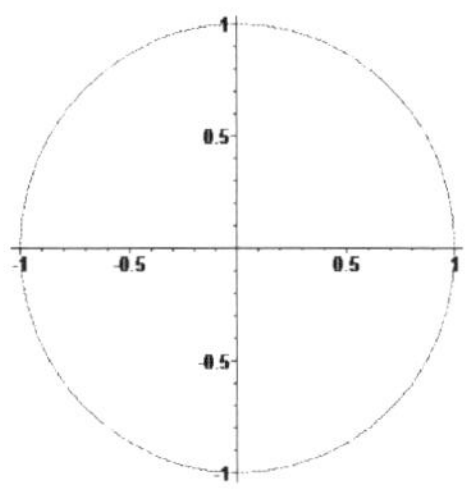

8. Arcos(-$\frac{\sqrt{3}}{2}$) =

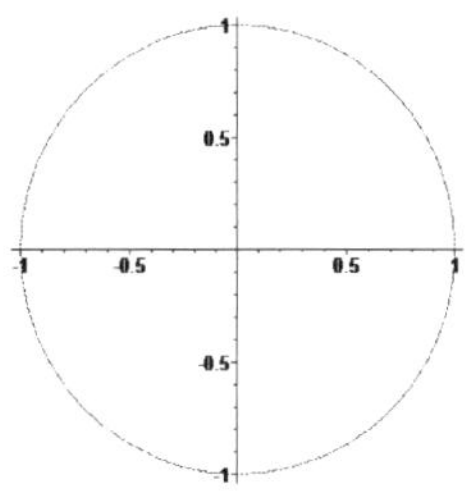

9. Arcsin($\frac{\sqrt{2}}{2}$) =

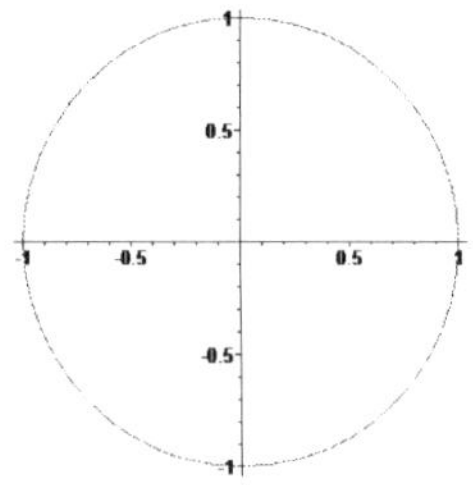

10. Arcos($-\frac{\sqrt{2}}{2}$) =

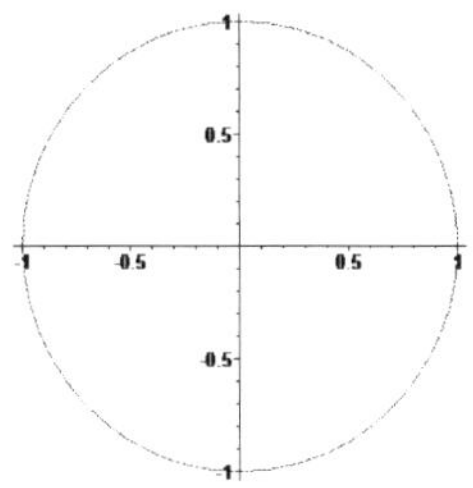

11. Arcsin($\frac{\sqrt{2}}{2}$) =

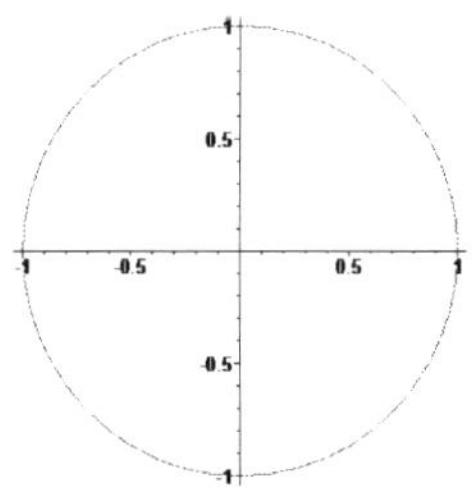

12. Arcsin(-1) =

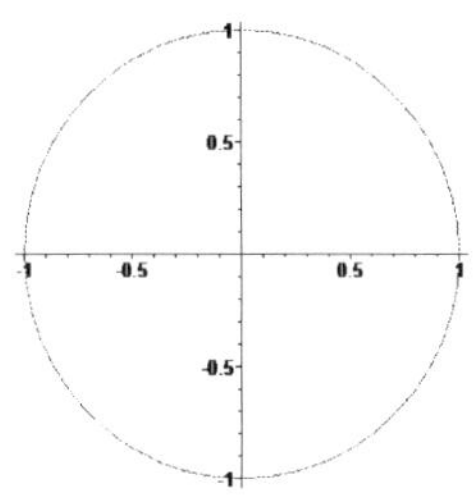

13. Arcos(-1) =

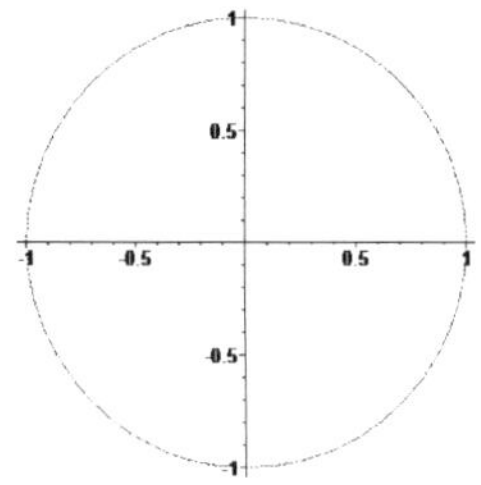

14. Arcsin(0.2) =

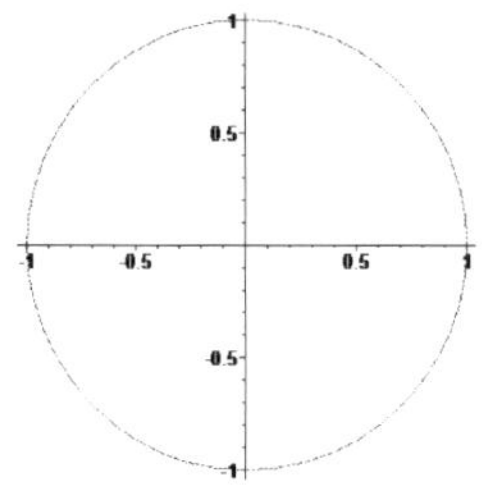

15. Arcos(-0.4) =

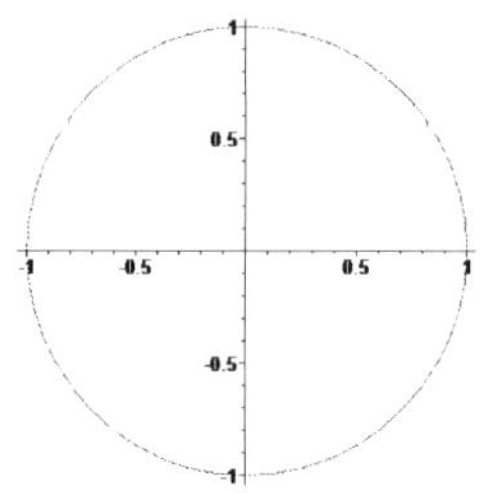

16. Arcsin(1/5) =

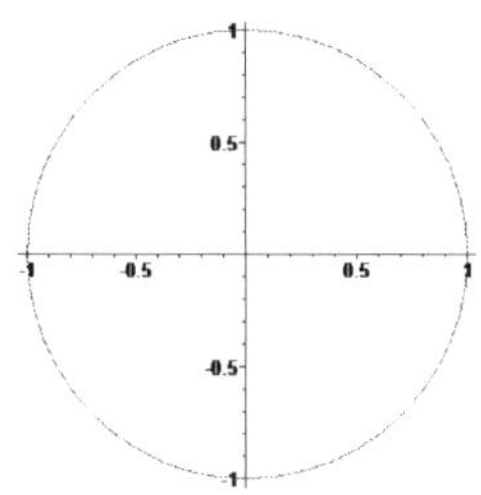

17. Arcos(-5) =

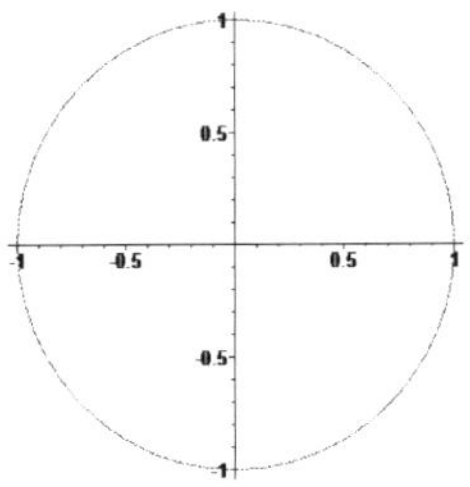

18. Arcsin(0.9) =

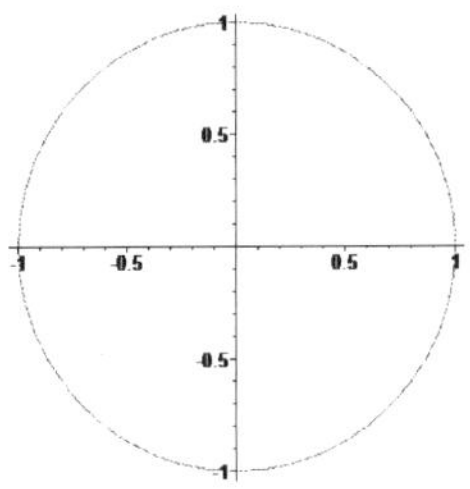

19. Arcsin(-2.4) =

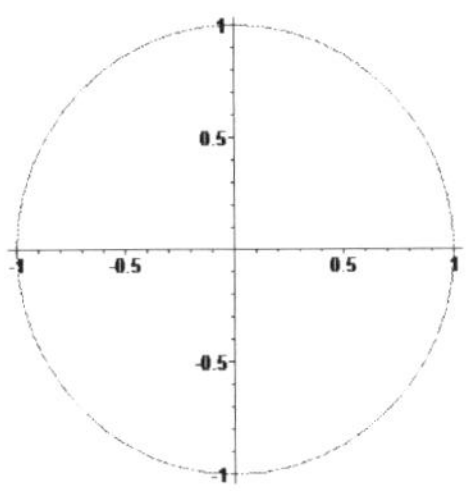

20. Arcos(0.05) =

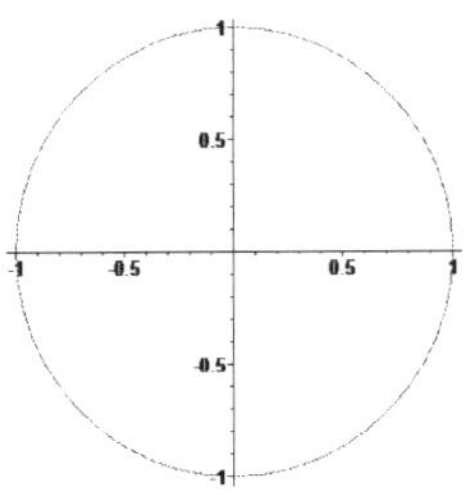

21. Arctan(-5) =

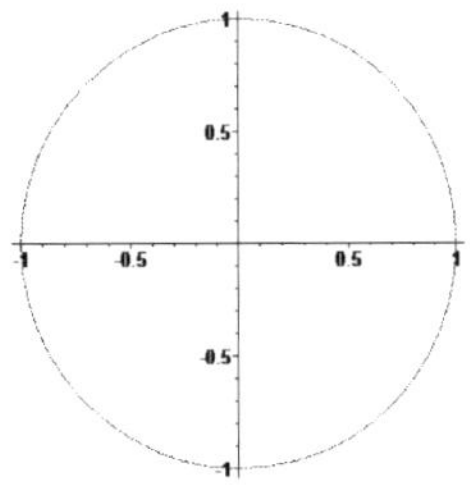

22. Arctan(1) =

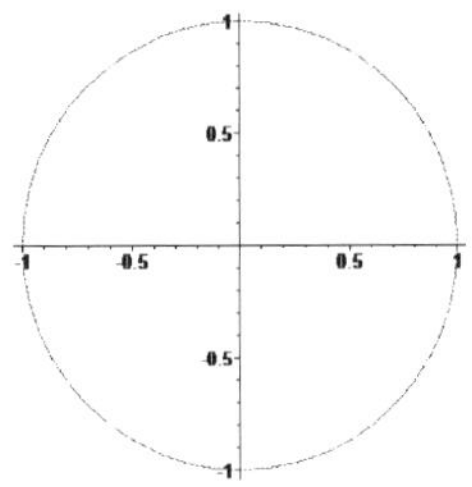

23. Arctan(-2.4) =

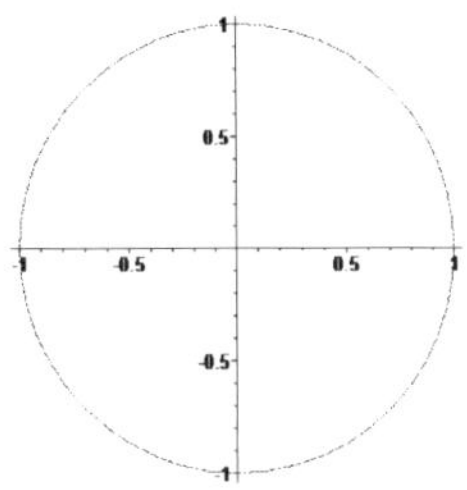

24. Arctan($\frac{1}{\sqrt{3}}$) =

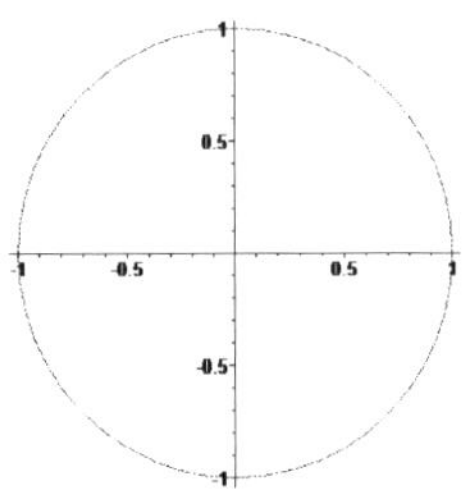

25. Arctan($-\sqrt{3}$) =

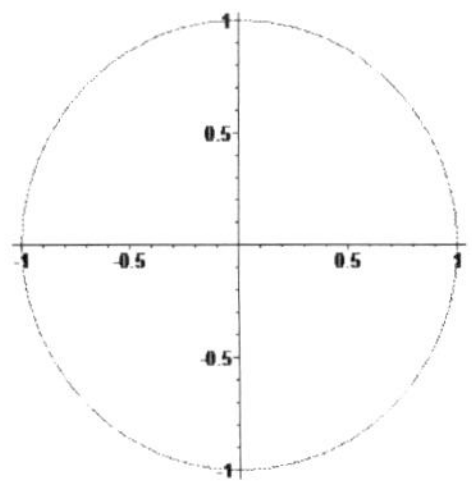

26. Arctan($\sqrt{3}$) =

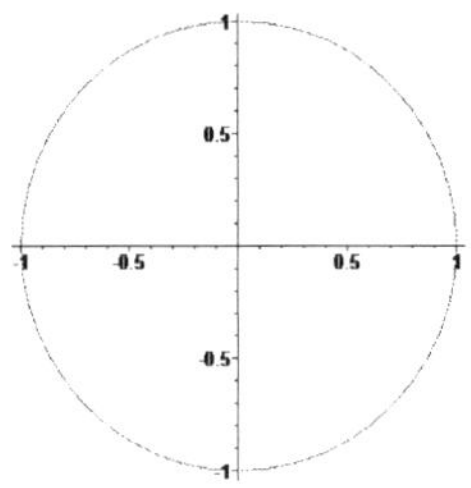

27. Arctan(-1) =

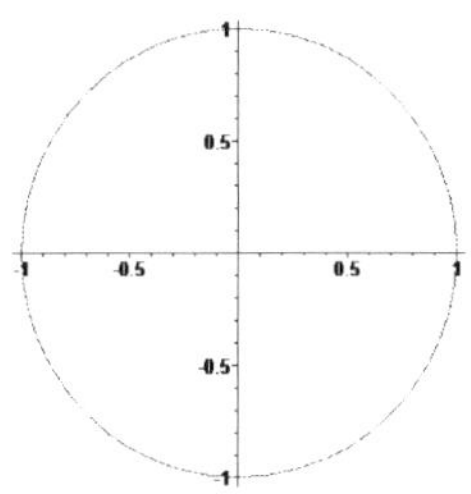

Evaluate:

28. $Arc\sin\left(\frac{-1}{2}\right)$

29. $Arc\cos\left(\frac{\sqrt{3}}{2}\right)$

30. $Arc\tan(0)$

31. $Arc\cos\left(\sin\left(\frac{\sqrt{3}}{2}\right)\right)$

32. $\cos\left(\arcsin\left(\frac{2}{5}\right)\right)$

33. $\sin\left(\arcsin\left(\frac{\pi}{5}\right)\right)$

34. $\csc\left(\arcsin\left(-\frac{2}{7}\right)\right)$

35. $\cos\left(\arctan\left(\frac{3}{4}\right)\right)$

36. $\csc\left(\arccos\left(\frac{2\sqrt{5}}{5}\right)\right)$

3.7. – TRIGONOMETRIC EQUATIONS

1. Find a few solutions of the equation: Sin(x) = 1

   Degrees: x_1 = ____ x_2 = ____ x_3 = ____ x_4 = ____

   Radians: x_1 = ____ x_2 = ____ x_3 = ____ x_4 = ____

2. Find a few solutions of the equation: Cos(x) = $\frac{1}{2}$

   Degrees: x_1 = ____ x_2 = ____ x_3 = ____ x_4 = ____

   Radians: x_1 = ____ x_2 = ____ x_3 = ____ x_4 = ____

3. Conclusion, In general trigonometric equations have ___________ solutions.

4. Cos(x) = –2

5. Solve: Sin(3x) = $\frac{1}{2}$, $0 \leq x \leq 2\pi$

6. Cos(2x – $\frac{\pi}{4}$) = –1, $0 \leq x \leq 2\pi$

   Solution(s): x = ____

7. $\text{Sin}(2x^{\circ} - 100^{\circ}) = -\frac{\sqrt{3}}{2}$, $0 \le x \le 360^{\circ}$

8. $\text{Cos}(\frac{\pi}{3}x) = -\frac{1}{2}$, $2\pi \le x \le 4\pi$

9. $\text{Sin}(\frac{\pi}{4}x) = 2$, $2\pi \le x \le 4\pi$

10. $\text{Sin}(2x) = \frac{1}{3}$, $0 \le x \le 2\pi$

11. $\text{Sin}(\frac{3\pi}{7}x) = -\frac{1}{2}$, $0 \le x \le 2\pi$

12. $\text{Sin}(\frac{\pi}{4}x - \frac{\pi}{2}) = -\frac{1}{2}$

13. $\text{Cos}(\frac{\pi}{5}x) = -\frac{1}{\sqrt{2}}$

14. $2\text{Cos}(\frac{1}{5}x) = 1$

15. $4\text{Sin}(3x^{o} - 5^{o}) = -\frac{2}{5}$

16. $\text{Sin}(4x^{o} + 20^{o}) = \frac{1}{\sqrt{2}}$

17. $-\text{Tan}(\pi x) = \frac{1}{\sqrt{3}}$, $0 \leq x \leq 2\pi$

18. $\text{Tan}(\frac{2\pi}{7} x) = \frac{1}{\sqrt{3}}$

19. $\text{Tan}(2x^{o}) = 5$, $0 \leq x \leq 360^{o}$

20. $\text{Tan}(2x^{o}) = -1$

21. $\text{Tan}(3x) = \sqrt{3}$

22. $\text{Tan}(2x - \frac{\pi}{3}) = 1$

23. $\sin(x)\cos(x) + 2\cos(x) = 0$

24. $(\cos(x))^2 + \cos(x) = 0$

25. $\tan(x)\sin(2x) + \sin(x)\cos(x) = 0$

26. $(\cos(x))^2 + \cos(x) - 2 = 0$

27. $2(\sin(x))^2 + \sin(x) - 1 = 0$

28. $2(\sin(x))^2 - 7\sin(x) + 6 = 0$

29. $2(\tan(x))^2 - 6\tan(x) + 4 = 0$

3.8. – 3D GEOMETRY

1. Sketch each one of the solids and fill the blanks.

    a. Cuboid Volume =__________ Surface Area = __________

    b. Right pyramid Volume =__________ Surface Area = __________

    c. Right prism Volume =__________ Surface Area = __________

    d. Right cone Volume =__________ Surface Area = __________

    e. Cylinder Volume =__________ Surface Area = __________

    f. Sphere Volume =__________ Surface Area = __________

    g. Hemisphere Volume =__________ Surface Area = __________

2. In the design process of a certain lamp the following diagram is obtained.

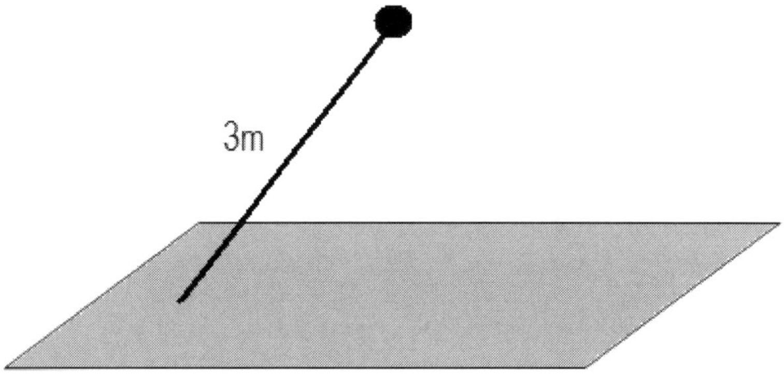

Assuming the sun is directly above the lamp and length of the shadow on the ground is 2.5 meters.

a. Find the angle between the lamp and the ground.
b. Find the height of the lamp above the ground.

3. Given the following diagram (not to scale): ABCD is a rectangle AB = 20 cm, BC = 12 cm, EA = BF = 14 cm. EM = 5 cm.

    a. Find the angle between NB and the base ABCD.
    b. Find the length of the segment MC.
    c. Find the area of MNBC
    d. Find the volume of the cuboid.
    e. Find the surface area of the cuboid.

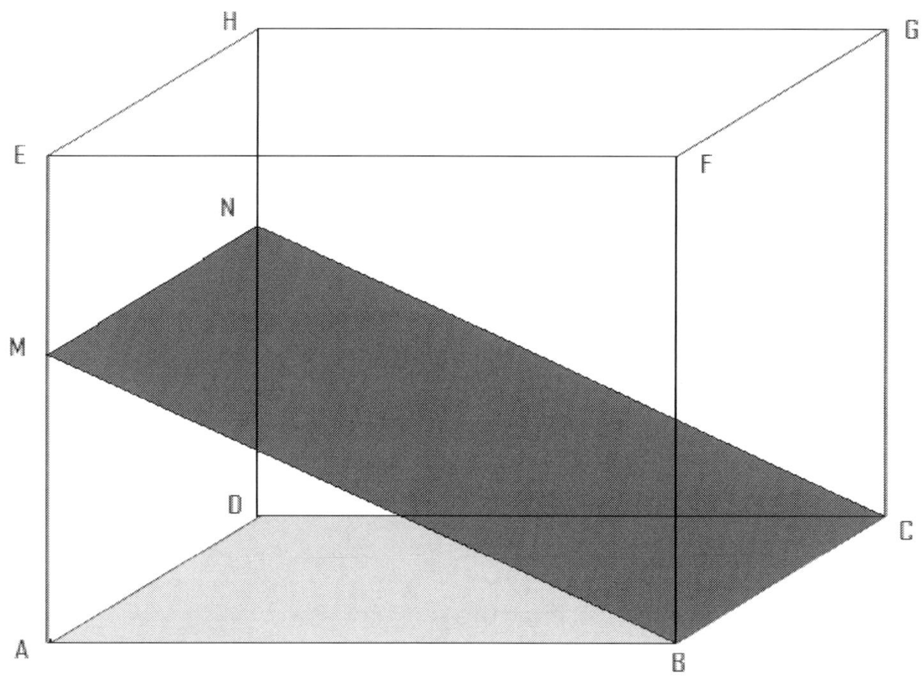

4. Given the following diagram (not to scale): ABCD is a square AB = 10 cm. CG = BF = 12 cm. M is the midpoint of DB.

   a. Find the length DB.
   b. Find the angle between DG and the base ABCD.
   c. Find the angle between GM and the base ABCD.
   d. Find the area of BDG.

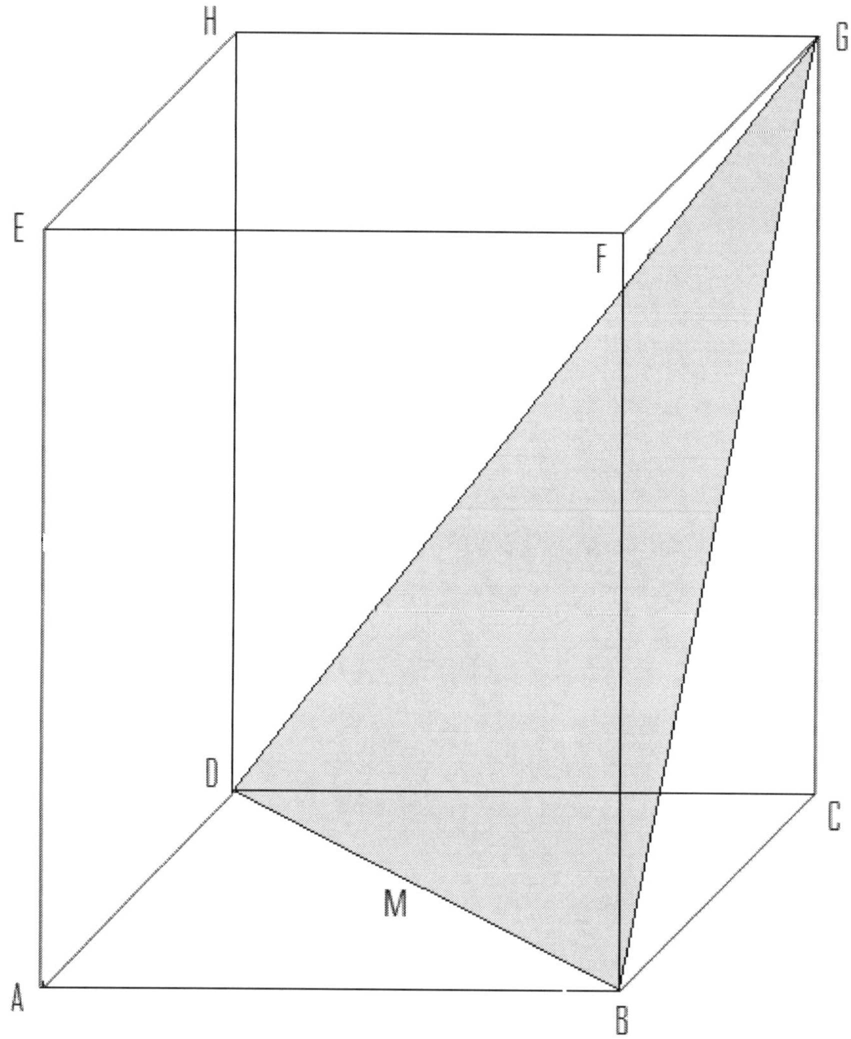

5. In the design process of a modern building a sphere of 5m radius is put on top a cylinder with a radius twice as big. The height of the building is 30m.

   a. Find the volume of the sphere.
   b. Find the height of the cylinder.
   c. Find the volume of the building.
   d. Find the surface area of the building that that is exposed to fresh air.

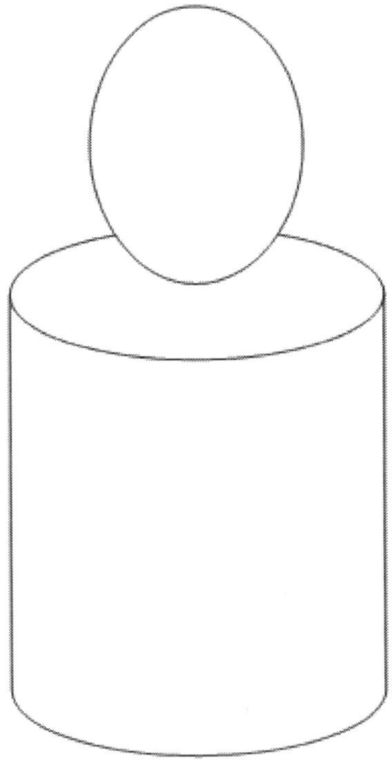

6. Given the following right prism. AB = 12cm, AE = 15cm.

Find:

a. The length of AD.
b. The length of ED.
c. The length of AF.
d. The angle FAB.
e. The surface area of the prism.

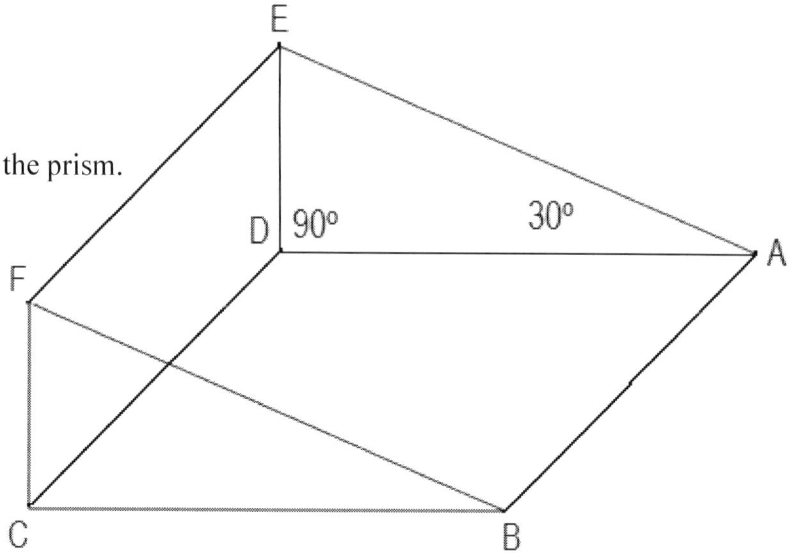

7. An old tower is made of a cone put on top of a cylinder. The radius of both is 5m. The height of the cylinder is 10m. The height of the cone is 60% of the cylinder's height.

    a. Find the height of the tower.
    b. Find the volume of the tower.

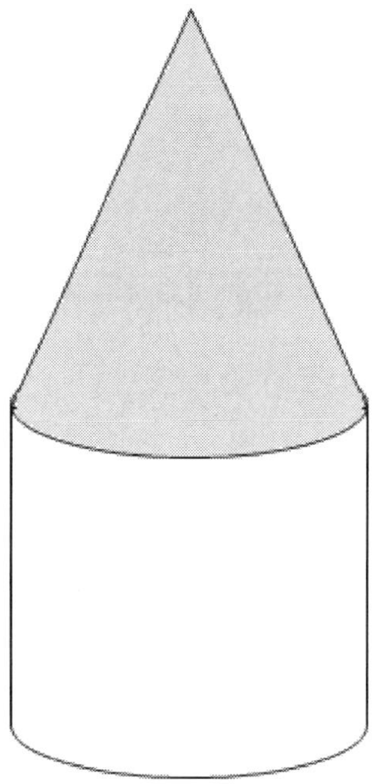

8. Given the following diagram (not to scale): ABCD is a rectangle AB = 9 cm. BC = 7 cm. EF = 10 cm is the height of the right pyramid.

Find:

a. The length AE.
b. The length AF.
c. The angle between AF and the base ABCD.
d. The length MF.
e. The angle between MF and the base ABCD.
f. The area of FBC.
g. Find the volume of the pyramid.
h. Find the surface area of the pyramid.

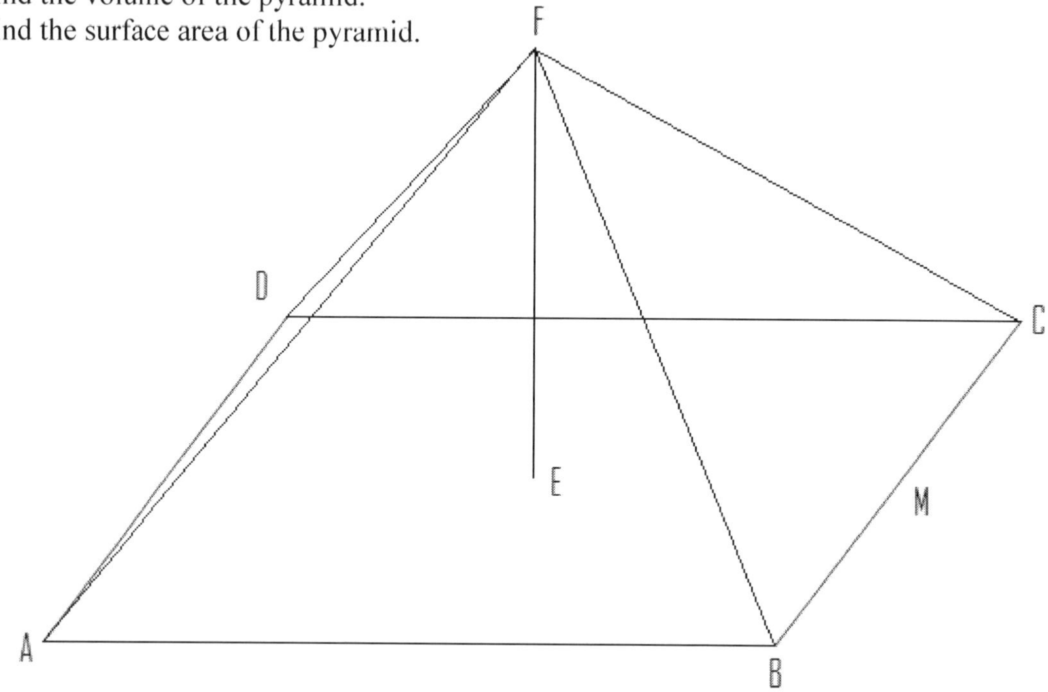

Printed in Germany
by Amazon Distribution
GmbH, Leipzig

26637407R00176